The Landscapes of Common Land

History and Ecology in Norfolk and Beyond

Tom Williamson

Windgather Press is an imprint of Oxbow Books

Published in the United Kingdom in 2025 by
OXBOW BOOKS
81 St Clements, Oxford OX4 1AW

and in the United States by
OXBOW BOOKS
1950 Lawrence Road, Havertown, PA 19083

© Windgather Press and Tom Williamson 2025

Paperback Edition: ISBN 978-1-914427-33-6
Digital Edition: ISBN 978-1-914427-34-3 (epub)

A CIP record for this book is available from the British Library

All rights reserved. No part of this book may be reproduced or transmitted in any form or by any means, electronic or mechanical including photocopying, recording or by any information storage and retrieval system, without permission from the publisher in writing.

Printed in the United Kingdom by Short Run Press

Typeset in India by Lapiz Digital Services, Chennai.

For a complete list of Windgather titles, please contact:

United Kingdom	United States of America
OXBOW BOOKS	OXBOW BOOKS
Telephone (0)1226 734350	Telephone (610) 853-9131, Fax (610) 853-9146
Email: oxbow@oxbowbooks.com	Email: queries@casemateacademic.com
www.oxbowbooks.com	www.casemateacademic.com/oxbow

Oxbow Books is part of the Casemate group

Front cover: Photograph by Tom Williamson

The Publisher's authorised representative in the EU for product safety is Authorised Rep Compliance Ltd., Ground Floor, 71 Lower Baggot Street, Dublin D02 P593, Ireland.
www.arccompliance.com

Contents

Acknowledgements   iv
List of Figures   v
Abbreviations   vii

1. Introducing Common Land   1
2. Environments and Origins   21
3. Commons and Communities   44
4. Industry, Trade and Recreation   68
5. Enclosure and Survival   91
6. The Later History of Common Land   121
7. Common Heaths   142
8. Fens, Greens and Marshes   165
9. Comparisons and Conclusions   192

Bibliography   220
Index   228

Acknowledgements

This book grew out of a project, 'Wildlife in Common', which was run by the Norfolk Wildlife Trust with the financial support of the National Lottery Heritage Fund between 2018 and 2021. I would like to thank the staff of the NWT for all their help and support, especially Gemma Walker, Ben Newton and Helen Baczkowska; and project volunteers including Margaret Dowland, Pauline Hull and Colin Needham for the many hours spent surveying at Southrepps; Teresa Rogers, Stephanie Witham, Michelle Hoare, Harriet Smith, Karen Wright, Mike Baldwin, Peter Norton and David Kennedy. My thanks also to the staff of Norfolk Record Office, Northamptonshire Record Office and Hertfordshire Archives and Local Studies.

Gerry Barnes and Charlotte Jarvis undertook invaluable archive research; Richard Malt introduced me to Hoe Common; and John Fielding showed me Fritton Common and Hales Green from the air. Many other people have provided help, advice or information, over many years, including Keith Bacon, Sarah Birtles, Alan Bull, Patsy Dallas, Rob Liddiard, Andrew Macnair, Karen Morley, Sam Neale, Tracey Partida, Jo Parmenter, Anne Rowe and Nicola Whyte. But my greatest debt, as ever, is to Liz Bellamy.

Figures and photographs are by myself and Liz Bellamy (assisted by the camera drone) except: 9.5, by Glyn Baker; 5.6, English Heritage; 2.5, 4.2, 4.5 and 8.8, John Fielding; 1.5, 2.1, 2.2, 5.8, 9.2 and 9.3, Andrew Macnair; 1.3 and 1.4, Mike Osbourne/Norfolk Wildlife Trust; 4.1, the Tate Gallery, London; 9.1, courtesy Tripadvisor.

Figures 2.3, 2.8, 3.1, 3.2, 3.4, 3.5, 4.6 and 7.7 are reproduced courtesy Norfolk Record Office; 9.4 with the permission of Hertfordshire Archives and Local Studies; 5.8 is copyright of the Ordnance Survey; 7.9 is copyright Norfolk County Council. Figures 1.1 and 1.2 are based on UK Environment Agency data.

All Lidar imagery, whether reproduced directly or used to generate maps or diagrams, is derived from UK Environment Agency open-source data or reproduced with the permission of the National Library of Scotland. All extracts from historic Ordnance Survey maps are likewise reproduced with the permission of the National Library of Scotland.

List of Figures

0.1.	Principal places and commons in Norfolk discussed in the text.	viii
1.1.	Registered commons in Norfolk.	8
1.2.	The distribution of registered common land in Egland.	10
1.3.	Roydon Common.	11
1.4.	New Buckenham Common.	12
1.5.	Norfolk: soils.	13
2.1.	Faden's *Topographical Map of the County of Norfolk*, re-drawn and georectified.	22
2.2.	Common land shown on Faden's 1797 map of Norfolk, overlain on soils.	25
2.3.	Detail from Waterman's map of Gressenhall, 1624, showing geese and cows grazing.	28
2.4.	St Peter's, Kimberley, one of the many isolated parish churches in Norfolk.	31
2.5.	Aerial view of Fritton.	32
2.6.	Detail from Faden's map, showing the area around Morley St Botolph and Morley St Peter.	33
2.7.	Landscape regions in England.	38
2.8.	Village plans in northern and western Norfolk.	40
3.1.	Fen 'doles' at Upton, as depicted on the tithe map of 1839.	51
3.2.	Detail from Waterman's map of Gressenhall, 1624, showing 'plantings' on the common.	54
3.3.	The remains of a 'planting' on Fritton Common.	55
3.4.	Brisley Green, as shown on the tithe map of 1838.	57
3.5.	Map drawn up in connection with a boundary dispute between Flitcham and Newton.	61
3.6.	Fritton Hall, Fritton Common.	64
4.1.	The post mill on Mousehold Heatth, as depicted by John Crome in c. 1816.	70
4.2.	Billingford mill on Billingford Common.	71
4.3.	Extraction pit associated with the lime kiln on Alderford Common, Swannington.	74
4.4.	Lidar image of Alderford Common, Swannington.	74
4.5.	Wymondham marketplace.	77
4.6.	Churches and marketplaces at East Dereham and Holt.	78
4.7.	The staithe at Stokesby.	80
4.8.	Holt Heath, as depicted on Faden's *Topographical Map* of 1797.	86
5.1.	Church Green, Old Buckenham.	97
5.2.	Kelling Heath.	100
5.3.	Poor's allotments in the Ant valley.	110
5.4.	Registered commons originating as poor's allotments, staithes and surveyors' pits.	112

5.5.	Broome Heath, Ditchingham.	114
5.6.	The site of Dickleburgh High Common.	115
5.7.	Impact on the modern landscape of lost commons at the junction of Wymondham, Little Melton and Wramplingham.	116
5.8.	The disposition of common heaths on the Holt–Cromer ridge.	117
6.1.	Alfred Munnings, *Crostwick Common: Woman with Donkey and Geese* (1904).	125
6.2.	School Common, Southrepps.	132
6.3.	Lane in Saxlingham Nethergate registered as a common.	138
6.4.	The village pond at Yelverton.	139
7.1.	Heather, gorse and acid grassland on Kelling Heath.	144
7.2.	Crostwight Heath.	149
7.3.	Church Hill Common, Ringland.	150
7.4.	The round barrow on Alderford Common, Swannington.	152
7.5.	Bronze Age barrows on Gallow Hill Common, Kelling.	153
7.6.	Extraction pits on Crostwight Heath.	157
7.7.	Notice prohibiting removal of sand, gravel and gorse.	158
7.8.	The remains of the Second World War radar station on Barrow Common.	159
7.9.	First World War training trenches on Hoe Common.	160
7.10.	Earthworks of probable Home Guard machine gun position, Southrepps.	160
8.1.	Boughton Fen.	166
8.2.	Lidar image of the turf 'doles' in Leziate Fen.	169
8.3.	Part of the network of enclosures, defined by turf banks, on Southrepps Common.	170
8.4.	Plan of the earthworks on Southrepps Common.	171
8.5.	One of the many 'pingos' on Foulden Common.	172
8.6.	Shotesham Common, recently cut for hay.	174
8.7.	The saltern mound on Marsh Common, North Wooton.	177
8.8.	Aerial view of Hales Green.	180
8.9.	Cattle grazing on Harpers Green, Brisley.	181
8.10.	Earthworks on Fritton Common.	184
8.11.	Hales Green, as depicted on the First Edition Ordnance Survey 6-inch map of 1884.	186
8.12.	'Planting' of pollarded oaks, Church Green, Old Buckenham.	188
9.1.	Windmill and former brickpits on the common at Brill, Buckinghamshire.	194
9.2.	Common land in Hertfordshire.	197
9.3.	Hertfordshire: commons and soils.	198
9.4.	Aston End, Hertfordshire, as shown on the tithe map of 1840.	201
9.5.	Patmore Heath, Albury.	205
9.6.	Northamptonshire: medieval land use.	206
9.7.	Northamptonshire: 'open-field pasture'.	208
9.8.	The configuration of 'open-field pasture' in west Northamptonshire.	209
9.9.	Northamptonshire: village plans and infilled greens.	210

Abbreviations

HALS – Hertfordshire Archives and Local Studies
NHER – Norfolk Historic Environment Record
NRO – Norfolk Record Office
Nmptn RO – Northamptonshire Record Office
TNA – The National Archive, Kew

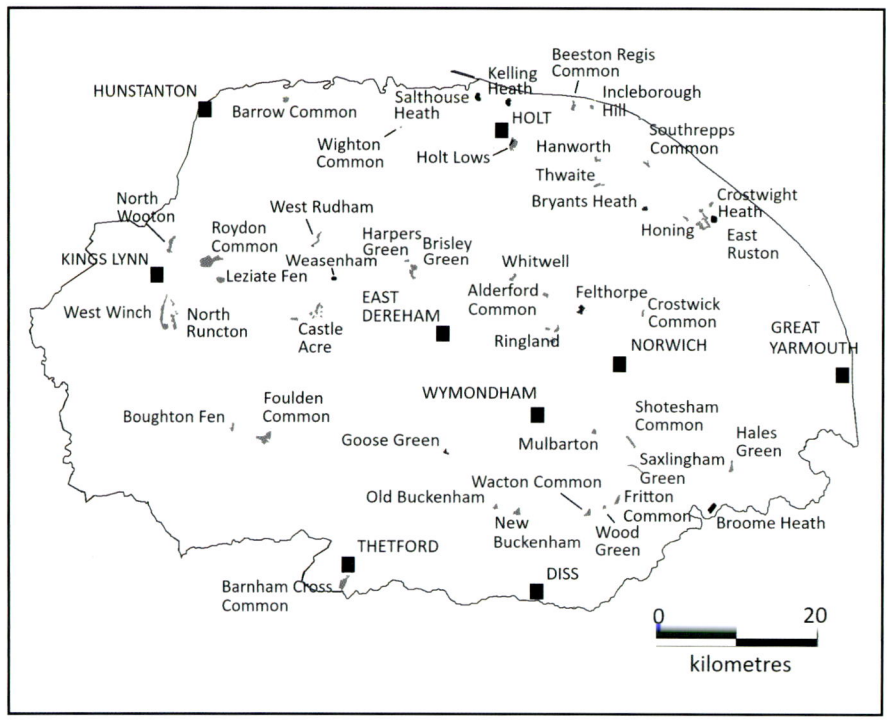

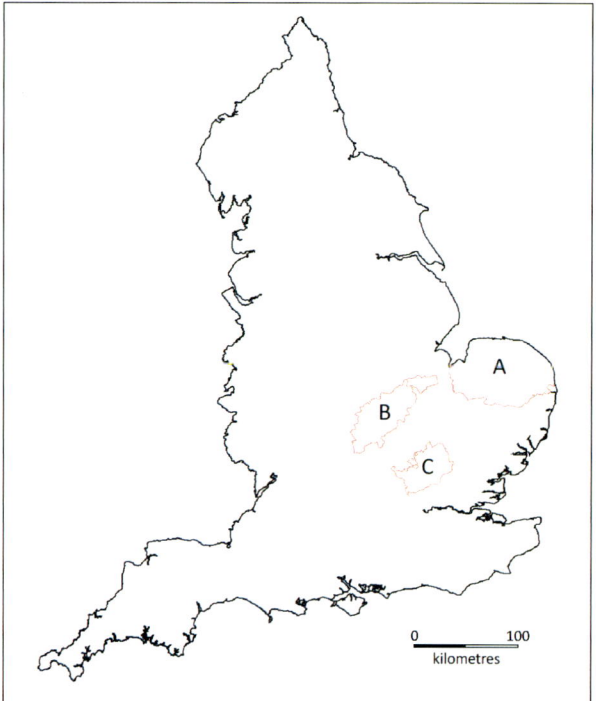

FIG. 0.1. Top: principal places and commons in Norfolk discussed in the text. Bottom: the locations of Norfolk (A), Northamptonshire and the Soke of Peterborough (B) and Hertfordshire (C) (modern county boundaries).

CHAPTER I

Introducing Common Land

Thinking about Commons

This book is about common land. It focuses, largely but not exclusively, on the county of Norfolk. And it is written, firmly but again not exclusively, from the perspective of landscape history, for my central concern is with commons as places and environments. In the chapters that follow I shall explore how and when the various parcels of land now described as 'commons' came into existence; discuss their morphology, distribution and location in the landscape; and examine how they were exploited and managed at various times in the past, and how this has shaped their archaeology, appearance and ecology. We begin in the Middle Ages but continue our story to the present day, examining the wholesale disappearance of commons, through enclosure, in the course of the post-medieval period; the traces left in the landscape by lost examples; and the profound changes experienced by the survivors since the late nineteenth century in terms of use and legal status, and the impact this has had on their visual and environmental character. An approach that begins with place and nature – with the physical, the archaeological and the ecological – is not, it should be emphasised, one which marginalises people. Much of this book is concerned with economic and social history. However interesting and important commons may be in terms of their natural history, they were created and defined by individuals and communities and shaped by their actions. The kind of approach adopted in this book does not neglect the economic, the social or even the cultural; it simply considers them as embedded in, or entangled with, the natural world.

And this, in turn, explains the restricted geographical focus of this study. Every region, every district in England has its own particular environmental character, born of geology, soils and climate. Each also has its own agrarian and social history, shaped in part by the limitations imposed and possibilities presented by that character, and in part by the nature of its contacts with other areas, in terms (for example) of market opportunities or cultural influences. The social and the natural interact, the one shaping and influencing the other, with common land forming an important part of the mix. The history of commons can only be understood in terms of these broader contexts but this becomes difficult if too wide a spatial focus, embracing too great a range of environments and histories, is adopted. While undertaking a detailed study of a limited area will allow the full complexity of the influences shaping common land to be understood, the outcome will be a history specific to that area. Yet if the one chosen is sufficiently varied in terms of soils, agriculture and social structure then observations can be made that may have a more general relevance. Which is all a long-winded way of saying that this is a book that examines commons in Norfolk, but it is not just about Norfolk commons, and in the final chapter some attempt is made to assess the wider relevance of conclusions drawn by looking briefly at the experience of other parts of England.

The approach adopted is hopefully different enough from that taken in the most recent academic study of common land, Angus Winchester's monumental (yet accessible) *Common Land in Britain: a History from the Middle Age to the Present Day*, to make this book worth reading, and not only by those with a particular interest in Norfolk.[1] Winchester's book comprises a comprehensive national account of the history of commons and commoning, embracing Scotland as well as England and Wales, which is followed by a clutch of detailed local studies from places widely scattered across the three nations. This book, in contrast, has a spatial focus that is intermediate in character: neither local nor national, but regional. It also adopts a more environmental and geographical approach which makes it, perhaps, closer in spirit to the great predecessor of Winchester's volume, W.G. Hoskins and L. Dudley Stamp's *The Common Lands of England and Wales* of 1963.[2] There are no other comparable studies. In this respect commons, which for much of history provided most of the grazing land in England (as well as providing fuel and other resources), stand in sharp contrast to arable fields, a subject on which historians, geographers and archaeologists have penned a vast number of books and articles embracing form, management and organisation.[3]

This perhaps over states the case for neglect, however, and for four main reasons. Firstly, there have been a number of important articles which discuss the common land of particular local areas.[4] Secondly, because the management of common grazing land, and arable, were to varying degrees integrated in the past – most closely in various forms of communal, open-field farming – studies of fields often, of necessity, include some consideration of commons, even if this is restricted to their role in sustaining the livestock on which arable farming depended. Thirdly, common land and its history have been discussed in works by historical ecologists, naturalists and environmental historians, although usually as one aspect of studies with a different primary focus, or a wider remit. The great historical ecologist Oliver Rackham thus engages usefully with commons on a number of occasions in his *History of the Countryside*, as do Ian Simmons and Nigel Webb, for example, in their studies of moorland and heathland respectively.[5] But lastly and most importantly common land – and more specifically its loss, together with that of open fields, through enclosure and especially parliamentary enclosure in the eighteenth and nineteenth centuries – has long held the attention of social historians. A long line of writers and researchers have portrayed enclosure as a form of organised class robbery which proved disastrous to small landowners, cottagers and the landless poor.[6] Most such studies are equally or more concerned with the enclosure of open fields than of commons; and in some, such as Keith Snell's *Annals of the Labouring Poor*, the impact of enclosure is examined as one part of a wider study of the experiences of the poor in England in the eighteenth and nineteenth centuries.[7] But in a number of works commons, and their disappearance, have a more central role. These range from scholarly studies like Jeanette Neeson's *Commoners: Common Right, Enclosure and Social Change in England, 1700–1820*, published in 1993, to more popular and overtly political treatments, including Ian Angus' powerful *The War Against the Commons: Dispossession and Resistance in the Making of Capitalism* and Peter Linebaugh's *Stop, Thief!: the Commons, Enclosures, and Resistance*.[8]

This brings us to why common land is such an important subject, worthy of academic research. It looms large in most people's experience of the countryside, providing one of the few opportunities to roam freely, unconstrained by fences and 'private property' signs, across uncultivated, seemingly wild and natural terrain. Surviving tracts of common land act as powerful reminders of a world we have supposedly lost: a pre-capitalist world in which local communities lived in close relationship to nature and managed the exploitation of the resources it provided for the common good. Capitalism, slowly at first and then more rapidly in the course of the eighteenth and nineteenth centuries, robbed us all of this shared inheritance. The spread of private property curtailed our freedom to roam, denied access to formerly shared natural resources and led to their exploitation in unsustainable ways. Such stories have an understandable appeal at a time of social and environmental crisis, in a country in which the gulf between rich and poor yawns ever wider, species of wild plants and animals once common are in sustained decline, and most people live in sprawling cities and only rarely have the opportunity of experiencing the wilder face of nature. When they do, moreover – and which they can even in the crowded south of England in the more remote recesses of Epping Forest, for example, or in the larger of the Chiltern commons – the experience serves as a powerful reminder of expropriation and loss.

It is not, therefore, surprising that common land possesses a symbolic significance, and that these kinds of narrative have become deeply entrenched in popular culture. In reality it is, as we shall see, very debatable whether common land was ever freely and equally enjoyed by all, or that its enclosure was the principal and decisive factor in the emergence of an industrial proletariat. Yet such things are repeated freely, as accepted and self-evident truths, by otherwise respectable and responsible communicators and journalists in otherwise respectable and responsible newspapers and other media. Common land was 'stolen' from the 'common people' by wealthy landowners.[9] Enclosure acts were responsible for 'carving up ancient common land into private estates. Thousands of farm labourers were forced out of work and took to the new industries – and city slums'.[10] Although the critical examination of such beliefs does not form a major part of this book it is necessary, in order to understand the real character of common land, to pay some attention to who owned commons, who was allowed to exploit them, and how equitably the resources they provided were distributed, and this I shall do in the chapters that follow.

Rather more attention will be paid, however, to the other main way in which commons loom large in public discourse and public experience – as tracts of wild, 'natural' land. In the sense that they are uncultivated areas which often serve as important refuges for wildlife such a characterisation is obviously true, and a significant number are today categorised as National Nature Reserves, Sites of Special Scientific Interest, County Wildlife Sites and the like. But many of these places, in order to fulfil their allotted role, are quite intensively managed by their custodians to maintain them in their 'traditional' state and prevent areas of heath or fen, for example, from regenerating to secondary woodland. This, as we shall see, has been the fate of most areas of common land in lowland England since the middle decades of the twentieth century. Where some form of 'traditional' management is not maintained and 're-wilding' has duly occurred, the resulting scrub and woodland may sustain as many species as the habitat or habitats they have replaced but there will usually be a decline in local and regional biodiversity arising from the disappearance of some of the more specialist species characteristic of, or dependent upon, what was there before. Commons accordingly raise interesting questions not so much about how our dwindling reserves of non-urbanised land should best be managed for the benefit of wildlife, but concerning what we actually mean when we employ those often used, but seldom defined terms 'nature' and 'natural'. Moreover, the situation is rendered more complicated, as we shall see, by the fact that what we might think of as the 'traditional', managed state of particular commons or varieties of common has often changed over time – sometimes in the course of the last few centuries – as a consequence of changes in population pressure, fuel use or agricultural economics. Commons, even those now in a derelict state, are part of an essentially human world. Their natural histories are entwined with their human histories and must be understood in these terms.

What is a Common?

While the particular character and extent of common land displayed much local and regional variation, its essential definition has for centuries been a matter of shared national law, whether common or statute. But the law relating to commons has changed over time, and most dramatically in the second half of the twentieth century. As a result, the question 'what is a common?' now has two rather different answers, which we might characterise as the 'traditional' or 'historical', and the 'modern'.

Traditionally, a common was an area of uncultivated land owned by one individual or institution, but over which a defined group, the 'commoners', enjoyed rights of access or use, principally for grazing livestock but also in other ways. These were generally described by the terms *estovers*, the right to take wood, and vegetation like rushes, for fuel and other purposes; *turbary*, the right to dig peat, again for fuel: *piscary*, the right to take fish from ponds and streams; and *common of soil*, the right to dig stone, clay, sand or gravel.[11] The character, scope and extent of such 'common rights' were decided by local custom, rather than national law, and varied significantly from area to area and from place to place. The owner of the common was the lord of the manor, except in royal forests where commons were generally owned by the Crown. Already by the time of Domesday many vills or townships – that is, the villages or local communities forming the lowest fiscal and administrative unit recognised by the state and which, in the more populous areas of England, were fast becoming the equivalent of the 'parish' as local churches proliferated – contained more than one manor. In such circumstances the lord (or lady) of the largest and oldest manor in the parish was usually regarded as the owner of all the commons, and their use was managed and regulated by decisions taken in his or her manorial court. This was not invariably the case – the lords of other manors sometimes claimed ownership of some of the commons, often perhaps where parishes had come to embrace more than one vill. But it helps to explain why commoners, regardless of which manor they held their farms from, could usually make use of all the commons in a parish; and why over time land originally attached to particular manors – as the 'waste of the manor' – came to be associated with particular parishes. Indeed, by the sixteenth century this association had grown so strong that legislation passed by the Tudor government for the relief of poverty allowed parish officials – the overseers of the poor and the churchwardens – to enclose portions of common land to provide accommodation or other facilities for the poor.

There were also significant changes over time in the way commoners held their own farms, and in concepts of land ownership more generally. Medieval Norfolk was distinctive in having large numbers of free tenants – individuals who might attend, and be subject to the rulings of, the manorial court but who were effectively freeholders, owners of their land. Most farmers, however, were 'dependent' or 'customary' tenants, the people Domesday describes as 'villeins' – holding the larger farms – and 'bordars' – with smaller areas of land. Their tenurial situation was more complex. In one sense they were tenants, in that they rendered rents and services for their holding and usually made a payment or 'fine' to the lord when it changed hands. But the terms of their tenure were customary and traditional, as recognised by the manorial court, there was an assumption that sons would inherit from fathers, and farms or parts of them could be bought and sold. From the later Middle Ages customary tenures developed into different forms of 'copyhold', their varying character the consequence of how existing local differences evolved in the new economic and social circumstances of the fourteenth and fifteenth centuries.[12] On some manors farmers came to hold their land 'by inheritance', and the fines paid when sons succeeded fathers, and other dues, might be fixed, steadily declining in value with the passing decades as a consequence of inflation. There was, after several centuries, little to distinguish these kinds of copyholds from freeholds. Elsewhere, however, copyholds only guaranteed possession for a number of successive lives, a single life, or even a term of years, and lords might also have greater scope for raising fines and rents.[13] In these circumstances lords tended, over time, to absorb copyhold farms into their 'demesnes' – their own freehold property. They could then be rented out as larger units to leasehold tenants, under terms and conditions privately agreed.

Those readers whose main interest is in natural, rather than social and economic, history may find this discussion of the overlapping institutions of manor, township and parish, and of the multiple property interests in peasant farms, complicated and confusing. But this is because they are complicated and confusing, not least because they varied from area to area and, as noted, changed over time. Indeed, much else in the medieval and early post-medieval landscape seems, from a modern perspective, to have involved multiple and shifting layers of rights, ownership and jurisdictions. In most parts of the country, alongside the common land owned by one individual but exploited collectively by others, there were other forms of agricultural land managed in broadly analogous ways. Much of the arable land lay in various kinds of 'open field' in which the holdings of proprietors took the form of narrow, unenclosed and intermingled strips, the cultivation of which might be subject to varying degrees of collective management, and which were grazed in common after the harvest, and usually when they lay fallow.[14] Meadows likewise often took the form of unfenced strips, usually privately owned but sometimes allocated by lot each year, which were similarly thrown open for communal grazing once the hay had been cut and removed.[15] Such areas were not commons, for they comprised parcels of land occupied and cultivated by private individuals who enjoyed the exclusive benefit of the primary crop they produced. But they obviously shared many of the features of common land and their management similarly fell under the jurisdiction of the manorial court. There were, moreover, some grey areas – 'doles' of common fens, for example – where the distinction between a 'common', and a communally managed hay meadow, was distinctly fuzzy (below, p. 52).

A strong historical tradition, beginning in the writings of Henry Maine and Paul Vinogradoff in the late nineteenth century, has argued that the roots of common land lie in concepts of shared tribal ownership.[16] In the early Anglo-Saxon period, according to this view, the uncultivated 'wastes' had been regarded as the joint property of the local community; only with the rise of local lordship in the centuries leading up to the Norman Conquest, and with the progressive elaboration of the manorial system in its aftermath, did the idea of lordly ownership of the commons become established. It is perhaps more accurate to say that in the sixth, seventh and eighth centuries, when population levels were unquestionably very low and reserves of uncultivated land extensive, nobody bothered or thought much about who had rights to use it, and to what extent. One early Anglo-Saxon law code refers to the management of communally managed hay meadows, divided into strips, but none says anything about the regulation of common land.[17] There are signs that in some areas, by the ninth century, there was a clear notion that certain areas of waste belonged to particular communities and, by implication, were reserved for their sole use.[18] But only as the population rose steeply and the extent of open waste dwindled markedly in the centuries either side of Domesday did it become imperative to formally define rights over what remained. With local lordship and a system of manors now in place, the principal lords in each vill became the recognised owners and their dependent tenants, and lesser freehold owners, received rights of use. It was at this point that 'commons' as such came into existence.

In terms of national law, as opposed to the situation negotiated locally, on the ground, the key piece of legislation was one section (Chapter 11) of the Statute of Merton of 1236, the provisions of which, as Winchester has described, essentially clarified and codified the existing situation in local custom and the common law.[19] The preamble explains that the new ruling was a response to the problems experienced by manorial lords in attempting to exploit the full potential of the 'residue of their manors' – that is, the uncultivated wastes – because attempts to 'approve' or enclose portions, presumably for the creation of deer parks and managed woods as much as new areas of agricultural land, had been opposed in law by commoners. Henceforth, the statute ruled, such opposition would be considered invalid if it could be shown that they had been left with 'sufficient' pasture for their tenements.[20] In fact, the actual wording of the statute refers only to knights, granted sub-manors, and free tenants; but that it was taken, and presumably intended, to apply to all tenants is clear from the wording of a later statute, that of Westminster of 1285, which describes how Merton had 'granted that the lords of wastes, woods and pastures, might approve the said wastes, woods and pastures, notwithstanding the contradiction of their tenants, so that the tenants had sufficient pasture to their tenements' which they were able to freely access. This new legal measure extended this principle to the inhabitants of neighbouring townships, in cases where areas of waste were shared.[21]

These pieces of legislation confirmed, by implication, that the lord was the owner of the commons. But equally important was the recognition that rights of common were attached to, or 'appurtenant to', the holdings or farms of tenants; and that, in the last resort, they were limited to an entitlement to graze only as many livestock, or to take only as much of the other resources provided, as was necessary for the agricultural viability of the holding. This implies in turn that where commons were extensive such limits would not apply; and that there was a shared notion of the numbers of sheep, cattle etc. required to make a holding of a particular size viable (in terms of traction, dung etc.) and to keep its owner's family fed. There is also, perhaps, a further implication: that the size of tenements varied, and with it the extent to which their holders might enjoy the resources afforded by the common. As we shall see, various subsequent pieces of national legislation made changes to the ways commons might be administered and used but did not, until the Commons Registration Act of 1965, affect the basic definition, established in the Middle Ages, of what a common actually was.

That Act, however, established a new definition, what I described earlier as the 'modern' definition of common land.[22] As I shall explain in Chapter 6, those responsible for drawing it up were primarily interested in the preservation of areas of open, uncultivated land, and of ensuring free public access to them for recreation. These ends were in part secured through the compilation of a comprehensive and legally definitive list of such land and the rights claimed over it, the 'Commons Register'. But the terms set out for defining what areas of land should be included, and the way in which the process of registration was carried out, changed – to an extent which varied from region to region across England – the body of areas categorised and protected as 'common land'. This was partly because the parcels registered could include not only 'land subject to rights of common' but also 'waste land of a manor not subject to rights of common', a new concept intended to cover cases where common rights had lapsed or remained unclaimed; and partly because the task of identifying potential candidates for registration was devolved to local communities, rather than being allotted (for example) to a team of experts. The outcome was the omission from the register of some land parcels that had traditionally been common land and the inclusion of others that had not, the latter including, in particular, various kinds of land allotted to parish officers for 'public' purposes when commons were enclosed by acts of parliament, such as pits for supplying gravel for the repair of the roads or areas set aside to provide fuel for the poor. 'Commons' of this kind are particularly numerous in Norfolk, accounting for around 27 per cent by number, and 18 per cent by area, of registered examples (Figure 1.1). In all, around 45 square kilometres of common land were registered in the county but of this nearly half comprises coastal mudflats, sandbanks and saltmarshes, mainly in the north-west, over which claims to take shellfish and other natural products were asserted. As

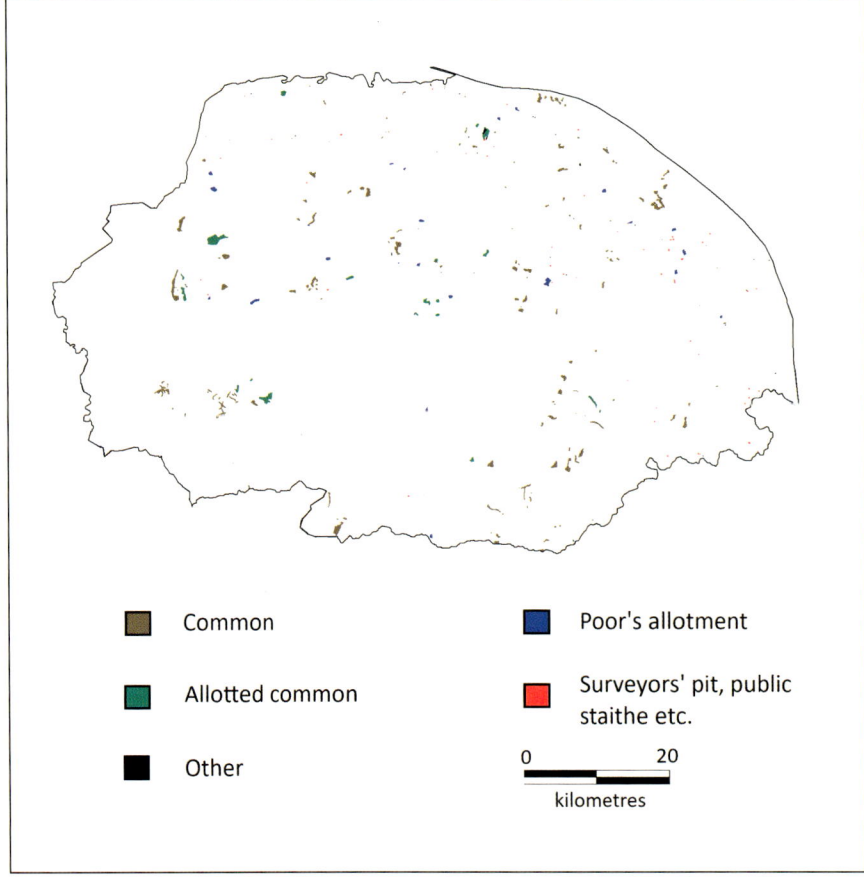

FIG. 1.1. Registered commons in Norfolk (current county boundaries). 'Allotted' commons are those recognised and regulated by enclosure awards. See below, pp. 96–100.

these have no physical expression in the landscape and have never really been considered as common land in the past, they will not be further discussed here; our concern will be with the remaining 22.76 square kilometres. This is made up of over 350 individual areas of land – it is impossible to provide a precise figure due to the problems posed by such things as conjoined commons – ranging in size from tiny plots covering less than a hundred square metres to huge examples like Brisley Green (59 hectares), Foulden Common (109 hectares) or Roydon Common (196 hectares). The mean average size, of around 6.5 hectares, reflects the predominance of examples towards the lower end of the size range, and especially of those covering between 1 and 4 hectares.

When I come to discuss the appearance, landscape, ecology and archaeology of present day common land my primary focus will be on 'registered' commons: firstly because these areas are thought of and treated as common land by local people, and local government, today; and secondly because those examples which are registered but not traditional commons, but parish pits, poor's allotments and the like, were usually carved out of more extensive areas of common land at the time of enclosure, have not been ploughed up or otherwise much changed since, and therefore retain something of the ecological and archaeological character of their progenitors. For the same reasons, I will also pay some attention to a number of areas which are similar in character to the various forms of 'registered' common, but which for some reason were never registered as common land under the 1965 Act, although they now have free public access under a more recent piece of legislation, the Countryside and Rights of Way Act (2000), such as East Ruston 'Common', Salthouse Heath and Broome Heath in Ditchingham.

The Norfolk Context

The county of Norfolk is, for a number of reasons, a particularly good place to study common land. It is blessed with excellent research resources, in the form of a superb record office and actively maintained Historic Environment Record and Biodiversity Information Service, and it has commons that are visually stunning and full of archaeological and biological interest, several of them actively managed by the Norfolk Wildlife Trust. It is also a well studied county, with archaeological and natural history societies founded in the nineteenth century, and a proud tradition of amateur research more generally, as well as being home to the University of East Anglia, established in 1963 on the edge of Norwich. Not surprisingly, much important research has been published into, or bearing directly upon, the county's commons. This ranges from the seminal articles published by W.G. Clarke in the early decades of the twentieth century in the *Transactions of the Norfolk and Norwich Naturalists' Society*; through the slim but important volume on *Commons in Norfolk* produced by members of the Norfolk Research Committee in 1988; to a clutch of PhD theses and MA dissertations completed by students at the University of East Anglia in the opening decades of the present century.[23] Of these the most important by far is Sarah Birtles' 'A Green Space Beyond Self-interest: The Evolution of Common

Land in Norfolk, c.750–2003' (2003), a work that has greatly informed my own thinking on a range of important matters.[24] Nicola Whyte's 'Perceptions of the Norfolk Landscape c. 1500–1750' (2005) also has much to say that is original and useful about common land; Keith Bacon's 2003 thesis on enclosure in north-east Norfolk is particularly informative on its disappearance; Jo Parmenter's study of the wetland vegetation of the Norfolk Broads contains much information about the management of common fens; while MA dissertations by Karen Morley and Alan Bull have both, in their different ways, cast important new light on the clayland commons in the south of the county, and that by Patsy Dallas has illuminated the local customs relating to tree planting on commons.[25] Although this book is based on my own fieldwork and archival research I have also, shamelessly and with pleasure, drawn heavily on all this earlier work.

Norfolk is a good place to study commons for other reasons. It boasts today a density of registered commons around average for England as a whole, roughly halfway between that of the Midlands, where commons are thin on

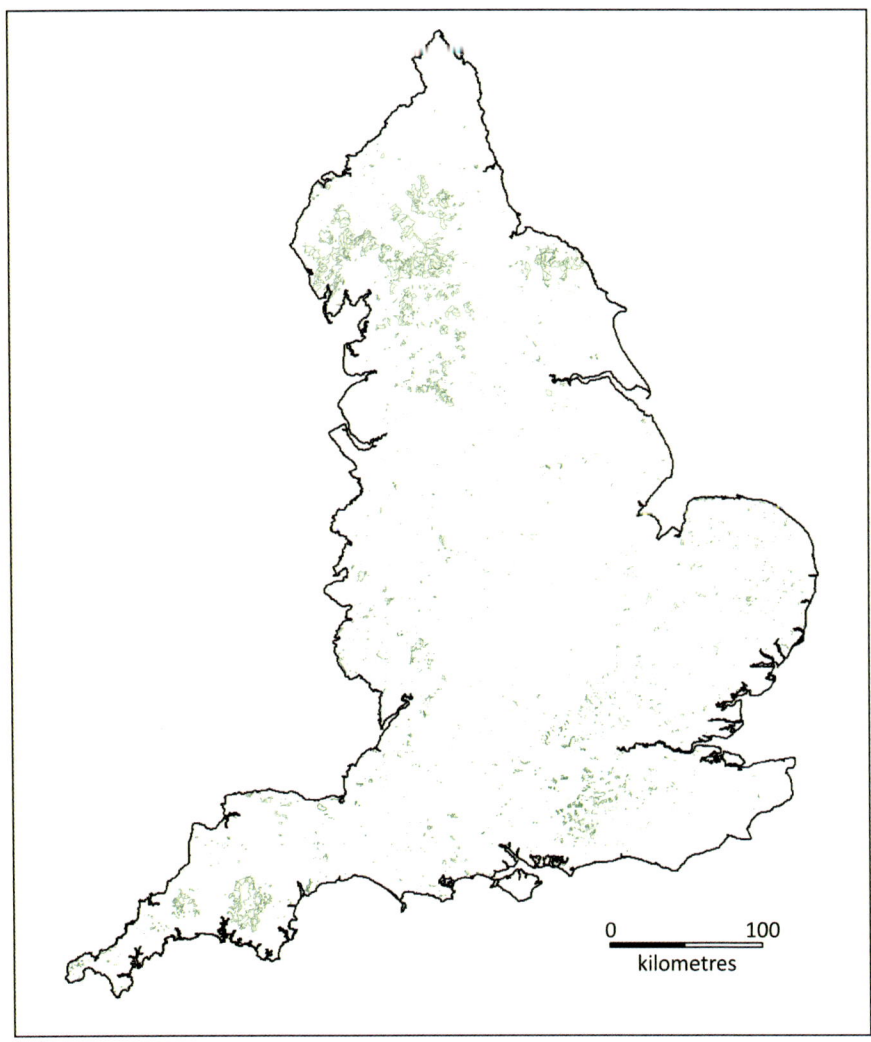

FIG 1.2 The distribution of registered common land in England.

1. Introducing Common Land 11

the ground, and upland counties like Cumbria, where they are particularly extensive (Figure 1.2). It is true that it provides few opportunities to examine urban commons, or the recent fate of common land in suburbanising areas. Norwich, King's Lynn and Great Yarmouth are major urban centres but most of the county remains surprisingly rural, with only a thin scatter of market towns, although its present character in this respect in some ways belies its past – in the Middle Ages Norfolk was the most densely settled county in England, and between the fifteenth and the mid-eighteenth centuries home to an important rural textile industry. On the other hand, the county displays remarkable variations in geology and soils, which were, and to an extent still are, associated with equally remarkable variations in the character, and extent, of common land.

Commons are, and were, 'semi-natural habitats'. Their character was shaped both by the way they were exploited and managed and by the natural characteristics of the sites they occupy, in terms of soils, geology and drainage. The two interacted in complex ways. Grazing was the most important use of most commons and its effects on the vegetation were determined by soil type. On the more acid, freely draining sites some kind of heathland developed, dominated by heather and grasses like sheep's fescue, but often with only a limited range of other herb species (Figure 1.3). On the chalky boulder clays which cover much of Norfolk, in contrast, sustained grazing under traditional conditions produces

FIG. 1.3. Roydon Common, a Norfolk Wildlife Trust reserve and arguably the best preserved heathland common in the county.

a sward featuring grasses like cock's-foot (*Dactylis glomerata*), common bent (*Agrostis capillaris*), red fescue (*Festuca rubra*), meadow fescue (*Lolium pratense*), and Yorkshire fog (*Holcus lanatus*) and wildflowers like common knapweed (*Centaurea nigra*), common bird's-foot-trefoil (*Lotus corniculatus*) and meadow rue (*Thalictrum flavum*), accompanied by rarer types, most notably varieties of orchid (Figure 1.4). In the past such differences were exacerbated by the kinds of livestock grazed on the commons. Sheep, the most important stock on light acid land, graze more closely than the cattle and horses which are better suited to the poorly draining soils of the boulder clays. But commons, as already noted, were not only exploited as grazing land. They also provided raw materials, and in particular domestic fuel, for local communities, and here, too, the natural characteristics of the site were of fundamental importance. Heathland commons often overlay deposits of gravel, widely used for road surfacing and similar purposes, or sand, used in a wide variety of ways; while pits dug on clayland commons provided the raw material for making wattle-and-daub or bricks. Heaths supplied bracken, cut for cattle bedding, and an abundance of fuel in the form of heather, gorse and bracken; clayland commons afforded rather less in the way of useful

FIG. 1.4. New Buckenham Common: neutral grassland typical of Norfolk's clayland commons.

materials, mainly wood lopped from pollarded trees. Commons fens, associated with deposits of waterlogged peat on valley floors, supplied their own particular range of resources, the exploitation of which – mainly by cutting and digging, rather than grazing – shaped their ecology in complex ways.

The geology of Norfolk, like that of other counties in eastern England, is characterised by relatively soft young rocks. Across much of the county the underlying 'solid' geology comprises chalk, which in the west is exposed as a low escarpment. It dips gradually from west to east and in the eastern third of the county becomes buried beneath the much younger 'Crag' deposits, gravels, clays and shelly sands laid down between 3.5 and 1.6 million years ago. Only in the far west of the county, in a narrow band running beside the Fens and the Wash from Stoke Ferry to Hunstanton, are formations earlier than the chalk exposed, principally the mudstones of the Gault Formation, the sandstones of the Carrstone, the Leziate Sands and the Kimmeridge Clay. All this solid geology is, however, largely obscured by much later 'drift' deposits, laid down during the successive glaciations of the Pleistocene period, and it is these which form the parent material for most of the county's soils (Figure 1.5).[26] The centre, south and south-east of the county are covered by deposits of boulder clay or till, the surface of which forms a slightly tilted plateau, falling gently to the east with the dip of the underlying rocks. Most of this material – essentially, that portion lying to the south of the modern A47 running west from Norwich towards King's Lynn – comprises the Lowestoft Till, a chalky clay giving rise to

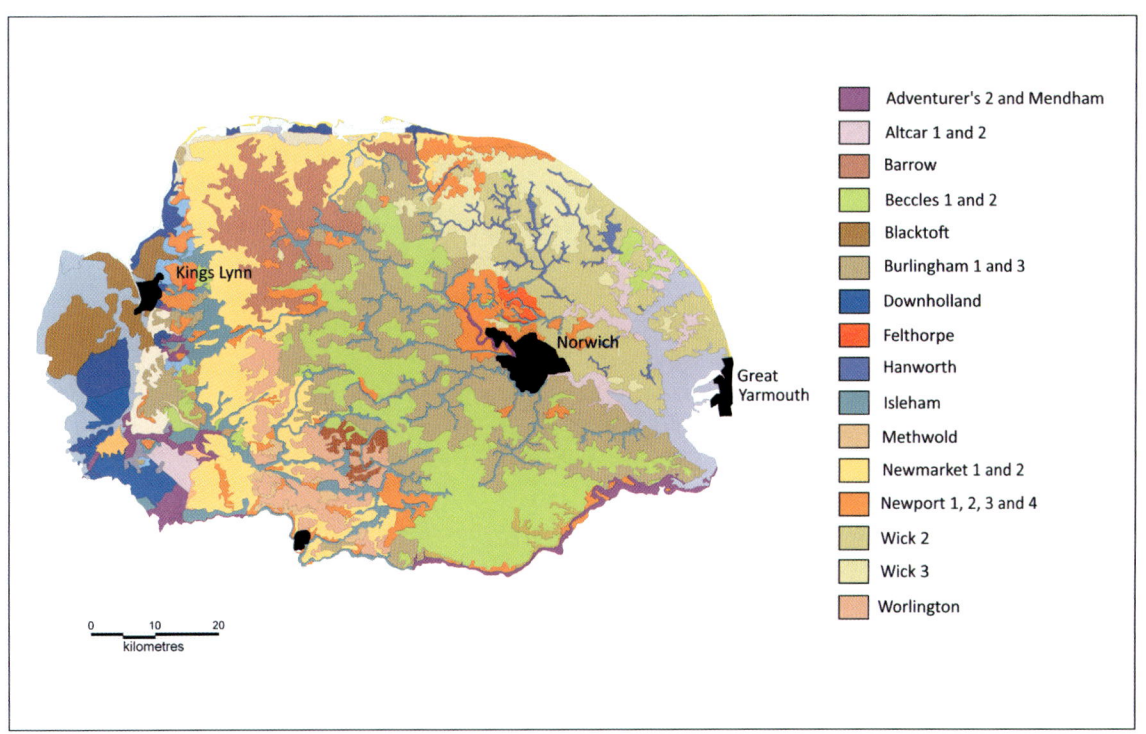

FIG. 1.5. Norfolk: soils. Only the most important soil associations, or those closely associated with common land, are shown on the key.

poorly draining but fertile soils – principally those of the Beccles 1 Association.[27] To the north of the A47, however, the Lowestoft Till gives way in places to the Sheringham Till, in which the chalky clay is interbedded with significant layers of sand and gravel which, where exposed on the surface, produce acidic soils, as well as being overlain in places by quite extensive patches of sands and gravels of the Briton's Lane Formation. The till plateau is often treated as a single entity in studies of Norfolk's landscape but this distinction between the northern section, and the central and south-eastern, is reflected in many aspects of the historic landscape, not least the character of common land, which before the nineteenth century was more extensive towards the north, and included areas of heath. Whatever the particular characteristics of the till, the plateau is dissected to varying degrees by rivers and stream which have in places cut through to the underlying chalk or Crag, and on the valley sides of which the clays are sandier and the soils – principally those of the Burlingham 1 Association – are anyway better drained because of the gradient.[28]

The north-east of the county also boasts scattered areas of boulder clay, some (the Weybourne Town till) silty and calcareous, others (the Bacton Green Till) less so, but is mostly characterised by glacial sands and gravels – especially those of the Briton's Lane Member and the Happisburgh Formation – which are associated with acid, heathy soils. All these formations are, however, covered by extensive areas of *loess*, thin, wind-blown silty deposits laid down during the Devensian glaciation. These give rise to some of the most tractable and fertile soils in England (those of the Wick 2 Association) and in the eleventh and twelfth centuries parts of north-east Norfolk boasted the highest population densities in England. In the south-west of the county, in contrast, wind-blown or aeolian deposits take a very different form. Here, although the underlying chalk is exposed in places on the lower ground, it is mostly buried under thick deposits of cover sand, accompanied in places by glacial outwash sands and gravels, the combination making for one of the most arid and agriculturally marginal areas in southern Britain, generally referred to as Breckland. The landscape here is dominated by the leached, acidic soils of the Worlington, Methwold, and Newport 3 and 4 Associations and still characterised by areas of now mainly private heath, interspersed with commercial conifer plantations. Further north, in north-west Norfolk, the exposures of chalk are more extensive but the higher ground is again covered in deposits of glacial, mainly wind-blown sand, albeit much thinner and mixed in places with chalky till. This, too, was traditionally a district of heaths, although they were here more easily reclaimed and converted to arable than was the case in Breckland.

There are other areas of dry, acidic soil in the county, generally associated with various forms of glacial sand and gravel. One extends as a broad, intermittent band from Norwich northwards to the sea, where deposits of surface *loess* are much more patchy than in the areas lying to the east, and features particularly extensive tracts of poor, heathy land (Newport 3 and 4 and Felthorpe Association soils) between the city and Cawston, and on the high 'Holt-Cromer Ridge' which runs just inland from the coast. Another, rather narrower strip of heathy, acidic land runs north–south between Hunstanton and Downham Market in the west of the county, on the eastern edge of the Fenland and the Wash. It is associated with pre-Cretaceous sands and sandstones as well as with glacial deposits, and in some places posed an additional challenge to farmers in the form of a high water table. In general the geological complexity of this particular stretch of countryside produces a diverse range of soils, including heavy clays, which are especially extensive in the area around Downham Market.

Deposits of glacial origin account for most of the county's surface deposits, and thus provide the parent materials for most of its soils. But in some places post-glacial or Holocene deposits dominate, peats, silts and clays resulting from complex changes in relative land/sea levels which have occurred since the end of glaciation – most notably in the level reclaimed wetlands of Fenland in the far west of the county. The southern part of this district (which extends far into the adjacent counties) is occupied by deposits of peat, while the northern portion, close to the Wash, comprises alluvial clay. On the other side of the county, in the district known as the Norfolk Broads, a similar contrast is apparent, albeit on a much smaller scale, with extensive areas of alluvium and clay towards the sea, in the great marshland triangle (a former estuary) lying immediately inland from Great Yarmouth generally referred to as the Halvergate Marshes, but with peats of the Adventurer's, Altcar and Mendham Associations occupying the valley floors of the rivers (Yare, Bure, Waveney, Ant, Thurne and Chet) draining in to this. Areas of peat also occur in river valleys more widely, across the county, especially where gradients are low and flows sluggish, although in many places more alluvial soils predominate.

Readers may be forgiven for finding this somewhat compressed account of Norfolk's soils and geology confusing. But it is essential for understanding why commons, and different kinds of common, were located and distributed in the ways that they were, for underneath this complexity a simple principle structured the development of the medieval landscape, including the distribution of common land. Almost everywhere in the county the most agriculturally attractive soils were to be found on the sides of the principal valleys. The main areas of common land were, and are, located on the drift-covered uplands, where the soils formed in poorly draining clays, or in acid sands and gravels, posed problems for early cultivators; or else on valley floors, where the depth of peat deposits made the land unsuitable for meadows. A broad understanding of Norfolk's geology is also important for another reason. The environmental character of commons as this developed over time was shaped, as already intimated, by the interaction of natural and social factors. Common land was embedded in local societies that displayed considerable variations in such things as the relative power enjoyed by manorial lords on the one hand and commoners on the other, in the distribution of land and wealth within the farming community, and in the extent to which agriculture was carried out on communal or individualistic lines. All these might have an influence on common land, and like population density – another major factor – were themselves closely related to soils and geology.

This is another immensely complex topic which must, of necessity, be discussed here only briefly and baldly. The most obvious spatial distinction within Norfolk, and the one noted by topographers from as early as the sixteenth century, was between the boulder clays in the centre and south-east of the county, and the light lands in the north and west. In the latter areas, chalk was exposed on the lower ground but on the higher was obscured by various kinds of mainly acidic, sandy drift. In the sixteenth and seventeenth centuries these were areas of 'sheep-corn' husbandry.[29] The arable mainly took the form of communally managed 'open fields' in which the lands of farmers lay intermingled as narrow, unhedged strips; settlement took the form of loosely nucleated villages, with dwellings clustering around springs or some other supply of water in this generally arid landscape.[30] Nutrients were rapidly leached from the porous soils and fertility could only be maintained by grazing flocks of sheep on the heaths or fallows by day, and closely folding them on the arable by night, when it lay fallow or before the spring sowing, where they dunged or 'tathed' it. But yields were always uncertain on these relatively poor if easily worked soils, and so too the fortunes of farmers. In the early Anglo-Saxon period these had been core areas of settlement but their relative importance declined over subsequent centuries. By medieval times they were characterised by comparatively low population densities and strong manorial lords, who took pains to ensure that their land received more than its fair share of the available manure through the institution of the 'foldcourse'. The manure was a manorial monopoly: the tenants might benefit from the dung dropped as the sheep roamed over the fallows but they could only enjoy the intensive night-folding in return for a cash payment.[31] The sheep were organised into flocks dominated by the lord's stock and under the care of his shepherd. But because there were usually several manors in a vill each had its allotted 'foldcourse' which included both heath and arable. There are signs that foldcourses became more rigid and formalised in late medieval times, and that in the twelfth and thirteenth centuries some peasants may have had the right to erect folds, but even then the system had been dominated by manorial lords.[32] The character of the system changed from the late Middle Ages, moreover. Lords, or the commercial flockmasters to whom they leased their rights, increasingly used foldcourses not to improve arable yields but as a way of farming sheep, and there were frequent complaints about the increasing size of the flocks and the detrimental effects this was having on the feed available for the tenants' livestock.[33]

The grip of large landowners on the agricultural landscape increased steadily, through the post-medieval centuries, on these light lands, especially where they were resident in a parish, and in places – most notably in Breckland – in which the most extensive areas of acid, sandy soils were found. They used every opportunity to take into their hands the farms of those holding by the more insecure forms of copyhold, especially by increasing the 'fines' paid when holdings changed hands through inheritance; they bought up the lands of neighbouring freeholders, great and small, and of those holding by the more secure forms of copyhold. In some places, by the eighteenth century, they had acquired every acre of land in a parish, sometimes in several contiguous ones, with the exception of the vicar's glebe. With no other common right holders the open fields and commons could be enclosed and the landscape rearranged at will, often with a park being laid out around the mansion and extensive plantations established, and the land leased out as large farms on fixed terms, commonly of 14 or 21 years. But more often the dominance achieved by large landowners was only partial, while at the interstices of great estates, usually on favourable soils in major river valleys, some so-called 'open' parishes existed in which much landed property remained in the hands of small proprietors. In many places, therefore, open fields and commons survived until they were enclosed by parliamentary acts, usually in the second half of the eighteenth century but sometimes in the early nineteenth. Enclosure, however it was achieved, was followed by the destruction of most areas of heathland where the sandy drift lay thinly over the chalk. The new farming methods of the 'agricultural revolution' – the cultivation of fodder crops like turnips and clover, in rotation with courses of cereals, in the arable fields – ensured that they were longer required as reservoirs of nutrients, transferred to the arable by the folding flocks. Where, however, the sands lay deeper, in Breckland, the scale of reclamation was more limited.[34]

The development of farming communities, and of the landscape, on the boulder clay plateau in the centre and south-east of the county was very different. These more intractable soils were, for the most part, opened up for cultivation rather later in the Anglo-Saxon period than the light lands to the west: before the ninth century settlement and cultivation were largely restricted to the lighter soils of the principal valleys, and even at the time of Domesday large areas of the plateau clays comprised wooded waste. Partly for this reason, partly because of the greater fertility of the land, and in part as a consequence of other factors, the power of local lords was weaker here. Manors with dependent tenants always existed – the numerous deer parks and enclosed coppiced woods which characterised the area by the thirteenth century were all manorial assets – but there were significant numbers of small freeholders and, as tenures evolved through the later Middle Ages, many dependent tenants came to hold their land by secure forms of copyhold. Even in the eighteenth and nineteenth centuries there were few really large, continuous landed estates.[35] There were other important differences. The clay plateau carried a 'perched' water table which could be accessed almost anywhere by shallow wells, so that farms and cottages tended to disperse widely across the landscape, often hugging, as we shall see, the margins of common land. Moreover, while open fields were extensive in the Middle Ages they were generally less continuous than in the west, especially on the most level land, where the soils were particularly poorly draining. Here they were interrupted by woods, parks, ribbons of settlement, commons, and by patches of hedged fields that had been enclosed directly from the 'waste'. There were no foldcourses here. Indeed, cattle were always more important than sheep in the local economy and became steadily more so in the course of the fifteenth, sixteenth and seventeenth centuries, as farmers came to specialise in dairying and bullock rearing, gradually enclosing their arable land and laying it to pasture. By the late eighteenth century, when prices swung back in favour of cereal production and the arable acreage began to expand once again, open fields had largely or entirely disappeared in most parishes and parliamentary enclosures were mainly concerned with the removal of commons.

It is not possible to provide a potted agrarian history of all the various geological areas and districts briefly noted in the previous pages. Suffice it to say that in broad terms, areas of light, leached land displayed some, but not necessarily all, of the features I have described for Breckland and north-west Norfolk – an emphasis on sheep husbandry, strong manorial control, late survival of open fields and the eventual emergence of large landed estates; while clayland areas displayed a bias towards cattle, tended to lose most of their open fields before the eighteenth century and were characterised by weaker lordship and a broader base of landownership. One distinctive area of the county, however, differs significantly from both. North-east Norfolk, with its fertile and tractable loams, was similar to the boulder clays in that it was never an area of large landed estates, but of small freehold proprietors and minor gentry. Moreover, while some sizeable villages existed from medieval times, settlement was, for the most part, similarly dispersed. But it differed from the claylands in that the cultivation of cereals continued to be the main business of farming and in many parishes open fields were only gradually and partially removed, significant areas surviving into the early nineteenth century when they were enclosed by parliamentary acts. Foldcourses were virtually unknown; sheep were kept in significant numbers but cattle were of more importance in the economies of many farms. This was not a reflection of the particular character of the rich *loess* soils, but of the fact that the area was interdigitated with 'Broadland', or the Norfolk Broads. The fertile uplands were dissected by the wide valleys of rivers and streams containing ample reserves of fen and marsh that were more suitable for grazing cattle than sheep.

Conclusion

As the above discussion should have made clear, Norfolk has a more varied character than outsiders often appreciate. Its admittedly muted topography belies a geographical diversity that has, over time, engendered remarkable contrasts in farming systems, landholding patterns and social organisation, themselves interrelated in complex ways. Common land, as I have emphasised, forms a key part of this ever-changing matrix. How its varied landscapes were shaped by the interaction of the natural, the social and the agrarian forms the subject of the rest of this book.

Notes

1. A. Winchester, *Common Land in Britain: a History from the Middle Ages to the Present Day* (Woodbridge, 2022).
2. L. Dudley Stamp and W.G. Hoskins, *The Common Lands of England and Wales* (London, 1963).

3   See, for example, A.R.H. Baker and R.A. Butlin (eds) *Studies of Field Systems in the British Isles* (Cambridge, 1973); D. Hall, *The Open Fields of England* (Oxford, 2020).
4   One excellent example being D. Pannett, Commons of the Stiperstones Mining District, *Shropshire History and Archaeology* 95 (2020), 61–82.
5   O. Rackham, *The History of the Countryside* (London, 1986); I.G. Simmons, *The Moorlands of England and Wales: An Environmental History, 8000 BC–AD 2000* (Edinburgh, 2003); N. Webb, *Heathlands* (London, 1986).
6   J.L. and B. Hammond, *The Village Labourer, 1760–1832* (London, 1911).
7   K.D.M. Snell, *Annals of the Labouring Poor: Social Change and Agrarian England, 1660–1900* (Cambridge, 1985).
8   J.M. Neeson, *Commoners: Common Right, Enclosure and Social Change in England, 1700–1820* (Cambridge, 1993); I. Angus, *The War Against the Commons: Dispossession and Resistance in the Making of Capitalism* (New York, 2023); P. Linebaugh, *Stop, Thief!: the Commons, Enclosures, and Resistance* (San Francisco 2014).
9   Time Bandits, *Guardian*, Nov 3, 1999; Fences against the people: Once we had monuments and common land, but next week the travellers will again be barred from Stonehenge, *Guardian*, June 19, 1995.
10 This Week in the 1800s, *Guardian*, Dec 13, 1999.
11 H. Bracton, *On the Laws and Customs of England*, ed. and trans. S.E. Thorne, Vol. 3 (Cambridge, Mass., 1977), 167; E.F. Cousins and R. Honey, *Gadsden on Commons and Greens* (London, 2012), Sections 2.34–2.49.
12 E. Kerridge, *Agrarian Problems in the Sixteenth Century and After* (London, 1969), 32–64.
13 Kerridge, *Agrarian Problems*, 64–82.
14 Baker and Butlin, *Studies of Field Systems in the British Isles*; Hall, *The Open Fields of England*.
15 A. Brian, The Allocation of Strips in Lammas Meadows by the Casting of Lots, *Landscape History* 21, 1 (1999), 43–58.
16 H.S. Maine, *Village-Communities in the East and West* (London, 1871); P. Vinogradoff, *Villainage in England* (Oxford, 1892).
17 D. Whitelock (ed.), *English Historical Documents. Vol. I, c.500–1042* (London, 1955), 68–9.
18 Winchester, *Common Land*, 37.
19 Winchester, *Common Land*, 27.
20 Records Commission, *Statutes of the Realm*, Vol. 1 (London, 1810), 2–3.
21 *Statutes of the Realm*, Vol.1, 46–7.
22 Commons Registration Act, 1965 c. 64.
23 W.G. Clarke, The Commons of Norfolk, *Transactions of the Norfolk and Norwich Naturalists' Society* 9 (1909–1914), 52–70; W.G. Clarke, The Natural History of Norfolk Commons, *Transactions of the Norfolk and Norwich Naturalists' Society* 10 (1914–1919), 294–318; M. Manning (ed.), *Commons in Norfolk* (Norwich, 1988).
24 S. Birtles, A Green Space Beyond Self-interest: the Evolution of Common Land in Norfolk, c.750–2003, unpublished PhD thesis, University of East Anglia, 2003.
25 N. Whyte, Perceptions of the Norfolk Landscape c. 1500–1750, unpublished PhD thesis, University of East Anglia, 2005; K. Bacon, Landholding and Enclosure in the Hundreds of East Flegg, West Flegg and Happing in Norfolk, 1695 to 1832, unpublished PhD thesis, University of East Anglia, 2003; K.E. Morley, The Origins and Development of Common Land in the Boulder Clay Region of Norfolk, unpublished MA dissertation, School of History, University of East Anglia, 2003; A. Bull, Five Clayland Commons: the Development, Survival and Ecology of a Relic Landscape, unpublished MA dissertation, School of History, University of East Anglia, 2020; P. Dallas, Wood Pasture in Norfolk:

The Relationship Between Trees, Animal Husbandry and the Changing Agricultural Landscape from the First Millennium AD to the Age of Improvement, unpublished MA dissertation, University of East Anglia, 2005.
26 G.S. Boulton, F. Cox, J. Hart and M. Thornton, The Glacial Geology of Norfolk, *Bulletin of the Geological Society of Norfolk* 34 (1984), 103–22; B.M. Funnell, Geological Background, in T. Ashwin and A. Davison (eds), *An Historical Atlas of Norfolk*, 2nd edn. (Chichester, 2005), 4–5; G.P. Larwood and B.M. Funnell (eds), *The Geology of Norfolk; Transactions of the Norfolk and Norwich Naturalists' Society* 19, 6 (1961); J.R. Lee, M.A. Woods and B.S.P. Moorlock (eds), *British Regional Geology: East Anglia*, 5th edn. (Keyworth, 2015).
27 C.A.H. Hodge, R.G.O. Burton, W.M.C. Corbett, R. Evans and R.S. Seale, *Soils and their Use in Eastern England* (Harpenden, 1984), 117–21.
28 Hodge *et al.*, *Soils and their Use*, 132–5.
29 B.A. Holderness, East Anglia and the Fens, in J. Thirsk (ed.), *The Cambridge Agrarian History of England and Wales Vol. 5* (Cambridge, 1984), 197–238; S. Wade Martins and T. Williamson, *Roots of Change; Farming and the Landscape in East Anglia, c. 1700–1870* (Exeter, 1999), 7–33.
30 E. Martin, and M. Satchell, *Wheare most inclosures be. East Anglian Fields, History, Morphology and Management*, Anglian Archaeology 124 (Ipswich, 2008).
31 K.J. Allison, The Sheep-Corn Husbandry of Norfolk in the Sixteenth and Seventeenth Centuries, *Agricultural History Review* 5 (1957), 12–30; J. Belcher, *The Foldcourse and East Anglian Agriculture and Landscape, 1100–1900* (Woodbridge, 2020); M.R. Postgate, The Field Systems of Breckland, *Agricultural History Review* 10 (1957), 80–101.
32 M. Bailey, *A Marginal Economy? East Anglian Breckland in the Later Middle Ages* (Cambridge, 1989), 43–5.
33 M. Bailey, Sand into Gold: The Evolution of the Foldcourse System in West Suffolk, 1200–1600, *Agricultural History Review*, 38, 1 (1990), 40–57.
34 Wade Martins and Williamson, *Roots of Change*, 34–43.
35 Wade Martins and Williamson, *Roots of Change*, 21–5, 49–52.

CHAPTER 2

Environments and Origins

Students of Norfolk's landscape are fortunate in having at their disposal one of the best of the many privately produced maps of English counties that appeared in the second half of the eighteenth century. William Faden's *Topographic Map of the County of Norfolk* was published in 1797 and mainly surveyed between 1794 and 1795, before the great wave of parliamentary enclosure acts swept away most of the county's common land.[1] A further benefit, for those with a particular interest in commons, is that they were mapped more accurately than most other features of the landscape, including woods and plantations or even the ornamental parks of great landowners.[2] This almost certainly reflects the current interest in enclosure and 'improvement'. The wealthy and middle-class individuals who constituted Faden's customers would have been particularly interested in the common 'waste', ripe for privatisation, in their neighbourhood – although the fact that commons were open and in effect public spaces, which could thus be surveyed (as it were) from the inside, may also have been a factor. In all, around 65,000 hectares (c. 160,500 acres) of 'commons and heaths' are shown on the map (Figure 2.1). Interestingly, this is close to the 144,846 acres of wastes, warrens and sheep walks which Nathaniel Kent estimated existed in Norfolk in 1794.[3]

Faden, however, unquestionably omitted several extensive areas of common land, for the map also has a separate category of 'Fens and Marsh Lands', most of which were enclosed property but some not. Common fens were, at this time, particularly extensive in Broadland but were widely distributed, throughout the county, on the peaty floodplains of rivers and their principal tributaries. Most are shown as common land but some, as we know from other sources, were included in this other category, especially in the valleys of the Ant, Thurne and Bure in the northern parts of Broadland. On the other hand, not all of the 'heaths' that the map lumps together with commons were, in fact, common land. In particular, many are labelled as 'warrens' that is, private rabbit farms, especially on the deep sandy soils of Breckland in the south-west of the county.[4] Faden shows no less than 21 examples of warrens that are clearly shaded as 'waste' (usually with the 'lodges' which provided accommodation for the warrener and a place to process carcasses and store skins and equipment), some covering more than 1,000 hectares and most of which were established between the fourteenth and the seventeenth century. In areas like Breckland, where common heaths were extensive relative to the number of farms, the provisions of the Statute of Merton left manorial lords free to enclose portions for this purpose. In some cases, however, the land occupied by the warren may

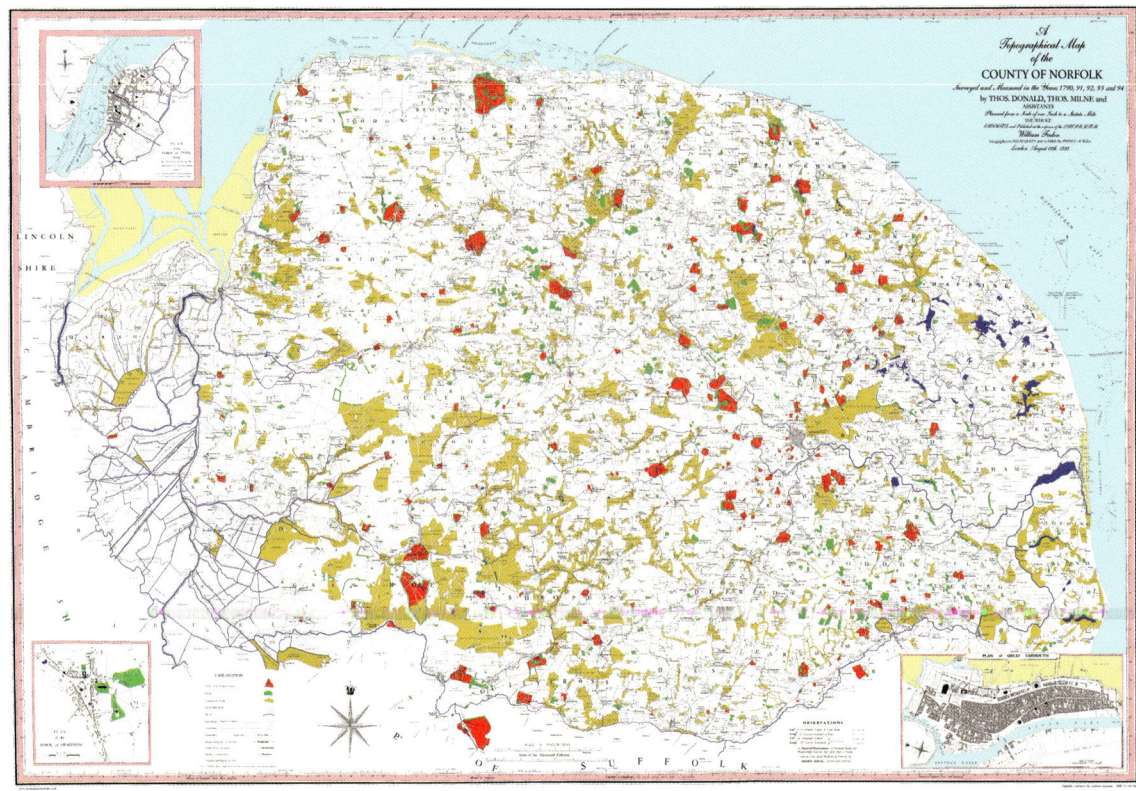

FIG. 2.1. William Faden's *Topographical Map of the County of Norfolk* of 1797, re-drawn and georectified by Andrew Macnair. 'Commons and Wastes' are shown in yellow.

have been neither physically nor legally enclosed, the rabbits simply sharing the grazing with the livestock of commoners. A royal grant of 'free warren' (permission to enjoy exclusive hunting rights over a tract of land) permitted manorial lords to establish colonies of rabbits on the 'waste' regardless of the impact that this might have on the grazing available to the commoners. In the words of the lawyer Harting, 'no action will lie against a lord of the manor for keeping coneys on land over which he has a right of warren'.[5] In such circumstances, commoners may have preferred a partial enclosure of the common, as the only way of limiting the depredations of the voracious animals. In some cases, commoners continued to enjoy certain rights within warrens but these were no longer 'commons' as this term is usually understood. Whatever the circumstances in particular cases, for these and other reasons – including errors in surveying which were the inevitable consequence of contemporary techniques and equipment – it is impossible to use Faden's map to provide an accurate estimate of the extent of common land at this time, and any attempt to do this using local maps would be incredibly time consuming and would face a similar range of challenges. We can reasonably assume, however, that in the 1790s commons still accounted for between 10 and 12 per cent of Norfolk's land area.

As the example of rabbit warrens suggests, both the extent and the configuration of common land in the county changed significantly between the thirteenth and the eighteenth centuries, and as we shall see, there were many ways in which individual commons might be whittled away or encroached upon. In a number of parishes, moreover, some or all of the commons had been removed altogether, through some kind of formal enclosure process, by the time Faden's map was surveyed. Indeed, the map itself refers to examples recently lost. The words 'Common inclosed' thus appears in Old Buckenham, a parish subject to an enclosure award of 1791; 'Thelton Common inclosed' is written across the area covered by the parish of Thelveton, with similar words describing Carleton Rode Common (enclosed by parliamentary act in 1777) and Banham Common (enclosed by an act of 1789). At least 46 enclosures by parliamentary act, dealing with land in 55 parishes, were made in Norfolk in the period before Faden's map was surveyed, most of which removed common land as well as open arable.[6] All this said, there are good grounds for believing that, in broad terms at least, the shape and distribution of commons shown on the map resemble those which had emerged many centuries earlier. In particular, archaeological fieldwalking surveys – involving the meticulous collection of artefacts lying around on the surface of the ploughsoil – have repeatedly shown that farms came to be established on the common edges surviving in the landscape today, or existing at the time of enclosure, in the course of the eleventh, twelfth and thirteenth centuries, leaving no doubt that these particular common boundaries, at least, have remained fixed since this time.[7]

Topography and Morphology

Faden's map, for all its faults, is a good place to begin an investigation of the county's common land not only because it allows us to see at a glance broad patterns of distribution but also because it reveals, in a way that an early map of an individual parish cannot, how a particular common, with its own name, often formed one portion of a wider tract, extending into neighbouring parishes, or part of a long chain of interconnected areas of uncultivated land. These might ramble across the landscape for many kilometres. In the 1790s it would have been possible to walk from Attleborough to the edge of Thetford (for example), around 20 kilometres as the crow flies, without leaving a common. Whether forming elements of such wider networks, or existing as more discrete components of the landscape, commons displayed variable but often complex shapes. Some formed continuous, uninterrupted blocks but others were filled with numerous 'islands' of private ground. Common edges might be staggered, indented and irregular but frequently formed smooth, concave, inward-bending arcs, with the common narrowing towards 'funnels' where roads entered them. Such smooth transitions, with roads gradually widening to 'become' commons, neatly reflected the legal situation, medieval law considering both to be part of the 'waste' of the manor.[8] There was, accordingly, no neat distinction between a wide road and a narrow linear common – a form which was particularly associated with the clay plateau in the south of the county. There was, however, usually a physical barrier, to prevent stock wandering off the common, which before the introduction of cattle grids in the second half of the twentieth century took the form of a gate. A few still exist at the entrances to surviving commons, as at the south-western corner of Hales Green, where Litchmere Road enters the common. The former presence of others is signalled by gateposts, as where Snakes Lane meets Fritton Common (half buried in a hedge) or at the western end of Whin Common in Denver (against the wall of a house).

Relatively narrow ribbons of common land followed bands of peat in the floors of stream and river valleys, although these as noted earlier were not fully recorded by Faden's map, which also omits many of the more extensive wetland commons that could also be found, on the floodplains of major valleys. In general, however, the largest commons were located on the higher ground, on interfluves, often forming parts of chains which ran close to the watersheds between drainage basins. As parish boundaries often ran through similar marginal terrain, dividing the land of communities whose arable fields were clustered on the more amenable soils of the valley sides, such commons were often shared – 'intercommoned' – between two or more neighbouring parishes, as indeed were some of the larger of the low, wetland commons. Such arrangements afforded fertile grounds for disputes over the fair allocation of resources and even when, and if, the common in question came to be divided by a physical boundary, there might be arguments over its precise course. Parishes often had 'high' commons, on interfluves, and 'low' ones, on floodplains, although Norfolk's muted topography ensured that this distinction was limited and confused, not least by the fact that streams often had their sources in damp, peaty concavities in heathy uplands, where the two kinds merged.

Although many individual commons thus comprised more than one type of habitat, there is no doubt that the overwhelming majority of Norfolk's common land comprised heath. Nearly 70 per cent of the common land mapped by Faden occupied soil types, as mapped by the Soil Survey, formed in deposits of sand or gravel, and characterised by high levels of acidity – especially those of the Methwold, Worlington and Newport Associations (Figure 2.2).[9] There is no doubt, moreover, that many examples apparently occupying other soil types were, in reality, associated with more localised pockets of acid ground, for the broad categories ('Associations') used in the published soil maps display much localised variation. Two of the largest areas of heath existing in the county at the end of the eighteenth century, Mousehold Heath and Stock Heath, thus overlay soils mainly mapped as 'slightly acid loams' (Wick 3 Association) and as a mixture of 'slightly acid loams' and 'seasonally wet clays and loams' (Beccles Association) respectively.[10] The complex drift geology of Norfolk ensured that lenses and patches of sand and gravel were widespread in otherwise more loamy and clayey deposits. Only in the south of the county does the Lowestoft Till

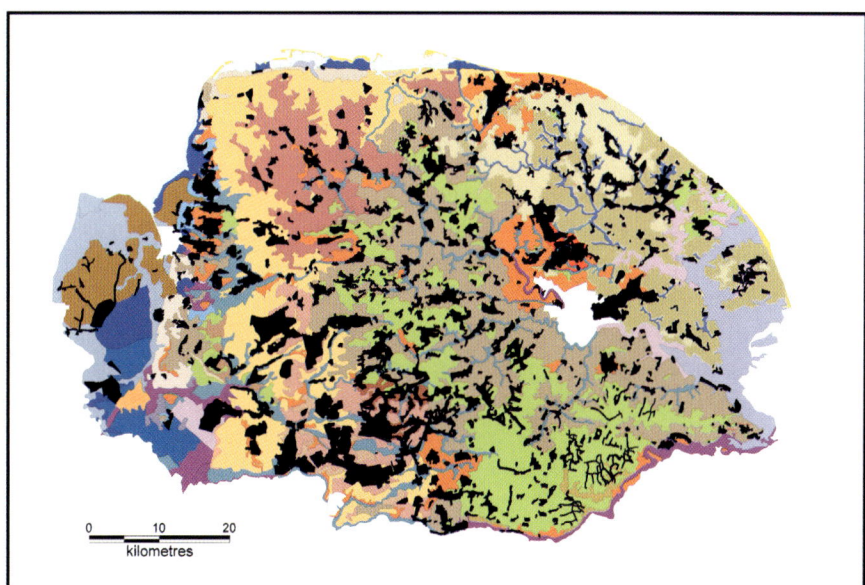

FIG. 2.2. 'Commons and wastes' shown on Faden's 1797 map of Norfolk, overlain on soils. Key as for Figure 1.5.

form a more homogenous deposit of lime-rich calcareous clay, and it is noteworthy that commons of any kind were relatively few in number, and limited in extent, in this area.

The predominance of heaths is, more generally, reflected in the names given to the various commons shown on Faden's map, although there is no doubt that this greatly oversimplified local nomenclature, often describing examples as 'Common', prefixed with the name of the parish in which it lay, where more local maps used terms like 'Green', 'Heath' or 'Moor' and provided more idiosyncratic prefixes. Thus Faden's 'Morley Common' appears on Thomas Waterman's 1629 map of Morley as 'Garsing Common', the former word an old, Middle English term for 'grazing', while 'Morley Bottom' is given as 'Southwoode Moore'.[11] In a similar way, the common described as 'Titshall Snath' on a 1727 survey of Tibbenham is named 'Titshall Common' by Faden, while 'The Bushes' is 'Aslacton Common'.[12] Around 38,794 hectares are simply described as 'common' on Faden's map, but of the rest, 16,620 hectares were 'heaths', only 2,519 hectares were 'greens' and a mere 781 'moors'. Heaths were particularly extensive in Breckland, in the south-west of the county; on the strip of sandy land extending along the eastern margins of Fenland and the Wash; in the area between Cawston and Norwich; and on the moraine ridge between Holt and Cromer. In earlier times much heathland had also existed in the 'Good Sands' region of north-west Norfolk, but had largely been reclaimed during the previous century or so, by large estates keen to embrace the principles of the 'agricultural revolution' (the sandy drift here lay thinly over the chalk, and the soils of the Barrow Association were more easily marled and brought into cultivation).[13] Most of the largest areas of common land depicted by Faden, moreover, were either labelled as 'heath', or largely overlay one of the more 'acidic' soil associations, as mapped by the Soil Survey. On the clay plateau, in contrast – and especially toward the south – common land was less extensive and more fragmented. All this suggests that it was soil acidity, far more than seasonal waterlogging, that discouraged the cultivation of certain areas of land and ensured their survival as commons, although much *permanently* waterlogged land was occupied by 'low' commons, the extent of which, as we have seen, is somewhat under represented on Faden's map.

Most of the commons bearing the name 'green' depicted on Faden's map are associated with poorly draining clay soils – especially those of the Beccles Association – and were thus a particular feature of the till plateau in the centre and south of the county. A significant minority, however, were amongst the relatively small number of 'low' commons mapped by Faden, and occupied slightly peaty, silty loams on valley floors – soils of the Hanworth and Isleham Associations – or the northern Fens – the Blacktoft Association.[14] Faden's map thus suggests, and a plethora of early maps confirm, that 'green' was the term traditionally given to damp commons on seasonally, but not permanently, waterlogged ground. The few areas labelled as 'Moor' by Faden are likewise mostly associated with poorly draining clay soil. Although 'moor' is today usually employed to describe an area of heather-grown upland, the Old English term *mor* had a more general sense of 'tract of desolate land'.[15] There are a total of 128 places described as 'green' on Faden's map, covering in all 2,519 hectares. They range in size from 0.8 to 190 hectares, with an average area of 19.7 hectares. The 62 named 'heaths', in contrast, covered no less than 16,620 hectares, ranging in size from 9.7 to 2,168 hectares, and with an average size of 268 hectares. The average 'heath', in other words, was over 13 times the size of the average 'green'. The 465 'commons', as we might expect from Faden's rather general usage of the term, fall in between these extremes, with an average size of 83.4 hectares and a range of 0.8 to 1,957 hectares. But there was another and perhaps more important distinction between these different types of common. A high proportion of heaths – just under 40 per cent – have no houses at all around their margins, compared with only 4 per cent of greens; 'commons' once again fall in between these extremes, with around 27 per cent lacking any associated dwellings. This pattern reflects the fact that heaths were generally associated with light, porous geological formations, which in many cases extended well beyond their margins, making it difficult to establish farms and cottages because of problems of water supply. On the kinds of heavy clay where most 'greens' could be found, in contrast, water was more easily obtained, from shallow wells.

The Uses of Common Land

Most commons were primarily used for grazing livestock but what was pastured, and by whom, varied from area to area and to some extent over time. Many commons were grazed by the demesne livestock – the animals of the manorial lord, or the individual who was renting his demesne – alongside those of the commoners. But in a few cases, as at Eccles, the demesne livestock were excluded and on many more, especially in the west of the county, foldcourses existed and the lord enjoyed rights of 'sheepwalk', meaning that only he could graze sheep there or the number the tenants could put on was limited, their stock being largely or entirely restricted to cattle, horses and poultry, principally geese.[16] In general terms the livestock grazed on commons reflected their wider importance in the local economy. Sheep thus predominated on the heathy commons in the north and west; they had less need of regular watering than horses or cattle and lived well on the acid grassland and heather. Cattle were, in contrast, always more important on the boulder clays of south and central Norfolk and, together with horses, were better suited to the lush damp grazing of the clayland commons than sheep. A list of the animals run on Fritton Common, drawn up in 1725, typically details two geldings, nine mares, fourteen foals, six cows, three heifers and eight colts.[17] Sheep were not entirely absent. Randall Burroughes, who farmed at Wymondham in the 1790s, grazed both mares with young colts and sheep on the local commons.[18] Cattle and horses also predominated on the common marshes, which could be found scattered along the floodplains of the principal rivers. In both cases, the manorial courts often stipulated the date on which grazing could commence, to prevent livestock 'poaching' the land and damaging the young grass growth, as on the common marsh of Heigham Holmes in Potter Heigham, where it was stated in 1632 that 'the saide inhabitants … do feede it as their common or waste from the 24th day of June yearely till the eighth day of September'.[19]

The kinds of livestock grazed by large farmers and manorial lords were different from those grazed by poor cottagers. The accounts of eighteenth-century writers like Arthur Young leave no doubt that their priority everywhere was a dairy cow, to provide daily milk for the household, and geese, to provide a family feast on special occasions, and it is likely that the same was true in earlier periods (Figure 2.3). The evidence suggests, however, that by the late nineteenth century the cows of the poor were increasingly being replaced by donkeys, cheaper to buy and able to consume a greater range of the common vegetation. Capable of pulling a small cart, they provided commoners with access to local towns and allowed them to run various kinds of full or part-time businesses. Geese, however, continued to be widely kept well into the twentieth century.

In addition to grazing, Norfolk commons supplied local people with a variety of domestic fuels. In the early Middle Ages many had been wooded but by the time our records become abundant, trees, and the firewood they produced, were limited and generally the subject of particular arrangements to which we shall return. Of more importance were gorse ('furze' or 'whin'), heather ('ling'), broom and bracken, cut from heaths, and a variety of combustible materials dug from the surface of both fens and heaths and usually described as 'flags' or 'turf', although the precise meaning of these terms seems to have varied over time and space. Heaths provided what are sometimes described in the documents as 'dry

FIG. 2.3. Detail from Thomas Waterman's map of Gressenhall, 1624, showing geese and cows grazing on the common.

ground flags', usually comprising blocks of heather, complete with fibrous roots, but in some cases apparently turfs in the modern sense – the soil was shaken off and the matted roots and dry grass burnt, a fuel used by the poorest households. The word 'turf' usually referred to peat, a fibrous, combustible material formed as plants died in waterlogged conditions and only partially decayed *in situ*, which was dug from 'turbaries' in fens that could be found on private land as well as on commons. It was mainly dug in the summer, when the ground was drier, manorial courts commonly restricting extraction to the months of May, June and July. Marshall in 1787 described how the individual blocks of peat ('turves'), when first cut, were 4 inches square, drying to 3¼ inches, and 'from two to three feet long, or of a length equal to the depth of the moor'.[20] Rather cheaper firing, again essentially a fuel for the poor, was provided by the unconsolidated material on the surface of the fen, scraped off before the true peat was extracted, which was also often referred to as 'flag' rather than 'turf' (although confusingly, flag can also be used for irises or rushes gathered to provide cheap lighting).[21]

Common fens provided a range of other resources. Some, the drier examples, were mown for rough marsh hay as 'fen meadows', or cut in late summer for 'litter', principally used for cattle bedding, in place of the more usual straw. Mixed with dung and urine, it made excellent manure for arable land, contributing 'to the great fertility of much of this country'.[22] 'Bolder' or bulrush (*Typha latifolia*), 'gladdon' or lesser bulrush (*Typha angustifolia*), club-rush (*Schoenoplectus* spp.) and yellow flag (*Iris pseudacorus*) were woven into baskets, mats and horse collars.[23] In c. 1803, during an investigation into common rights in Irstead, John Morton of Ludham claimed 'He had always cut Boulder and Gladding [gladdon] on Irstead Broad for a Right of a Cottage he was owner of at Irstead'; he was described as a 'bedmat and collar ma'er'.[24] More importantly, reed (*Phragmites australis*) was harvested from permanently waterlogged areas for use as a thatching material. In contrast to hay and litter, it was cut in the winter and spring; the regulations for managing the commons of Ludham, Catfield and Potter Heigham, drawn up in 1677, typically ordered that 'no reed be cut upon any of the said commons before the day after St Andrew [30 November] under penalty of 6sh 8d for every fathom so cut'.[25] It was the dead stems of the plant, rather than the young growth, that were harvested. They were cut below the surface of the water, as close to the roots as possible:

> It being an idea, even unto a proverb, that one inch below the water is worth two above it; for the part which now appears green changes to a blackish brown, and becomes as hard as horn; whereas that which grows above the water is brittle, and of a more perishable nature.[26]

Sedge – that is, saw-sedge (*Cladium mariscus*) – was also harvested from the more waterlogged areas, principally for making the ridges of roofs – it is extremely pliable when dry – although it was also used on its own to thatch hay and corn ricks and poorer dwellings. Suffling, writing in the 1880s, also recorded that local labourers made leggings 'of twisted sedge, to keep off the weather'.[27] Sedge was cut in the summer months rather than in the winter and spring and on a longer rotation than reed, usually at intervals of three years, in order to obtain the long stems required for ridging.

Common Land and Settlement

There is something paradoxical about common land. On the one hand it produced a range of resources which were of vital importance to the members of local communities, including the larger farmers, at least in the period before the eighteenth century. But on the other hand, commons occupied land which, viewed from the perspective of arable production, was marginal or sub-marginal in character; land that could not be cultivated, or which was unrewarding to cultivate, because of soil acidity or waterlogging. This said, it is important to emphasise that it was rare for an individual common to correspond closely with an area occupied by a particular soil type; in the case of Norfolk's 'upland' commons, at least, boundaries did not usually mark significant changes in soil character. But they did on occasions coincide with those of parishes or townships, indicating differences in pressure on resources or perceptions of land potential on the part of neighbouring communities or manorial lords. The extent and configuration of common land, in Norfolk as elsewhere, were thus broadly influenced by environmental factors, but in detail shaped by social and economic circumstances. They were, in particular, closely related to the ways in which settlement developed during the eleventh, twelfth and thirteenth centuries.

The evidence of fieldwalking, aerial photography and other archaeological approaches leave no doubt that in the Roman period fields and farms were widespread on all soil types, on heavy clays and acid sands and gravels. By the middle of the fifth century it is clear that settlement had retreated to the most easily worked and rewarding soils, mainly located in the principal river valleys, a change which probably reflects both a demographic decline and a significant regression in agricultural technology.[28] The area under cultivation began to expand once again from the seventh century, and by the tenth century large areas of land, including some of the heavier clays, were once more under cultivation. All Norfolk parishes seem to contain at least one, and sometimes two or three, settlements which were in existence by the time of the Norman Conquest, comprising compact clusters of dwellings. Some were the halls of local lords or thegns, accompanied by the homes of tenants and slaves, others the residences of free peasant families which might likewise, in some cases, be accompanied by the homes of slaves and dependants. In many cases, such settlements were fixed in the landscape for centuries, usually occupying sites beside the most fertile and easily cultivated soils and with a good water supply. Most, in the last centuries of the Anglo-Saxon period, acquired a church, initially of wood, paid for by a local lord or in some cases groups of wealthy freemen.[29] Churches were a statement of status as much as an expression of faith; they cost money to build and also needed to be endowed with glebe land for the support of the priest, while moves had to be made to appropriate the tithes formerly paid by local people to some more distant 'minster' – the term given to the older, sparser network of semi-monastic churches, sustained by extensive *parochiae*. The system of parishes that had emerged in Norfolk by the twelfth century thus fossilised earlier patterns of secular land holding; parishes were conterminous with the estates of single local lords, or with the combined properties of a group of free peasant families.

As population continued to grow, farms to proliferate, and the area under cultivation to expand onto the more problematic soils, existing settlements did not simply grow *in situ* and equally in all directions. Increasingly, from the eleventh century, new farms were placed on the margins of the residual fragments of the uncultivated 'wastes', or on the roads leading towards them. In some cases the original settlement by the church grew in an asymmetrical fashion, expanding towards, and then around the margins of, a neighbouring common. Elsewhere new houses were attracted to areas of uncultivated ground more remotely located so that the old focus failed to grow, remaining as a small group of houses or simply as a 'hall–church complex', a pairing of church and manorial site. But in many places, perhaps especially where extensive tracts of unploughed pasture lay at a significant distance, the original settlement site was abandoned altogether, as all the inhabitants decamped to a common edge, leaving the church alone in the fields (Figure 2.4). Archaeological investigations in the immediate vicinity of such isolated churches invariably reveal evidence of settlements abandoned in the eleventh or twelfth centuries, and which often originated as early as the eighth; the earliest occupation on common edges, in contrast, almost always seems to post-date c. 1000.[30]

Large scale enclosure in the post-medieval period has ensured that, while Norfolk can boast many examples of churches that stand alone, or almost alone,

2. Environments and Origins 31

FIG. 2.4. St Peter's, Kimberley, one of the many isolated parish churches in Norfolk.

in the fields, there are only a few places where we can still see, as it were, the other half of the equation: a nearby green or common surrounded by a girdle of farms and cottages. Fritton in the south of the county is a striking survivor (Figure 2.5). The church of St Catherine stands in isolation, at a height of around 40 metres OD, the ground to the north comprising well-drained clays on land that slopes gently away towards a tributary of the river Tas. Settlement has migrated to the margins of what is now Fritton Common, a fragment of a more extensive tract of uncultivated land that had formerly occupied the higher, flatter, more poorly draining ground to the south. Faden's map, surveyed when Norfolk's commons were still extensive, shows many similar examples of this pattern, as well as variations on the same theme, where for example green-edge houses, and church, were connected by a short ribbon of roadside settlement. It also vividly conveys an impression of how commons were the tattered remnants of once much larger areas of grazing land, otherwise eroded by the expansion of cultivation. The isolated churches of Morley St Botolph and Morley St Peter were surrounded by areas of open farmland which were bounded in turn by a ring of large commons, to the margins of which most farms and cottages had migrated (Figure 2.6). The farmland areas appear almost to have been 'punched' out of a once continuous tract of uncultivated ground. Common boundaries, that is, are best understood not as the edges of the commons themselves, but as the margins of areas of cultivated land, which – whether developing gradually, or created at a stroke as an intake received as a grant – were fenced off from the surrounding grazing lands of the waste.[31] This may provide a partial explanation for the curving, concave boundaries that, as noted earlier, are a feature of so many commons, in Norfolk as elsewhere. They reflect the economies of fencing such intakes from the 'waste', rough approximations to the circular shapes which would have enclosed the greatest surface area

FIG. 2.5. (opposite) Aerial view of Fritton (courtesy John Fielding). The church of St Catherine, at the bottom of the picture, has been left isolated by the migration of settlement to the margins of Fritton Common, centre-top.

FIG. 2.6. Detail from Faden's 1797 map of Norfolk, showing commons and settlements in the area around Morley St Botolph and Morley St Peter in the central Norfolk claylands. Note the isolated churches and the curving common boundaries which define the edges of ovoid intakes from the waste.

for the shortest length of hedge and ditch. It also explains why neighbouring commons are, or were, directly linked by public roads which gradually widen as they 'funnel' into them (see Figure 2.6). These represent the boundaries between adjacent intakes, residual slithers of common land retained in order to allow the continued movement of livestock from one part of the dwindling wastes to another. Larger ovoid intakes might have a parish church, marking a settlement newly established in the tenth, eleventh or twelfth centuries, close to their centre; smaller and later examples were associated with farms placed on their peripheries, located in the usual way on a common edge.

Commons and Woods

The name of Morley – the *mōr lēah*, or 'barren upland clearing' – was coined several centuries before the boundaries of the local commons began to be fixed in the landscape. But it is likely that even at this time, in the eleventh or twelfth centuries, many commons still carried significant amounts of tree cover – they were 'wood pastures', or grazed woodland. When Faden's map was surveyed one of Morley's commons was still called 'Hookwood'; the map of the parish surveyed by Thomas Waterman in 1629 names another as 'Southwoode Common'.[32] Other clayland commons in the centre and south of the county carried similar wood-related names, including Diss Heywood and Badley Moor (OE *leah*, 'wood' or 'clearing'); 'Horsefrith Common' (Old English *frid*, 'wood') is so named on Waterman's 1624 map of Gressenhall.[33] On the late-settled, poorly draining clay soils the presence of common wood-pastures is perhaps unsurprising. But the evidence is equally abundant from heathland commons.

While many, on the sandier soils especially, may have remained free of trees since first cleared in prehistory, some – mainly overlying soils formed in gravelly deposits in the east of the county, and especially those of the Newport 4 Association – appear to have been wooded in the early Middle Ages. The name of Stock Heath features the Old English word *stocc*, 'tree stump'; that of the vast Mousehold Heath to the east of Norwich incorporates *holt*, another Old English term for 'wood'. Domesday implies that there was still a substantial wood here but in the thirteenth century the agent of the bishop of Norwich complained that it was proving difficult to restrain the tenant's use of the area and the trees were disappearing. By the end of the century, documents refer to Mousehold *Heath*.[34] There are other examples. In 1239 Robet de Hauteyn granted lands to William Lincoln in Taverham, a heathy parish near Norwich, along with 'common of pasture for 8 sheep, 6 beasts, in the woods, except in the park of the said Robert'.[35] In the late sixteenth century the inhabitants of nearby Marsham accused James Brampton of erecting a foldcourse 'where he ought not', and asserted that he had 'felleth downe woode growinge upon the common contrarye to the custome of the mannor'.[36] By the eighteenth century the commons in both of these parishes consisted entirely of open heaths. Evidently the environmental character of the various kinds of common land when first described or illustrated in the eighteenth and nineteenth centuries – as clayland pastures or open heathland – may be a poor guide to the situation in the eleventh or twelfth centuries, when commons were first becoming fixed in the landscape, or even in much later periods. The degeneration of common woods to open pasture was the consequence of the fact that, as trees died, were blown down or felled, any replacements – whether planted or self-sown – were unlikely to survive, given the intensity of the grazing. Nevertheless, some commons appear to have retained a significant number of trees into the eighteenth or nineteenth centuries. This was partly because the process of attrition was slow, but mainly because in many places, as we shall see, it was halted or reversed, as both manorial lords and commoners possessed rights to fence in or otherwise protect new trees they had planted on commons (below, p. 53).

As the example of Mousehold suggests, the 'woodland' recorded by Domesday, in Norfolk at least, mainly took the form of wood pasture, rather than the kind of intensively managed coppice-with-standards woodland we are familiar with today as 'ancient woodland'. In Norfolk, as in neighbouring counties, Domesday records woodland in terms of the numbers of pigs it could support, reflecting an assumption that most was used for *pannage* – that is the autumn fattening of herds of swine on nuts and acorns – with the implication that sheep, goats and cattle were grazed at other times of the year. Domestic livestock of all kinds do tremendous damage to coppiced woods, browsing off and eventually killing the shoots of the regenerating stools, and were usually rigorously excluded by substantial banks, surmounted by hedges or fences; such woods were always private property, a part of the manorial demesne, and tenants usually enjoyed no common rights over them.[37] Domesday's woodland, in other words, represents the more densely timbered areas of the uncultivated 'waste' a short time before common boundaries began to be fixed.

So far as the evidence goes, as the cultivated area continued to expand through the twelfth and into the thirteenth century manorial lords enclosed portions of such land, managing them more intensively for the production of wood and timber. At Bradenham in 1226 it was reported that the lord of the manor had 'about the wood… raised one earthwork for the livestock, lest they eat up the younger wood'.[38] Where uncultivated land was still particularly extensive or manors were in the hands of particularly powerful individuals rather larger areas of the wastes might be taken into private ownership, securely enclosed, and used as hunting parks. The establishment of parks and coppiced woods, the fixing of common boundaries, the drift of farms and cottages to the margins of commons and, perhaps, the allocation of common rights between and within communities should all be seen as parts of the same process of differentiation and definition, driven by population growth, the proliferation of farms, economic expansion and the increasing power of manorial lords, which may have begun in some areas of Norfolk as early as the eleventh century, but which continued in others into the thirteenth. It was a process common to other areas of England and one which, as Christopher Dyer has demonstrated, involved innumerable legal disputes, and episodes of direct action, on the part of local communities against enclosures and intakes, both before and after the Statute of Merton.[39]

Not surprisingly, medieval woods, parks and commons sometimes formed continuous or near-continuous blocks which are often still apparent on William Faden's county map. The largest, which might extend over several square kilometres, were to be found on high, remote ground, on the watersheds between major drainage basins. In the area between Hindolveston, Fulmondeston, Melton Constable, Barney, Swanton Novers, Gunthorpe and Thursford, for example, the late eighteenth-century landscape was dominated by the vast, rambling area of Stock Heath and its associated commons – Fulmondeston Common, Hindolveston Common, and Orbury Common. Attached to these were a number of areas of ancient woodland – including Swanton Novers Wood – together with an extensive block of private wood pasture, Fulmondeston Severals, which had probably (like the coppiced woods) been severed from the surrounding commons at an early date. To the east lay the landscape park surrounding Melton Constable Hall, which existed as a deer park by the seventeenth century, and which had probably originated in the twelfth or thirteenth centuries.[40] The area occupied high ground between the headwaters of the Glaven, Bure, Stiffkey and Wensum and its marginal character is reflected in the fact that the hundreds of Eynesford, Gallow, Holt and North Greenhoe all converged on Stock Heath. A similar cluster of woods, parks and commons lay to the south-east, to the west of North Elmham, between the Wensum, the Nar and the Panford Beck. Here Faden's map shows that Elmham Heath, Brisley Green, the deer park (with medieval origins) at Elmham and Horningtoft Wood all lay contiguous and must have originally formed one single area of 'waste' which also probably included Colkirk Common and Colkirk Wood, lying a little further to the west.

Yet while these various features of the landscape could often be found clustering in the same areas, on the heavier or more acidic soils onto which settlement expanded from the eleventh century, there were nevertheless subtle differences in their distributions. In particular, woods tended to be found towards the *margins* of the difficult upland soils, on the edges of the principal valleys, whereas commons were more widely distributed, with many of the larger examples occurring towards the centre of interfluves.[41] This pattern, which is especially clear where the uplands between valleys are occupied by boulder clays rather than by sands and gravels, has been noted elsewhere. Warner, for example, has describe how in north-east Suffolk medieval commons tended to occupy the central sections of the boulder clay plateau, with the enclosed woods lying towards their edges;[42] while Witney has observed how, by late medieval times, most woodland within the Weald of Kent and Sussex clustered around the district's periphery rather than, as we might expect, towards its centre.[43] This, she suggested, reflected practical economic factors, and in particular access. Areas of woodland were enclosed from the common swine-pastures, and more intensively managed, in places from which their products could be transported to markets with relative ease. In contrast, it was almost impossible to move loads of wood and timber from the central parts of the Weald in wintertime because of the poor condition of the clay roads.[44] In medieval Norfolk similar processes may have been at work. Manorial lords, residing for the most part in long established settlements located beside areas of tractable soil in major valleys, established woods in places from which wood and timber could be easily transported to their own homes, or to more distant markets.

Woodland and Champion

We must be careful not to view the drift of farms to common edges entirely in terms of a movement to the wooded upland margins. It was more than a form of colonisation, for the expansion of cultivation in the course of the eleventh, twelfth and thirteenth centuries regularly leap-frogged patches of unappealing or intractable ground, leaving pockets of uncultivated land which likewise acted as magnets for settlement. So, too, did fens and marshes on the floors of valleys, many lying in the heart of areas that had been settled and cultivated for centuries, and often only a stone's throw from the parish church. This expansion, and relocation of settlement towards, and around, areas of common land – 'common edge drift' – has never been satisfactorily explained. As the landscape began to fill up with small peasant farms, a location beside a common, close to the grazing and other resources that it offered, evidently made more sense than it had done earlier in the Saxon period, when settlements had been fewer. Most had then probably been occupied by lords or wealthy freemen owning slaves, or by extended kin groups able to share the daily tasks of farming, including management and supervision of livestock and their movement to and from common pastures. The individual peasant living at the time of the Norman Conquest, cultivating his own holding with the labour of his immediate family, perhaps found it more difficult to find the time to do such things; certainly, some later sources emphasise how small landowners living at any distance from a common might be unable to exploit their rights to use it (see below, p. 45). At a time when common rights were becoming more carefully defined, moreover, proximity may have helped secure the use of these dwindling remnants of the 'waste'. Whatever the explanation, there is no doubt that the spread of farms and cottages around the edges of greens and commons was a key theme in the development of medieval settlement not only in Norfolk, but also more widely.

Those familiar with the Norfolk countryside may query this last statement, for while the dispersal of settlement to the margins of commons was unquestionably important across much of the county – and is still manifest in today's post-enclosure landscape in the plethora of scattered farms and cottages, and isolated churches – there were areas where it is much less apparent. On the light, well-drained soils of the north and west, settlement was (and is) more 'nucleated' or clustered in character, with most or all of the dwellings in a parish lying in close proximity, forming villages.[45] This contrast in settlement patterns corresponds, to a significant extent, to the variations in field systems and agricultural practices outlined earlier between the north and west of the county, and the south and east; and is part of a wider national pattern, although on this larger scale rather less obviously related to variations in the natural environment (Figure 2.7).[46] In the Middle Ages, and to an extent until the early nineteenth century, a broad band of England running diagonally from Yorkshire and Durham in the north-east to Dorset and Hampshire on the south coast was 'champion' countryside. On the poorly draining clays of the Midland vales, as much as on the light, freely draining chalk soils of Wessex or the Yorkshire and Lincolnshire Wolds, farms were clustered in villages and their land lay scattered, as small strips, through the arable fields of the parish, within which farming was organised on highly communal lines. The south-east of England, in contrast – including much of East Anglia – was 'woodland' country. Farms were more widely dispersed across the landscape and cultivated their own enclosed fields, or strips that lay close at hand, rather than widely dispersed, and in fields whose management was often less tightly controlled by the community.

For generations historians, geographers and archaeologists have debated the origins of these (and other) variations in the character of the English rural landscape. They have been interpreted as reflections of the areas settled by different ethnic groups after the fall of the Roman Empire; as the consequence of variations in early medieval population density or social and economic structure; or as the outcome of environmental influences on agricultural practices.[47] As they are not central to the principal concerns of this book, such matters cannot be discussed in detail here. But two observations that may have some relevance can usefully be made. The first is that, in Norfolk as elsewhere, differing forms

38   *The Landscapes of Common Land*

FIG. 2.7. Landscape regions in England. (a) the boundaries of Howard Gray's 'Midland System', of extensive communal open fields. (b) Oliver Rackham's distinction between the 'planned' countryside, created by eighteenth- and nineteenth-century enclosure, and the 'ancient' countryside. (c) the 'Central Province', of strongly nucleated settlement, as defined by Roberts and Wrathmell (2000). (d) densities of dispersed settlement mapped by Roberts and Wrathmell (2000). Note the varying approach taken by these authorities to northern and western Norfolk.

of settlement emerged gradually, mainly in the period between the tenth and the thirteenth century, as the population grew rapidly, and were largely a consequence of the extent to which new farms dispersed away from existing sites as the frontiers of cultivation expanded – hugging the margins of surviving fragments of 'waste', for example – rather than being established in immediate proximity to existing dwellings. And secondly, while landscape historians, geographers and archaeologists often draw a simple distinction between 'villages' and 'dispersed' settlements, this rather oversimplifies a more complex situation. The latter could take a variety of forms and even in Norfolk might include dwellings strung out along the sides of roads or farms surrounded by their own fields, as well as common-edge clusters; while most areas of dispersed settlement, including those in Norfolk, contained some recognisable 'villages' alongside their scattered farms and hamlets. But above all, 'nucleated' and 'dispersed' did not represent alternative forms of settlement so much as the ends of a spectrum.

This is particularly clear in Norfolk, where many of the 'villages' in the west and north resemble, as depicted on the earliest surviving maps, rather loose agglomerations of settlement, clusters of farms or discrete hamlets that only pass as villages because of the wide expanse of surrounding land, devoid of farms and cottages, separating them from the next loose cluster. Indeed, this – together with the associated 'intermediate' character of these areas' field systems – explains why researchers have differed over whether these areas (together with the western parts of Suffolk) should be considered as 'woodland' or 'champion' (Figure 2.7). Until the parliamentary enclosure of 1854 the village of Heacham, for example, largely comprised a scatter of dwellings around a complex collection of rambling, interconnected commons, with the church, accompanied by a small cluster of houses, standing slightly removed.[48] The plans of villages in the north and west of the county had often, by the time they were first mapped in the seventeenth, eighteenth or nineteenth centuries, been significantly modified by a variety of late medieval and post-medieval changes related to the poor nature of the local soils and the power of local lords; by shrinkage, enforced depopulation, or the creation of extensive parks and gardens. It nevertheless remains clear that most once exhibited a similar loosely nucleated form and simply represent the consequences of a dispersal of settlement that was more restricted than that which took place in the south and east of the county. In this area dominated by permeable geological formations, settlement remained tethered close to places where water was freely available.

In some places, 'villages' emerged as settlement dispersed around the margins of a single large common, but not more widely. On the chalk uplands of northwest Norfolk some of the higher ground is capped by deposits of boulder clay but only in a few places, where they fill concavities in the chalk surface, are these of sufficient depth to provide the kind of reliable water supply they afford in the centre and south of the county. Such areas also provided better grazing than surrounding, drier soils. At Great Massingham we can still see how, in response to these influences, settlement did not disperse far across the landscape, the church and principal farms hugging a series of greens (Figure 2.8a).[49] The artificially straight northern boundary of the largest of these suggests that it had once extended further in this direction. More importantly, even a cursory examination reveals that what are now in effect four separate greens, were two before nineteenth-century encroachments, and was originally one. This was divided, at some unknown earlier date, by the insertion of a substantial block of houses and gardens, while two further 'islands' of dwellings appeared elsewhere. In other places this process went further. Indeed, many of the larger villages, with the most complex plans, including Docking and Binham, have at their heart a large green which has been infilled to varying extents and the same is true of some smaller places (Figure 2.8b). The main part of the village of South Creake,

40   *The Landscapes of Common Land*

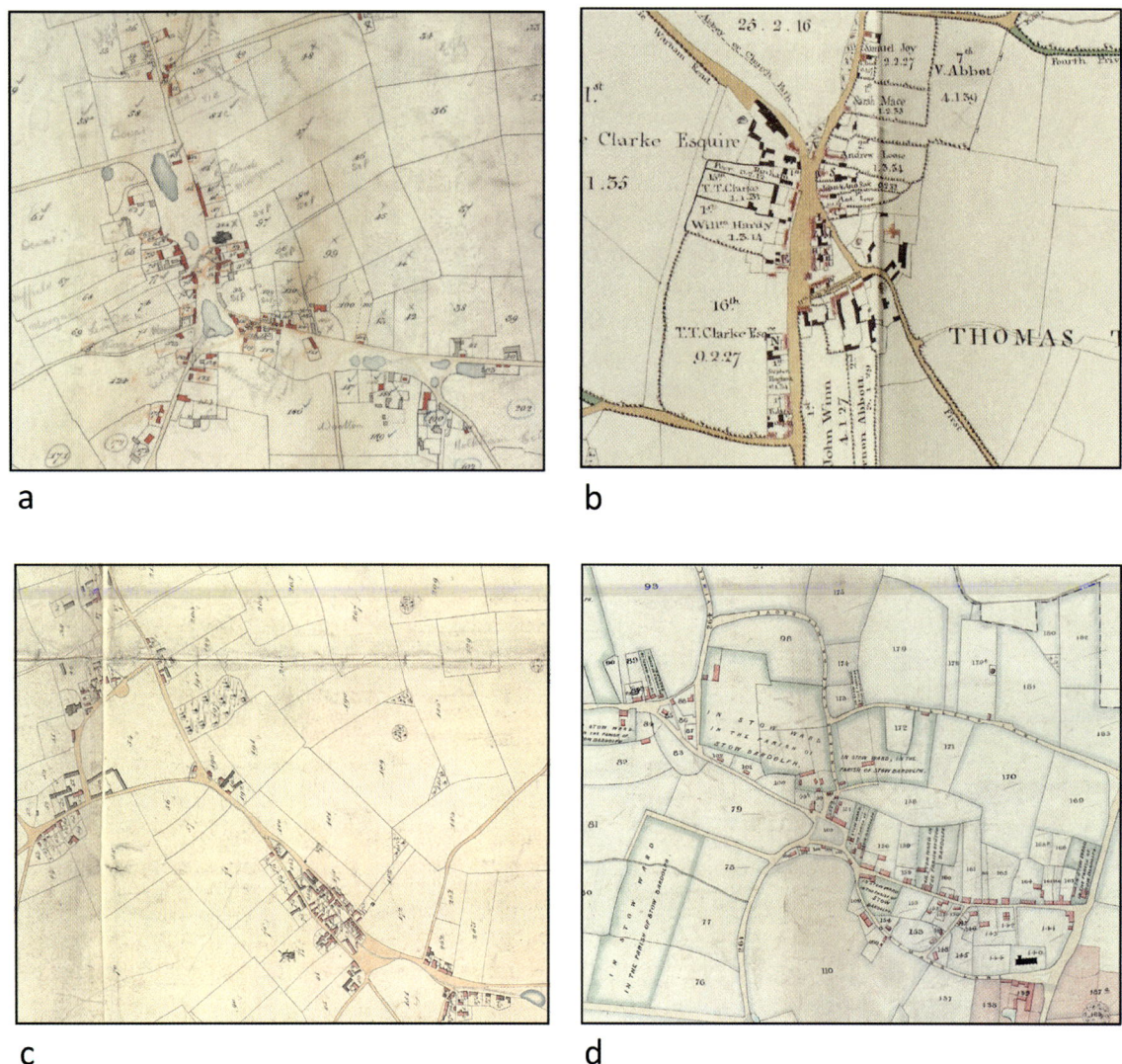

for example, occupying a ribbon of damp ground on the floodplain of the river Burn, appears to comprise a single infilled common (Figure 2.8c), as does the centre of Wighton. There were probably many other examples in the area in the early Middle Ages which, because of the scale of post-medieval changes, have left less obvious traces in the landscape.

Not all areas in the west of the county are characterised by permeable geological formations and obvious restrictions in water supply. On the margins of the Fens and the Wash the geology is complex and includes extensive areas of low-lying sandy land with a high water table, and deposits of both Gault and boulder clay. Yet here early maps depict a similar repertoire of village plans, with settlement clustered around a single large common (Stradsett) or several

FIG. 2.8. (opposite) Village plans in northern and western Norfolk, shown on the tithe maps of c. 1840. (a) Massingham, a village ranged around a large green partly colonised by 'islands' of houses. (b) Binham and (c) South Creake, where the main section of the village comprises a large infilled green. (d) Wimbotsham, with houses scattered around the margins of several small greens and former greens.

neighbouring greens (Wimbotsham) (Figure 2.8d), or else exhibiting clear signs of infilled central greens (Wereham).[50] The emergence of 'villages' in such places must reflect more subtle hydrological influences or social or agrarian factors militating against dispersal, as seems to have been the case elsewhere in England's 'champion' (below, p. 209). Nor were greenside agglomerations the only elements in these villages of clustered dispersal. As in areas of more widely scattered settlement in the county, some farms or manors might represent foci with pre-Conquest origins, as revealed by the programme of research at Sedgeford;[51] while medieval expansion often simply spread farms and cottages thinly along the sides of roadways. But everywhere in Norfolk it is likely that the majority of dwellings, by the thirteenth century, stood beside commons, a clear reflection of their importance in the lives of farmers and cottagers, and the advantages that accrued from dwelling in their immediate proximity.

Notes

1. W. Faden, *A Topographical Map of the County of Norfolk* (London, 1797).
2. A. Macnair and T. Williamson, *Wiliam Faden and Norfolk's 18th-Century Landscape* (Oxford, 2010), 86–9.
3. W. Kent, *General View of the Agriculture of Norfolk* (London, 1794).
4. M. Bailey, The Rabbit and the Medieval East Anglian Economy, *Agricultural History Review* 36 (1988), 1–20; A. Mason and J. Parry, *The Warrens of Breckland* (Thetford, 2010); T. Williamson, *Rabbits. Warrens and Archaeology* (Stroud, 2007), 100–9.
5. J.E. Harting, *The Rabbit* (London, 1898), 57.
6. W.E. Tate and M. Turner, *A Domesday of English Enclosure Acts and Awards* (Reading, 1978), 178–9, 187.
7. A. Davison, The Field Archaeology of Bodney, and the Stanta Extension, *Norfolk Archaeology* 42 (1994), 57–79; A. Davison and B. Cushion, The Archaeology of the Hargham Estate, *Norfolk Archaeology* 53 (1999), 257–74; A. Davison and A. Fenner, *The Evolution of Settlement in Three Parishes in South East Norfolk*, East Anglian Archaeology 49, 1990; A. Rogerson, Fransham: An Archaeological and Historical Study of a Parish on the Norfolk Boulder Clay, unpublished PhD thesis, University of East Anglia, 1995; P. Wade-Martins, *Village Sites in the Launditch Hundred*, East Anglian Archaeology 10, 1990.
8. Rackham, *History of the Countryside*, 265–7.
9. Hodge *et al.*, *Soils and their Use*, 270–9, 368–70.
10. Hodge *et al.*, *Soils and their Use*, 117–19, 346–9.
11. NRO PD3/111.
12. NRO PET 1009/12.
13. Wade Martins and Williamson, *Roots of Change*, 34–43.
14. Hodge *et al.*, *Soils and their Use*, 124–7, 212–13.
15. A.H. Smith, *English Place Name Elements*, Vol. 2 (Cambridge, 1956), 42–3.
16. Bailey, Sand into Gold, 40–57.
17. NRO/ MS14081/ 36A4.
18. S. Wade Martins and T. Williamson (eds) *The Farming Journal of Randall Burroughes of Wymondham, 1794–99,* Norfolk Record Society Vol. 58 (Norwich, 1995), 22, 87, 121.
19. NRO DN HAR 3/1, p. 31.
20. W. Marshall, *The Rural Economy of Norfolk*, Vol. 2 (London, 1787), 98.

21 C. Wells, Post-Medieval Turf-digging in Norfolk, *Norfolk Archaeology*, 43/3 (2000), 469–82, at 470–1.
22 A. Young, *General View of the Agriculture of the County of Norfolk* (London, 1804), 76.
23 R. Malster, *The Broads* (Chichester, 1993), 29.
24 NRO MC121/238–40.
25 NRO Ms 19424, 103X4.
26 Marshall, *Rural Economy*, Vol. 2, 89.
27 E.R. Suffling, *The Land of the Broads* (London, 1885), 211.
28 C. Scull, S. Brookes and T. Williamson, *Lordship and Landscape in East Anglia AD 400–800: The Royal Centre at Rendlesham, Suffolk and its Contexts* (London, 2024), 268–70.
29 R. Morris, *Churches in the Landscape* (London, 1989), 230; P. Warner, Shared Churchyards, Freemen Church Builders and the Development of Parishes in Eleventh-century East Anglia, *Landscape History* 8 (1989), 39–52.
30 Davison, The Field Archaeology of Bodney; Davison and Cushion, The Archaeology of the Hargham Estate; Davison and Fenner, *Evolution of Settlement*; Rogerson, Fransham; Wade-Martins, *Village Sites in the Launditch Hundred*.
31 T. Williamson, *Environment, Society and Landscape in Ealy Medieval England* (Woodbridge, 2013), 156–60.
32 NRO PD3/111.
33 NRO Hayes and Storr 72.
34 Rackham, *History of the Countryside*, 299–303.
35 F. Blomefield, *An Essay Towards a Topographical History of the County of Norfolk* (London, 1805), Vol. 2, 247.
36 A. Hassell Smith and J. Baker (eds), *The Papers of Nathaniel Bacon of Stiffkey* Vol. 2 (Norwich, 1983), 242–3.
37 G. Barnes and T. Williamson, *Rethinking Ancient Woodland: The Archaeology and History of Woods in Norfolk* (Hatfield, 2015), 38–44, 59–61.
38 O. Rackham, The Ancient Woods of Norfolk, *Transactions of the Norfolk and Norwich Naturalists' Society* 27 (1986), 161–77, at 168.
39 C. Dyer, Conflict in the Landscape: The Enclosure Movement in England, 1220–1349, *Landscape History* 28 (2006), 21–4.
40 NRO Hayes and Storr map 82, M3; T. Williamson, *The Archaeology of the Landscape Park; Garden Design in Norfolk, England, c.1680–1840* (Oxford, 1998), 261–3.
41 Barnes and Williamson, *Rethinking Ancient Woodland*, 44–6.
42 P. Warner, *Greens, Commons and Clayland Colonization* (Leicester, 1987).
43 K.P. Witney, The Woodland Economy of Kent, 1066–1348, *Agricultural History Review* 38 (1998), 20–39.
44 Witney, Woodland Economy, 20.
45 A.G. Louverre, The Atlas of Rural Settlement GIS, *Landscapes* 11, 2 (2010), 21–44, at 36; Martin and Satchell, *Wheare Most Inclosures Be*; Rackham, *History of the Countryside*, 3; B.K. Roberts and S. Wrathmell, *Region and Place; a Study of English Rural Settlement,* English Heritage (London, 2002),147–73.
46 G.C. Homans, *English Villagers of the Thirteenth Century* (Cambridge, Mass., 1941), 21; Rackham, *History of the Countryside*, 3, 164–79; B.K. Roberts and S. Wrathmell, *An Atlas of Rural Settlement in England* (London, 2000).
47 See, in particular: B.M.S. Campbell, Commonfield Origins – the Regional Dimension, in T. Rowley (ed.) *The Origins of Open Field Agriculture* (London, 1980), 112–29; R. Dodgshon, *The Origins of British Field Systems: An Interpretation* (London, 1980); H.L. Gray, *English Field Systems* (Cambridge, Mass., 1915); G.C. Homans, The Explanation

of English Regional Differences, *Past and Present* 42 (1969), 18–34; C. Lewis, P. Mitchell-Fox and C. Dyer, *Village, Hamlet and Field: Changing Settlements in Central England* (Macclesfield, 2002); B.K. Roberts and S. Wrathmell, Peoples of Wood and Plain: An Exploration of National and Local Regional Contrasts, in D. Hooke (ed.) *Landscape: The Richest Historical Record* (Birmingham, 2000), 85–96; J. Thirsk, The Common Fields, *Past and Present* 29 (1966), 3–29; and Williamson, *Environment, Society and Landscape*, 125–83.

48 NRO C/Sca 2/146; NRO DN/TA 649.
49 NRO DN/TA 162.
50 NRO BL 14/54 (Stradsett, 1689); NRO HARE 6812/1–2 (Wimbotsham, c. 1620); NRO NRO DE 38 (Wereham 1840).
51 N. Faulkner, G. Rossin and K. Robinson (eds) *Digging Sedgeford: A People's Archaeology* (North Walsham, 2014).

CHAPTER 3

Commons and Communities

Commoners

It was rare in Norfolk for commons to be exploited equally, by all the inhabitants of a particular place. Common rights were not anyway owned, in and of themselves, by individuals. They were instead, at least in theory, attached to particular dwellings, or even to their sites, one eighteenth-century document from the county declaring that 'a farm, house or cottage, though pulled Down, or destroyed shall retain its rights of Commonage'.[1] Even in areas like Broadland, where parishes often included particularly extensive areas of common marsh and fen, rights to their use were usually attached to only some, not all, of the properties, the oldest in the parish. As the regulations drawn up in the seventeenth century for Potter Heigham put it, 'none but ancient tenements shall presume to reap any profit' from the manorial wastes.[2] The 'commoners' were thus a specific and circumscribed group that did not necessarily include all the householders in a community.

In many places this had probably been the situation at the point when 'commons' as such, with defined rights and limits, first came into existence, in the twelfth or thirteenth centuries. It certainly became the case almost everywhere in Norfolk in the course of the sixteenth and seventeenth centuries, as local populations increased and new cottages proliferated. It is true that some of these properties came to possess common rights. In Burgh St Margaret on Flegg in 1606, for example, the occupiers of eight newly erected cottagers were each fined 3d for illegal use of the common, but deemed thereafter to enjoy full common rights, subject to the same duties and obligations of existing commoners.[3] But the effects of such concessions in increasing the numbers of common-right holders were often outweighed by a more important development. From the fifteenth to the eighteenth century the number of separate farms tended to decline, albeit to varying extents in different parts of the county.[4] Tenements were purchased by neighbouring freeholders or, if held by the more insecure forms of 'copyhold', acquired by a variety of means by manorial lords and their lands added to one or more of the estate farms. What had been independent farms thus declined to the status of cottages, occupied by labourers or artisans who would be left, at best, with only a residue of the original rights to use the parochial common. When commons were finally enclosed by parliamentary acts in the eighteenth and nineteenth centuries individuals frequently claimed compensation for multiple rights exercised over the commons. When the mid-Norfolk parish of Shipdham was enclosed in 1809, for example, John Platfoot claimed rights to common pasture, to cut flags and furze (gorse) for fuel, and to excavate clay for repairs, attached to three commonable tenements, together with 'the planting of trees standing upon the said common pasture, opposite and adjoining the said premises respectively'.[5]

Not that the resources provided by the parochial commons had ever, in most cases, been shared equally between commoners. Where commons were particularly extensive commoners might be allowed to graze unlimited numbers of livestock. But over time restrictions were usually enforced, in order to allow a fair allocation of the herbage and to maintain it in a healthy condition. In the Middle Ages commons in Norfolk, as elsewhere, seem to have been regulated 'levant and couchant'. The number of livestock commoners could graze was related to the winter carrying capacity of their holding; to the number of animals that could be kept on hay, beans and other fodder grown on the holding, in yards and pens during the period, usually from October until March, when commons were closed to grazing. Such an arrangement shaded off easily into an informal recognition of the numbers of stock that tenements of a particular size 'ought' to keep, and thus graze on the common. Cornford, in her study of the commons of Flegg, found that 'seventeenth-century evidence from Clippesby suggests that a holding of 6 or 8 acres (c.2.5–3 hectares) was expected to support two or three cows', and thus to enjoy the common grazing required to sustain them.[6] But by this time population growth, reduction in the area of commons and increasing production for the market were beginning to erode such neighbourly agreements or lax and liberal arrangements. In some parishes, the number of stock that commoners could graze continued to be subject to vague regulation well into the nineteenth century; there are references to common rights 'levant and couchant' in Denver as late as the early twentieth century.[7] In a few parishes there was virtually no regulation, even on the eve of enclosure, as in Holm Hale where, according to Young in 1804, the 36 commoners could turn 'what horses and cows, and geese they please' onto the extensive common they shared with the inhabitants of Necton and West Bradenham ('but no steers, sheep or hogs').[8] But in the course of the post-medieval centuries the commons in many parishes came to be 'rated' or 'stinted' – that is, each commonable tenement was allocated a fixed number of stock it could graze.

A document drawn up in 1751 by the lord of the manor, the 18 principal owners and 18 principal tenants in Earsham described how the extensive commons 'in an unstinted state' were overgrazed and 'of very little value'.[9] Lack of proper regulation meant that animals were being turned onto the commons by 'intruders from other parishes' to the general detriment of the people of Earsham but especially 'of the honest poor, of such as are really settled inhabitants of the Parish'. Of particular interest, given the phenomenon of 'common edge drift' discussed in the previous chapter, is the statement that:

> Such persons who can live in cottages near the Commons turn on an unlimited number of geese to the destruction of the feed for cattle, whilst they who are not

conveniently situated can make no use of the commons whatsoever. When the Commons are rated, each occupier of a cottage would have his real right, and that clearly defined.[10]

At Snetterton in 1775 a stint was agreed because 'disputes and differences' had arisen between commoners, and the commons were being grazed by those without common rights, again including inhabitants of neighbouring parishes.[11]

In some places, as at Snetterton, each commonable property was given a specific number of stock it could graze, complicated in this case by the fact that one farm was given the exclusive use of one of the commons (together with the right to run four 'cattle' on the rest). More usually, each commonable tenement was allocated a certain number of 'goings', which conveyed the right to run a defined number of stock. In the case of Earsham, each 'going' allowed the commoner to:

> Feed, or depasture on the said commons, either one horse, or cow beast, or two one year old horses, or neate Beasts, or five Weathers, or four Ewes, and their Lambs, or one Gander, two Geese, and their Goslings.[12]

'Goings' were like shares – in 1834 it was said that the common at Swardeston was 'so Cal'd, because it is held by particular Tennure, or Shares'.[13] And, like shares in a company, different amounts were held by different commoners. Similarly, where simple numerical stints were imposed, they varied from tenement to tenement. As the document drawn up when the Snetterton commons were 'rated' in 1775 put it, 'it being reasonable that such persons as occupy a greater share of Lands and Tenements in the said Parish should have and keep a larger number of cattle than those who have less'.[14] Stints were accordingly based on the yearly value of farms, as ascertained by an agreed valuation, or on actual rental values. At Earsham one 'going' was allotted for every £5 of annual rental value and the list made on the basis of this calculation reveals that, unusually, only 13 of the 86 houses in the parish had no pasture rights. Of the rest, 31 possessed between 1 and 2½ 'goings'; 29 had allocations of between three and six; and 13 more than this, one as many as a dozen.[15]

The two broad approaches to regulating the use of commons – by levancy and couchancy, and by stint – were thus perhaps more closely related than we sometimes assume, for stints were, in effect, calculated on the basis of the perceived productive capacity of the various common-right dwellings. Such a procedure fossilised at a certain moment in time inequalities of use that had always existed in most places, for a common managed according to the rules of levancy and couchancy would by definition be grazed disproportionately by the animals of the largest farms, with the greatest acreages. And in the medium and longer term the allocation of formal stints usually exacerbated such inequalities, for everywhere the number of 'goings' attached to the various dwellings became fragmented, as properties were divided by sale or inheritance, and accumulated as, over time, commonable tenements were acquired in whole or part by neighbouring farming families, or by the local squire, and rented out, minus some or all of their stint, as cottage accommodation, in the manner already described. Indeed, while in theory common rights were attached to particular tenements, in practice they were sometimes alienated from them and bought and sold as private property.[16] By the time we see them for the first time in our documents stints were generally very unequal. In 1725 one farmer had the right to run 6 'great beasts' on Fritton Common; one could run 5; two, 4½; two, 4; two, 3; two, 2; six, 1; and one, a half.[17] At Swardeston in 1843 there were 45 goings; one individual exercised 13, another 6, two had 4, seven 2 and four 1. Most were tenants, rather than owner-occupiers: there were, at the time, more than 60 households in the parish so the 15 commoners comprised a small minority of the population.[18]

By the eighteenth century, and probably for long before, there seems to have been a general assumption that, where commons had not been formally stinted, the owner of a cottage with common rights, but with only a little land attached, had the right to turn a single cow, and perhaps a few geese, onto the common. As the examples already discussed suggest, by the time of enclosure the proportion of properties in any parish with common rights varied considerably, to judge from the evidence of enclosure awards and maps and the comments of writers like Arthur Young, but in the south and east of the county especially might often exceed 70 or even 80 per cent. These figures, however, provide a misleading impression of the number of poor households able to legally exercise such rights, because where commonable properties had been acquired by neighbouring farms, large landowners or commercial graziers living in another parish, and rented out as cottages, there was no guarantee that the owners would allow the tenants to use them. At Holm Hale in 1804 there were 36 common-right houses, nearly two-thirds of the properties in the village, but Young described how 'There is not one cottager that has a right of his own; all farmers and tradesmen … The cattle are all turned on by the proprietors, and not by the cottagers to whom the houses are let; they have not a cow in the town; but keep geese, and cut flags'.[19] This said, many cottagers without legal rights used commons as a source of fuel and even, in those places where they were extensive, for grazing a few livestock. The strict legal interpretation of how a common should be used is often a poor guide to the realities of rural life, on the ground. In Thompson's words, 'custom as praxis – village usages – generally afforded greater latitude for the exercise of minor rights than will be found in a formal view of the law'.[20] But even in the eyes of local custom, as overseen by manorial courts, such uses were not really *rights*, for they were enjoyed only by permission, often only tacitly given, and could be terminated if they conflicted with the interests of commoners.

Rights and Regulation

In most places, commoners had the right to use all of the commons in a parish, but occasionally they were limited to particular ones, usually those near or adjoining their houses. The tenants of Downham Hall manor in the north of Wymondham, for example, always seem to have enjoyed rights over the commons in their immediate vicinity, but not on others in the parish.²¹ There are some indications that this situation may have been more usual in the Middle Ages. The eighteenth-century historian Francis Blomefield described how Boyland Green in Bressingham 'is so called from *Boyland Hall*, which stands on the west side of it, and anciently was appropriated to be fed by the tenants of that manor only'.²² But even if they had the right to use all the commons, in practice, where a number of discrete areas of common land existed, the smaller farmers and commoners in particular seem to have grazed livestock on, and extracted fuel and other resources from, the nearest.

Conversely, some or all of the resources of particular commons, usually extensive ones, might be shared between the inhabitants of several communities. The 6,000-acre (c. 2,500-hectare) Mousehold Heath was shared by Norwich and 10 rural parishes to the east, while in Broadland the tracts of fen in the Thurne valley were jointly exploited by Ludham, Catfield and Potter Heigham and those in the Ant valley by Neatishead and Irstead.²³ In the south-west of the county, where the heaths of Breckland met the vast peat fens, there were ample reserves of both types of common. An extent for the Bishop of Ely's manor of Feltwell, drawn up in 1277, included among its possessions:

> a certain common pasture … in length one league and more, and in breadth a good furlong, where the villages of Methwold, Wilton, and Hockwold have a right to common, and the other lords of this town, as the bishop and the lords of this town have a right to common in the common pastures of Methwold, Hockwold, and Wilton … but no one ought or can dig, cut heath, &c. but the Bishop, and his tenants only.

Here the livestock appear to have run together over the whole area of the common but in South Fen, also the Bishop's property, the lords and tenants had full rights but the towns of Wilton and Hockwold could only intercommon within certain bounds.²⁴

In a host of ways, the use of common land was controlled and regulated; we need to resist romantic notions of commons as fragments of wilderness, exploited freely. Those entitled to use the common could only do so if they followed particular rules and agreed to undertake particular duties, including the maintenance of the boundaries between commons and their own property. In most cases they were also obliged to make an annual payment. Sometimes this was to the manorial lord, a particularly clear recognition of his role as owner. At West Harling in the 1730s commoners still paid '*bosage,* which is 1*d.* a head yearly for all cows and great cattle that feed on the commons'.²⁵ More usually the sums paid went towards routine maintenance and the supply of particular services, overseen by a 'pindar' elected annually from among the commoners, which might include supervision of livestock. Charges were usually levied on each animal put onto the common. They were sometimes fixed – at Cantley in the early eighteenth century commoners paid 3s. for every bullock grazed on the common marsh, the large amount reflecting the costs of maintaining the drainage works.²⁶ More usually they varied from year to year, the commoners at Earsham, for example, paying the Common Reeve 'so much per head … on all Cattle &c as shall be necessary to defray all necessary Repairs, expenses, & disbursements of each year touching the said Common'.[27]

The body responsible for the management of common land, and thus the first stage in the arbitration of most disputes concerning its exploitation, was the manorial court, attended by commoners and presided over by the steward of the manorial lord. In most Norfolk villages there were several separate manors, and authority over such matters resided with the 'leat' court, that is, that of the principal and generally oldest manor. In a few cases, some control was exercised by the court of a manor in another vill, whose lord claimed the right to profit from particular aspects of management or resources, inherited from the distant past. The manor of Attleborough thus claimed in the sixteenth century superior jurisdiction over the commons and wastes in a whole host of surrounding places – Attleborough, Besthorpe, Hargham, Wilby, Snetterton, Illington, Larling, Shropham, Breckles, Rockland, Great Ellingham, Roudham, Brettenham and Kilverstone – with the right to impound stray animals and to fine people overstocking a common or using it illegally.[28]

Manorial courts made their judgements primarily on the basis of 'custom', or established precedent. While in theory this involved adherence to practices or principles established 'time out of mind' custom was not fixed or immutable but could be adapted to new circumstances; as in the civil law courts following the principles of common law, new precedents could be set. But manorial courts were not the only arbiter of disputes concerning common. Both the lord's ownership of the common, and the commoners' rights to use it, were forms of property and so unresolved disputes might escalate to the public courts, and perhaps especially in a famously litigious county like Norfolk. So, too, could disagreements over the use of commons shared between neighbouring communities, if these could not be resolved through negotiation.

Manorial courts worked hard to ensure that the commons were exploited by individual commoners fairly, responsibly, and in a manner that did not impinge on the rights and interests of neighbours. People were fined for failing to properly maintain, as custom generally demanded, sections of common boundary lying against their own lands; for blocking access ways; for minor encroachments; and for a wide variety of selfish or slovenly behaviour, as when in 1653 William Gore was fined for allowing 'his bullock to lye dead upon the common of West Wynch which died of a disease called garart which was to the common annoyance'.[29] Prosecutions for overstocking the commons, or for illegally enclosing sections of them, were especially frequent. In October 1603 the court of the manor of Banyardes in Chedgrave fined John Marten for 'overburdening the common pasture called Lyvesheath with more beasts than he ought, according to the limitations of his tenure'. The following year it ruled that John Ufflete, gentleman, had:

> enclosed parcel of the common of Chetgrave called Laies Heath namely 3 acres and occupies the same severally to the lord's disinheritance and to the great prejudice and

damage of the lord's tenants and of the inhabitants of Chetgrave. He is amerced 12d, and ordered to throw open the said parcel of common by the annunciation, on pain of 10s.[30]

Where, as was usually the case, commons supplied a range of different resources, courts attempted to ensure that the untimely or excessive exploitation of one did not reduce the availability of the others. This was a particular problem with common fens, where stock might need to be excluded from areas cut for litter or thatching materials and, in particular, where the digging of peat needed to be controlled, for this could create extensive areas of open water, reducing the amount of grazing that was available and the quantity of litter or hay that might be cut. At Martham in 1404 two men were fined by the manorial court for digging peat from part of the parish common land which should have been left for hay; in 1509 the court forbade the extraction of peat from all the commons in the parish, except Cess Heath and parts of South Fen.[31] Manorial courts were also concerned to ensure that the various resources, especially peat, were exploited only to support the domestic economy of commoners, prohibiting, in particular, their sale to outsiders.[32] They also attempted to prevent commoners taking more than was due to them.

'Doles' and 'Plantings'

Regulating the grazing on commons was a relatively straightforward matter. At intervals the animals would be 'driven' or herded together by officers appointed by the manorial court and the numbers belonging to the various holdings checked against their agreed allocation, with fines being levied for infringements. Ensuring the correct distribution of the materials cut or dug from the common was more difficult, for this really required a level of surveillance, and a degree of regular and repeated measurement, that was beyond the competence of the community or its court. One solution was to divide part of the common into strips called 'doles', occasionally 'severals', that were allocated to individual commoners, from which they could cut or dig fuel and other materials. Doles were a particular feature of common fens but were also found on many heaths. A list of the 'doles' on the commons of Hemsby, drawn up in 1639, included both 'whin [gorse] doles' on the upland commons and wetland doles like those which 'abutteth upon Smale fenn towards the south & begineth within Dole of the lady of this Mannor', the latter also an indication that some 'doles' formed part of the manorial demesne.[33] In theory the doled land remained part of the common land of the manor, and the strips were unbounded so that livestock could still roam freely across them; in the case of the Hemsby list, the doles were said to be 'Common of Hemsby as concerning the feed Thereof', but the 'sweepedge', or cut material, was considered 'the freehold of the persons hereafter named'. Peat was the main fen commodity allocated in this way but other resources, especially reeds – sometimes but not always from flooded peat cuttings – were also extracted in this way. In the manorial records of medieval Hemsby there are references to 'reed doles', 'rush doles', 'moor doles' and 'flag doles'.[34] In nearby Fleggburgh a document of 1588 describes the layout of the reed doles within Reed Fen.[35] On common heaths, in contrast, doles seem to have been largely about regulating the extraction of various kinds of fuel: the cutting of gorse and heather, and sometimes the digging of 'flags'.

The practice of doling was well established by the fourteenth century – there is a reference to a 'turbary called West Dole' in Gillingham in 1316.[36] But it seems to have developed in different ways on heaths and fens. Doles may originally have been seen as temporary allocations and even as they became permanent they seem initially, like common rights, to have been attached to particular properties, passing with them as they changed hands through sale or inheritance. Heath doles generally retained this character and, remaining as part of the common, had largely disappeared from the landscape by the end of the eighteenth century. Those on Mousehold Heath, for example, referred to in sixteenth-century documents, appear to have reverted back to open heathland by the time of enclosure.[37] Fen doles, in contrast, had a longer and more independent life. Although in some places, such as Honing, they continued to be regarded as common land, in others they became separated from the tenements to which they were originally attached and began to be treated as parcels of private land. The difference between heath and fen doles in this respect may reflect the fact that the materials harvested from the latter were of greater commercial value, while the common grazing they provided (and thus their value to the wider community) was considerably less. As early as 1394 John Roth granted 'a parcel of marsh called a fendole' in Gillingham.[38] Doles could then be accumulated – in the early sixteenth century William Docking of Dilham bought two acres in 'Twelve Men Dole' from Robert Eche and five acres from William Blome – and amalgamated into larger blocks of

FIG. 3.1. Fen 'doles' at Upton, as depicted on the tithe map of 1839.

private fen or marsh.³⁹ In some Broadland parishes the drainage ditches or 'dykes' enclosing parcels of grazing marsh have a 'strippy', parallel, slightly sinuous appearance suggesting that they evolved through the consolidation and enclosure of bundles of narrower, unfenced 'doles', most notably in the parishes of Langley and Gillingham, the latter perhaps representing the 'turbaries of divers men' referred to in a deed of 1391.⁴⁰ Progressive amalgamation and privatisation served to remove most systems of fen dole from the landscape by the nineteenth century but there were a few survivors, mainly in Broadland. The Upton tithe map of 1839 shows that the whole area of 'Upton Doles', now 40 hectares of reedbeds and wet woodland lying to the north-east of Upton Broad and managed by the Norfolk Wildlife Trust, was then divided into a mass of privately owned strips, without physical boundaries, the narrowest less than 7 metres wide (Figure 3.1).⁴¹ Similar arrangements are depicted by the tithe maps in Surlingham, in the area around Surlingham Broad and (less well preserved) in Rockland St Mary and Honing, but elsewhere only the occasional example of a single open strip, or a small groups of strips, survived to suggest their former presence.⁴² Enclosure acts usually treated surviving doles not as common land but as pieces of private property, albeit ones over which, as with arable strips in the open fields, common rights of grazing and access might need to be removed.

Fen meadows might also be doled. At Earsham, for example, the 'dooled meadow' on the fen was closed to grazing by the fen reeves from Christmas day until 'the time of mowing', which was to be no later than 1 August, with livestock being allowed into the area on the last day of the month, allowing time for the grass to grow. It was then grazed by the livestock of those possessing shares there, 'allowing to each acre thereof a share or going for two horses, or Cow beasts, and so in proportion for any greater or lesser Quantity'.⁴³ At nearby Denton in 1757, similarly, a list was drawn up of 'The names of the land holders and the tenants belonging to Staple and Marsh meadows with their several contents and number of Beasts goings apportioned to everyone for the feed of the latter crop. At the rate and estimation of two beasts to one acre', although here the date on which stock were allowed onto the land was fixed as the 'Feast day of St Bartholomew', or 24 August.⁴⁴ At both places, typically, the doles were treated as private property when the parishes were enclosed by parliamentary act and ignored by the commissioners; in spite of much consolidation, large numbers of unhedged strips still survived when the tithe maps were surveyed in 1839.⁴⁵ But as we have seen, in Norfolk as elsewhere meadows of more conventional type, occupying more silty floodplain soils, might also be divided into strips, owned by different individuals, resembling the properties in arable open fields. It is unclear, in fact, where we should draw the line between such common meadows, and fen 'doles' – or what this blurred boundary may suggest about the origins of the former.

'Doles' were not the only way in which commoners came to exercise very private property rights over the commons. In the previous chapter I noted how many commons were wooded in the Middle Ages, but became progressively less so over time because, as trees died or were felled, it was difficult to replace them. New trees were vulnerable to grazing livestock on open land exploited by a multiplicity of commoners. But even on the eve of enclosure many commons retained some trees and a few boasted significant numbers. William Faden's map of Norfolk shows, schematically, trees on a number of heaths (including Stock Heath, Stratton Strawless Common and Walsham Heath) and a few clayland commons (including those at Haddiscoe, Topcroft, Woodton). Moreover, many of the examples that are shown as completely treeless, such as the various commons in Mattishall, we know carried trees at the time because of the claims for compensation made when they were enclosed by parliamentary acts a few years later, which in this particular case occurred in 1801 and with claims that included Mrs A.M. Bodham's of Mattishall Hall for the value of '100 trees and pollards upon part of the said commons and waste lands, called South Green, opposite the said mansion'.[46] This location of the trees in the vicinity of a residence is significant, a recurring feature of such claims, and by no means restricted to manorial halls like this. Those made when Shipdham was enclosed in 1809, for example, included one by John Mendham for four trees 'standing and being on the said common, in front of the said messuage' and one by the Earl of Leicester in respect of five commonable tenements he owned for:

> All trees, and all bushes and thorns planted or set by him or his predecessors, or his or their tenants, upon the said commons and waste grounds, contiguous or near to any of his said messuages or farms, which have been usually lopped, topped, pruned, or cut by him or his predecessors, or his or their tenants.[47]

The significance of this is explained by the eighteenth-century historian Francis Blomefield who described how, in his home parish of Fersfield 'The tenants have liberty to cut down timber on their copyholds, without licence and also to plant and cut down all manner of wood and timber on all the commons and wastes against their own lands, by the name of an outrun'.[48] He describes similar customs in the nearby south Norfolk parishes of Kenninghall, Diss and Garboldisham;[49] they were clearly widespread, at least on the claylands of southern and central Norfolk, and perhaps elsewhere in the county where houses were clustered around the margins of commons. At Pulham in the late sixteenth century, for example, it was stated that 'The tenantes of the said manor have used to make benefitt of the trees growing upon the common near their houses which were planted by themselves and their predecessors';[50] while a manorial survey of Gressenhall, made in 1579, described how each of the farms had one or more 'plantings' on the common, a map from 1624 showing these as areas of trees bearing the name of the owner and located close to his home (Figure 3.2).[51] The few surviving remains of such 'outruns' or 'plantings' suggest that they mainly comprised pollards, cropped every five to ten years for firewood, poles for hedge laying or other practical uses on the farm (Figure 3.3). Whether timber or pollards, such trees were not a communal resource, jointly exploited by commoners, but private property attached to particular tenements and reserved for the sole use of their owner.

FIG. 3.2. Detail from Thomas Waterman's map of Gressenhall, 1624, showing cattle grazing in the 'plantings' on the common.

Lords and Commoners

There was an obvious inherent tension between the lord's perception of the common as his private property and the commoner's view of it as a resource to be jointly exploited under the regulation and supervision of the lord's court. Disputes naturally arose over the respective rights each party might enjoy, disputes that might rumble on for decades and escalate to the public courts. One notable example erupted in the 1680s between the commoners of Irstead and Neatishead and their manorial lord, the Bishop of Norwich, over the common fens in the valley of the river Ant and its tributaries. They claimed not only 'Common of Pasture of all Commonable Cattle' but also the right to:

> Take cut and carry away Fodder Rushes Reed and Sedge growing in any of the said Fenns for their cattle and repairing the said messuages and also Liberty of Fishing in a certain water there called Alder Fenns and in all other the Broads and Waters in Irstead aforesaid.

But the bishop was keen to protect his rights to the fish and other resources provided by the flooded peat workings.[52] The dispute continued in the public courts, on and off and under new manorial owners, into the early nineteenth century.[53] Other disputes, however, involved attempts by the lord to enclose portions of a particular common, change its boundaries in some way or even relocate altogether something he evidently viewed as his personal property.

In Fersfield in the southern claylands at the end of the fifteenth century a common of 110 acres (45 hectares) in the south of the parish was taken into

3. Commons and Communities

the lord's hands and divided into fields and a replacement Great Common was laid out, joining together two existing commons called Fersfield Geen and Old Green. In the words of the historian Blomefield, whose home parish this was:

> and thus they continued 'till *Thomas* Duke of *Norfolk*, in the Time of King *Henry* VIII. desiring to make his Great Park at *Kenninghall*, in which his Palace stood, every way compleat, inclosed 44 Acres of *Fersfield Green* into the said Park … Upon this the Inhabitants petitioned his Grace for relief, who ordered his Bailiff thereupon to assign them other Lands, to the full Value and Quantity of their Land Inclosed.[54]

This decision was not carried through and the commoners took the Duke to court, eventually receiving a ruling that an equivalent amount of demesne land should be added to the common. As this was being laid out, however, the Duke was attainted and the manor seized by the Crown – whereupon the commoners reappropriated the 44 acres (18 hectares) of Fersfield Green originally taken into the park. The story did not end there, however. At the start of the seventeenth century, in Blomefield's words, '*Thomas* Earl of *Arundel* and *Surrey*, desirous to perfect the park, and to make the demeans of his manor of *Fersfield* as complete as they were before this common was seized by the inhabitants, came

FIG. 3.3. The remains of a 'planting' of pollarded oaks in the south-western corner of Fritton Common.

to agreement with them' by which, in return for a variety of payments, they allowed the 44 acres to be incorporated once again within the park, and the lands previously agreed to be annexed to the common in compensation.[55]

The case is an interesting one, not least in showing the limits of lordly power. Even as nationally important a figure as the Duke of Norfolk could not ride roughshod over the wishes of his commoners. On the other hand, in this and similar cases there is no suggestion that the commoners opposed, or felt that they had a right to oppose, this reorganisation of manorial property. Their concern was the provision of an equivalent area of land over which their common rights could be exercised. We should also note that the potential loss to the commoners, 44 acres, was considerable and therefore contestable in law under the provisions of the Statute of Merton. In numerous other cases smaller parcels of land were alienated from the manorial commons with the formal agreement of the manorial court. Lords could benefit from such grants by charging an annual 'quit rent' on the property so created. Commoners could not easily oppose them where commons were extensive, and often had little incentive to, not least where they met some pressing personal need, as perhaps at Middleton in 1777, when the widow Elizabeth Cary was given permission by the manorial court to enclose 8 perches (200 square metres) of land and build a cottage on the manorial waste; or Ditchingham in the seventeenth century, where there is a reference to a 'cottage long since built on a piece of waste ground ... for the habitation of John Colman, a poor man'.[56] At Brisley the tithe map of 1838 shows a number of tiny, irregular parcels of land scattered around, and projecting in from, the edge of the vast common. Ranging in size from 13 to 30 perches (325 to 750 square metres), all were described by the tithe schedule as 'gardens' or 'garden taken from the waste' and were owned by individuals who possessed no other property but rented cottages in the parish (Figure 3.4).[57]

A list of encroachments made on the commons in Fulmodestone and Stibbard, drawn up in 1809 when the two parishes were enclosed, itemises no less than 32 examples in the former and 33 in the latter, an astonishing number given that, by implication, only those made within living memory were included. Ranging in area from 10 perches (250 square metres) to three quarters of an acre (0.3 hectares), most appear to have been additions to fields but eight were for one or more gardens, one for extending a garden to provide space for a stable, while three were to provide space for cottages. Not all appear to have been made with the sanction of the manorial court, given that, in the case of Fulmondeston, nearly a third were ruled as still forming part of the common by the enclosure commissioners.[58] It is not surprising, then, that surviving commons often display irregular, 'crenellated' boundaries as a result of grants made for such gardens, as the sites for new cottages, or for the extension of yards, orchards and gardens around existing common-edge premises. But signs of encroachments on the waste are more widely present in the landscape. Cottages were often built on small plots taken in from the kind of broad roadway, or narrow, linear common, especially characteristic of the claylands of south and

FIG. 3.4. Brisley Green, as shown on the tithe map of 1838. The tiny encroachments protruding in from the green edge are mainly the gardens of poor cottagers living elsewhere in the parish.

central Norfolk. They are easily recognised today, the house standing with long axis parallel with the road, occupying a narrow piece of land similarly ranged, the rear boundary of which continues as that of the road at one or both ends. Often such linear commons were narrowed in another way. Existing fields were extended into them, which is why roads sometimes widen or contract slightly at the points where they are met by a field boundary.

Not all encroachments made with the permission of the lord and manorial courts were small. Larger intakes were also sanctioned, either to provide space for industrial premises, as discussed below, or to create new areas of agricultural land, as at Besthorpe in 1643 when 20 'inhabitants of Besthorpe and owners of Estates' permitted John Howse to enclose a portion of the common 'with pale ditche hedge or otherwise'.⁵⁹ Such encroachments can appear as sizeable projections extending into, or island within, areas of common land. Sometimes added security was given to such agreements by having them formally enrolled by the Quarter Sessions magistrates. The eighteenth-century court records confirm that most encroachments were small – around half covered 3 acres (1.2 hectares) or less – but where commons were extensive they might be larger, such as the 60 acres (24 hectares) enclosed at Aylmerton in 1776.⁶⁰ Alternatively, formal legal agreements to an encroachment might be drawn up, outside the manorial court, between the principal parties concerned, such as that made in 1787 by Henry Hobart, 'Lord of the several manors of Wymondham Grishaugh, Wymondham Cromwells and Rustons in Wymondham & the several other Persons owners & occupiers of lands and tenements … to enclose a part of the waste or common of Wymondham containing by measure 11a [acres] or [roods] 25p [perches]'.⁶¹

The role of manorial lords as the owners of common land was far more than a legal fiction and they or their representatives generally tried assiduously to make what money they could, or otherwise benefit, from this portion of their property. Some of the ways they exploited commons were very different to those enjoyed by commoners, such as the right to take game or establish a rabbit warren, or to profit from the fines levied for the infringement of common rights by the manorial court. Others were similar and shared, if in some cases enjoyed in greater abundance, including the right to graze livestock or dig and remove fuel and other materials. Some rights were easier to assert than to successfully exercise, notably that of planting timber on the manorial waste, for trees could be difficult to protect, especially where commons were shared between several parishes. In the middle of the eighteenth century William Windham, lord of the manor of Attleborough, had around 500 oak trees planted on Hookwood Common in Morley. He seems to have been able to protect this valuable investment from his own manorial tenants but the common was shared with the people of Morley and Deopham, who freely lopped the trees for fuel, converting them to pollards, claiming that they had a customary right so to do.⁶²

People in the past were clear that the manorial lord was the owner of common land and the extent to which commoners were able to freely exercise their rights over it or prevent portions from being alienated was determined less by legal theory than by the hard realities of life on the ground. Even where enclosures or encroachments were on such a scale that they could be contested under the terms of the Statute of Merton, commoners might often have been unwilling to make an enemy of the most powerful individual in the locality, on whose custom, patronage or support they might need to rely in other contexts; and whatever the position in abstract legal terms, rich men then, as now, possessed the resources required to triumph in the courts of law. Common rights were only as strong as the community of commoners asserting them. Where this was made up largely or entirely of people who held by one of the more insecure copyholds; and, in particular, where the land was poor and thinly peopled, and farm incomes low; then the power of lords over the manorial wastes was correspondingly great. This appears, in particular, to have been the case on the poor soils in Breckland, and to an extent on the light lands of north-west Norfolk. Here, as we have seen, large landowners in the late Middle Ages often established large commercial rabbit warrens on the manorial wastes and successfully asserted foldcourse rights. In such areas rights to use the commons might not be confidently claimed so much as couched as humble requests. In 1752 the tenants of the 'commonable tenements and cottages' in Shouldham Thorpe drew up a letter in which they 'begged the favour' of Sir Thomas Hare, 'owner of all the commons and waste grounds … to cut flags for their fuel next winter'.[63] In 1791 the inhabitants of Cockley Cley similarly sought permission to cut 'flaggs for our necessary firing'. Their request was granted but subject to conditions; each household could only take four cartloads and were charged 4d for the favour, and instructed not to 'cut dig or stubb up any of the whinns' growing in particular specified locations.[64] In such circumstances common land does seem to have been regarded very much as the lord's property, exploited by commoners with his permission.

'Foreigners'

Relationships between lords and commoners were not always antagonistic. Where one group of commoners was in dispute with another over the exploitation of an area of intercommoned waste, manorial lords often took a lead in proceedings, in part because of the threat to their own property rights but also because in the medieval and early modern world the protection of tenants was a socially accepted duty of lordship. Because, as we have seen, commons often flowed uninterrupted from one parish to another, without any hedge or other physical barrier along the boundary, there were ample opportunities for arguments, fights and legal cases over individual acts of trespass. Barbara Cornford, in her study of the commons of Flegg, described the numerous presentments made in the late medieval court rolls for Martham of individuals from adjoining parishes for grazing on the common, including in 1398 that of the communal shepherd for the adjacent parish of Rollesby.[65] In nearby Burgh St Margaret the 'foreigners' from Billockby accused of the same crime included, in the sixteenth century, the lord of the manor.[66] Such cases feature prominently in the documentary record, but so too do ones in which neighbouring communities collectively contested the use of a common on their shared boundary. Numerous such disputes were resolved informally but some ended up in the public courts, such as that which erupted between Litcham and Kempstone in the 1590s;[67] or that concerning the claims of the men of Tibenham to share, with Winfarthing and Banham, rights to graze on Banham Outwood, part of the vast (485-hectare) Banham Heath, as well as on the adjoining area of Banham Green (on the grounds that the two were not physically separated by ditches or fences), a claim rejected by the courts in 1625. The commons of Boyland Green, Whitehouse Green, Piddock's Green, and the Great Green all straddled the boundary between Shelfhanger and Bressingham, and commoners in both parishes claimed the right to use them. But the Shelfhanger men began to claim exclusive rights, sporadically impounding Bressingham cattle, until the case was taken to the Court of Chancery in 1704, which ruled in 1714 that only Boyland Green was intercommoned, the others being the sole preserve of the men of Bressingham.[68]

Where parish boundaries running across open commons were not marked by continuous hedges, but only by a series of landmarks, the annual ceremony of 'beating the bounds', vital for establishing parish rights and parochial obligations, often took on a particular significance in such contests. A major dispute developed at the turn of the seventeenth century between the inhabitants of Flitcham and West Newton over the limits of their respective rights to graze, and to cut turf and flags, over the extensive common that straddled their shared parish boundary. For the court case the men of Flitcham drew up a map showing the 'true' course of the parish boundary, passing over 'Sweete Hills', a probable barrow, and its line 'as Nuton men pretend'.[69] The case was of sufficient local importance for the map and its many annotations to have been carefully copied more than a century later, in what to modern eyes is a more readable form (Figure 3.5).[70] One witness described how there had formerly been agreement over the bounds 'but … of late years the inhitants of Newton have of late come further south in their pambulacon'. New, illegitimate boundary marks had been created but the court was unconvinced, ruling that 'the Nuton men in their drift may come no farther southward than unto Sweete Hills'.[71]

Some disputes over shared common continued on and off for centuries. That between the commoners of Carleton Rode and New Buckenham began in the fourteenth century. The men of Carleton Rode claimed the right to graze their livestock as far as the windmill on the common, a site still marked by Windmill Garage, located in the middle of the surviving New Buckenham Common.[72] As this point lay much closer to the New Buckenham end of the common – less than 200 metres from the nearest farms in that parish, but nearly a kilometre from the closest in Carleton Rode – the claim was successfully contested. But in the 1560s there were renewed arguments, this time also over how far beyond the parish boundary running across the common the men of New Buckenham could graze; cattle were seized and fighting occurred.[73] In 1593 the case was taken to the Court of Exchequer, the New Buckenham Commoners submitting, in 1597, a fine manuscript map in support of their case, which still survives in Norfolk Record Office.[74] In 1601 the court ruled that they did indeed have the right to graze cattle over 100 acres (40 hectares) on the Carleton side of the boundary but the following year a group of Carleton men, led by Heny Rame, impounded several of their animals, and were themselves prosecuted for contempt.[75] New Buckenham Common remains open to this day but Carleton was enclosed in 1778, with the commoners of the former claiming that the consequent loss of common rights necessitated a significant reduction in the number of livestock they could put on the common.[76]

FIG. 3.5. Early eighteenth-century copy of a map drawn up in c. 1617 in connection with a dispute between the inhabitants of Flitcham and Newton in west Norfolk concerning rights on the common straddling the boundary between the two parishes.

The State of the Commons

Eighteenth-century writers on agricultural 'improvement' frequently bemoaned the condition of common land, in Norfolk as elsewhere, characterising it as rough and neglected, offering few useful resources and occupied by half-starved livestock, as a consequence of the poor management provided by commoners and manorial courts. Some modern academics have followed them, seeing resource depletion and environmental degradation as the inevitable consequence of joint exploitation, the 'tragedy of the commons'.[77] Such land was better enclosed, divided into privately owned and individually managed parcels, so that it could be made more productive. But these arguments are simplistic and misleading, not least because they conveniently ignore the fact that most of this land survived as common precisely because it was agriculturally problematic due to soil acidity or seasonal or permanent waterlogging. Even employing the new techniques of the 'agricultural revolution', including systematic marling and various kinds of land drain, it was often impossible to farm economically even when it had been enclosed, and in many cases nobody bothered to try, the land remaining as heath and fen. In fact, the available evidence tends to suggest that most commons were reasonably well managed and did what they were supposed to do in terms of providing grazing, fuel and materials for commoners and to an extent the wider community, often affording fuel for the poor and, as we shall see, other resources, such as gravel for repairing the public roads. The current derelict, overgrown appearance of most surviving examples is as misleading as the comments of contemporary advocates of enclosure. On 'wet' commons in particular management often extended well beyond the enforcement of regulations and the fining of miscreants and 'foreign' trespassers. At Martham in the sixteenth century the commoners paid annually for 'casting, carting, or other repairing or drayning of the common', while at Cantley in the early eighteenth century a rate was levied 'for the repairs of the Walls, Banks, Sluices, Ditches, Drains, Gates and Fences of the Said Common'. Commoners had to pay 3s a year for each bullock grazed on the marsh, a custom changed in 1728 to a more flexible system, by which a committee of five, chosen by the commoners, decided what works were required and fixed the yearly rate accordingly.[78]

Manorial courts generally tried hard to prevent overgrazing, and probably with increasing success as, in the course of the post-medieval period, formal 'stints' came to be more widely employed. The various pasture rights listed at Earsham in the 1750s suggest that 304 'goings' were grazed on the common fens and clayland greens. Their total acreage was estimated at just over 300 acres, exclusive of various 'small Common Spotts and Broad Roads', suggesting a stocking density very close to 1 acre per 'going'; that is, one cow or horse, two young of the same, five sheep or four with lambs per acre.[79] A document drawn up in 1725 lists two geldings, nine mares, fourteen foals, six cows, three heifers and eight colts grazing on the 66-acre Fritton Common; another, drawn up in the same year but after the common had been 'rated' or stinted, stipulated that a total of 45½ 'great beasts' – each of which might be substituted by five sheep – could be grazed there, roughly equivalent to 1.5 acres per 'going'.[80] The 1791 enclosure act for the 43-acre Town Green at Old Buckenham laid down seven stints of 'two great beasts and no more', and 18 of 'one great beast and no more', equivalent to c. 1.3 acres per mature cow or horse; while at Snetterton the new stint established in 1778 allowed 79 'great beasts' to be grazed on 76 acres.[81] In the early nineteenth century seven cows, a horse, two pigs and 24 geese were grazed on the 10½-acre St Mary's Common in Swainsthorpe.[82] These stocking rates are all comparable to those laid down in the written agreements drawn up when private pastures were leased out in the post-medieval period, those for the drained marshes to the west of Yarmouth in the seventeenth and eighteenth centuries, for example, commonly stipulating no more than one fat bullock, two young cattle or five sheep per acre.[83] We need to remember, of course, that on some of these commons the amount of grazing available to the livestock was reduced by the presence of pits and ponds, and by the shade cast by closely packed trees in 'plantings'. The quality of the sward may have been reduced by poor drainage or soil acidity. These figures, moreover, cannot take account of any additional, informal or illegal, use of the grazing made by the local poor without common rights, which Arthur Young notes as a feature of commons at Fincham, Saham and Ovington, Northwold, and on Smeeth Fen in Marshland, and implies occurred elsewhere.[84] Yet even allowing for all this, there is little suggestion that commons were, in general, chronically overgrazed, although we should note that the situation at Earsham had been different before the stint was imposed. Commons were, after all, principally managed by small and medium-sized famers who surely knew what they were doing. Commons were not uncontrolled spaces, freely used by anyone, but regulated ones, exploited in defined ways by defined groups of people. As Ostrom has argued, in such circumstances collective exploitation has no necessary association with resource depletion.[85]

It seems likely that over-grazing, where it occurred, was often the result of the exercise, or abuse, of seigneurial rights, rather than arising from the activities of the commoners themselves. On the poor, light lands in the north and west of the county manorial lords often established rabbit warrens on commons and enjoyed monopoly rights to graze sheep there which, in the fifteenth and sixteenth centuries in particular, they exploited with particular vigour, overstocking or 'overcharging' their foldcourses. Attempts to assert these latter rights into new areas of the county appear to have been one of the triggers of Kett's rebellion in 1549 (below, p. 93). Both could have a serious impact on the condition of common, which could lead to arguments and litigation. Typical was the dispute which occurred during Elizabeth's reign at Cawston in Norfolk.[86] This was a complex legal case, one part of which involved accusations that a warren, originally contained within the bounds of the adjacent Jerbridge Park, was expanding across the common heath, partly because the boundary between the two areas had not been adequately maintained. New 'burrowes' or breeding mounds (pillow mounds) had been constructed on the heath itself 'where there were never any before' and numerous 'falls' or traps had been dug, as well as holes to extract rabbits and ferrets. The commoners complained of the damage being done to the grazing on the common, as well as to the adjacent arable land, by the rabbits. The warreners argued that the area of the warren had always included the heath, as well as the land within the park, and that there had long been 10 'old and ancient' breeding mounds there. Clearly referencing the provisions of the Statute of Merton, they alleged that the commoners had 'a sufficient comon for the feede of ther great cattell in the said great heath of Cawston notwthstandinge the number of conyes there as the same ten[a]ntes in former tyme have had'. The poor condition of the heath, they asserted, was in reality due to the activities of the commoners themselves, and especially to their habit of allowing the poor to cut turfs as fuel for their fires. The state of the heath suggests, however, that the warreners and their rabbits were mainly to blame, one witness describing how:

> Sand and gravell is cast upp in such great heapes upon the playne grownd by reason of the digging therof that ther will noe grasse growe upon the said grownde in a verie long tyme and ... the digging now lately used is a great hindrance to the inhabitants of Cawston as well in the fede of the cattell as in dangering ther said cattell.[87]

Conclusion

Medieval and later records are full of disputes over common land, whether within communities over management issues, the fair allocation of resources and who should be included in their distribution; between different groups of commoners, over the use of a shared common; or between commoners and their manorial lord. To some extent, of course, this simply reflects the fact that most of our documents were generated by various kinds of court dealing with problems and infringements. Such evidence accordingly needs to be understood within the context of an evolving legal system and the gradual increase over time in the strength of state authority and the independence of the public courts. An apparent increase in legal disputes over commons in the sixteenth century, for example, probably reflects an escalation of this process under the regime of the Tudors, as much as the increased pressure on commons resulting from rapid population growth and the development of a more market-oriented economy. This said, particular aspects of commons seem to have been almost designed to generate contention. There was an essential vagueness about commons; about how to measure, and thus ensure an equitable distribution of the resources they offered and, in some cases, over the boundaries of the land subject to particular rights. But fundamentally disputes arose from the fact that, even in the Middle Ages, commons were not a 'common treasury' of natural, unoccupied land, jointly and freely exploited for the good of all. Every common was someone's personal property and the rights asserted by others over it were individualistic rather than communal in character, and could on occasions – as with 'plantings' – morph into a type of private property.

FIG. 3.6. Fritton Hall, Fritton Common. The houses clustering around Norfolk commons do not solely consist of small cottages but include large freehold farms and even the residences of the gentry, the principal users of commons.

For while historians sometimes characterise the history of commons as a continuing struggle between a lordly elite and 'communities', or even between rich and poor, it is better understood in terms of competing property rights within unequal local societies. The wealthier common-right holders or their tenants always enjoyed a disproportionate access to their resources which they preserved from the encroachments of others in the community through the rules laid down by the manorial court; they made common cause with manorial lords in resisting the claims of neighbouring groups of commoners, but might – if they possessed sufficient wealth and confidence – take them to court, when assertions of lordly ownership seriously damaged their own interests. The importance of the 'middling sort' in the history of common land, at least in the post-medieval period, is manifested with peculiar clarity in the landscape of today. The sixteenth, seventeenth and eighteenth-century houses strung out around the margins of commons include some cottages (post-dating 1700 – earlier examples have not usually survived), as well as what were formerly small farms. But these are interspersed with large farmhouses, often still with extensive ranges of agricultural buildings, which then as now were the homes of a prosperous middle class, the principal users of the common (Figure 3.7). By the time they came to be enclosed, commons had, for centuries, been firmly embedded in local systems of inequality.

Notes

1. NRO MEA 7, 25, 661X1.
2. NRO MS 19424, 103X4.
3. B. Cornford, The Commons of Flegg in the Middle Ages and Early Modern Periods, in M. Manning (ed.), *Commons in Norfolk* (Norwich, 1988), 14–20, at 20.
4. Wade Martins and Williamson, *Roots of Change*, 76–80.
5. NRO BR 90/14/2.
6. Cornford, Commons of Flegg, 14.
7. NRO PRA 433/1–35, 380x.
8. Young, *General View Norfolk*, 130.
9. NRO MEA 7, 25, 661X1.
10. NRO MEA 7, 25, 661X1.
11. NRO HNR 155/7.
12. NRO MEA 7, 25, 661X1.
13. NRO MCC 2973.
14. NRO HNR 155/7.
15. NRO MEA 7, 25, 661X1.
16. NRO PRA 433/1–35, 380X1.
17. NRO MS 14082.
18. NRO MC 2973.
19. Young, *General View Norfolk*, 130.
20. E.P. Thompson, *Customs in Common* (London, 1991), 150.
21. Blomefield, *Topographical History*, Vol. 2, 506.
22. Blomefield, *Topographical History*, Vol. 1, 72.
23. NRO MS 19424, 103X4.
24. Blomefield, *Topographical History*, Vol. 2, 188–9.
25. Blomefield, *Topographical History*, Vol. 1, 299.

26　NRO MC 76/1.
27　NRO MEA 7, 25, 661X1.
28　Blomefield, *Topographical History*, Vol. 1, 519.
29　Cambridge University Library CH (H) 109; D. Higgins, West Winch Common, in Manning, *Commons in Norfolk*, 21–8, at 23.
30　MC 2265/2, 1008X7.
31　NRO DCN 60/22; Cornford, Commons of Flegg, 18–19.
32　NRO MS 19424, 103X4.
33　NRO MC 1559, 1, 815X4.
34　Cornford, Commons of Flegg, 16.
35　NRO MS 2506 2F1.
36　NRO GIL 1/67, 716X6.
37　TNA E178/7153.
38　NRO GIL 1/17, 716X3.
39　NRO KC 1/105, 391X5.
40　NRO GIL 1/15, 716X3.
41　NRO PD 255/29.
42　NRO PD 611/33; NRO PD 256/16.
43　NRO MEA 7, 25, 661X1.
44　NRO Fx 394.
45　NRO DN/TA 209; NRO DN/TA 564.
46　NRO PD 670/23.
47　NRO BR 90/14/2.
48　Blomefield, *Topographical History*, Vol. 1, 95; P. Dallas, Sustainable Environments: Common Wood Pastures in Norfolk, *Landscape History* 31 (2010), 23–36.
49　Blomefield, *Topographical History*, Vol. 1, 220, 263; Dallas, Sustainable Environments.
50　NRO NAS II/17.
51　NRO MR61 241X1; NRO Hayes and Storr 72.
52　NRO MC 121/238.
53　NRO MC121/238–40.
54　Blomefield, *Topographical History*, Vol. 1, 88.
55　Blomefield, *Topographical History*, Vol. 1, 88.
56　NRO MC 3597/20, 1082X6; NRO PD 301/57.
57　NRO DN/TA 409.
58　BR 90/16/9.
59　Morley, Common Land, 69–70; NRO 13964a.
60　NRO C/Sce 1/1; C/Sce 1/13; C/Sce 1/15; C/Sce 16.
61　NRO, KIM 3/21/5; Morley, Common Land, 56.
62　NRO MEA 2/111, 652X6.
63　NRO HARE 3147, 2202/6.
64　NRO MC 2667/19/3, 991X2.
65　Cornford, Commons of Flegg, 18.
66　NRO MS2517 2F2.
67　NRO PD 459/1.
68　TNA C 6/384/104; NRO PD 111/154; NRO PC 25/1.
69　NRO FLT 407.
70　NRO MS4291.
71　NRO MS4291.
72　NRO MC 343/105, 735X7.
73　NRO MC 343/105, 735X7; NRO PD 540/92; NRO PD 254/168.

74 NRO PD 254/169–74; NRO MC 22/11.
75 NRO PD 254/175–6, 181; NRO PD 540/96.
76 NRO MC 343/121–2, 735X9.
77 G. Hardin, The Tragedy of the Commons, *Science* 162, 3859 (1968), 1243–8.
78 NRO MC 76/1.
79 NRO MEA 7, 25, 661X1.
80 NRO MS 14081, 1408 and 14084, 36A4.
81 NRO BR 90/1. NRO HNR 155/7.
82 NRO DUN (C) 56–57, 499X5.
83 T. Williamson and A. Yardy, *Broadland: Shaping Marsh and Fen* (Hatfield, 2024), 155.
84 Young, *General View Norfolk*, 107, 138–9, 147–8 and 156.
85 E. Ostrom, *Governing the Commons: The Evolution of Institutions for Collective Action* (Cambridge, 1990).
86 Whyte, Perceptions, 178–80; TNA E134/43&44Eliz/Mich7.
87 TNA E134/43&44Eliz/Mich7.

CHAPTER 4

Industry, Trade and Recreation

So far, I have discussed common land mainly in terms of its exploitation as a source of grazing and fuel. But this is only part of the story. As both landscapes and habitats, commons were also shaped by a host of other activities and uses, especially during relatively recent times. These were associated in part with particular resources that commons had to offer, in terms of fuel or raw materials. In part, however, they simply arose from the character of commons as relatively unencumbered spaces, free of crops and property, interconnected by roads and accessible to people from far and near. Commons served as semi-public spaces within which crowds could gather, within a landscape that was otherwise largely private. In addition, in the course of the post-medieval period these open areas, administered and regulated by the local community, acquired new social roles, and came to be used in a variety of ways for the relief of the poor. The character and impact of all these things can be reconstructed in part from documentary sources but once again much can be learnt from archaeological evidence, and from that provided by the landscape itself, in terms of morphological patterns and spatial relationships.

Commons and Industry

Although we tend to think of commons mainly in rural, or at least agricultural, terms, in Norfolk as elsewhere they were often the location for industrial enterprises. Some were small scale activities, probably carried out by commoners. Linen production was an important industry in medieval and early modern Norfolk and required the 'retting' or rotting of the hemp in water-filled pits in order to liberate the fibres. As this process produced a noxious smell and toxic effluent, pits were sometimes placed on commons, away from houses, although even on the common their presence in large numbers might be considered a nuisance by manorial courts, as at West Runton in the sixteenth century.[1] The name of Bleach Green in Pulham suggests the presence of another textile production process best carried out at a distance from habitations. But more importantly, commons were often chosen as the sites for windmills. William Faden's map of the county, published in 1797, shows numerous examples standing isolated on common land, or in what appear to be intakes that have sundered two adjacent commons. The list is indeed a long one, with examples shown in Aldeby, Ashby, Attleborough, Bacton, Banningham, Bedingham (two), Billingford, Blofield, Bressingham, Briston, Burnham Overy, Burston, Caston, Cawston, Cranworth, Diss, East Harling, East Rudham, Ellingham, Emneth, Fakenham, Frettenham,

Garboldisham (two), Gaywood, Gooderstone, Great Dunham, Honing, Kenninghall, Mattishall, Moulton, Mulbarton, Mundham, Necton, New Buckenham, North Elmham, Oulton, Plumstead, Poringland, Ranworth, Ringland, Scottow, South Lopham, Southrepps, Strumpshaw, Thompson, Tivetshall (two), Tunstead, Watton, Weeting, West Caistor, Wheatacre, Witton, Wramplingham, Wymondham and Yelverton. Indeed, around a third of the windmills shown on the map stood on common land. Others are depicted on local maps which had been removed before Faden's map was surveyed, were established afterwards, or were simply missed by his surveyors, like the example on Marlingford common depicted on the tithe map of 1838.[2] The names given to some commons hint at their former presence elsewhere, as at Mill Moor, Carbrooke. Mills provided dramatic incidents in these open landscapes and artists of the Norwich School were, in the first half of the nineteenth century, drawn irresistibly to particular examples, including the old postmills on Mousehold Heath and New Buckenham Common (Figure 4.1). Sometimes the mill stood alone on the common but often it occupied an island of enclosed ground which included yards, sheds and a mill house or cottage. Whatever the case, windmills were a familiar, characteristic component of the landscapes of common land.

Windmills were not, of course, communal structures, built by commoners, but private ones, erected by, or with the permission of, the lord of the manor. Some of these sites, although not of course the mills themselves, may have originated in the Middle Ages, when milling was a manorial monopoly and customary tenants were obliged to use the lord's mill to grind their grain. The mill on New Buckenham Common, for example, is referred to in a sixteenth-century dispute, where its relocation from an earlier site within New Buckenham Castle, in the previous century, is described.[3] Others had doubtless been first erected in the post-medieval centuries, permission being granted, presumably with the acquiescence of the manorial court, in return for an annual payment or quit-rent which was often fixed, declining gradually over time with inflation (a mere 15 shillings *per annum*, in the case of the New Buckenham mill in 1789).[4]

Commons were good places to erect windmills. As well as saving the use of land which might otherwise be employed in growing crops, such a location was convenient for the farms scattered along the common edge, yet usually far enough away from them to negate the risk of fire – mills were always burning down. In addition, by late medieval times many commons – their central areas at least – were fairly open and free of trees, providing appropriately windy sites.

The association of mills and common is less obvious today than it was in Faden's time, mainly because of the enclosure and disappearance of commons, but also due to the wholesale loss of windmills from the landscape since the late nineteenth century.[5] But Billingford mill, in the far south of the county, still stands alone and undivided from the surrounding common, although originally enclosed within a small yard (Figure 4.2). Built in 1859–60 to replace an earlier post mill, it was the last windmill in the county to operate commercially, only finally closing in 1956.[6] In the west of the county, on the edge of the Fens,

FIG. 4.1. The post mill on Mousehold Heatth, as depicted by John Crome in c. 1816.

Denver Mill, erected in 1835 but again replacing an earlier postmill, stands within what is clearly an intake from the adjacent Sluice Common.[7] In most cases, even where a common still survives, the mill has gone. The post mill on Ringland's Church Hill Common, drawn in elevation on the tithe map of 1839, has left no obvious trace of its former presence: destroyed in a gale in 1858, its machinery was sold and its site cleared.[8] But sometimes the memory of a mill on a common lives on in local nomenclature. A small island of enclosed ground in the middle of New Buckenham Common is occupied by an eighteenth-century cottage and what is now Mill House Garage, marking the site of the mill which ceased working in 1890 and was demolished in 1920.[9] In Southrepps, Mill Common gets its name from a mill, demolished at the end of the nineteenth century, which stood within a complex of yards separating it from the main area of Southrepps Common. Conversely, there are a number of places where

4. *Industry, Trade and Recreation* 71

FIG. 4.2. Billingford mill still dominates the landscape of Billingford Common (courtesy John Fielding).

mills, originally erected on common land, are now surrounded by farmland as a consequence of enclosure, as at Frettenham, or Garboldisham, where the post mill is of mid-eighteenth-century date and thus the same structure as that shown on Faden's map.[10]

The erection of mills on commons had limited impact on the other ways in which they were used and virtually none on their ecology. Other forms of industrial use had a much greater effect. They were drawn to common land because of the fuel or raw materials it provided, which were either in short supply in the surrounding landscape or could only be extracted, or exploited, in a manner that interfered with farming and other activities. In Norfolk, the most important was brickmaking. In the sixteenth and early seventeenth centuries the demand for bricks was generally low and most brickworks were small and often temporary affairs, established to meet the needs of an individual building project. As the use of bricks and tiles spread, with increasing speed from around 1700, larger and more permanent units of production developed, and a high proportion of those shown on William Faden's 1797 county map were to be found either beside or actually within areas of common land. Instances of the former relationship were more numerous, with examples at West Runton, Heacham, Honing, Staunton Heath in Hoe, Shingham Heath in Beechamwell, Guist, Hethel, Lynford, Gillingham, East Harling, Pulham and Needham Market, and no less than three in close proximity to Stock Heath. But Beeston Heath, Harpley Common, South Acre Common, Mousehold Heath, Thompson Common and Weeting Heath all had brickworks on them, which in some cases continued to exist long after their enclosure. Local documents and maps reveal many other examples. When the manors of Langley and Buckenham were sold in 1739 the property included 'All that Brick Kiln Situate upon Hassington Common with liberty of digging Brick and Tile Earth there'.[11] On an early nineteenth-century survey of Sir John Lombe's estates, a brickyard leased to one William Ketteringham is described which stood immediately adjacent to Stanton Common in Hoe.[12] The locations of others are indicated by names such as Brick Kiln Common in Thompson. As Robin Lucas noted in his important study of the subject, 'the maps show that brickmaking either on or by the side of common land was unexceptional and, indeed, frequent' in post-medieval Norfolk.[13]

To some extent, the association of brick-making and commons reflects the use of the latter as a source of clay. But most of these brickworks were associated with heathland, located on sandy and gravelly soils, rather than on what are clearly significant deposits of clay. While sand was also needed for brick making, and while many of these brickworks were doubtless exploiting very localised deposits of serviceable brickearth (tolerable bricks could be fired from a wide range of geological materials available in East Anglia), the real attraction was probably the fuel that such commons afforded. Heather, broom, gorse and even bracken were all regularly used for firing bricks, tiles and pottery. When Blickling Hall was constructed in 1617–21, for example, more than a million bricks were fired in kilns entirely fuelled with gorse and broom faggots brought from the heaths at nearby Cawston and Saxthorpe (although Blickling also appears to have had its own 'Furze Close', to judge from an estate map of 1729).[14] It has been suggested that the vitrified bricks so common in seventeenth, eighteenth and even some nineteenth-century buildings throughout England, and often used in a decorative fashion, may have been the consequence of using such fuel: 'the high proportion of vitrified headers was probably a consequence of using firing materials, such as heather and gorse, which gave off fumes containing potash'.[15] Leases and other documents refer to the fuel used to fire kilns as much as they do to clay or sand. When, in 1626, Edmund Hamond and William Ditcher leased from Sir Arthur Capel a kiln for making 'brickes, tyles, and other merchantable stuffe and wares', they were given permission to 'break soil and dig sand, and take sweepage and brakes upon the commons and pasture' in South Wooton.[16]

Where kilns produced pottery, rather than bricks and tiles, the association of kilns and common heaths was less close. There certainly are examples of pottery kilns, known from archaeological evidence, that were placed on common edges, like that in the far north of Potter Heigham parish (TG 40742111), producing pottery in the fourteenth and fifteenth centuries, which fronted onto Catfield Heath.[17] Some lay far from any known common – like the medieval kilns at Clippesby and Langhale, or the post-medieval example at Cringleford – but many were to be found in the general area of extensive common heaths, although unlike brick kilns, not actually on or beside them – most notably the numerous medieval potteries scattered through the parish of Grimston, generally within 500 metres of the extensive Grimston Heath.[18] The difference reflects the fact that for pottery production, in contrast to brickmaking, raw materials were more important than fuel. Pots required good quality clay and kilns were placed close to an adequate supply of this, rather than to the source of their fuel, which was more easily transported.

Other industries might also be fuelled with gorse, broom, bracken and heather, including lime burning, and Faden's map shows two examples of lime kilns on common land, at Sustead and on Alderford Common in Swannington. The latter was never enclosed and the kiln continued to operate into the twentieth century.[19] Its remains still survive, surrounded by numerous pits, now engulfed in woodland and scrub, which cover nearly half the surface area of the 44-acre (17-hectare) common (Figures 4.3 and 4.4). This example raises, in acute form, the question of how such industries could develop on common land, given their impact on the interests of common right holders, in terms of loss of grazing and depletion of fuel reserves. In part the answer lies in the fact that their environmental impact was perhaps not as great as we might expect. The pits at places like this developed over a long period – not all were open, and denuded of vegetation, at the same time – and the demands made on gorse and heather were often small-scale and sporadic. Until the end of the eighteenth century bricks were often burnt in 'clamps' – in covered stacks, carefully interspersed with the fuel – rather than in true kilns, which used more fuel. Brickworks were, more importantly, often operated by local farmers, and run on a discontinuous or sporadic basis, in response to specific orders from customers, and the same was true of some lime kilns.[20] Nevertheless, the consumption of gorse and heather and in some cases the excavation of pits must have been on a significant scale and, while manorial custom often allowed tenants to dig clay or other materials for use on their own holdings, it did not permit commercial extraction. For this, the agreement of the manorial court was required, at least in theory. The fact that it was often granted indicates, once again, the dominant position of manorial lords in the management of commons. In some cases, indeed, large landowners ran their own brickworks on common land, including Sir Edward Paston, who used his rights as lord of the manor of Blofield to establish one on Mousehold Heath in the 1580s; and the Lothians of Blickling, who by the early nineteenth century were operating one beside White Top Common.[21] But there are also signs that the manorial permission required for such activities was only granted, in some cases, after certain benefits for the commoners had been negotiated. When John Last was given permission in 1734 to erect and operate a brick kiln on the commons of Gillingham and Aldeby, he

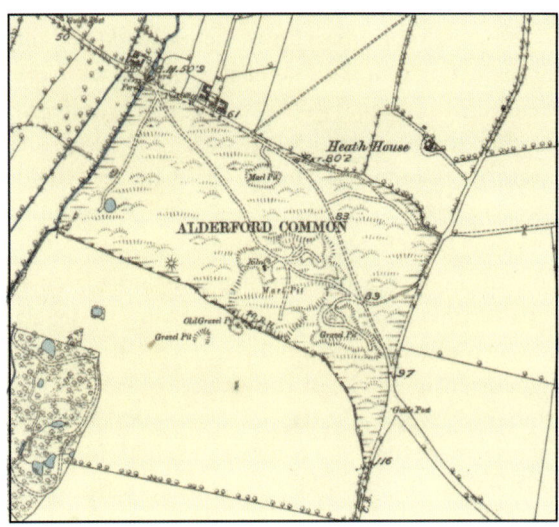
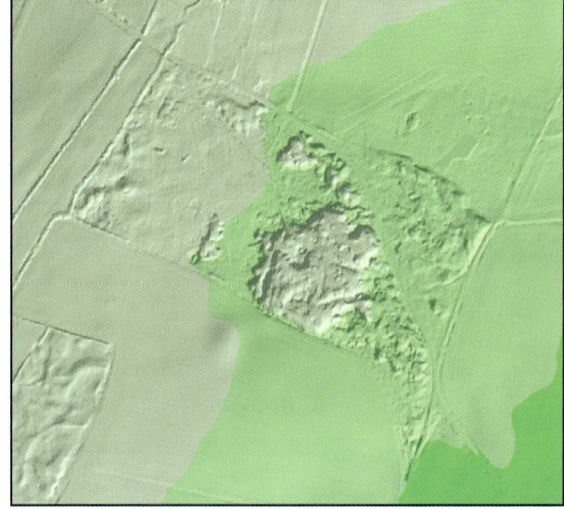

agreed to 'furnish Sir Edmund Bacon and his tenants' with bricks, pamments and roofing tiles at reduced rates.[22] At Stibbard in 1809 it was reported that William Buckenham had been allowed to dig brickearth on the common in return for two guineas a year paid to the poor of the parish (although he had 'not paid any for 10 or 12 years').[23]

FIG. 4.3. (opposite) The great extraction pit associated with the lime kiln on Alderford Common, Swannington.

Surviving commons, as we shall see, are often riddled with extraction pits. Many were clearly formed by the small-scale removal of materials for use on commoners' farms but on some heaths, such as Crostwight Heath, a quarter or more of the surface area is covered with pits of varying sizes and depths which have been dug for the removal of sand and, in particular, gravel. Some of the larger pits may have been dug by the parish highways surveyors to obtain materials for the repair of the local roads, using a communal resource for the public good. But others may be examples of private enterprise, working with manorial sanction – some perhaps to provide material for the various new turnpike roads that were established in the county from the late seventeenth century (in the case of Crostwight, that running from Norwich to North Walsham, created by an Act of 1797, which passed some 4 miles (6 kilometres) to the west).[24] The largest pits ever dug on common land in Norfolk (although no example remains so located) are the 'broads', the shallow freshwater lakes found on the floodplains of rivers in east Norfolk, which were formed by the flooding of medieval turbaries. Most appear to have been dug on the manorial 'waste' and, often covering 25 hectares or more, clearly represent commercial production, although whether this was mainly by lords, by commoners, or by others working under licence, remains unclear.[25]

Fairs, Markets and Towns

The use of commons as places for hosting large gatherings of people, non-agricultural in nature and including many who were not the holders of common rights, can be traced back to the Middle Ages. Greens in the centre of settlements might thus provide space for religious or semi-religious gatherings more extensive than that afforded by the churchyard, as at West Wereham where, as Cromwell described in 1829, the small common to the west of the church, with its well dedicated to St Margaret, was 'much frequented in the times of Popery. Here, on St. Margaret's Day, the people regaled themselves with ale and cakes, music and dancing. Alms were given, and offerings and vows made'.[26] Many commons became the locations for yearly fairs. Fairstead Green in Diss was the site of a fair from the thirteenth century, held every year (in Blomefield's words) 'upon the eve, day, and morrow after the feast of St. *Simon* and *Jude*, and three days following'.[27] Fairland in Wymondham was the site for the fair which King Stephen granted the Prior in the twelfth century, which was held 'on the eve, day, and morrow of the *nativity* of the *Virgin Mary*'.[28] But fairs on commons were not only a feature of market towns like these. Fair Green in Middleton, for example, was the site of a fair held by Blackburgh Priory from 1244; there were 'fairsteads' on common land at Cley (across the road from the parish church) and Briston; an annual fair was held on Banham Green from 1338 until 1873; while regular livestock fairs were held on commons at Southrepps and Gressenhall, as well as on Hempton Common, just outside the town of Fakenham.[29]

FIG. 4.4. (opposite) Alderford Common, Swannington. Typically, the Lidar image (right) indicates a scale of extraction even greater than that suggested by the 1880s 6-inch Ordnance Survey map.

At both Diss and Wymondham the fair took place on a common located a short distance away from the area where the weekly market was held, and this was the situation at other market towns, such as Hingham. This, however, raises the difficult question of the relationship of medieval *markets* – more frequent, usually weekly, assemblies of traders and customers – and common land. By the fourteenth century there were around 140 legally recognised markets in Norfolk.[30] Some were small affairs, held at places that remained as villages. But many were held at settlements that had developed into towns, clustered around a central marketplace. It is often stated, or implied, that markets were established by manorial lords, by obtaining a royal charter, and that urban development was often initiated at the same time, as a combined package of economic investment, with plots for shops and workshops being established around a newly laid out marketplace.[31] But it is likely that legal recognition, in the form of a royal charter, did not usually signal the inception of markets, while some important markets were never officially 'chartered', but were simply held by 'ancient prescription' – that is, had existed time out of mind. Most markets in fact appear to have developed organically as commercial trade expanded in the course of the eleventh, twelfth and thirteenth centuries, and often at places where people already gathered regularly for other reasons. The receipt of a charter simply marked the point when the manorial lord began to benefit from its existence by charging tradesmen 'tolls' for being allowed to set up stalls.

There seems little doubt that informal assemblies of tradesmen would have taken advantage of an accessible open space and indeed, most marketplaces do not exhibit a neatly planned, rectangular appearance but instead resemble areas of common land. Once 'islands' of encroachment have been removed, created as impermanent stalls gradually became more substantial in character, most exhibit the same funnel entrances, the same roughly triangular or 'biconcave' form, as many commons. Wymondham is a typical case. The original endowment given to the Abbey here by William D'Albini in 1107 included, according to Blomefield, 'all the amercements of their own tenants, whether they were amerced in his *leet* or in the *market court*'. Although Blomefield also notes that the right to hold a market was granted by King John in 1203 this reference, if correct, indicates pretty clearly that the market was already in existence nearly a century earlier.[32] It was certainly in existence by 1180, when the marketplace is referred to in the foundation charter of the chapel of St Thomas. It seems likely that the market grew up organically, serving visitors to the abbey or its predecessor *minster*, and the layout of Wymondham and its marketplace reflects this.[33] The town, rather than having a 'planned' appearance, looks much like any other common-edge settlement, its marketplace and 'Fairland' clearly once a single tract of open land, sundered by a large 'island' of encroachment (Figure 4.5). The abbey church stands at a distance, echoing the relationship of many more rural parish churches, standing apart from settlement clustered around a common.

The plan of Holt, in the north of the county, is in many ways similar (Figure 4.6); here regular markets may have developed as people gathered to

4. Industry, Trade and Recreation

FIG. 4.5. The shape of Wymondham's marketplace strongly suggests that it originated as an area of common land. The area of grass, top right, is Fairland Green, the common where the annual fair, established in the twelfth century, was held (courtesy John Fielding).

attend the hundred court held at this important royal manor. At East Dereham, similarly, the church (again in origin an ancient minster) stands back from a common-like marketplace (Figure 4.6). But, just as some rural churches had areas of common land beside them, around the margins of which settlement expanded, so too many towns – Swaffham, Aylsham or North Walsham – have church and marketplace in immediate proximity, although with the latter generally displaying a classic common-like shape. The similar character of commons and marketplaces is particularly clear where places with medieval markets never really developed into true towns. The village of Snettisham to the north of King's Lynn, for example, resembles many others in Norfolk, with (before twentieth-century expansion) most of the houses clustered around a green, and the parish church standing almost alone some 500 metres to the east. A market was held here in the Middle Ages and the green is still known as the Market Place.

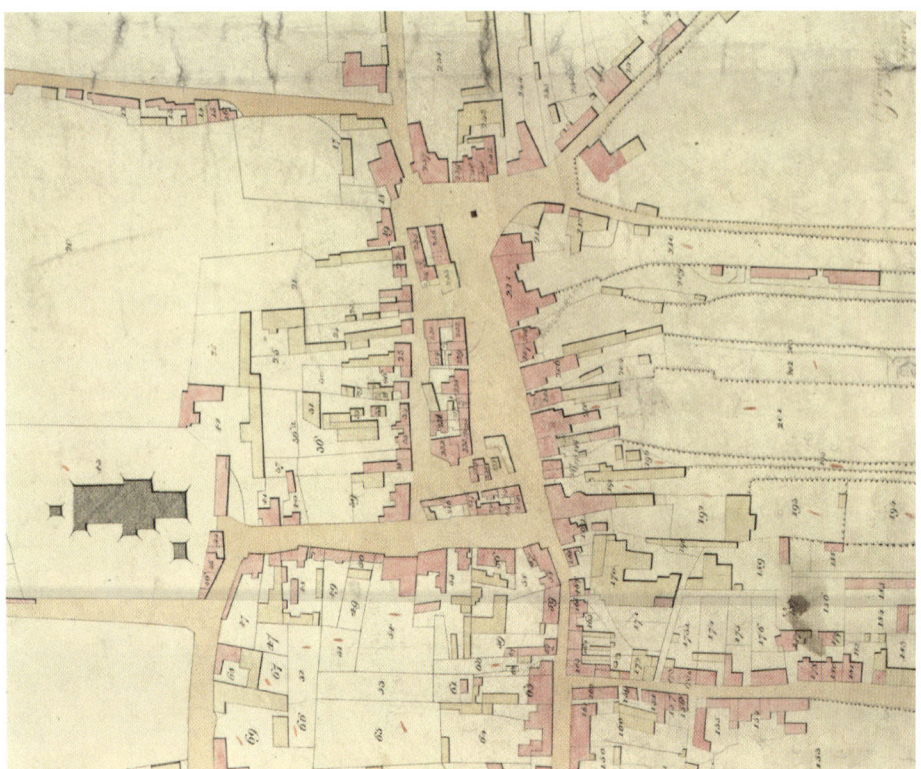

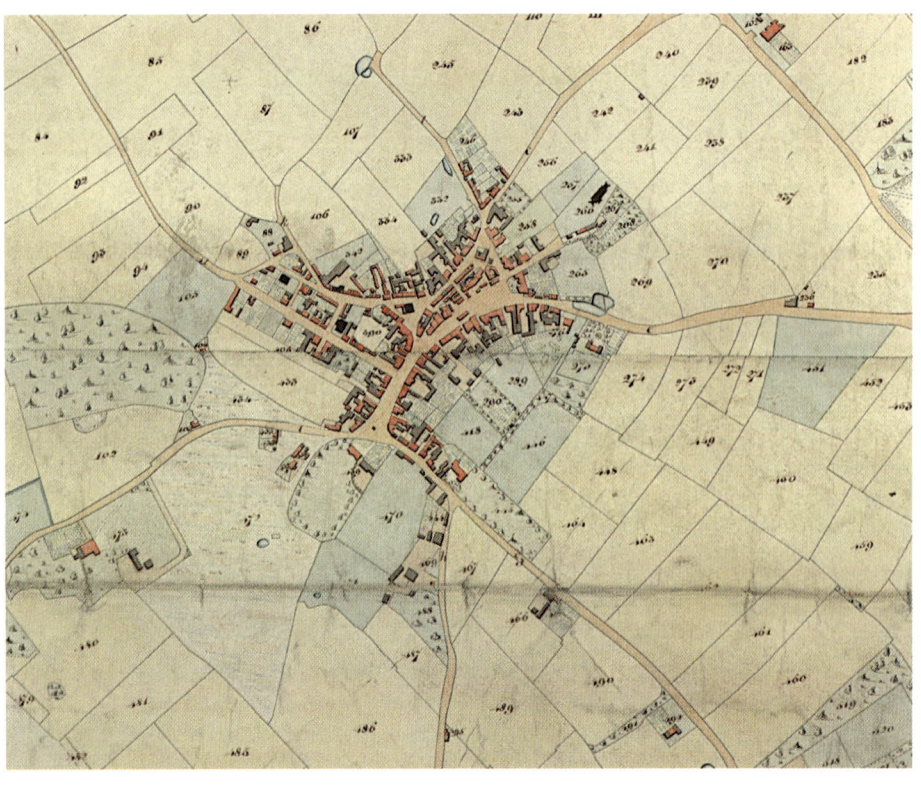

FIG. 4.6. The plans of the towns of East Dereham (above) and Holt (below) echo those of innumerable rural settlements in Norfolk, with parish church standing at a distance from a marketplace, in both cases partially infilled, that had clearly originated as a common.

There are some examples of 'planted' towns, certainly or probably established by lordly initiative on new sites unrelated to places of earlier importance, in Norfolk. But even these had an intimate connection with commons, for their establishment required an area of open, uncultivated and untenanted land. The town of Harleston still forms part of the parish of Redenhall and, originating in the grant of a market charter in the thirteenth century, its plan essentially comprises a large filled common, a small remnant of which survived to serve as the marketplace. More striking, because it is more obviously 'planned', is New Buckenham, which was founded by William D'Albini II in the 1140s, to accompany his new castle.[34] The latter stood in the parish of Old Buckenham, apparently on the edge of a large tract of common waste. The town, which was given its own tiny parish, was clearly placed on part of this open tract, with much of the rest surviving to this day as New Buckenham Common. In short, just as it is impossible to understand the development of medieval rural settlement in Norfolk – or arguably elsewhere – without considering the role of commons, so too are the history and morphology of towns, and of common land, intimately connected.

One other important association between commons, and commerce, needs to be briefly mentioned. The interconnected rivers and lakes of Broadland developed from an early date as important arteries of trade, plied by small sailing craft – keels and, later, wherries. There were accordingly numerous public 'staithes', or landing places, where cargoes could be loaded and unloaded. The overwhelming majority were found where public roads run alongside rivers for some distance, or cross them by bridge or ford; or on areas of common land running down to the water's edge. Most of the latter were removed by parliamentary enclosure although the staithes usually survived, either on the same site or on some neighbouring one, allotted by the enclosure commissioners (below, p. 113). The old association can still, however, be seen in the few places where waterside commons remain unenclosed – at Coltishall, Stokesby, Chedgrave, and less clearly at Thorpe St Andrew and Reedham (Figure 4.7).[35] It is easy to see why staithes should have grown up in these locations. Tidal rivers, and other navigable watercourses, are in legal terms highways: 'the right of navigation … is a right of way for all the public for all purposes of navigation, trade, and intercourse'.[36] But there was, and is, no general right to moor, or to load and unload, on the banks of a watercourse. There are only defined places 'appropriated by usage, grant or statute' for the purposes of landing or embarking. Where a public highway, or a common to which there was *de facto* public access, met a navigable river, there would need to be a place, and a public right, to tranship goods and people, given that both road and river were effectively highways (at least for local inhabitants), and a boat cannot navigate a road, nor a vehicle drive along water. Such staithes were particularly likely to develop on riverside commons, where there was ample space to manoeuvre vehicles or stack cargoes. Coastal landing places were also closely associated with common land; Morston Quay on the north coast of the county remains a registered common.

Gibbets and Gallows

If greens and commons lying close to important settlements, and encircled by dwellings, might in some cases become the locations for markets and fairs, the larger and more remote examples sometimes developed other public uses. Such lonely, liminal spaces were, in particular, considered appropriate places for the erection of gibbets, structures on which the bodies of executed criminals were displayed, to serve as a warning to others. The gibbeting of executed criminals – usually murderers – originated in the Middle Ages but was essentially a post-medieval practice. It seems to have peaked in the 1740s, shortly before the Murder Act of 1752 denied churchyard burial to all murderers and made it obligatory for their bodies to either be treated in this manner, or handed over for medical dissection by anatomists. It was finally abolished in 1825.[37] Gibbet sites were normally used only once, chosen in part to be near to where the miscreant had committed their crime.

Gibbets comprised a tall post, usually 10 metres or more in height, which supported a cross beam from the end of which an iron cage, containing the criminal's corpse, was suspended on a short chain. Once erected, they might stand for 10, 15 or more years, long after the gibbeted body had disintegrated, and formed prominent and long-lived landmarks in these often open, windswept landscapes. This explains why they are so clearly and carefully depicted

FIG. 4.7. The green at Stokesby, one of the few survivors of the many waterside commons in Broadland once used as staithes, or landing places. The building in the foreground originated as a small warehouse

on William Faden's county map of 1797. Nine examples are shown, almost all on commons – Badley Moor, Mousehold Heath, Methwold Heath, Holt Heath, Bradenham Heath and Kettlestone Heath; the example shown at West Dereham also stood on a common, although this is not apparent from the map.[38] There were many other examples, either not shown by Faden, or abandoned before or erected after his map was surveyed. In 1797 the body of the murderer William Suffolk, for example, was gibbeted on common land in North Walsham.[39] In most cases, the gibbets seem to have been placed towards the centre of the common, and often where it was crossed by a major road.

The reasons for the close association of gibbets, and the larger and more remote areas of common land, were complex. Gibbeting was intended to convey a strong social message, to deter others from committing similar crimes to the executed miscreant. Gibbets therefore needed to be placed in public places and in locations where they were widely visible. Commons crossed by public roads fulfilled these requirements, while on treeless moors and heaths the grim message they conveyed was reinforced by the starkness of their setting. The stench produced by the decaying body made it necessary to place them at a distance from habitations, making small greens and commons unsuitable for the purpose. But deterrence morphed easily into public spectacle, especially at a time when notorious criminals often achieved a measure of celebrity. Gibbets when first erected often drew large crowds and therefore needed to be placed where growing crops and other property could not be damaged. When James Cliffen was hung in a gibbet on Badley Moor in March 1785, following his execution in Norwich for murder, so many people came to see the body that the place resembled a fair, with booths erected to serve alcohol, leading to 'many hilarious scenes'.[40] On 4 April Parson Woodforde of Weston Longville noted in his diary: how 'it being fine weather', he rode 'to Baddeley Moor where Cliffen stands in Chains'.[41] But in addition, the choice of remote commons for gibbet sites also emphasised the marginalisation of the criminal, even in death; and as Nicola Whyte has noted, most if not all not only stood on commons, but on or close to where these were crossed by parish boundaries.[42] Cliffen's gibbet on Badley Moor thus stood on the boundary between Yaxham (where his crime had been committed) and Mattishall; that on West Bradenham Common, on the boundary between that parish and Holme Hale; while the gibbet on Methwold Heath stood on the boundary between Methwold and Feltwell. Those on Martham Common and Kettleston Common were similarly positioned.

As Whyte has also noted, the association of criminal execution, and boundaries, took another form. In the medieval period gallows were numerous, in Norfolk as elsewhere, because many local lords held the right to execute convicted criminals on their manors, in addition to the rights exercised by the hundred courts. In some cases the sites at which those convicted by the latter bodies were executed had originated in the pre-Conquest period as *cwealam-stow*, places of public execution, often conveniently located next to the meeting place of the hundred court and, like them, often placed on or beside prehistoric earthworks.[43] A few examples were later re-appropriated as the sites of gibbets, such as Gallow Hill in Thetford. Whyte has highlighted the strong association between gallows sites and parish boundaries, a relationship which again served to emphasise, in spatial terms, the social marginality of the condemned.[44] And, because ribbons of common land often survived along the boundaries between parishes – but also because spectators needed to be accommodated without damage to crops or property – gallows sites were also often to be found on commons. One of the Bronze Age barrows on Salthouse Heath – actually in the parish of Kelling, and c. 170 metres from the boundary between the two parishes – is called Gallow Hill, while 'Galley Hill' – its name surely derived from a lost barrow – was an area of common heath in East Wretham, beside the parish boundary. The First Edition Ordnance Survey 6-inch maps show that in the early twentieth century the round barrow called Gallows Hill stood on the remains of Snetterton Heath, close to the junction of the three parishes of Snetterton, Hargham and Eccles.

Sport and Recreation

Village greens, and other small commons forming the centres of settlements, may have been used in the past for informal sports and recreations but perhaps, before the nineteenth century, on a limited basis. The traditional East Anglian game of 'Camping' – a kind of football, which took a variety of often violent forms – was sometimes played on common land.[45] The famous but probably mythical early eighteenth-century match between Norfolk and Suffolk, in which 300 people participated and several are said to have died, is supposed to have taken place on Diss Common; in 1806 a match was planned, but aborted, on Crostwick Common.[46] But the game generally took place in enclosed 'camping closes', some privately owned, some the property of the church or a village trust, that at Edgefield belonging to 'Edgefield Single Men' according to the tithe apportionment of 1845.[47] Some commons, in the eighteenth and early nineteenth century, may have been used on a regular and organised basis for cricket matches – certainly, part of Brisley Common, or Green, is specifically labelled as 'Cricket Ground' on the tithe map of 1840 (above, Figure 3.4).[48] But the popularity of cricket at a local, grassroots level probably post-dated the enclosure of most commons, and the sport was initially promulgated by large landowners, many of whom, in the course of the nineteenth century, established pitches within their parks. The First Edition Ordnance Survey 6-inch maps from the 1880s show examples in the grounds of Quidenham Hall, Rackheath Hall, Bayfield Hall and Houghton Hall; others certainly existed, in the parks at Lexham and Holkham for example, that are not shown.

So far as the evidence goes, the sporting use of commons was more often associated with the larger and more remote examples, rather than village greens, and with the social elite, rather than with the commoners themselves. Diaries and correspondence make it clear that, at least by the eighteenth century, those holding the required property qualification shot freely over common land, with little if any regard for the livestock of commoners. It is possible that the role which heaths, in particular, played as game cover reduced the enthusiasm of landowners for their enclosure and reclamation. In 1780 Abel Smith, a tenant of the Merton estate, got into trouble for having 'cleared all the furze off Wether Heath, which leaves it as naked as Lincoln Inn Fields for the preservation of game'.[49] The open, uncluttered character of the more intensively grazed heaths, in contrast, invited other kinds of recreational use. Regular horse racing events were thus held on Swaffham Heath, to the south of the town, from at least 1721.[50] Some time later a cricket pitch was laid out in the centre of the course where, in 1797, a Norfolk county team took on an 'All England' side. Race meetings continued to be held until 1864, four years before the heath was enclosed in 1868.[51] The race course on the heathland common to the south of the north Norfolk town of Holt was in existence by 1732, when, in a race held on 4 July, 'Sweetlips', 'Jilting Peggy' and 'Small Hopes' all competed.[52] The common was enclosed in 1810 but race meetings continued until 1844, presumably on another site as the tithe map of 1839 describes the original venue as 'old race course'.[53] 'Old Race Course' continued to be marked on the 6-inch Ordnance Survey map until 1905. Horse races were also held on Mousehold Heath, just outside Norwich, from early in the eighteenth century and, on a more regular basis, from the 1840s, something still remembered in the name of Racecourse Plantation in Thorpe St Andrew.[54] Horse racing in a less organised or regular form took place elsewhere. 'Throngs of people' assembled on Mulbarton Common in the middle decades of the nineteenth century 'in Whitsun week, to witness pony and donkey races, and other sports and amusements'.[55]

The large racing events held on common heaths were instigated and patronised by members of the landed elite: Lord Orford, Colonel Townshend and Captain Vernon were, in the 1750s, patrons of the Holt races; the eighteenth-century patrons of the Swaffham races included the Duke of Devonshire, the Duke of Kingston, Lord March, Lord Portmore, Lord Orford, Sir J. Lowther, Earl of Oxford, Lord Clermont, Lord Offery, Lord Stradbroke and Sir Jacob Astley.[56] But the attendees included individuals from all social ranks. Indeed, urban populations clearly found their own amusements on nearby commons, in the absence of any lead provided by the local elite. Mousehold Heath, on the doorstep of Norwich, was noted for wrestling, archery, gambling and general unruly behaviour. MacMaster has described how, in October 1767:

> Some ten thousand were reported to have attended a contest – significantly this was a 'Holy Monday' and the workplaces were deserted – between a waterman, Robert George, and a worsted-weaver and 'noted bruiser', John Todd. In July 1845 a prize-fight was held between Jim Woods and the 'Norfolk Slasher', Ben Clarke, for £5 a side.[57]

The heath provided a welcome recreational space for the poorer elements of the city population, but such activities disturbed the city's nineteenth-century elite, keen to preserve the peace and uphold public morality, and were the main reason why they worked hard to effect the enclosure of its last surviving portion, nearest to the city, and its conversion into a public park, against the spirited opposition of the inhabitants of the suburb of Pockthorpe (another, interestingly, was the increasing disfigurement of the heath by brick-making).[58]

Poor Houses and Allotments

As we have seen, from the fifteenth century, in Norfolk as in most parts of England, there was a steady reduction in the number of independent properties, whether copyhold or freehold, as these – together with their common rights – were bought up by neighbouring farms, or acquired by large estates. At the same time the rural population increased, the rate of growth slowing in the late seventeenth and early eighteenth century, but resuming after 1750 and reaching unprecedented levels by 1800. In the course of the eighteenth century, moreover, opportunities for employment in the county were significantly reduced by the contraction of the rural textile industry. As population growth outstripped the supply of work, agricultural employment, if it could be obtained at all, was often temporary and insecure. The landless poor gradually became – at a rate which varied over time, and to an extent that varied from place to place and area to area – a large if not dominant proportion of the population, unable in particular to survive on their own resources at times of illness, when widowed, or in old age.

In the late Middle Ages significant levels of poor relief were delivered by the Church but in the wake of the Dissolution an expansion of private charities was insufficient to meet the scale of the problem and the government was eventually obliged to make the care of the local poor the responsibility of individual parishes. Acts passed in 1597 and 1601 laid the foundations of a system that endured for more than two centuries, by which a rate levied on those dwelling in each parish was used to support the 'impotent poor' – the old, infirm, ill or very young who were unable to undertake productive work – with money payments, assistance in kind, housing and even medical treatment.[59] In theory, the parish officials called Overseers of the Poor were also empowered to find work for the able-bodied but, while they usually made strenuous attempts to find apprenticeships for the children of the poor, were less keen to establish the kinds of make-work schemes sanctioned by the Acts; for most of the labouring poor, unemployment was seasonal, rather than permanent or long term, and they, too, generally received some kind of temporary support. The 1597 Act laid down that the poor rate required to support parochial relief was to be paid by 'every Inhabitant, and every Occupier of Lands in the said Parish'. Parochial relief accompanied, but could not in theory be replaced by, the support provided by the one or more charities that had been established over time by private benefactors in most parishes, usually in the form of income from land, which was used by the overseers and churchwardens to provide the poor with fuel, bread, cash payments or other benefits.

Both the 1597 and the 1601 acts permitted and encouraged parishes to enclose portions of common land to provide housing for the poor,[60] the 1601

Act allowing churchwardens and overseers to 'erect, build and set up in fit and convenient Places of Habitation, in such Wastes or Commons, at the general Charges of the Parish ... convenient Houses of Dwelling for the said impotent poor'.[61] Through the seventeenth and eighteenth centuries, in Norfolk as elsewhere, numerous small parish 'poor houses', providing accommodation for a handful of elderly or infirm individuals, were accordingly erected on commons under the direction of parochial charities, or by the overseers of the poor, such as the 'house for the use of the poor' which was built on one of the commons in East Tuddenham some time before 1682.[62] Cottages for homeless families might also be provided; no less than five had been erected on Wells Green in the same parish by 1786.[63]

The provisions of the 'Old Poor Law', established by the acts of 1597 and 1601 and updated by various subsequent administrative measures, made individual parishes responsible for maintaining their own poor and sick.[64] But as the rural population continued to grow, and poverty increase, through the eighteenth century groups of parishes began to combine, under the terms of an act passed in 1722, to erect larger 'poor houses' or 'work houses' which provided both accommodation and employment. By 1776, 24 such institutions had been created in Norfolk.[65] Numbers increased still further after the passing of Gilbert's Act in 1782, which empowered individual hundreds, or groups of 'incorporated' hundreds, to erect larger workhouses. Not surprisingly, these new forms of institution were also often built on the open space provided by common land. Faden's map of 1797 specifically labels a total of 17 examples, many of which occupy encroachments on commons, including those at Rollesby (built to serve the incorporated hundreds of East and West Flegg), Smallburgh (for the Hundred of Happing), Heckingham (for Loddon and Clavering), Wicklewood (Forehoe), Gressenhall (Launditch and Mitford) and Holt (for Holt Hundred, and sharing the common, in typical fashion, with both a racecourse and a gibbet) (Figure 4.8). Finally, the New Poor Law of 1834 brought in a universal system of 'Unions', based on hundreds or groups of hundreds.[66] Eight of these used workhouses from (and a few perpetuated the boundaries of) earlier Unions but a dozen new ones were built, and much of the earlier local provision was rendered redundant. At Ashwellthorpe in 1845 the overseers rented out 10 acres of land 'which was enclosed from the waste for the use of the Workhouse 55 years ago', using the income to help the poor: 'the Workhouse was sold after the formation of Depwade Union'.[67] At Hindolveston, similarly, the overseers were leasing out 'the *Workhouse land*, enclosed from the waste, under Gilbert's Act'; while at Foulsham 'the old *Workhouse*, which was built on the waste in 1782' had been 'divided into tenements'.[68] The workhouse at Holt, 'built on the heath in 1779' had now also been sold, with the income 'applied to the poor-rates'.[69] The new, post-1834 workhouses, in marked contrast to the earlier ones, displayed no close relationship with commons, largely because, by the time they were built in the 1830s, most had been enclosed.

FIG. 4.8. Holt Heath, as depicted on Faden's *Topographical Map* of 1797. Note the rabbit warren, prominent pit, workhouse, racecourse – and gibbet.

Once again, wholesale enclosure has made the association of earlier poor houses of various kinds, and common land, less obvious than it would have been in the past – coupled with the fact that the small parish poor houses have long since become private dwellings with few if any obvious signs of their original purpose. The house now called Rose Cottage, for example, standing in what is clearly an intake from Thwaite Common, was built by the Thwaite Trustees for the Poor and in 1841 was still owned by them and occupied by 'John Payne and others'.[70] It is noteworthy that here, as in several other cases, the common commandeered as the site for a parochial poor house did not lie near the centre of the parish in question, or form the focus for the principal settlement within it, but instead lay towards the edge of the parish, on or close to the parish boundary. The 'middling' elements in the community, while perhaps happy enough to provide for the old and infirm, may have preferred to place them at arms length, spatially marginalising the socially marginal.

There were other ways in which common land was pressed into the service of poor relief. In 1756 a parliamentary act, mainly concerned with the encouragement of tree planting by facilitating the enclosure of portions of the waste by manorial owners, also permitted their partial enclosure to provide gardens for the poor or, as we would say, 'allotments'.[71] In Dickleburgh, for example, sometime in the eighteenth century, 9½ acres were enclosed from Seamere Green as gardens, while at nearby Pulham St Mary the Virgin 10 acres were enclosed from South Green at the end of the century, partly used for a new poorhouse and partly divided into 73 allotments for the use of the poor.[72] Legislation also allowed intakes to be made from the common and leased out to private individuals, with the income being used to help the local poor. The tithe maps, surveyed around 1840, show a number of examples of such 'parish land' or 'town land' enclosed from adjacent commons, as beside Crow Green in Long Stratton, or the two intakes from Morningthorpe Common owned by the Trustees for the Poor.[73] But it is likely that on the eve of enclosure the main way in which commons contributed to the relief of the poor was through the informal use they were allowed to make of many examples, especially as a source of fuel. It is hard otherwise to account for the way in which, when finally enclosed by parliamentary awards, the poor were so often provided with an allotment, on which they could continue to cut fuel and also, in some cases, graze a few livestock.

Conclusion

A host of other non-agricultural activities occurred on common land, including military training. The name 'The Buttlands' applied to greens and commons in Wells, Aylsham and elsewhere recalls their use for archery training by local militias in the Middle Ages or later. There are records of archery practice on Litcham Common; of the presence of archery butts on one of the greens at Shelfhanger; while in 1543 and 1618 the manorial court ordered the repair of the butts on West Runton Common.[74] Parson Woodforde went with his nephew in 1777 'to see the Dragoons exercise on Mousehold Heath about 3 miles from Norwich', and in 1793 observed a 'Regiment of soldiers' marching there for the same purpose.[75] The Cavalry Barracks, established in 1791, and the Britannia Barracks, built in the 1880s, were both placed on land taken out of the heath, and located where they were because of the space it afforded for training. As we shall see, military activity during the First and Second World Wars has left significant archaeological traces on many common heaths in Norfolk. Conversely, in 1549 Kett's rebels famously camped on Mousehold Heath, and greens and commons generally provided arenas for public protest, as for example during the Burston School Strike in 1914, when lessons were held on Burston village green. Nor should we forget the role of those greens and commons ringed by houses as spaces for informal recreation and socialising as well as for more organised community events, such as the meal for the parish poor of roast beef and plum pudding held on Brockdish Common to celebrate the peace, 1801.[76] May Day festivities are presumably remembered in the name of Maypole Green in Toft Monks.

Commons in the past, as well as being more intensively managed and exploited agriculturally than most of their survivors, were also often much busier, less 'natural', in character, used in ways which are easily forgotten but which in some cases might have a profound, even disfiguring, impact on their appearance and ecology. These various uses, moreover – industrial, commercial, social and recreational – have much to tell us about how the character and roles of common land were understood in the past and how this changed over time and about the balance of power between manorial lords and commoners; and in particular about how, in local societies displaying increasing levels of inequality, commons gradually acquired an important role in the relief of the poor. The latter thus came, in the eyes of many communities, to have some claim on the commons. Above all, perhaps, a consideration of these additional uses and activities adds a further level of complexity to these contested landscapes, for some of them – crowds amassing to watch a race or to picnic under a gibbet – must have had negative effects on the 'core', agricultural uses of the commons in question, although our sources appear to be silent on how commoners regarded such intrusions.

Notes

1. G.F. Leake, *The Commons of East and West Runton* (Norwich, 1991), 7.
2. NRO DN/TA 144.
3. NRO MC 343/105, 735X7.
4. *Norwich Chronicle*, 20 June 1789.
5. H. Apling, *Norfolk Corn Windmills* (Norwich, 1984).
6. Apling, *Norfolk Corn Windmills*, 25–8.
7. Apling, *Norfolk Corn Windmills*, 33–6.
8. NRO DN/TA 560; *Norfolk News*, Saturday 13 March 1858; *Norfolk Chronicle*, 2 April 1859.
9. Norfolk Windmills Trust, https://www.norfolkmills.co.uk/Windmills/new-buckenham-postmill.html: accessed 11.11.2024.
10. Apling, *Norfolk Corn Windmills*, 192.
11. NRO BEA 9/3, 433 X 5.
12. NRO NRS 4109.
13. R. Lucas, Brickmaking on Norfolk Commons, *Norfolk Archaeology* 43, 3 (2000), 457–68.
14. NRO MC3/45; Map of 1729, Blickling Hall, no catalogue number.
15. A. Cox, *A Survey of Bedfordshire Brickmaking: History and Gazetteer* (Bedford, 1979), 28–9.
16. NRO BIR 67, 397X2.
17. NHER 8388.
18. NHER 6589 and 9406. For Grimston, see; NHER 1075, 1105, 3580, 3582, 3584, 3586, 3588, 11789.
19. NHER 7443.
20. Lucas, Brickmaking, 462.
21. Lucas, Brickmaking, 461.
22. NRO GIL 2/17, 717X8.
23. NRO BR 90/16/9.
24. A. Davison and R. Joby, Early Roads and Turnpikes, in T. Ashwin and A. Davison (eds), *An Historical Atlas of Norfolk*, 3rd edn. (Chichester, 2005), 154–5.
25. C. Jarvis, The Making of the Broads, in T. Williamson and A. Yardy, *Broadland: Shaping Marsh and Fen* (Hatfield, 2024), 197–208.
26. T.K. Cromwell, *Excursions in the County of Norfolk* (London, 1829), Vol. 2, 145.

27 Blomefield, *Topographical History*, Vol. 1, 4.
28 Blomefield, *Topographical History*, Vol. 2, 517.
29 C. Barringer, Markets and Fairs in the 18th and 19th Centuries, in T. Ashwin and A. Davison (eds), *An Historical Atlas of Norfolk*, 3rd edn. (Chichester, 2005), 138–9; Blomefield, *Topographical History*, Vol. 9, 34 (Middleton); NRO DN/TA 445 (Cley); C. King, The Leisure Activities of the Rural Working Classes with Special Reference to Norfolk 1840–1940, unpublished PhD thesis, University of East Anglia, 2015, 53 and NRO, PD 552/45 (Banham); for the others see King, Leisure Activities, 53–8.
30 D. Dymond, Medieval and Later Markets, in T. Ashwin and A. Davison (eds), *An Historical Atlas of Norfolk*, 3rd edn. (Chichester, 2005), 76–7.
31 M. Beresford, *New Towns of the Middle Ages* (London, 1967); K. Lilley, *Urban Life in the Middle Ages 1000–1450* (Basingstoke, 2002), 47–9.
32 Blomefield, *Topographical History*, Vol. 2, 509–10.
33 A. Rogerson, Wymondham Before 1107, in P. Cattermole (ed.) *Wymondham Abbey: A History of the Monastery and Parish Church* (Wymondham, 2007), 2–15; T. Williamson, The Landscape, in Cattermole, *Wymondham Abbey*, 172–85.
34 B. Ayers, Medieval Planned Towns, in T. Ashwin and A. Davison (eds), *An Historical Atlas of Norfolk* (Chichester, 2005), 74–5; R. Hoggett, *New Buckenham, Norfolk: Landscape and Heritage Statement* (New Buckenham, 2018), 45–54; R. Liddiard, The Castle Landscapes of Anglo-Norman East Anglia: A Regional Perspective, in C. Harper-Bill (ed.), *Medieval East Anglia* (Woodbridge, 2005), 33–51; P. Rutledge and T. Rutledge, *New Buckenham: A Moated Town* (New Buckenham, 2002).
35 Williamson and Yardy, *Broadland*, 291–9.
36 A.S. Wisdom, *The Law of Rivers and Watercourses* (London, 1979), 58.
37 S. Tarlow, The Landscape of the Gibbet, *Landscape History* 36, 1 (2015), 71–88.
38 N. Whyte, The Deviant Dead in the Norfolk Landscape, *Landscapes* 4, 1 (2003), 24–39.
39 *Norfolk Chronicle,* 25 March 1797.
40 *Norfolk Chronicle*, 26 March 1785; *Norwich Mercury,* 26 March 1785.
41 J. Beresford (ed.), *The Diary of a Country Parson: The Reverend James Woodforde, Vol. 2, 1782–1787* (Oxford, 1926), 182.
42 Whyte, Deviant Dead, 24–9.
43 A. Reynolds, The Definition and Ideology of Anglo-Saxon Execution Cemeteries, in D. Boe and F. Verhaeghe (eds), *Death and Burial in Europe* (Bruges, 1997), 33–41.
44 Whyte, Deviant Dead, 31–3.
45 D. Dymond, The Game of Camping in Eastern England, *The Local Historian* 51 (2021), 2–15, at 5–6.
46 *Norfolk Chronicle*, 19 July 1806.
47 NRO DN/TA 912.
48 NRO DN/TA 409.
49 NRO Petre Box 17, bundle 1.
50 *Stamford Mercury*, 8 June 1721.
51 Racecourses, Here Today and Gone Tomorrow, http://www.greyhoundderby.com/Closed%20Courses%20New.html, accessed 14.11.2024.
52 C. Buxton, Eighteenth and Early Nineteenth-Century Race Grounds in Norfolk and Suffolk, unpublished MA dissertation, School of History, University of East Anglia, 2005; Racecourses, Here Today and Gone Tomorrow, http://www.greyhoundderby.com/Closed%20Courses%20New.html, accessed 14.11.2024.
53 NHER 33478; NRO C/Sca 2/165; NRO DN/TA 494.

54 Racecourses, Here Today and Gone Tomorrow, http://www.greyhoundderby.com/Closed%20Courses%20New.html, accessed 14.11.2024.
55 W. White, *History, Gazetteer, and Directory of Norfolk, and the City and County of Norwich* (Sheffield, 1845), 697.
56 Racecourses, Here Today and Gone Tomorrow, http://www.greyhoundderby.com/Closed%20Courses%20New.html, accessed 14.11.2024.
57 N. MacMaster, The Battle for Mousehold Heath 1857–1884: 'Popular Politics' and the Victorian Public Park, *Past and Present* 127 (1990), 117–54, at 121.
58 MacMaster, Mousehold Heath, 127.
59 P. Slack, *The English Poor Law, 1531–1782* (Cambridge, 1990).
60 Birtles, Green Space, 115–21; S. Birtles, Common Land, Poor Relief and Enclosure: The Use of Manorial Resources in Fulfilling Parish Obligations 1601–1834, *Past and Present* 165 (1999), 74–106; Morley, Common Land, 61.
61 43 Eliz, c2 (1601).
62 NRO PD 297/79; NRO PD 447/79
63 Birtles, Green Space, 118.
64 J. Crowley and A. Reid (eds), *The Poor Law in Norfolk, 1700–1850* (Ely, 1983); D. Dymond, Workhouses Before 1834, in P. Wade-Martins (ed.), *An Historical Atlas of Norfolk* (Norwich, 1993), 142–3; Slack, *English Poor Law*.
65 Dymond, Workhouses Before 1834.
66 A. Digby, Poor Law Unions and Workhouses, 1834–1930, in T. Ashwin, and A. Davison (eds) *An Historical Atlas of Norfolk* (Chichester, 2005), 148–9.
67 White, *Directory*, 700.
68 White, *Directory*, 348, 351.
69 White, *Directory*, 741.
70 NRO DN/TA 563.
71 29 Geo. II c. 36.
72 Birtles, Green Space, 119–20; NRO PC 15/30; NRO C/Sca 2/90; NRO DN/TA 714; NRO DN/TA 12.
73 NRO DN/TA 492. NRO DN/TA 140.
74 Birtles, Green Space, 158; Leake, *East and West Runton*, 9.
75 J. Beresford (ed.), *The Diary of a Country Parson: The Reverend James Woodforde, Vol. 1, 1758–1781* (Oxford, 1924), 82 and 135.
76 NRO MC 2329/1, 958X1.

CHAPTER 5

Enclosure and Survival

The overwhelming majority of common land which existed in Norfolk at the end of the eighteenth century, so prominently displayed on William Faden's county map of 1797, had by the middle of the nineteenth century been *enclosed* – that is, converted into parcels of land which were privately owned, and over which no-one else had rights of use or access. Enclosure, so defined, was of course not a new phenomenon of this period. As we have seen, commons as they existed by the thirteenth century represented the fragmentary remains of much more extensive tracts of open land, exploited by groups of individuals, that had gradually been encroached upon, turned into fields, parks or coppiced woods, over the previous decades. With ownership of and rights to these residual fragments now more tightly defined, further attrition seems to have slowed, although it did not cease, with innumerable encroachments and intakes being sanctioned by manorial courts. Manorial lords were bound by law to leave sufficient common land to meet the needs of commoners, so that while in most parishes its area contracted significantly over time, there were few in which they were able to remove it entirely. The scale of enclosures increased markedly, however, from the sixteenth century.

Early Enclosure

Enclosure did not only affect commons, but also the arable open fields which covered, in various forms, much of the county by the thirteenth century. In this case enclosure converted properties in the form of unhedged, scattered strips, subject to varying extents to communal use and regulation, into consolidated blocks of private land. There were significant differences in how all this was achieved in different parts of the county. On the claylands in the centre and south the enclosure of open fields mainly occurred in a gradual or 'piecemeal' manner. Over time, individuals bought and sold land until they possessed a number of contiguous strips, which they could then fence or hedge and remove from the routines of communal cultivation; or large landowners gradually bought up the strips of small freeholders, enclosing in a similar manner as they did so. Piecemeal enclosure, because it involved the gradual hedging or fencing along the margins of groups of strips, tended to preserve in simplified form the rather irregular, sinuous pattern of boundaries in the old landscape.[1] In the west and north of the county, field systems were generally more complex and rigidly organised and here they were more likely to survive until the eighteenth century, when they were removed by parliamentary enclosure, with the common land of the parish usually, although by no means invariably, being enclosed at the same time. In other parts of the county parliamentary enclosure was primarily concerned with common land, and in most parishes dealt with only small areas of open arable that had escaped piecemeal enclosure, or with residual rights of grazing on the fallows of land that had been so enclosed.[2]

In many parishes, however, the area of common land had already been considerably reduced before the advent of parliamentary acts, through large scale partial enclosures which were more extensive than the kinds of encroachments described in Chapter 3, although the line of distinction is a fuzzy one. They were carried out through formal legal agreements between the relevant parties, sometimes backed up by a writ from the Court of Chancery. In 1599, an agreement was thus drawn up between King's College, Cambridge, lords of the manor of Horstead; their 'farmer' or long-term tenant of the manorial demesne; and the many common-right holders, for the enclosure and division of a proportion of the heaths and commons in the parishes of Horstead and Stanninghall and the termination of rights of common grazing on the arable, 'soe the whole Towne and lande within the same might be imployed to the best Improvement of all and every the saide persons … being to them much more profitt then the former use of the same'.[3] Similarly, in 1623 the 500-acre (200-hectare) Great Heath in the parish of Great Melton was enclosed by agreement, with Edmund Anguish, lord of the manor, receiving an allotment of 70 acres (c. 28 hectares), and the rest being divided between the commoners. The various other commons in the parish, extending over more than 250 acres (c. 100 hectares), survived until the parliamentary enclosure of 1818.[4] The 1623 enclosure was opposed by farmers in the adjacent parish of Wymondham, who claimed rights of common on the heath, but was confirmed by a Chancery decree in 1624.[5]

A number of these early enclosures by agreement dealt with common marshes and fens in Broadland. At Aldeby in 1614 lord and tenants agreed to enclose 'all such marshes rushe grounds and reede grounds … as nowe bee or are reputed to bee or might be used or fedd in common'. Most although not all of these commons were allotted as private parcels to the lord, and to the landowners in proportion to the commonable rights claimed on the basis of land held on the adjacent 'upland', with 20 acres being set aside 'for charitable and good uses to and for ye benefitte of ye said towne only'.[6] In 1676, similarly, an agreement was made to enclose the Great Marsh in Langley, while a document of 1678 refers to 'one marsh late parcell of the Common called East Marsh' in the adjacent parish of Hardley.[7]

Early enclosures in this area, as elsewhere in the county, were not always amicable. At Clippesby in 1573 there were disputes when the lord of the manor fenced off part of the common and took it into private ownership. In 1589 six Ormesby yeomen brought a legal action against Sir Edward Clere, Lord of the manor, for obstructing their access to the common and enclosing 30 acres for his own use.[8] The famous rebellion led by Robert Kett in 1549 had many causes but was unquestionably in part a response to enclosure, beginning with the tearing down of hedges planted around land taken in from a common in Hargham. But the rebels' opposition was to illegal, unilateral enclosures made without due process, rather than enclosure *per se*, although Kett, a wealthy Wymondham yeoman, had himself been fined in the manorial court for the unauthorised enclosure of common land.[9] They also objected to the overstocking of foldcourses, and thus commons, by manorial lords and flockmasters, and to attempts by the former to assert foldcourse rights where none had existed before.[10] The rebellion was proceeded by anti-enclosure riots and protests elsewhere in England in the late 1540s, stimulated both by the illegal acts of landowners in an increasingly commercial society and by the government's own attempts to restrain enclosures which, in the 'champion' Midlands, were associated with the conversion of arable to pasture and the depopulation of villages.[11]

In fact, the evidence suggests that illegal enclosure of commons, and certainly the most blatant violations of the terms of the Statute of Merton, were relatively rare in early modern Norfolk and, where they occurred, were often successfully contested by commoners. It is of course true that some of the 'agreements' to enclose, of the kind just noted, may have involved a measure of coercion. It is also true that commoners must have struggled hard against a legal system controlled by the local gentry. As the commoners of Middleton, fighting to preserve their common, complained to Protector Somerset in 1547, it was hard to obtain an impartial judgement of their case against their lord because of the 'color of his worship and estymacon and also of the grete favor p[ar]tiality frendship and alliance towarde hym born and shewed in the said County and elsewhere'.[12] But, as we have also seen, most areas of common land in existence in the fifteenth century remained extant in the late eighteenth and, to judge from the evidence of Faden's map, there were only a few parishes in which commons had been removed in their entirety.

Only from 1746 did legal changes allow lords to enclose portions of the manorial wastes, even if opposed by commoners claiming violation of the Statute of Merton, and then only for the purpose of planting trees.[13] Faden's map shows a number of plantations within areas of common land which were probably established by landowners taking advantage of this legislation. Several still survive although, with the common since enclosed, they are now surrounded by fields, such as Common Plantation in Aylmerton. Quaker's Wood in Marsham, however, is still bounded by a large area of Marsham Heath, preserved as a poor's allotment and now managed as a nature reserve, but never registered as a common. Such enclosures, while legal, were not always meekly accepted. In 1775, the fences surrounding Sir Jacob Preston's new plantation on Smallburgh Common were forcibly torn down by the commoners, although the plantation survived, and is shown on Faden's map.[14]

As just noted, there were a few Norfolk parishes where common land was removed in its entirety by legal agreements between lords and commoners, rather than by parliamentary enclosure. The historian Francis Blomefield described in 1739 how there were over 150 acres (60 hectares) of common land in Thelveton, a parish of only 1,057 acres (c. 430 hectares).[15] But none is shown on Faden's map, surveyed around 1794, on which the words 'Thelton Common inclosed' are written across the area covered by the parish. A few years earlier, in 1780, a deed of agreement for enclosing all the commons here was drawn up between just two people, the lord of the manor, Thomas Havers, and 'John le Grys, yeoman'.[16] But where commons were completely removed it was usually because the manorial lord had acquired all the land in a township: the common rights were thus monopolised, and land could be enclosed at will. Blomefield described how in the Breckland parish of Kilverstone 'There were above 200 acres of common and heath, on which the inhabitants commoned, but now every thing belongs to the lord'.[17] Such enclosures were rare, and a particular feature of the light lands in the north and west of the county and especially of parishes which formed the heartlands of large landed estates such as Holkham, Houghton or Raynham.

Parliamentary Enclosure

Although we must not underestimate the extent to which piecemeal attrition, monopoly ownership, illegal encroachment and formal enclosure agreements reduced the extent of common land, the vast majority of Norfolk's commons survived into the late eighteenth century, and were then removed by parliamentary enclosure. This process originated in the seventeenth century but only became widely used in the middle decades of the eighteenth. The landowners in a parish or – especially in Norfolk – a small group of parishes, would draw up a petition to parliament, requesting an enclosure. This needed the support of the majority of owners, but this was calculated on the basis of acres owned rather than simple numbers, with the bar fixed at two-thirds by an act of 1773. A bill would be read twice in the House of Commons and, having been referred to Committee and passed, and been approved by the Lords, would receive Royal Assent.[18] The Inclosure Act of 1773 and, in particular, the General Inclosure Act of 1801 standardised and simplified the process, the latter now establishing four-fifths of land owned by value as the required majority. Most Norfolk Commons were enclosed after the latter piece of legislation was passed, through acts which made use of the standardised format it established. Further acts, in 1821, 1835, 1845 and 1859, made additional modifications to the procedure.

The act having been passed, commissioners were appointed to oversee the enclosure process. They surveyed the open fields and commons and calculated the value of the land owned by each proprietor, and they invited claims for common rights enjoyed, and for the value of any property lost or harmed by the enclosure. The commissioners then set about allocating to the individuals concerned (and to institutions like village charities) one or more carefully surveyed parcels of land ('allotments') in lieu of their stake in the previous landscape. The lord of the principal manor received an allotment, commonly a twelfth of the total area of the enclosed land, as owner of the soil of the commons; the rector, or other tithe owner, received land to compensate for loss of tithes; and some was usually allocated for public purposes. Of particular importance for the history of Norfolk's commons, because they often later came to be confused with them, were the allotments made for the parish poor, in recognition of the benefits they had derived from the commons, albeit usually on sufferance rather than by legal right; and to the parish highway surveyors, on which materials required for road maintenance might be dug. The commissioners established new public roads across the enclosed areas or – more rarely in the case of common land – confirmed existing ones, but defined their limits with hedges and/or ditches; and new private ones, to provide proprietors with access to their allotments. Where extensive wetland commons were enclosed, the awards often established arterial drains, to feed water from the ditches around individual allotments into some larger stream or river, like 'The Drain or water course which we have caused to be made over the great Common in Bressingham aforesaid for the purpose of Draining and carrying water from off the same Common' described in the enclosure award for Bressingham (1802).[19] When the extensive common fens and marshes of Broadland were enclosed they often went further, establishing bodies called Drainage Commissions to maintain flood defence works and erect drainage windmills on plots of the former common.[20]

The allotments had to be physically enclosed – by hedges and ditches or by water-filled dykes, depending on location – within 12 months of the award. The activities of lawyers and surveyors cost money, which later enclosures especially sometimes raised by selling off portions of the enclosed land. In the case of Elsing no less than nine separate parcels of the former common, totalling 73a. 3r. 13p., were allocated for this purpose in the award of 1848; 10 plots of land, 'part of the commons and wastes of Dickleburgh' were sold to pay for its enclosure in 1855.[21]

The key feature of parliamentary enclosure was that it could be carried through even if the majority of landowners opposed it: it required not a majority of landowners, but the agreement of those who held most of the land in a township.[22] In the famous words of the Hammonds, 'the suffrages were not counted, but weighed'.[23] Not surprisingly, it brought about the removal of almost all surviving open fields and the overwhelming majority of commons, in Norfolk as elsewhere in England. Somewhere between 21 and 23 per cent of the country's land area was probably enclosed in this way in the eighteenth and nineteenth centuries, with most activity occurring in two great waves, concentrated in different areas. The first, peaking in the 1770s, was principally focused on places where extensive areas of open-field still existed, especially on the heavy clay soils of the Midlands. The second, which occurred during the Napoleonic War years, was more concerned with the enclosure of common land, including moorland grazing in the upland areas of England, although it also removed much open-field land, especially on the lighter soils of southern and eastern England. This second wave was driven by the high prices of the War years, and a patriotic fervour for reclamation and 'improvement'.[24]

The earliest parliamentary enclosure in Norfolk was for Stokesby, where the common marsh was enclosed by an act passed in 1720.[25] Over the following 143 years there were more than 300 further acts, the last (in 1863) enclosing Saxlingham common. As Turner has noted, ranked in terms of the numbers of awards,

Norfolk is the third most affected county, after the West Riding of Yorkshire and Lincolnshire. But, because many enclosures here removed only small areas of residual open land, it ranks only fourteenth in terms of county area enclosed by act, around 21 per cent, slightly below the overall national average.[26] Acts enclosing significant tracts of open fields as well as commons were markedly concentrated on the light soils in the west of the county and, to a lesser extent, the fertile loams of the north-east. In the majority of Norfolk parishes, especially on the claylands, open fields had, as already noted, often been drastically reduced or removed altogether by earlier piecemeal enclosure. Parliamentary enclosure was thus concerned with common land alone, or with common land accompanied by only small pockets of residual open arable. This said, given the extent of surviving open fields in some western parishes in the county, and the limited extent of common land in many clayland ones, open arable accounts for around three quarters of the land enclosed by act in the county, commons only a quarter.[27] Not surprisingly, given what has already been said about the national pattern, most Norfolk enclosure acts fall within the second, 'Wartime' wave of activity. The minority of examples pre-dating 1793 mainly dealt with large areas of open field, in the west of the county. The vast majority of Norfolk commons disappeared after 1793 and most between 1800 and 1820.

The Survival of Common Land

Why, it might be asked, if parliamentary enclosure was such a powerful tool for landscape change, did so many commons manage to survive in Norfolk? This question cannot be addressed without discussing a curious phenomenon, seldom noted by historians. While in some cases commons survived because the parishes in question were simply unaffected by enclosure, in a significant number of others, acts were passed which removed the open fields but left some or all of the commons in place, albeit with their use more formally regulated, and usually with some change in their legal status. The passing of an enclosure act did not, in other words, necessarily lead to the complete disappearance of common land in a particular place.

Church Green in Old Buckenham is one of the finest of Norfolk's clayland commons, extending over more than 40 acres (17 hectares), ringed by houses, and still retaining some of its peripheral 'plantings' of pollarded trees (Figure 5.1). The parish was enclosed under an act of 1790 but this, while removing the other commons, left Church Green intact.[28] It was allotted jointly to 25 listed individuals, all of whom were owners of a 'Dwelling house adjoining the green', and who had formerly enjoyed 'right of pasturage upon the said common'. In other words, the Green continued to exist but rather than being regarded as manorial waste, owned by the lord of the manor, it was now in effect a piece of shared property. Seven of the joint owners were permitted to keep 'two great beasts and no more', the rest 'one great beast and no more'. 'No steers of any kind' were to be allowed on the Green, and a mare with a foal were to be counted as one animal. All stock were to be branded with the

5. Enclosure and Survival 97

FIG. 5.1. Church Green, Old Buckenham, allotted to the commoners as a piece of joint property when the parish was enclosed in 1781.

owner's initials and could be put on the Green from 20 May but were to be taken off on 2 February, presumably to allow a good flush of spring growth. In a document separate from the enclosure award the Commoners agreed to the new arrangements, writing that 'we do hereby order direct and appoint that the said Church Green shall at all times forever hereafter be stocked with such number of Horses Cows and other Cattle by the several proprietors before named, their heirs and assigns'.[29] The Enclosure Act also ordered that:

> A proper person shall be yearly chosen by a majority of the Proprietors present, at a meeting to be called for that purpose by notice given in the church of Old Buckenham aforesaid, after divine service the preceding Sunday, to take the care of the beasts; and that his wages and all other charges and expenses attending the management of the said green, and the fences and gates to the same belonging, shall be borne and paid by the Proprietors having rights thereupon, or their tenants, rateably and in proportion to their respective rights.[30]

The act also included measures to prevent any increase in the area under trees, at the expense of open pasture, ordering that 'It shall not be lawful for any of the said proprietors, their Heirs or Assigns, at any time hereafter, to extend any of their plantings further than they now are upon the said green'. It established that the arrangements for managing the common could, in the future, be altered and amended by a majority decision of the proprietors, and over the following decades some changes may have been effected, for the tithe award of 1843 lists 28 people as owning 'undivided 39ths of the Common called Church Green', each person having between one and three divisions.[31] Assuming that each 'share' was equivalent to the right to turn one 'great beast' onto the common, this was a slight change from the 32 shares, divided between 25 proprietors, originally established.

East Dereham, enclosed in 1815, is a similar case. Most of the town's extensive commons were removed but Neatherd Moor and Potter's Fen survived, reserved for the use of those holding 'ancient messuages' in the town, while Etling Green also remained, the 16 rights to its use shared between the farms scattered around its margins. All still survive as registered commons.[32] Other well known Norfolk commons have a similar history. In North Runcton the enclosure of 1839 left all the commons in the parish, 102 acres (41 hectares) in all, open and the joint property of the common right holders, accounting for the series of registered grass commons which survive here on the edge of the Fens.[33] The magnificent Foulden Common, 140 hectares of acid grassland, partly colonised by secondary woodland, and an important SSSI, likewise owes its survival to the fact that the enclosure act of 1782 left it untouched, together with the 20-hectare Borough Fen, which also survives as a registered common, the tithe apportionment of 1840 simply giving the owner of both as 'Common lands of Foulden' and the occupiers as 'The several owners of pasturage rights of cattle'.[34] Here, by implication, the common seems to have remained the property of the manorial lord, as was the case at Whitwell (enclosed in 1804);[35] while at Boughton (enclosed in 1803) the enclosure created a particularly complex situation. Most of the commons were removed but Boughton Fen was allotted to:

> The Lord or Lords of the Manor Boughton, Overhall and Netherhall, for the time being, the Rector, the Churchwardens, and Overseers of the Poor of the said Parish of Boughton for the time being; and to the Proprietors within the aforesaid Parish of estates of the yearly value of £25; and to their respective successors for ever … for the purpose of providing and supplying to the occupiers of each of the Commonable Messuages or Tenements now standing in the said Parish of Boughton, for the time being, and to the occupiers of each of the three following Cottages in Boughton, one belonging to Loom Brook in the occupation of Edward Whittrick and two belonging to, or in the occupation of, George Lewis and William Fincham, a quantity not exceeding nor not less than 4000 turves or flags, of the usual dimensions, for fixing in every year, and for the tenants and occupiers of all the commonable messuages now standing in the Parish of Boughton, to use and enjoy right of common pasture over the said allotment, with such kind and number of stock as is hereinafter mentioned. For each of the commonable messuages, that is to say, 2 cows or 3 head of young stock under 3 years old, or 1 cow with 2 calves under 1 year old, or 2 geldings or 2 mares, with or without foals not exceeding 8 months old. And we, the said Commissioner, direct that the said allotment may be stocked and fed from 12th May until 11th October in every year and that from 14th February until 12th May in every year, the allotment shall not be stocked or fed with any kind of beasts or cattle whatsoever.[36]

The iconic Barrow Common close to the north coast of the county, with its magnificent views out to sea, is different again. When the parish of Brancaster was enclosed in 1755 it was allotted, not to all the commoners in the parish, but only to the poorer cottagers, those with houses worth less than £5, in compensation for their loss of grazing rights over the open fields. They, rather than the lord of the manor, were identified as the owners in the tithe apportionment of 1841.[37] This was clearly an alternative to providing a mass of tiny allotments to the owners of commonable cottagers. Broadly similar stinted commons for the use of the poor were created by parliamentary enclosures at Kelling (Figure 5.2), Salthouse and Shotesham, although only the two commons in the latter parish are registered as common land today; 60 acres out of the 300 enclosed were here preserved for the use of all cottagers in the parish, not just those with existing common rights.[38] The tithe apportionment of 1842 describes the two parcels as 'common', and gives no proprietor, with the implication that ownership continued to reside in the lord of the manor.[39] Those for Kelling and Salthouse, in contrast, give the poor of the parish as owners.[40] There was clearly a fine line between a residual area of common land allotted for the use of the poor, and the larger poor's allotments created by parliamentary enclosures at place like East Ruston (below, pp. 106–7). Holt Lowes in Holt, where the owners were the 'Trustees for the owners of houses under the value of ten pounds' may have been little different to a poor's allotment.[41]

Some commons allotted by enclosure acts have particularly complicated histories. That at Litcham is the survivor of no less than three parliamentary enclosures. The first, in 1760, was solely concerned with the removal of grazing rights over the arable; a second, in 1770, also enclosed part of the common land in the parish, allocating three of the remaining areas – Litcham Heath, Clay Pit Moor and Granson Moor – for the use of the principal farmers and a fourth, South Common, to those with common-right cottages but little or no other land.[42] The last, in 1856, enclosed the three farmers' commons, leaving that of the cottagers, which survives today. In this case, the lord of the manor appears to have remained as owner.[43] Other examples are even more complicated. What is now Dersingham Common seems initially, by the enclosure of 1781, to have been retained for the use of all those with commonable tenements, together with other commons in the parish.[44] But by 1840 it was used as a fuel allotment, the tithe apportionment giving the owners as the Trustees for the Poor, with 'the Poor' as occupiers, while a further act of 1857 enclosed a substantial area in the north-east of the common, leaving the rest – 76 acres (31 hectares) in the hands of the trustees.[45] Billingford near North Elmham was enclosed by an act passed in 1806 and under the award of 1809 most of the commons were removed.[46] However, an area of just under 52 acres remained as a 'Cow Pasture', which 25 proprietors had rights to use, one of whom was the Earl of Leicester, the largest landowner in the parish and lord of the manor. This survived until 1864, when it was enclosed by a second act and divided between a smaller number of rights holders, there having been some amalgamations of properties in the intervening period, and the First Edition Ordnance Survey 25-inch map of 1883 shows it divided into 14 parcels, varying in size and accessed by broad driftways.[47] But it is still named on this and subsequent maps as 'Billingford Common' and on the Second Edition 25-inch map of 1904 most of the enclosures are shown as covered with gorse and heather, circumstances which presumably explain why (with the exception of its eastern section) it came to be registered as common land in 1982.[48] Other examples include the two commons at Brockdish, excluded from the enclosure award of 1825, and soon afterwards given by the lord of the manor to the parish, with management and ownership vested in trustees.[49]

FIG. 5.2. Kelling Heath, one of several Norfolk commons allotted for the use of poor cottagers at enclosure.

Many of the largest, most familiar and most ecologically important commons in the county thus lie in parishes that were enclosed by parliamentary acts, and were effectively established by them in their present form. Indeed, various kinds of 'allotted common' probably account for around a quarter, by area, of the registered common land in the county – 5.6 square kilometres – and nearly 30 per cent of such land which might be considered as 'real' common land, as opposed to poor's allotments, parish pits and the like. Evidently, even at the height of the enclosure movement not everyone was hostile to the concept of the shared occupancy and exploitation of land; the enclosure commissioners in all such cases must have been responding to the wishes of local property owners. These cases may throw some light on the more numerous places where commons survived simply because there was no parliamentary enclosure.

In some of these, failure to seek an act probably reflects the indifference or philanthropy of the manorial lord and dominant landowner, coupled perhaps with an appreciation of the sporting potential of unenclosed, uncultivated land. In Honing, the Cubitt family, to judge from the tithe apportionment of 1843, owned significantly more of the parish than the 75 per cent required to force an enclosure but their land was divided between 27 tenants, mostly in farms of between 40 and 100 acres, some of whom occupied 'common severals' and doles.[50] Estate policy here, unusually, evidently favoured the maintenance of relatively small tenancies, whether for paternalistic or economic reasons, or a mixture of both, and failure to enclose should perhaps be seen in this context. In some cases large landowners showed less enthusiasm for enclosure than the commoners. In 1841, for example, a letter signed by the copyholders of Fritton was sent to the lord of the manor and largest landowner in the parish, Frederick Paul Irby, asking for an enclosure.[51] His son Frederick William Irby inherited three years later and recalled in 1858 his father's strong opposition to the enclosure of the common, which he continued to share.⁵² But in most cases where no attempt was made to enclose it is likely that a majority of those involved, both manorial lords and common right holders, simply saw no economic advantage in such a move. Taking into account the costs of an enclosure, the common rights were more valuable to them than any allotment of land they might receive in lieu, whether in terms of their own farming businesses if owner-occupiers, or in terms of the rent they might charge tenants if not.

In this context, the high survival rate of clayland commons – affording better quality grazing than heaths or fens – is striking. This is most apparent in the south of the county, where there are a number of large examples – Wacton, Hales Green, Mulbarton – as well as numerous smaller ones – Howe Green, Stubb Green in Shotesham, Bracon Green in Bracon Ash. Particularly noteworthy is the magnificent cluster, almost conjoined, in the contigous parishes of Fritton, Morningthorpe, Shelton, Stratton St Michael and Stratton St Mary, all completely unaffected by enclosure acts – Fritton Common, Morningthorpe Common, Wood Green, Crow Green, Rhees Green and Shelton Common. But other important examples can be found as the clay plateau continues northwards, through central Norfolk – the magnificent Brisley Common and Harpers Green – and also where there are isolated, often tiny patches of clay soil in the west of the county, such as East Winch Common. Commons likewise survived in a number of places on valley floors where the soils of the Hanworth and Isleham Associations were more silty than peaty in character, as at Wighton, Brampton, North Wooton, Hanworth, Coltishall or Southrepps, again affording grazing of reasonable quality. The common fens found where flood plains were characterised by deep deposits of waterlogged peat, in contrast, were almost everywhere enclosed, those in Broadland with peculiar thoroughness. While rather more common heaths evaded enclosure, such as Alderford Common, Ringland Common or Crostwight Heath, they formed a smaller proportion of the total population of commons of this type. In Breckland, in particular, parliamentary enclosure effectively wiped out common heaths.

It is noteworthy that heaths and fens are similarly under-represented amongst those 'allotted commons' which enclosure acts allocated to common right holders, rather than to the poor. While some of North Runcton's extensive commons occupy damp sands of the Downham Association, others overlie clays, as do the entirety of Etling Green and Neatherd Common in East Dereham, Church Green in Old Buckenham and most of the commons at Litcham and Billingford, although the clays are more acidic in these two cases and the commons also extend onto silty floodplain land. Boughton Fen is, in fact, the only real exception to this general rule. Again the pattern is clear; those commons most valuable as grazing land were the most likely to survive. Parliamentary enclosure thus radically altered the relative proportions of different kinds of common in Norfolk, removing heaths and fens to a greater extent than clayland commons, although this shift was rather less marked in ecological terms because much heath and fen lived on in private allotments and, in particular, as poor's allotments.

The retention of common land may have made more sense to small and medium sized proprietors than to larger owners and manorial lords, and this may also have been a factor in their survival in clayland parishes, many of which, as we have seen, had a broad base of ownership (above, p. 17). The 769 acres (c. 310 hectares) of enclosed land in Wacton in 1840 were divided between 35 proprietors; the largest held 195 acres but there were no others with more than 70.[53] Not all, of course, were owner occupiers but most were resident in the parish and presumably aware of the circumstances of small tenants as well as their own financial interests. In Brisley in 1840 the 995 acres (402 hectares) were divided between 30 owners, the largest with only 185 acres.[54] In Morningthorpe, more typically, there was a dominant owner at the time of commutation in 1839, but he owned only 336 of its 972 acres (394 hectares).[55] Similar circumstances often pertained where parishes were enclosed by act, yet commons retained. The Earl of Albemarle was the principal landowner in Old Buckenham but he owned only a fifth of its nearly 5,000 acres (2,000 hectares) and there were well over a hundred other proprietors, 17 of whom owned more than 100 acres (but of whom only four owned more than 250).[56] This, however, brings us to the contentious issue of how enclosure affected small farmers and cottages.

Poor's Allotments and the Poor

According to a long line of historians, enclosure – and especially parliamentary enclosure – had a universally negative influence on these groups.[57] The allotments received by the smaller proprietors in lieu of land held in open fields, and rights enjoyed over common land, were of significantly less value to them than their use of the unenclosed landscape had been. They were also obliged to pay for hedging and ditching their new plots of land within a short period of time, and usually to contribute to other costs. Many were obliged to sell up, concentrating land ownership into fewer and fewer hands. The landless poor also suffered. The practice of gleaning across the open fields after harvest was curtailed, and they lost access to the fuel, wild foods and other resources they had routinely gathered from the commons, and the ability to graze any livestock there. In popular discourse, enclosure was legalised theft which robbed the poor of their independence and their birthright and brought about the proletarianisation of much of the rural population.

While there is much truth in these arguments, they need to be treated with caution. In most cases enclosure initially *increased* the number of small landowners in a parish, as those owning a cottage with common rights, but little land, usually received an allotment. The amounts varied but where commons were extensive might be as much as 3 or even 4 acres, reflecting the general assumption that, prior to enclosure, such properties had the right to run a cow on the common; Young thus described how, when the parish of Sharrington was enclosed, 3 acres were given 'to each cottage-right house, to enable the cottager to keep a cow'.[58] Where, conversely, commons were limited in area and claims were many, cottagers often received allotments of half or even a quarter of an acre. Such land could be used in other ways – for growing hemp, for example. But in the immediate aftermath of enclosure, cottagers, or their landlords, frequently cashed in, selling their diminutive parcels to neighbours. Shouldham for example was enclosed in 1794; 10 years later it was reported that 'Those cottages that had rights and allotments, are now let merely as houses, and the allotments laid to the farms'.[59]

In Norfolk overall there is little evidence for a significant overall decline in the number of small owners following the enclosure of common land. The commons of Rollesby, totalling 484 acres, were enclosed in 1816, together with 246 acres of residual open field. Fifty-nine people received allotments, mostly small plots of half an acre or more in lieu of common rights.[60] The enclosure map shows that John Ensor owned nearly two thirds of the land but the names of another 58 owners are attached to new allotments and to parcels already enclosed, covering more than a half of an acre; of these properties, nine covered between 20 and 100 acres.[61] The tithe apportionment drawn up 23 years later shows Ensor still owning two thirds of the parish.[62] The number of properties in the 20–100-acre range remained unchanged but the overall total of proprietors owning half an acre or more had declined slightly, to 50. A comparison of the two sources suggests this was largely a consequence of the sale, in the immediate aftermath of the enclosure, of small parcels allotted to cottagers, cashing in on a windfall. Indeed, the enclosure award shows that several such parcels had already been alienated before the enclosure process had been completed (mainly to Ensor).

In Moulton St Michael on the southern claylands around 92 acres of common land were enclosed in 1820 and allotted to 49 proprietors, many again receiving tiny plots of less than half an acre. The enclosure map shows that there were three large holdings in the parish, of over 100 acres, the largest of which covered around 235 acres.[63] There were: 14 medium-sized properties, in the range 20 to 100 acres; and 45 covering between half an acre and 20 acres. By the time the tithes were commuted in 1837 there had been a number of changes in the configuration of property in the parish: there were now four estates covering more than 100 acres (the largest largely unchanged); 15 of between 20 and 100 acres; and 37 of between half of an acre and 20 acres.[64] There was thus a slight decline in the number of very small owners, but as in Rollesby this was largely the result of cottagers selling off the tiny parcels allotted to them by the award.

In other parishes where commons were enclosed the pattern was broadly similar: some new owners, created by the allotment of land in lieu of common rights, soon sold up, but enclosure had little if any discernible impact on established landowners, large or small. When extensive areas of open field were enclosed, small landowners may well have been more adversely affected by the costs involved. But in Norfolk at least the enclosure of commons *per se* does not appear to have led to an avalanche of land sales. When assessing the impact of such enclosures on village society, on the fate of the poor and the survival of the 'peasantry', one complication is that only a minority of properties – a little over a third at Moulton, just under a half in the case of Rollesby – were actually owner-occupied, or farmed by a family member, while some of the 'small' owners, such as the Duke of Norfolk in Moulton, held extensive properties elsewhere. Allotments of former common land were, in most cases, simply attached to the nearest tenancy of the proprietor in question, so it is doubtful whether tenants were much disadvantaged by the change.

Those living in rented cottages, or owning ones without common rights, did not receive an allotment of land, although there is little sign that the enclosure commissioners worked strenuously to contest any claims made by such people. Indeed, in many parishes, evidence that common rights had merely been exercised was considered as legal proof of a claim.[65] They could, however, usually benefit from a 'poor's allotment' or 'fuel allotment' established by the enclosure award. These were parcels of former common land which were either leased out, and the income used to purchase coal or other commodities for the poor, or which they directly exploited as a source of domestic fuel, and sometimes in other ways.[66] Not all enclosure awards provided them. There were a few places like Hevingham where, as Arthur Young put it in 1804, 'The poor that had no rights, have no benefits'.[67] But the overwhelming majority did so, and by the middle of the nineteenth century over 250 parishes in Norfolk possessed one, sometimes in the form of several discrete land parcels.[68] They displayed much variation in size, ranging from tiny examples like Ashwellthorpe, with just under an acre and a half, to Grimston with nearly 193 acres, Marham with 200 and Feltwell with no less than 360.[69] Around half, however, covered between 10 and 30 acres (c. 4–12 hectares). In a few cases, as at Rockland St Andrew and Rockand All Saints, or Weasenham St Andrew and Weasenham St Peter, allotments were shared by adjoining parishes, anciently connected and jointly enclosed.[70] All allotments were managed by trustees, variously constituted but generally comprising the wealthier elements of the community. The Lopham enclosure award, for example, described how the poor's allotment was given to 'The Lord of the Manor of Lopham, and also to the Rector, Churchwardens, and Overseeers of the Poor … and to their respective successors for ever'.[71] This wording was typical, but in most parishes, in practice, churchwardens and/or the overseers of the poor controlled the allotments, and were generally recorded as their owners when the tithes were commuted in the years around 1840.

Awards sometimes stipulated whether allotments should be directly exploited by the poor, or rented out, but the wording of most allowed trustees a measure of discretion. The 1802 award for Bressingham typically described how 'the said allotments shall be employed for the purpose of raising fuel for the necessary firing of the said poor persons or be otherwise appropriated and the produce and profits existing there from applied for their use and benefit'.[72] At nearby Blo Norton, the allotment was made:

> for the benefit of poor persons settled and residing in the said parish and not occupying to the value of £15 a year. The land to be cut for providing fuel for the said poor or to be let and the profits arising therefrom to be distributed among them according to such regulations as the trustees should make.[73]

A little under half seem to have been rented out in their entirety, from the start, and the rest exploited directly, in whole or part (often one of several allotments in a parish, or part of a single allotment, would be leased out by the trustees and the income used to defray the fencing, drainage and other costs associated with those areas which were directly exploited).

The 'poor' were sometimes, as at Blo Norton, defined by the awards themselves, usually in terms of the annual rental value of the property they occupied (commonly less than £5 to less than £15 per annum). But more often the decision on who might use or benefit was left to the discretion of the trustees, perhaps reflecting an awareness that if fixed in such terms, inflation would, over time, steadily reduce the number of potential beneficiaries. The enclosure award for Snettisham, made as early as 1766, restricted the use of the allotment to those occupying property worth less than £2 per annum. By 1845 it was being used as a common pasture by all the parishioners, 'there being no poor in the parish occupying so little as 40s yearly value'.[74] While in most parishes all the settled poor could benefit from the allotment, in some – either immediately, or after a few years – disbursements might be more limited, the restrictions clearly reflecting the ideological perspectives of trustees. At Horsey in 1832 only five or six of the 'deserving' poor were beneficiaries; at Beighton, only families who had not claimed poor relief over the previous year.[75]

Where allotments were rented out, the income received was principally used to purchase coal (or occasionally peat or, as at Little Cressingham, firewood) for the poor. But a proportion of the income might be used in other ways. In Salhouse by 1845 it was partly used to buy 'blankets &c.', at Little Plumstead and Little Walsingham 'clothes &c', and at Deopham bread; while at Happisburgh and Wymondham some was simply distributed as cash payments, as it was at Fulmondeston, here specifically 'at Christmas'.[76] At Surlingham, £10 of the annual income was spent on 'schooling poor children'.[77] At a number of places *all* the income was shared amongst the poor as cash payments, commonly of between 3 and 6 shillings but reaching 8 shillings at Ingham in 1832, around £30 in modern money, so not a princely sum.[78] Whatever form disbursements took, the number of beneficiaries in most cases amounted to between a quarter and a third of inhabitants. At Ingham in 1831, for example, 37 out of 93 households received them, at Gaywood 50 out of 216, at Ashmanaugh 9 out of 35 and at Runham 17 out of 54.[79]

Where an allotment was a source of funds for the benefit of the poor, rather than an area directly exploited by them, trustees might seek ways of investing in it, in order to increase future income. Sometimes they did this directly, as at Sporle, where by 1845 the income from the allotment included the rent from a house that they had erected on it, or at Fincham, where they erected a barn to make the property more attractive to tenants.[80] Or they could do it indirectly, by letting the land on a long 'improving' lease. At Wood Norton the 18-acre poor's allotment awarded at enclosure in 1813 was leased two years later to John Miller, for a term of 40 years, who covenanted to 'improve the land, and to build a house upon it'.[81] Within a year he had erected a 'house, windmill, roundhouse, barns and stables' there. The tithe map of 1840 shows that the property, now occupied by William Long, had been divided into seven parcels, five of which were pasture, one arable, and one containing the mill and mill house.

Where allotments were directly exploited it was principally as a source of fuel; most, indeed, are referred to as 'fuel allotments' in nineteenth-century documents. The enclosure awards seldom state clearly the type they provided but references in the *Report of the Commissioners into Charities* of 1832 and White's *Directory* of 1845 suggest that around two thirds were dug for peat and the rest were divided equally between those affording heathland firing – mainly gorse (furze or whins), but also heather (ling) – and those that afforded both ('furze and flags', 'turf and whins', 'turf and furze'). Firewood is scarcely mentioned, one of the few exceptions being West Lexham, where 5 acres of 'oak stubs' provided the poor with fuel.[82] As we have seen, gorse, heather and peat had long been cut from commons and used as domestic fuel but, as Wells has shown, the use of peat especially expanded significantly in Norfolk in the second half of the eighteenth century as the rural population, and the numbers of the poor in particular, grew rapidly.[83] Although wealthy households might use gorse and perhaps heather as oven firing, they mainly burned wood or, especially near the coast or navigable waterways, coal brought by sea from the north-east of England. Peat, gorse and heather were, by the late eighteenth century, the fuels of the poor. The quantities allowed to each household varied but, where peat was concerned, were almost always between 3,000 and 5,000 turves a year. In some parishes, including Stoke Ferry and Wretton, the amount allowed might vary with the size of the family.

Fuel allotments, whether peat grounds or heaths, often provided some secondary resources. The cutting of sedge or reeds is often referred to in contemporary documents but, more importantly, most afforded some rough grazing. White in 1845 described how the fuel allotments at East Dereham, Hassingham and Ludham were also used by the poor for grazing unspecified livestock, while those at Tottenhill and Grimston were used by them for feeding geese; that at Scarning for both geese and cattle; and that at Beetley for geese and asses.[84] But more usually, any vegetation was grazed, or cut for hay, by one or more local farmers, in return for an annual payment. Fuel allotments providing turf were more likely to be grazed than those supplying combustible heathland vegetation, presumably because the growth of the latter would be damaged by livestock, which were accordingly excluded (trustees found other ways of making additional money from these: at Great Ringstead the right to shoot over the allotment was let; at Sedfeford, 'the right of killing rabbits').[85]

The marginal use of some fuel allotments by the poor for grazing shades imperceptibly into cases where grazing and fuel cutting were of more equal importance. In 1845 the allotment at Catfield comprised 57 acres 'on which the poor cut turves and graze cattle', while at Burgh St Margaret 40 acres of the huge 146-acre (59-hectare) allotment was rented out and the rest was 'used for cutting fuel, reeds &c., but the poor cottagers are allowed to turn cows upon it'.[86] In a small minority of cases, almost all in and around the Ant and Thurne valleys in Broadland, grazing seems to have been the *main* purpose of the allotment. Forty-one acres of the 78-acre allotment at Martham was said to be 'a pasture for the cows of the poor inhabitants'.[87] At nearby Potter Heigham, most of the allotment was grazed and the rent from the rest was divided between those too poor to keep a cow; at Hempstead a few kilometres to the north the only allotment was a 'poors pasture' of 9 acres; while at Repps-with-Bastwick the allotment of 19 acres was 'marsh land, on which the poor depasture their cows'.[88] At Thurne in 1832 there was a fuel allotment, partly rented out on a three-year lease and partly 'appropriated to the purpose of cutting fuel and fodder to be distributed amongst the … poor', but also a second allotment, which was

> Depastured by the cows of poor inhabitants of the parish … They pay 10s each and if they have a second cow they pay £1.10 in addition for the second. No person having an allotment sufficient to keep a cow is allowed to turn them out'.[89]

Such dual provision, of separate fuel and grazing allotments, was occasionally made elsewhere, as at Ashill.

The most comprehensive provision was made at East Ruston, where 300 acres out of the 771 acres of common land enclosed in 1810 were allotted to the poor in five contiguous blocks: 160 acres of North Fen Common; 40 acres of South Fen; 30 acres of Holmes Fen; 30 acres of The Fox and Hill Common; and 40 acres of the 'Common which lies next to the parishes of Happisburgh and Brunstead'.[90] Rules were drawn up in 1811, under the terms of the award, which regulated the use of the allotments, dividing the 'poor' into three categories: those with a cottage and less than an acre; those renting property worth less than £5 per annum, or between 1 and 10 acres; and those *owning* such property. The poorest could turn 'three head of stock and two brood geese and goslings, reared by them, unto the said allotments'; could dig up to 2,000 'upground flags' – heather – and up to 3,000 'fenground flags' – peat – each year; and could mow fodder on Burnt Fen for one day. Those in the median category were allowed to graze 'two head of stock, and two brood geese and goslings, reared by them' and to cut the same number of flags, but not to mow fodder. Those owning £5 properties or between 1 and 10 acres could only graze 'one head of stock and one brood goose and the goslings reared by it', and could cut only a thousand of each type of 'flags' each year.[91]

All such allotments, but especially those used for grazing, resembled true commons in that they were jointly exploited by defined groups of individuals, supplying them in some cases with a similar range of produce. They differed from them in that use was conditional on poverty rather than on ownership of defined properties, was enjoyed by permission rather than by right, and rather than being organised by the users themselves (albeit within the structure of the manorial court and, to varying degrees, under the control of the manorial lord) was in the hands of others. These trustees administered the finances of the allotment, receiving money from letting shooting rights or grazing – even the poor usually paid at least a nominal charge for this. The income from all these sources might be used, as at Pentney, to buy coals for the poor. But, meagre as it often was, it might be entirely absorbed in the maintenance of fences, access ways and the like. At South Lopham in 1832 the grazing was leased for £7 or £8 a year, an amount deemed to be 'not more than sufficient for keeping the drains and fences in repair'.[92] Allotments were not usually areas on which the poor simply foraged at will, unregulated, but were like commons managed environments; heathland allotments might, for example, be ploughed and re-seeded when supplies of gorse became depleted.[93] The period during which turf cutting was permitted was generally restricted, to avoid turning large areas into a quagmire. In 1801 the churchwardens and overseers in Old Buckenham, concerned about the 'great damage done to the Fen by the Improper Manner of Cutting', ordered that this should commence on 20 April and end on 1 August, after which the turf was presumably too dry to be removed in neat blocks. These dates were evidently subject to adjustment, with a document of 1839 delaying the commencement of cutting until the start of May and bringing forward its cessation to 20 July.[94]

Trustees were also keen to ensure an equitable distribution of fuel, to prevent individuals from selling to others, and to prevent fuel being taken by people with no right to do so. Achieving the last of these aims was made difficult by the fact that many of those in need of fuel were old, infirm, or otherwise unable to extract it themselves. Others had to dig or cut, and transport, the material on their behalf, providing a ready excuse for the unscrupulous. The Old Buckenham regulations of 1801 described how, on the first day of cutting, the trustees were to meet at the allotment at 9.00 in the morning 'to see that no person take for Himself any more Land or parcel of ground than is sufficient for one Hearth only'. In addition they ruled that nobody was allowed:

> To Carry for sale from off the aforesaid Fen or Other places Appropriated for Cutting of Firing without the Consent of us the Trustees. And we are Fully Determined to Commence an Action against any person or persons whomsoever shall either by themselves or their agents, enter upon the said Fen, or Other places Appropriated for Cutting of Firing as aforesaid, with any Waggon, or other Carriage, for the purposes of carrying off any Firing or Sedge or Rede from off the aforesaid Fen, without first being duly authorised by us the aforesaid Trustees.[95]

In 1839 the trustees drew up a list of all those allowed to dig peat on the allotment, and a second list, of individuals allowed to receive their allocation from 'cutters' sanctioned by the trustees.[96] There were 105 people on the first of these lists and 10 on the second. Given that the population of Old Buckenham was around 1,200 in the period, it seems likely that something approaching a quarter of the households in the parish were making use of the allotment.[97] A number of comments were made in the 1832 *Report of the Commissioners into Charities* about the poor state or illegal exploitation of allotments and in some parishes, such as Irstead or Neatishead, trustees simply undertook the cutting, transport and distribution of fuel themselves, covering the costs by letting the grazing, or part of the allotment itself.[98]

The factors influencing whether enclosure awards provided the poor of a particular parish with an allotment, and if so how large it might be and how it was used, were complex. Extensive allotments might, as at the towns of Attleborough, Thetford or Wymondham, reflect the fact that the parish, its population and the numbers of the poor, were all particularly large. There are signs that provision was generous in places, like East Ruston, where there were large numbers of relatively small proprietors, in which many of those receiving allotments were only marginally better off than those who did not.[99] But extent and distribution largely reflect the importance that the parish commons had, before enclosure, played in the lives of the poor, as a source of fuel and, in some cases, informal grazing, together with the quantity of the land enclosed which was too waterlogged or acidic to be of much use to landowners; the huge allotment of nearly 160 acres at Hevingham was candidly described by the 1832 *Report of the Commissioners into Charities* as 'very bad land'.[100] They were accordingly related closely to soils and geology. Parishes with more than 50 acres (c. 20 hectares) of allotments were noticeably clustered in the Broads, in the valleys of the Ant and the Thurne, where parishes like Burgh St Margaret, Catfield, East Ruston, Hickling, Ludham, Martham, Potter Heigham, Stalham and Sutton included large areas of floodplain peat within their boundaries (Figure 5.3). They were also to be found in a number of parishes containing extensive peat fens in the west of the county, such as Downham Market, Feltwell, Grimston, Marham, Northwold, Pentney, Shouldham, Shouldham Thorpe, while the adjoining allotments of 103 and 126 acres in North and South Lopham were contiguous with one covering 80 acres in the Suffolk parish of Redgrave, the whole corresponding to an extensive area of waterlogged peat, most of it now occupied by nature reserves, around the headwaters of the Little Ouse and the Waveney. Other large allotments were associated with extensive tracts of particularly acidic and infertile soils, especially those of the Newport 4 and Felthorpe Associations, with marked clusters in the area to the north of Norwich (Cawston, Felthorpe, Hevingham, Horsford, Horsham and Marsham) and around the eastern margins of Breckland (East Harling, Griston, Shropham, Ellingham, Shipdham, Tottington, Banham, Carbrooke, Bridgham and Saham Toney).

In all these places the commons had been large and much used by the poor for fuel and, in Broadland especially, grazing. At the other extreme, where commons had provided no resources for the poor, or commoners had prevented the poor from exploiting them, no allotment was made. Young, summarising the enclosure of 800 acres of common in Fersfield and Bressingham in 1804, simply noted: 'Poor. – Never cut any fuel on the common: no allotment.'[101] In between these ends of the spectrum lay the mass of small and medium-sized allotments, scattered along the peaty floors of small valleys, or corresponding to patches of sand and gravel, which prior to enclosure (and as parts of larger commons) had afforded firing for the poor. In broad terms, the extent and character of the uses which the poor had made of the commons were thus reflected in the size and use of the allotments they received at enclosure, suggesting a general

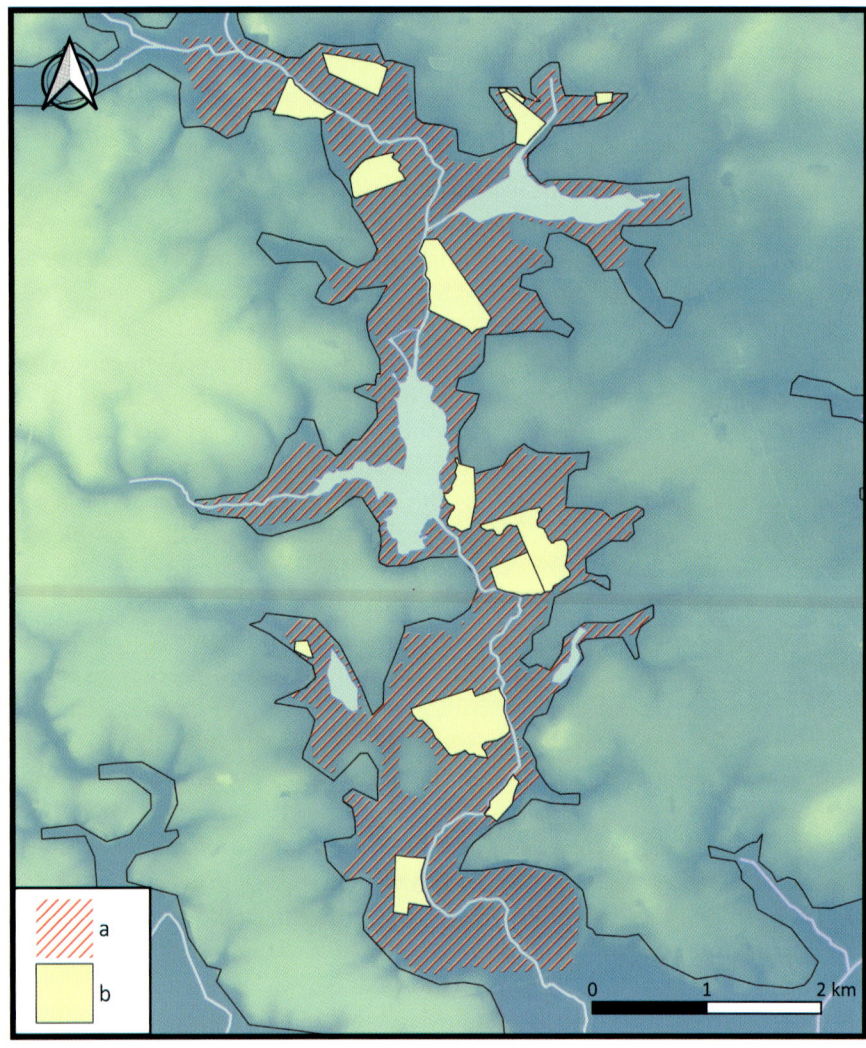

FIG. 5.3. Poor's allotments in the Ant valley. (a) areas of common fen enclosed by parliamentary acts; (b) poor's allotments.

belief that even though such exploitation was not based on legal rights it should nevertheless receive some recognition in awards.

Poor's allotments were a practical and cheap way of helping to alleviate the escalating problem of local poverty. Few commoners living in these close-knit rural communities would have been entirely indifferent to the physical needs of their poorer neighbours: even the most callous local farmer needed workers at least moderately well fed and warmed. But above all allotments were part of an unwritten bargain, the community offering compensation where the poor were deemed to have made significant use of a common (although providing nothing where they had not). Right from the start there seems to have been an expectation that the poor should, in the appropriate circumstances, receive an allotment. The earliest parliamentary enclosure in Norfolk, for Stokesby in 1720, was accompanied by one of the county's few enclosure riots. 'The poor inhabitants finding that no allotment was set out for their benefit under the Inclosure Act … proceeded in a riotous manner and insisted upon having some allotment given to them'.[102] The widespread provision of allotments served, like so much else in the process, to make enclosure appear fair, and thus to avoid such incidents of unrest. Nevertheless, and in spite of what writers like Young asserted, it is unlikely that allotments provided the same benefits to the poor as the commons had done. Even Young acknowledged, for example, that at Cranworth and Reymerston the fuel allotment was insufficient compensation, given that they had formerly also grazed geese on the common.[103] At Fincham, similarly, enclosure had ended the 'cottage cow keepers'.[104] But, as he also observed, many here had ceased to keep cows before the enclosure. For rural poverty was increasing before the advent of parliamentary enclosure, and was present in places and areas unaffected by it, driven by factors both long term – the development of an agricultural system increasingly capitalist in character, an inexorable increase in the numbers of landless labourers – and more immediate – rapid population growth that outstripped employment opportunities.

Many may have resented enclosure, sharing the views of an anonymous Ashill letter writer that local farmers 'rob the poor of their commons right, plough the grass up that God sent to grow'.[105] But, with the exception of the riots at Stokseby already noted, organised opposition to the parliamentary enclosure of common land in Norfolk seems to have been a largely urban affair, with strong protests mounted in defence of Norwich's Mousehold Heath in the 1860s and 70s, and over the enclosure of the commons at Swaffham and Fakenham in 1869 and 1870 respectively; at Fakenham the new fences were taken down and burnt.[106] All three came right at the end of the parliamentary enclosure period, and at a time, as we shall see, when educated opinion was moving strongly in favour of the preservation of common land (below, p. 134). Urban commons were much used for recreation, and for grazing the donkeys on which small businesses depended for making deliveries. In contrast, rural opposition is conspicuous by its absence. The loss of common land, even where allotments were provided, certainly did the poor no favours. But, as a visible and dramatic change in the physical landscape, it made a good scapegoat, then and since, for the ills of the rural poor. In reality, it was only one of the many difficulties that assailed them.

Fragments and Ghosts

Poor's allotments form an important part of the story of Norfolk's commons. They account for around 17 per cent by area of registered examples and, as fragments of the manorial 'wastes', they are often, in ecological terms, no different from surviving examples of 'real' commons; many are registered as Sites of Special Scientific Interest, such as Lopham Fen, or as County Wildlife Sites. Confusion of allotments and 'real' commons did not begin with the process of registration. It was natural for local people to think of these residual pieces of common land, especially the larger examples, exploited in the most diverse ways, as 'commons'. Goose Green in Little

Ellingham, for example, extending over some 30 acres (c. 12 hectares), is a fragment of a larger common of that name, allocated as a poor's allotment at the enclosure in 1769, but it was described as 'Common' in the tithe apportionment of 1839.[107] Several others, as at East Ruston or Marlingford, are so labelled on the Ordnance Survey 6-inch maps from the 1880s and 90s and are still so described locally today. But commons and poor's allotments display important differences as features of the cultural landscape. While many 'real' commons registered as common land in Norfolk have houses on their margins, this is rare in the case of poor's allotments, hardly surprising given that the latter represent fractions cut out of the former. For the same reason, while some poor's allotments have one or more curving, irregular boundaries inherited from the old common, most have boundaries as straight as those of the surrounding private allotments. And while most 'real' commons are, for reasons discussed earlier (above, pp. 23–4), crossed by public roads, there are no examples of registered poor's allotments where this is the case. Some have a public road running along one boundary; a few, along two boundaries; but many lie away from the public road network, accessed by a straight track (Figure 5.4).

Other examples of what are now registered commons in Norfolk were created in a rather different way by enclosure awards. No less than 48 originated as allotments made to parish highway surveyors as a source of material for repairing the roads. The maintenance of local highways, like the relief of local poverty, became the formal responsibility of individual parishes in the sixteenth century, organised

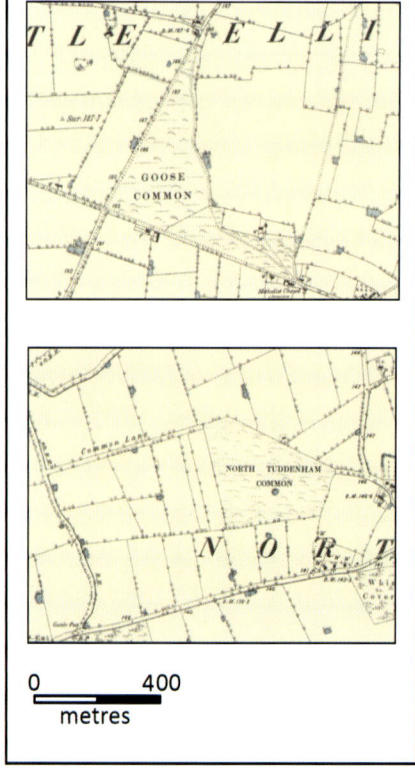
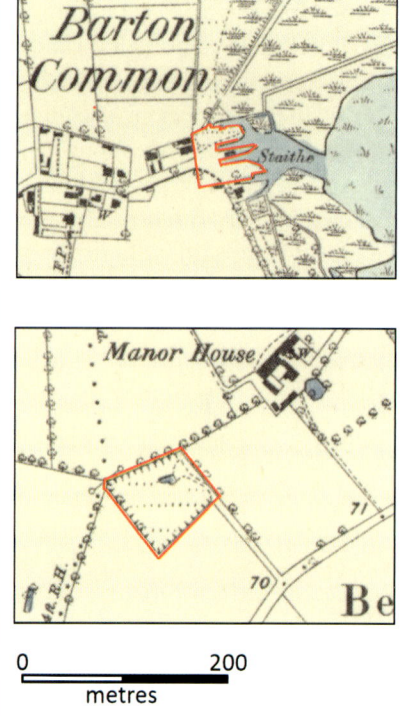

FIG. 5.4. Extracts from the First Edition Ordnance Survey 6-inch maps showing examples of registered commons originating as poor's allotments (left, Little Ellingham and North Tuddenham); village staithes (above right, Barton Turf); and Highways Surveyors' pits (below right, Beighton).

in a variety of ways and carried out with varying degrees of effectiveness and enthusiasm. The gravel and other material required was often, perhaps usually, obtained from pits dug on commons. It is not surprising, then, that enclosure awards usually allocated one or more areas to the parish highway surveyors which they could continue to use for this purpose; nor that, considered in some sense 'public', these sometimes came to be confused with common land. Most are parcels covering less than 2 acres (0.8 hectares), typically beside public roads and now occupied by secondary woodland, which are largely or entirely filled by a single large pit, as at Wheatacre, Burgh St Peter, Geldeston or Beighton. Often some kind of access ramp is still apparent. Elsewhere more casual and shallow surface extraction is indicated, as at Broome, Stody, Newton St Faith or Moulton. In a few cases pits appear to have become shallower over time, perhaps because they were later used as dumps for domestic refuse by District Councils.

In addition, enclosure Commissioners in Broadland often allotted an area of land as a public staithe, or landing place, 'for the conveyance of corn, manure and other goods to and from the river by owners and occupiers of the Parish'. This was usually where, prior to enclosure, one had already existed on the same site or nearby on the commons.[108] Such areas were usually placed in the care of the highways surveyors, or in that of a Drainage Commission established at the same time. But responsibility for maintenance then variously shifted, to parish councils or to the bodies that succeeded the Drainage Commissioners.[109] Much confusion developed, and persists, over the ownership and status of particular examples and, widely regarded as common land, seven have been registered as such: Irstead Staithe, Ormesby Staithe, Barton Staithe, Johnny Crowe's staithe in Catfield, Bastwick staithe in Repps-with-Bastwick, and both Upper and Lower Street staithes in Horning.

We should also note that in a few places private allotments made when commons were enclosed continued to be used and accessed by the public, with owners unwilling or unable to invest in measures to secure what was, in some cases, rough land of little economic value. Broome Heath, close to the southern boundary of the county, is bisected by the parish boundary between Ditchingham and Brome and until they were enclosed formed part of a much larger area of common land lying between the two parishes.[110] The two allotments that now comprise the heath were never physically divided from each other or subdivided and by 1840 only 4 acres (c. 1.6 hectares) were being cultivated.[111] By this time both allotments were the property of a single owner and in 1904 were acquired by Robert Carr of the Ditchingham estate who, shortly after the purchase, remarked in his notebook that, although the heath was freehold land which had been allotted at the time of the enclosures, 'it has never been fenced off and the public have an unrestricted passage across it'.[112] That use continues to this day, although under Section 1 of the Countryside and Rights of Way Act, not because the heath is a registered common (Figure 5.5).

In addition to these various fragmentary survivals, the Norfolk landscape is littered with the ghosts of commons which were entirely removed by parliamentary enclosure. Particularly noticeable are the number of minor place-names which feature the words 'common' and 'green' in the south and east of the county, on the boulder clay soils and on the fertile loams around Broadland. This is not because common land was especially extensive in these areas. It reflects instead the fact that common-edge settlements were more numerous here than in the north and west of the county, where farms and cottages tended to cluster in loosely nucleated villages. The names of former commons, that is, have lived on as the names of settlements once attached to them. It is in these same areas of the county, moreover, that traces of former commons are most clearly etched into the fabric of the modern landscape. Their presence is signalled most clearly by concentrations of ruler-straight roads and field boundaries within a wider matrix of less regular, more sinuous examples. The former are associated with the kinds of relatively species-poor, hawthorn and blackthorn-dominated hedges commonly created by eighteenth- and nineteenth-century enclosure, in contrast to the surrounding ones, older and more mixed in composition. In some cases, the division between the two is still marked by the gently curving, generally species-rich field boundaries marking the old common edge. In many places, however, such patterns have been blurred both by hedge removal in the twentieth century and by wholesale changes to the field pattern made immediately after enclosure, when the opportunity was often taken to amalgamate the new allotments with older fields beside them, removing or realigning sections of the old common edge and other long-established boundaries (something which – in this age of fashionable agrarian 'improvement' – was often more widely extended into the surrounding 'ancient enclosures'). Nevertheless, even in places much affected

FIG. 5.5. Broome Heath, Ditchingham, with one of the two round barrows in the background.

5. *Enclosure and Survival* 115

by such developments ruler straight roads will continue to signal the former presence of a common, sometimes with farms and cottages standing back from them, accessed by long straight drives or tracks, their position marking the line of the old common edge (Figure 5.6).

Houses thinly scattered around the margins of a large common were converted by parliamentary enclosure into a scatter of isolated dwellings surrounded by fields. But the new allotments were often built on and, where commons were small, they might within a few decades become largely or even entirely filled with houses, as for example at Little Melton or Hethersett. Indeed, what we think of as 'nucleated villages' in the south and east of the county often arose in this manner, echoing developments that occurred much earlier in the north and west of the county (above, p. 39). Where large commons with thinly settled edges occupied areas much affected by the kinds of subsequent changes to boundary patterns just noted, their impact on the modern landscape can still be profound, if subtle, as the example dissected in Figure 5.7, on the level claylands on the boundaries between Great Melton, Wramplingham and Wymondham, clearly illustrates. The pattern of roads and the location of a host of landscape features only make sense when viewed in the context of the lost commons, including farms, the sites of lost farms and cottages, and an area of pits and depressions, now covered by woodland, marking the location of a

FIG. 5.6. In spite of much modern field boundary removal, the site of Dickleburgh High Common is still clear in the landscape as an area of ruler-straight roads and boundaries, ringed by houses.

former brickworks. The house now known as Town Cottage was originally the Poor House for Great Melton, erected on a plot of land cut out of the common in 1791 and conveyed to the churchwardens and overseers by the lord of the manor, Sir John Lombe, with the agreement of the commoners.[113] Typically, it stood a few metres from the parish boundary, isolated from other properties. The hedges on the few surviving stretches of common edge are species-rich, with much hazel, dogwood and maple, and their ground flora includes abundant quantities of woodland herbs like dog's mercury and primroses.

On the light lands in the north and west of the county, where common-edge settlements were less prominent and – because open fields were extensive – the landscapes of entire parishes were often transformed by parliamentary enclosure, the ghosts of commons can be much harder to detect. But not always. In a

5. *Enclosure and Survival*   117

FIG. 5.7. (opposite) The impact on the modern landscape of lost commons at the junction of Wymondham, Great Melton and Wramplingham. Almost all the farms and former farms (circled in red) originally stood on the common edge. 1, pits of a brickworks shown on the Great Melton tithe map. 2, Great Melton poor house, built on an intake from the common in 1791. 3, earthworks of abandoned tofts fronting on the common edge. 4, site of cottage shown on nineteenth-century maps, now represented by a scatter of late medieval and post-medieval pottery. 5, area of pits probably associated with another brickmaking site.

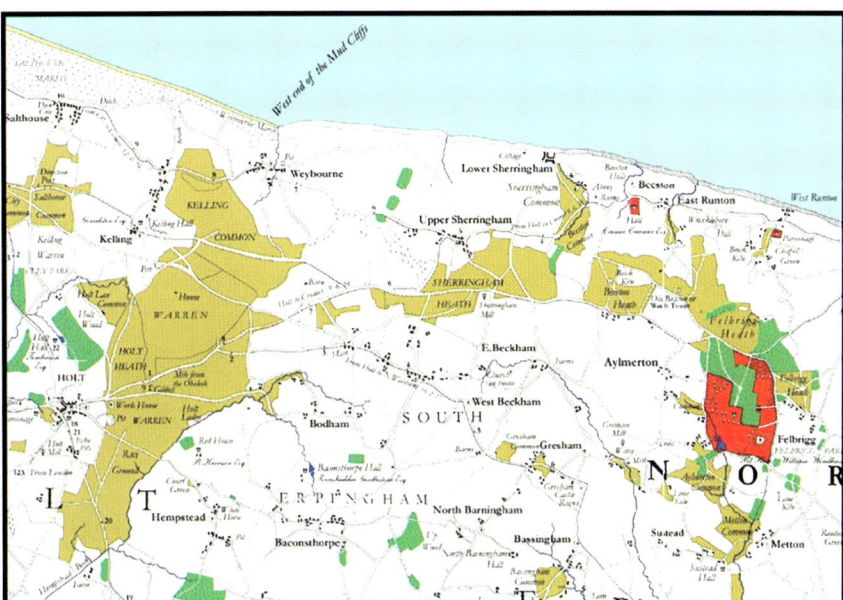

FIG. 5.8. The disposition of common heaths on the Holt–Cromer ridge in north Norfolk, as shown on Faden's county map (above), is strikingly mirrored in the disposition of woods and plantations shown on the modern Ordnance Survey map (below).

number of areas of particularly poor, acidic soil – as on the gravel ridge between Holt and Cromer – the pattern of commons shown on Faden's map is preserved, with striking accuracy, in the disposition of woodland depicted on the modern Ordnance Survey maps (Figure 5.8). This was planted on, or regenerated over, heaths which, although enclosed, were never converted to farmland. Despite the claims of some contemporaries, much common heathland, and most common fens, could never be successfully cultivated, or were so agriculturally marginal that cultivation ended with the agricultural depression of the late nineteenth century, and was never resumed. The enclosure of commons was, in many contexts, primarily about fashion, landscape aesthetics, social control and game preservation, rather than agricultural improvement.

Notes

1. S.R. Eyre, The Curving Ploughland Strip and its Historical Implications, *Agricultural History Review* 3 (1955), 80–94; T. Williamson, Understanding Enclosure, *Landscapes* 1 (2000), 56–79; J.A. Yelling, *Common Field and Enclosure in England 1450–1850* (London, 1977), 11–18.
2. M.E. Turner, Parliamentary Enclosure, in T. Ashwin and A. Davison (eds), *An Historical Atlas of Norfolk*, 3rd edn. (Chichester 2005), 130–2.
3. MC 208, 667X5.
4. NRO C/Sca 2/195 and 196.
5. NRO EVL 184, 454X7.
6. NRO MS 7458, 736. NRO MS 19913, 123X1.
7. NRO BEA 72–4, 435X6. NRO BEA 76/1.
8. Cornford, Commons of Flegg, 16.
9. A. Wood, *The 1549 Rebellions and the Making of Modern England* (Cambridge, 2007), 60–2.
10. Wood, *The 1549 Rebellions*, 56.
11. Wood, *The 1549 Rebellions*, 47–55.
12. Wood, *The 1549 Rebellions*, 58.
13. 29 Geo. II c. 36.
14. NRO MC 36/196, 543X2.
15. Blomefield, *Topographical History*, Vol. 1, 153.
16. NRO MS 1895, 2B7.
17. Blomefield, *Topographical History* Vol. 1, 544.
18. G.E. Mingay, *Parliamentary Enclosure in England: An Introduction to its Causes, Incidence and Impact 1750–1850* (London, 1997), 55–82.
19. NRO C/Sca 2/51.
20. Williamson and Yardy, *Broadland*, 190–1.
21. NROEVL 62, 447X6; NRO HNR 314/5.
22. Mingay, *Parliamentary Enclosure*, 60.
23. Hammond and Hammond, *Village Labourer*, 48.
24. M.E. Turner, *English Parliamentary Enclosure* (Folkestone, 1980).
25. NRO P/CH 1/19.
26. Turner, Parliamentary Enclosure.
27. Turner, Parliamentary Enclosure.
28. NRO PD 107/105.
29. NRO ACC 2018/107
30. NRO PD 107/105.
31. NRO DN/TA 736.
32. NRO Sca 2/87.
33. NRO Sca 2/233.
34. NRO PD 140/27; NRO DN/TA 302.
35. NRO C/Sca 2/326.
36. NRO C/Sca 2/47.

37   NRO PC 86/1; NRO DN/TA 483.
38   NRO C/Sca 2/241; Young, *General View Norfolk*, 152, 162.
39   NRO DN/TA 558.
40   NRO DN/TA 148; NRO DN/TA 100.
41   White, *Directory*, 740; NRO DN/TA 345.
42   NRO C/Sca 2/186.
43   NRO HNR 364/2. NRO PD 459/142.
44   NRO C/Sca 2/81.
45   NRO DN/TA 274; NRO C/Sca 2/82.
46   NRO C/Sca 2/270.
47   NRO C/Sca 2/35.
48   Association of Commons Registration Authorities, Reference 225/U/242: https://acraew.org.uk/sites/default/files/uploads/Norfolk/BILLINGFORD%20COMMON%20-%20BRECKLAND%20D%20NO.CL.96.pdf, accessed 1.6.2024.
49   E. Murphy, Brockdish Common, Norfolk: Historical Research for Present-Day Community Benefit, *Local Historian* 51, 1 (2021), 47–56.
50   NRO DN/TA 842.
51   NRO HRN/256/9
52   NRO HNR 267/12
53   NRO DN/TA 501.
54   NRO PD 664/22.
55   NRO DN/TA 140.
56   NRO PD 107/105.
57   Hammond and Hammond, *Village Labourer*; Linebaugh, *Stop, Thief!*; Neeson, *Commoners*; Snell, *Annals of the Labouring Poor*.
58   Young, *General View Norfolk*, 159.
59   Young, *General View Norfolk*, 181.
60   A further six received a cash payment in lieu of common rights.
61   NRO C/Sca 2/226.
62   NRO DN/TA 326.
63   NRO PD 489/20.
64   NRO DN/TA 19.
65   Young, *General View Norfolk*, 156, 180.
66   S. Birtles, The Impact of Commons Registration: A Norfolk Study, *Landscape History* 20, 1 (1998), 83–97; Birtles, Common Land; Birtles, A Green Space.
67   Young, *General View Norfolk*, 120.
68   *Report of the Commissioners Concerning Charities and Education of the Poor in England and Wales, Vol. XXIII, Norfolk* (London, 1832); White, *Directory*.
69   White, *Directory*, 393, 595, 620, 700.
70   White, *Directory*, 342 and 419.
71   NRO C/Sca 2/188.
72   NRO C/Sca 2/51.
73   NRO C/Sca 2/43.
74   White, *Directory*, 644.
75   *Report of the Commissioners*, 278, 30.
76   White, *Directory*, 436, 446, 653, 680, 688, 769 and 784.
77   White, *Directory*, 794.
78   *Report of the Commissioners*, 279.
79   *Report of the Commissioners*, 71, 265, 279, 307.
80   *Report of the Commissioners*, 524.

81 White, *Directory*, 361; Norfolk Windmills Trust, https://www.norfolkmills.co.uk/Windmills/wood-norton-smockmill.html, accessed 12.9.2024; NRO DN/TA 642.
82 White, *Directory*, 336.
83 C. Wells, The Role of Turf and Associated Fuels in the Nineteenth-Century Rural Economy of Norfolk, *Norfolk Archaeology* 43, 4 (2001), 630–42.
84 White, *Directory*, 312, 328, 340, 596, 627, 687, 773.
85 White, *Directory*, 642 and 643.
86 White, *Directory*, 301 and 768.
87 White, *Directory*, 303.
88 White, *Directory*, 304, 770, 774.
89 NRO P/CH1/51.
90 NRO C/Sca 2/226.
91 NRO KIM 5/13/9.
92 NRO PD 111/44.
93 White, *Directory*, 596.
94 NRO PD 107/70.
95 NRO PD 107/70.
96 NRO PD 107/70.
97 1,255 inhabitants are listed in the 1841 census.
98 *Report of the Commissioners*, 312–3.
99 No less than 48 private individuals received allotments when East Ruston the common was enclosed in 1810. There were 35 proprietors of more than 10 acres here in 1841; NRO DN/TA 525.
100 *Report of the Commissioners*, 247.
101 Young, *General View Norfolk*, 88.
102 NRO P/CH 1/19.
103 Young, *General View Norfolk,* 95.
104 Young, *General View Norfolk,* 107.
105 D. Dymond, *The Norfolk Landscape* (London, 1985), 216.
106 Dymond, *Norfolk Landscape*, 216; MacMaster, Mousehold Heath.
107 NRO DN/TA 503.
108 Williamson and Yardy, *Broadland*, 292–5.
109 As a result of the 1930 Land Drainage Act the property of parish Drainage Commissioners passed to the East Norfolk Rivers Catchment Board if they lay on a main river, or to the new local Internal Drainage Boards if they did not. Those on main rivers passed, in the late 1940s, from the East Norfolk Rivers Catchment Board to the East Suffolk and Norfolk Rivers Board; then, after 1977, to the Anglian Water Authority; before devolving in 1989 to the National Rivers Authority and finally, in 1996, to the Environment Agency.
110 NRO C/Sca 2/102; NRO C/Sca 2/100.
111 NRO DN/TA 361 and DN/TA.
112 NRO MC 166/238.
113 NRO PD 479/63 and PD 479/64.

CHAPTER 6

The Later History of Common Land

Survivals and Confusions

By the middle of the nineteenth century the overwhelming majority of Norfolk's commons had gone. A few, as we have seen, survived because they were formally recognised by enclosure awards; a scatter remained elsewhere, in parishes in which, for a variety of reasons, no parliamentary enclosure occurred. But these probably accounted for less than 4 per cent, by area, of what had existed half a century or so earlier, when Faden's map was surveyed. Yet as we have also seen, in many parishes in the county enclosure awards preserved a portion of the parochial wastes in an unimproved state as 'poor's allotments' on which, in many cases, some form of traditional management continued. In many ways the distinction between these two types of land is blurred, even meaningless. Enclosure acts created, at places like Brancaster, Kelling or Shotesham, 'commons' which were reserved for the use of cottagers; and some poor's allotments were not only used in similar ways to commons, but were described as such by local people. It is not surprising, then, that the famous Norfolk naturalist W.G. Clarke, who published his two important articles on the natural history and history of Norfolk commons in the *Transactions of the Norfolk and Norwich Naturalists' Society* in 1909 and 1918, made no real distinction between the two, effectively regarding 'fuel allotments, managed by trustees' as just one variety of 'the commons in Norfolk of the present day'.[1] The provisional list he prepared of such land in 1909 included commons that had escaped enclosure; examples allotted, often as some form of joint property, by enclosure awards; numerous poor's allotments; and a scatter of surveyors' pits and the like.

While Clarke noted these distinctions, they were less important to him than what such areas had in common. Firstly, they were all examples of uncultivated land that was 'accessible to the public … on which the botanist can wander unchallenged'.[2] Accordingly, poor's allotments still notionally managed by trustees might be considered as 'commons', while those leased out, with the proceeds used to benefit the poor, were not. Secondly, and more importantly, he emphasised that because surveyors' pits, poor's allotments and the like had all been cut out of common land and not subsequently much altered, they were effectively indistinguishable from them in terms of their natural history.

> Having never been cultivated and in many cases rarely subject to alteration by man, these commons are among the most interesting parts of the county to the naturalist, for on them to a much greater degree than elsewhere there has been an almost undisturbed succession of fauna and flora from post-glacial times.[3]

Because they have a shared early history, moreover, poor's allotments were as likely as commons to preserve archaeological evidence for pre-medieval activity.

Yet the extent to which these various kinds of land display ecological continuity with the pre-agricultural landscapes of the remote past should not be exaggerated. The character of common land was shaped by modes of exploitation and changed over time as, in particular, over the centuries wood-pastures gave way everywhere to open expanses of grass and heather. What we think of as the 'traditional' character of clayland commons, heaths or fens was the consequence of the ways in which they were used and managed; of the kinds of livestock that were grazed on them and with what intensity; of what fuels and other materials were removed from them and in what quantities. The present appearance, and ecological qualities, of such areas have accordingly been shaped by changes in exploitation which have taken place since the middle of the nineteenth century, and which in many cases have involved a decline in the intensity of management, so that commons have become wilder, rougher and usually less biologically diverse places, ultimately regenerating in many cases to secondary woodland. Only with conscious effort, driven by a concern for wildlife rather than the needs of farming and subsistence, has this progression in some places been slowed or reversed in the course of the last half century or so. Much about the landscapes of common land, in other words, can only be understood by examining their relatively recent history.

Nineteenth-century Changes

Changes in management in the nineteenth century are most clearly documented in records relating to poor's allotments, but similar developments also evidently occurred on many 'real' commons. In particular, as the century progressed fewer and fewer were cut for fuel. Trustees could, from the start, make significant changes to use or administration because the section of the enclosure award dealing with the allotment generally included a clause stating that it was to be used as a source of fuel for the poor or 'otherwise appropriated, and the Produce and Profits arising therefore applied for their use and benefit'. But their freedom of manoeuvre was increased by a succession of parliamentary acts. In particular, the Charitable Trusts Act of 1860 provided that the Charity Commissioners (constituted as a permanent body in 1853) could, under certain conditions, make an order for the establishment of a scheme for the administration of any fuel allotment, which might even extend to using the land in new ways; while the Commons Act of 1876 authorised them to allow allotments to be used as recreation grounds and allotment gardens, or exchanged for a piece of land of similar or equal value that could be so used.[4]

The proportion of allotments leased out for grazing, shooting or fishing, with the income received used to buy coals for the poor, slowly but steadily increased through the middle and later decades of the century. In some parishes, it is true, direct exploitation came to an end simply because reserves of usable peat had been exhausted or the flooded condition of the workings made continued extraction difficult or impossible. In 1832, it was said that at Sutton 'there is now very little remaining … The produce is now very small about 10 or 12 thousand turves is the utmost quantity now cut'.[5] By 1845 the workings were largely under water, as was the case with the 23-acre allotment at Surlingham, all but 7 acres of which was 'a morass, now let for cutting sedges, and fishing'.[6] But more generally it was encouraged by the steady improvement in transport systems, both locally and nationally, which lowered the cost of coal, a process that in Norfolk culminated with the arrival of the railways in the 1840s. Renting out the allotment and using the proceeds to buy coal saved trustees all the trouble of administering the cutting or digging – making sure that it was done at the proper time, that nobody took more than they were entitled to, and that the old and infirm, unable to extract fuel themselves, had someone to do it on their behalf. By 1832, at Happisburgh, Sea Palling, Caistor, Ludham, and elsewhere, allotments initially cut and grazed by the poor were already being rented out.[7] The trend continued, and intensified, through the second half of the century, with trustees often making use of the new powers vested in the Charity Commissioners. In 1875, for example, the Blo Norton trustees obtained a ruling from them that:

> The Trustees shall take steps to discontinue the gratuitous use of any portion of the land … by the poor inhabitants of the said Parish for the purposes of cutting and getting fuel therefrom, and they shall cause so much of the said land as has been so used to be let from time to time, either with or without the right of cutting fuel therefrom.[8]

Here, perhaps, there is an implication that some opposition to the change was anticipated. But there is no real evidence that the poor much objected to these new arrangements. Most presumably preferred a regular supply of coal to the opportunity to dig their own peat, or to cut their own gorse, from the allotment. Indeed, in some cases the initiative for renting out all or part of an allotment clearly came from the poor themselves. In 1859 a petition, signed by the heads of 43 pauper households, was sent to the Trustees of the Catfield allotment, requesting that they accept an offer made by Richard and William Riches to lease that part containing one of the village staithes for £8 per annum, with the proceeds to be distributed amongst them, although in this case it should be noted that many of the petitioners were members of the Primitive Methodist congregation of which William Riches was leader.[9]

Even where trustees did not make the change, cutting for fuel might be abandoned anyway as the price of coal fell. At Pentney, a few kilometres from the port of King's Lynn, it was reported in 1832 that no fuel had been cut from the allotment for two years.[10] Declining demand for gorse, in particular, led trustees to find new uses for allotments. By 1845 that at Litcham was divided into garden plots which were let to the poor; at Sloley the 11 acres were 'let to poor families', while in Fulmondeston the whole allotment was rented out 'in small parcels to labourers'.[11] This provision of early 'allotments', in the modern sense, took a further turn at Guist where in 1845 it was reported that 6 of the 30 acres had been

> Divided into twenty garden plots, let at rents amounting to £21, and the remainder is used by the poor for cutting fuel. On the garden plots there are eleven cottages, nine built by the tenant and two by the overseers.[12]

Allotments might also be significantly eroded in ways unsanctioned by trustees. Between 1822 and 1827 Robert Pollard, a wherryman, occupied a portion of the allotment at Catfield and built a thatched clay cottage on it. Unopposed, the land became his by adverse possession, a rector of the parish describing in 1881 how it had been 'successfully abstracted by encroachment years ago, the Trustees being asleep'.[13] By 1883 a pair of semi-detached cottages had been built beside it by the Riches who rented that section of the allotment used as a staithe, to house some of their employees. By 1905 they had also built a small warehouse and an ice-house where ice, gathered off Hickling Broad in winter, was stored and then taken by wherry to Yarmouth to be used in the fishing industry.[14] But more striking was the appearance across the rising ground on the southern half of the site, between 1842 and 1883, of more than a dozen squatters' cottages, set in small enclosures, apparently built with the acquiescence, but not the active involvement, of the trustees.[15] Constructed of clay and straw, sometimes with a brick skin, they disappeared in the middle decades of the twentieth century as their inhabitants were re-housed elsewhere, but the land remained divided into fields.[16]

Where allotments were divided into gardens, built on, or otherwise 'improved' they ceased to resemble common land, in any environmental sense. They disappeared as distinctive features of the parish landscape, in some cases only living on as parish charities. But the majority of directly exploited poor's allotments survived as parcels of unimproved land, although, with the passing decades, fewer and fewer were cut for fuel. By the end of the century, moreover, few cottagers kept a cow, reducing both the intensity with which these areas might be grazed and the number that were mown for litter or fodder; geese and donkeys were still often kept but many allotments were simply let for shooting (Figure 6.1).

The available evidence suggests that the history of common land in the nineteenth century broadly mirrored that of poor's allotments, but with some significant differences. Many commons, especially those on clay and alluvial soils or which were allotted to common-right owners by enclosure acts, continued to be managed communally, and used intensively, into the twentieth century. But the tithe apportionments for a number of parishes, including Beeston Regis, Harleston, Thwaite and Corpusty, record only one occupier of each area of common land, suggesting that the commons were no longer being grazed collectively but were instead being rented out to particular individuals by the manorial lord, presumably because the commoners as a group no longer had any interest in grazing them.[17] Elsewhere, as at Ringland, the occupiers are

FIG. 6.1. Alfred Munnings, *Crostwick Common: Woman with Donkey and Geese* (1904).

simply recorded as 'the poor', again suggesting a lack of involvement on the part of common-right farmers.[18] Indeed, in a number of places – Whitwell in 1824, Swainsthorpe around the same time – formal agreements appear to have been made between the lord of the manor and the village farmers giving poor cottagers the sole use of commons, so that they came to resemble the stinted commons established for the use of the poor by enclosure acts at places like Barrow or Shotesham, or some of the larger poor's allotments, especially in Broadland.[19] Once they had passed into the hands of the poor many such commons were gradually exploited less intensively through the second half of the century, as fewer cottagers kept a domestic cow, and as coal use became normal at the lowest social levels. As early as the 1870s it was reported that the local population has ceased to cut turfs on Whitwell Common because 'the houses and fireplaces of the commoners are unsuitable for the burning of turf'.[20] The traditional uses of such marginal land were being ended, not by enclosure, but by modernity.

Decline and Dereliction

In his two articles on common land in Norfolk, published in 1909 and 1918, W.G. Clarke discussed how various Norfolk 'commons' were being managed. His accounts suggest that those found on the claylands were still for the most part being actively grazed by commoners, mainly with cattle. Elsewhere the situation was variable. Castle Rising Day and Night Common, the various Castle Acre commons, Thornham Common, the Carr and the Heath in Great Massingham, West Winch 'Common', Foulden Common, Thornham Common and The Lowes and Spout Hills in Holt were all regularly grazed, while Ingoldisthorpe was grazed by the horses of the parishioners.[21] But in many other places he implies that grazing, if it occurred at all, was at a low level and desultory in character, especially on dry heaths. A number of 'commons', generally poor's allotments comprising wet heaths and fens, were also regularly mown, while a few were cut for other products. The Oxburgh Fuel Allotment, for example, was mown each year on a date fixed by the villagers: 'the man employed puts the litter in heaps and receives about 1sh. for each heap; these are numbered and the ownership for each is settled by drawing lots'.[22] Boughton Fen, Bressingham Fen, Burgh St Margaret Common, Flordon Common, Felthorpe Common, Guist 'Common', the Smallburgh Fens, were still mown each year for rough hay or litter, Kettlestone Common was both grazed and cut for rush and sedge, while on Marsham Heath and Buxton Heath '*Calluna* and *Erica* are still cut for besoms or sink-brushes, which are made by the villagers', and bracken was still harvested at Great Bircham and Bircham Tofts, and on Congham 'Common'.[23]

But there were few other places where such activities are mentioned and the role of commons and allotments as sources of domestic fuel had by now clearly dwindled markedly. Peat was still cut at Blo Norton Fen, on the allotments in South Lopham, and on Buxton Heath in Marsham: at the former, 'each rightholder has a strip 14 yards wide from road to river, the signal for beginning to cut peat the tolling of the church bell'.[24] Goose Green (a poor's allotment in Little Ellingham), as well as being grazed by 'large numbers of geese and ducks', was cut for furze.[25] But these are the only places where significant fuel cutting is mentioned. At Boughton turf was still cut but only 'to a small extent'.[26] At Old Buckenham the 'Poor have right of turf-cutting, never exercised',[27] while at Brumstead the allotment was still mown for hay and rushes, and cut for gorse and pea sticks, but no peat had been cut for fuel 'for the past ten years'.[28] Where, as was often the case, fuel allotments were leased for shooting little if any regular management, by cutting or grazing, was taking place.

Other writers in the first two decades of the twentieth century present a similar picture. The naturalist Maurice Bird described the history and management of East Ruston 'common' in an article published in 1909. Some mowing of the wetland areas was still being undertaken, as 'even if only fit for litter, rushes and mixed stuff are always saleable in this bullock grazing district'. But the use of the common for grazing had much declined.[29] The few cattle to be found were mainly the property of local farmers as 'the poor are too poor to buy a cow', and 'the grazing would be wasted if those who ought not did not make use of it'.[30] The geese and donkeys being grazed were mainly the property, not of the poor, but of local residents whose property exceeded the technical qualification for the use of the common. Above all, peat was no longer being cut on the lower, waterlogged areas, nor gorse from the drier, heathy parts. He suggested that the burning of peat had effectively ceased in part because, with the arrival of the railways, the price of coal had declined, and in part because the 'old specially constructed iron, large brick ovens and open chimneys have entirely disappeared' from the houses of the local people.

With traditional structures of management now often in abeyance, those commons and poor's allotments lying close to towns or large villages began to be regarded as an eyesore and a problem, places afflicted by fly tipping, dumping, fires and gypsy camps.[31] In 1907 Mulbarton Parish Council debated the future management of the local common and listed the various problems from which it currently suffered, including illegal grazing, manure heaps, and gypsy vans.[32] Three years later, when East Dereham Urban District Council applied, under the terms of recent legislation, for a scheme to regulate the use of Neatherd Moor, similar difficulties were described: 'At the present time it is a horrible nuisance, the pit full of dead dogs and dead cats, and broken glass bottles, rendering it dangerous to cattle and children which might stray into it'.[33] Their attempt to regulate the Moor was opposed by local people, who wanted its management to remain in the hands of the existing trustees.

By the turn of the twentieth century less intensive management of commons and poor's allotments was beginning to have a significant impact on their vegetation. Heaths began to become more infested with bracken. If allowed to grow to maturity the plant is unpalatable to livestock but if regularly harvested in the traditional manner, for bedding or firing, the young fronds can be consumed by sheep and cattle, which also keep the plant in check by treading. With declining numbers of stock, and a cessation of cutting, bracken spread unchecked across extensive areas of marginal, acidic land, whether common or private.[34] Clarke in 1908 described how bracken was 'certainly the dominant plant of the "breck" district, and on several heaths has usurped the position which heather occupied some 20 years ago. Bracken lacks its former economic importance'.[35] In 1914 it was said to be the principal plant on the heaths in other areas of Norfolk.[36] Gorse also increased. Bird described how at East Ruston, 'The best parts of the common for grazing purposes are now being much encroached upon by the spreading of furze ... there are not enough Donkeys to nibble down the gorse bushes'.[37] Regular cutting of gorse for fuel no longer encouraged the young growth most likely to be grazed by livestock. Clarke similarly described in 1918 how on Barnham Common near Thetford 'the original steppe flora has been greatly reduced by the encroachments of furze'.[38] Clarke reported in 1919 that many commons were partly occupied by areas of scrub dominated by gorse, but also containing hawthorn, blackthorn and brambles.[39] In 1914 natural regeneration of pine was noted on the allotments at Horsford and Horsham St Faith's, and Clarke in 1918 reported that seedlings of birch and pine, and sometimes oak, were 'common on many heaths'.⁴⁰ Indeed, the regeneration of woodland over poor's allotments seems in some cases to have been encouraged by trustees, to increase the value of the shooting rents or for other reasons:

> Horsford Heath was formerly manorial waste subject to common rights: the trees were suppressed as a matter of policy by the common-right holders, and villagers now living remember it an open heath. Since its allotment to the poor at the enclosure, the trustees have protected the seedling trees, and it is now open canopy forest, the small annual produce being divided amongst the poor.⁴¹

The Ordnance Survey 6-inch maps suggest that a number of poor's allotments, such as those at Bodham and Felthorpe, were by now much invaded by trees.

During the inter-war years heathland commons and fuel allotments were used even less intensively. Cutting of peat and gorse came to an end and the intensity of grazing declined still further. The larger farmers had less and less interest in exploiting the meagre grazing provided by this often poorly fenced marginal land, especially as the volume of road traffic increased; motorists appear to have been less assiduous in closing the common gates than local people on foot, horseback or cart. On some commons, encroaching scrub began to be managed by burning, a practice unrecorded in earlier times. Fens in particular were neglected, as the market for rough hay and litter contracted.⁴² In 1947 Petch, writing about the changing condition of those in the west of the county, described how:

> Many of these tracts of land are held in trust for the poor of the parish in which they lie, but their usefulness must have declined in recent years. They are now only a source of rough grazing, the cutting of sedge having been largely given up, and the digging of peat which was in vogue at the beginning of the century, abandoned.⁴³

Even grazing was in decline in many places. In the valley of the Gaywood River, Sugar Fen was said to be 'much invaded by birch and alder'; while Marham East Fen was 'not now grazed and is much overgrown'.⁴⁴

But clayland commons, in contrast to commons and allotments comprising heaths and fens, generally retained their economic importance. The successive editions of the 6-inch and 25-inch Ordnance survey maps published from the 1880s into the 1920s and 30s populate heathland examples with the symbols used to depict 'rough grazing and heather', or 'gorse', and show peat fens as waterlogged ground, in both cases sometimes with a scatter of deciduous or coniferous trees invading from neighbouring woods and plantations. Commons overlying clay (and most of those occupying silty floodplains), in contrast, are mainly shown without symbols, indicating that surveyors saw them as close-cropped pasture of reasonable quality, and in the few cases where trees are shown these are deciduous, located towards the margins, and evidently represent the remains of 'plantings'. In spite of the problems caused by road traffic and the increasingly depressed state of agriculture from the early 1880s – including much of the livestock sector from the 1890s – most of these commons evidently retained an economic importance that fens and heathland had, by the middle decades of the twentieth century, largely lost. Indeed, some enjoyed a short-term boost in value, and in some cases in the intensity of use, during the two world wars.

The War Agricultural Committee set up in January 1917, with 20 District Sub-Committees beneath it, made many direct interventions in Norfolk farming in an attempt to boost food production.[45] Farmers were instructed to plant at least 62 per cent of their tillage land with cereals and potatoes and ordered to plough up small areas of pasture. The Committee sometimes provided farmers with additional workers in the shape of prisoners of war and occasionally took over particular holdings that were either uncultivated, or badly farmed. There were 17,000 additional acres (c. 6,890 hectares) of cereals in Norfolk by the end of 1917 (a 4 per cent increase) and 3,000 acres (c. 1,200 hectares) of pasture had been ploughed up.[46] Little of this appears to have been common land, however. The committee asked Marsham parish council to bring the poor's allotment into cultivation, but with what success is unclear; and attempted to get the Smallburgh Sub-committee to take over and plough 30 acres of East Ruston 'Common', but abandoned the attempt due to cost and local opposition.[47] A threat to take over the Badley Moor poor's allotment in East Dereham in order to improve drainage, and thus the quality of the grazing, was abandoned when the trustees agreed to undertake the work themselves.[48] There is little evidence that other commons were affected but the use of clayland commons may have intensified, although that of heaths probably did not, to judge from the fact that the numbers of sheep in the county, the principal denizens of heaths whether private property or common land, declined by around 9 per cent between 1913 and 1917 (more than can be explained by the ploughing up of private pastures), while those of cattle rose slightly (by 1,180).[49]

The Second World War may have had a greater impact on common land in Norfolk. The County War Agricultural Executive Committees (WAECs) and the District Committees (DCs) under them could again order the ploughing up of pasture for crops and dispossess inefficient farmers, and work land directly. Ploughing-up targets were laid down and in Norfolk 25,000 acres (c. 10,100 hectares) of grass and derelict land was to be returned to arable.[50] Improvement of pastures, through re-seeding, liming or better drainage were also on the agenda although less of a priority. A number of commons were now ploughed up and either re-seeded or sown with arable crops, either on the initiative of the committees or as a result of private initiatives. Most were grazing commons occupying clay soils or floodplain silts: Brisley Green and Harpers Green in Brisley, Litcham Common, Neatherd Moor in East Dereham, Ridlington Mill Common, Thwaite Common, Wacton Common, and the common marshes at North Wooton. Only a handful of common heaths, such as West Rudham Common, and a few small fuel allotments comprising fen or heath – at Ashill, Tittleshall, Weasenham and Wellingham – were also affected.[51] Badley Moor in East Dereham was requisitioned with the intention of converting it to arable but in the end was left as pasture, although attempts, not entirely successful, were made to improve the drainage.[52] A number of other large commons were considered for requisitioning by the committee, including New Buckenham Common and Crostwick Common, but ultimately rejected.[53] Plans drawn up in November 1942 to cultivate Honing Severals were abandoned early the following year on the grounds that it was 'unlikely that sufficient labour would be available immediately for the debushing and clearing'.[54] In all, 13 commons and allotments were requisitioned and ploughed or improved by the WAEC, a total of 658 acres (266 hectares), alongside a few like Rudham Common by private initiative.[55] Many heathland commons and poor's allotments were used for military training, as we shall see, something that has left a profound mark on their archaeology (below, pp. 158–61). But on the whole, fens and heaths survived the war unscathed, continuing their slow decline into dereliction.

Rabbits and Regeneration

It is, however, important to emphasise that this decline was, indeed, remarkably slow. Today nature conservation groups in Norfolk fight an unceasing battle to preserve areas of heath from being invaded by scrub and trees. Where they are not grazed intensively, birch seedlings seem to spring up almost overnight. Yet the vertical air photographs taken by the RAF at the end of the Second World War suggest that heathland commons and poor's allotments, as much as the clayland commons on which grazing continued, still remained largely free of trees. And while in the early years of the twentieth century naturalists like Clarke and Bird noted the inexorable spread of gorse and scrub, the same photographs appear to suggest that on most common heaths extensive areas of grass and heather survived, something supported by contemporary observation, oral testimony, and ground-level photographs from the inter-war years (Figure 6.2).

Only from the 1950s does this situation appear to have changed; gorse now spread more rapidly across common heaths, accompanied to an extent by bramble and blackthorn, while colonisation by bracken also accelerated. Next, at a rate that varied from place to place, birch, Scots pine and oak invaded. June Batstone, born in Crostwight in 1931, typically recalled in 2018 how, in her childhood, 'The flat heath was mainly covered with heather – a wonderful purple sight in July'. By 1954, when she was married, 'Heather was still the dominant plant but some gorse and bracken grew, mainly at the roadside. It was easy to gather enough heather to cover the windowsills and generally decorate Honing Church for the event'. She did not visit the Heath again until 1974 and 'the change was amazing. There was much less heather. Gorse had become the dominant plant. There was also more bracken'. A decade and a half later and the common was largely wooded.[56] By 1988, when Norfolk County Council commissioned an aerial survey, places like Alderford Common, Church Hill Common in Ringland, Ringland Hills and School Common in Southrepps, all of which had been open expanses of heather and grass with scattered gorse in 1946, had largely regenerated to secondary woodland. And while most clayland commons still remained reasonably free of trees and scrub even some of these, including Marsh Green in Bracon Ash or Mulbarton Common, were also now mainly or entirely wooded.

There were some variations to this chronological pattern. Some common heaths, unlike that at Crostwight, were much infested with scrub and trees by the 1960s: some fuel allotments on sandy, heathy soils, such as Felthorpe 'Common' or the neighbouring Drayton Dewray, had already been extensively invaded by trees by the end of the nineteenth century. But for the most part, invasion by scrub and regeneration of woodland were delayed until well into the post-war period. In part, the slowness of succession may reflect the fact that on some heaths grazing or cutting continued, even if only at a low level of intensity, into the 1930s; and that in some places encroaching scrub was held in check by fire, intentionally or otherwise. But the most important retarding factor was probably the rabbit.

Rabbits had begun to escape from commercial warrens in Norfolk, and establish colonies in the wild, by the late Middle Ages: as early as 1388 a survey of Wilton in the west of the county described how 60 acres of arable were 'worth nothing by the year because of destruction of the coneys of the duke of Lancaster's warren there'.[57] But from the 1860s and 70s their numbers increased rapidly, more perhaps than in most counties. Norfolk had long been famed for its shooting and by the second half of the nineteenth century landed estates were being managed for game more intensively than ever.[58] On some, especially in the west of the county, rabbits were actively encouraged and protected as quarry.[59] Even where they were not, the success of gamekeepers – now armed with breach-loading, double-barrel shotguns – in destroying foxes, stoats, hawks, and other predators 'so that game birds may survive in abundance',[60] also served to boost their numbers. But more important was the impact of the agricultural depression, which began in the late 1870s, on this predominantly arable county. Where, on the poorest and most sandy soils, fields were abandoned, rabbits soon moved in. In 1885 the cost of the damage caused by rabbits on Sturston Hall and Stanford Home farms in Breckland was estimated at £335, over £20,000 in modern money.[61] As hedges were widely neglected due to declining farm incomes they became, in Lilias Rider Haggard's words, 'a formidable tangle of briar and thorn some eight feet through and twelve feet high … forming an almost impenetrable dwelling place for numerous rabbits'.[62] By the 1920s rabbits were abundant almost everywhere; Norfolk was, as she expressed it, a 'rabbit-infested country'.

132 *The Landscapes of Common Land*

FIG. 6.2. (opposite) Above: School Common in Southrepps, now occupied by secondary woodland, with Southrepps School top centre. Below: in the inter-war years the common was still open heathland.

Rabbits caused widespread damage not only to crops and pastures but also to young trees and woodlands: Nicholson in 1913 noted that they had 'a noteworthy selective influence on vegetation – seedling trees are suppressed and woodland fails to regenerate itself unless protected by netting'.[63] The increase in rabbit numbers coincided closely with the decline in the management of commons and poor's allotments by cutting and grazing but, as well as holding in check the spread of gorse, blackthorn, birch and other trees and shrubs, rabbits tended to shun young bracken (unlike sheep and cattle), encouraging its spread at the expense of heather and grasses. Commons were thus kept open as management declined, although those on acid soils often became increasingly dominated by bracken.

All this changed in the mid-1950s. By this time rabbits, throughout England and across much of Europe, were having a major impact on agricultural production. Attempts to control their numbers by trapping, poisoning and gassing had largely failed. In 1953, following experiments in Australia and Canada, the virus *Myxomatosis cuniculus* was deliberately and successfully introduced to wild rabbit populations in Europe and rapidly spread through France and then into England, transmitted principally by fleas.[64] In part as a consequence of the deliberate movement of infected animals, it was soon affecting rabbits throughout the country. 'The winter of 1955–6 was the turning point in the history of the rabbit. During that winter the population fell to a lower level than at any time since the medieval period.'[65] The rabbit was not, of course, entirely eradicated; by 1958 it was clear that a small percentage of the population was exhibiting signs of immunity, while those animals that nested, as some did, above the ground were less infested with the fleas that were the principal vector of transmission than the burrow-dwelling majority. In Norfolk in 1959 it was reported that 'in some places numbers have built up strongly, but in others rabbits are still entirely absent'.[66] Increases in numbers stimulated further attempts at elimination on the part of farmers and the Ministry of Agriculture, with the proliferation of local 'Rabbit Clearance Societies'. Localised recoveries continued to be reported into the 1960s; in 1962 it was said that 'Despite the efforts of Rabbit Clearance Societies and continued sporadic outbreaks of myxomatosis, the population is now in many areas higher than at any time since 1954'.[67] By the middle of the decade, however, a pattern of 'extreme fluctuations' in rabbit numbers was being recognised, as localised recoveries were checked by renewed waves of disease.[68] Rabbit populations at best recovered for only short periods in any locality before falling and overall, they remained a fraction of what they had been in Norfolk before the arrival of myxomatosis.

In 1969 George Garrod, in an article discussing the vegetation of Wretham Heath, described the impact of the decline in rabbit numbers.[69] He noted how, prior to myxomatosis, 'woody plants had generally been unable to establish themselves under heavy rabbit attack, and all but mature shrubs and trees were apt to be killed by barking in severe winters, but by 1960 young birches, now up to two feet high, were well established', together with some sallow and Scots pine. By the middle of the 1960s 'the progression towards tree and scrub was well marked'.[70] In the same period it was noted that the decline in rabbit numbers had led to the rapid spread of birch across Bawdeswell Heath, a derelict fuel allotment, which was only held in check by the regular mowing associated with the area's recreational use by local people.[71]

The loss of grass and heather to bracken, scrub and secondary woodland on the county's commons and poor's allotments that began with a decline in the intensity of management in the late nineteenth century was thus coincidentally slowed by an explosion in rabbit numbers, albeit to an extent that varied with the density of local populations, until the mid-1950s. The dramatic decline in rabbit numbers which then occurred was followed by rapid changes in vegetation. By the 1980s only those commons, mainly on the claylands, which were still regularly used by farmers for commercial grazing; or those few examples managed for wildlife conservation or recreation by regular cutting and grazing; remained largely open. The majority had by now become at least partly covered in scrub or woodland, with any open areas, in the case of heaths, choked with bracken.

New Roles and Registration

To understand the development of Norfolk's commons over the last half century or so we need to briefly adopt a national rather than regional perspective. The final phases of parliamentary enclosure in the middle and later decades of the nineteenth century were accompanied by a growing concern on the part of the social elite about some of its negative social consequences, especially in terms of reducing the recreational opportunities, and thus the health, of the urban and rural population. Common land began to be seen as a matter of concern to society as a whole and not merely to lords and commoners, or even the poor, of particular places. The 1845 Inclosure Act, as well as facilitating the enclosure of remaining areas of open land, also prohibited the removal of village greens and stipulated that some land should be set aside for recreation grounds and allotment gardens as part of any enclosure act.[72] Speaking in 1844, in the debate over the bill preceding the act, Sir Robert Peel argued the importance of having, near every town, 'an open space accessible to all', and that any consideration of the benefits of enclosing common land needed to set 'considerations of health, of innocent recreation, of moral improvement against the mere considerations of pecuniary gain'.[73] Bowing to the pressure exerted by groups like the Commons Preservation Society, alarmed by the enclosure for development of commons around expanding Victorian towns and cities – sometimes carried out unilaterally by the landowner under the guise of 'approvement', as sanctioned by the Statute of Merton – the 1876 Commons Act effectively permitted the enclosure of common land only where it could be shown to bring benefits to the community as a whole, while Section 29 prohibited the enclosure of all greens and commons lying in the immediate vicinity of urban areas.[74] The act also made provision for the regulation of common land in order to increase its value as amenity land, used by the general public. The latter section of the legislation proved largely ineffective but similar provisions included in the Commons Act of 1899 made more sense, given that the Local Government Act of 1894 had established a network of parish and district councils who could, if necessary, undertake the task. Indeed, the 1899 act gave parish councils the duty of managing all 'village greens', loosely defined, as well as the right to take over the running of poor's allotments, surveyors' pits and other 'public' land awarded at enclosure.[75] By now, enclosure had largely come to an end, the Law of Commons Amendment Act of 1893 effectively terminating the provisions of the Statute of Merton by stipulating that all enclosures by 'approvement' required the sanction of the Ministry of Agriculture.[76]

In 1925 the Law of Property Act gave the public full rights of access to all areas of common land within London or any other city or urban district.[77] But, with increasing leisure time, the spread of car ownership and the growing popularity of rambling and other healthy outdoor pursuits there was a widespread desire to similarly protect, and safeguard access to, more remote examples. As early as 1909, W.G. Clarke described Norfolk's commons as 'places remote from dusty roads where all may walk with freedom and view nature in the wildest aspects which such a county as Norfolk can furnish'.[78] But, as noted in his subsequent article of 1918, commons were areas 'accessible (*though not of legal right*) to the general public' [my italics].[79] The belief that *all* common land should be both protected and publicly accessible seems to have enjoyed increasing levels of public support through the 1920s and 30s, but the issue only really began to rise to the top of the political agenda during the immediate post-war decades. It is probable, as Sarah Birtles has suggested, that the need to over-ride the rights of owners, and common-rights holders (and, in the case of poor's allotments, trustees) during the national emergency of the Second World War engendered new approaches to common land in this period, although these can also been seen as part of wider changes in the balance between private rights and the public good, and in understandings of the role of the state in land use and land use planning.[80] It is no coincidence that L. Dudley Stamp, co-author with W.G. Hoskins of the first comprehensive study of the history and geography of common land in England – *The Common Lands of England and Wales*, published in 1963 – had earlier, in the inter-War period, directed the Land Utilisation Survey, summarising its findings, and making extensive recommendations for future land use planning, in the monumental *The Land of Britain: Its Use and Misuse*, published in 1948.[81]

The appearance of Hoskins' and Stamp's book came at the end of a decade or more of discussion, in government and elsewhere, of what the title of a parliamentary debate in 1956 termed 'Derelict Common Land'. Some politicians and lobby groups advocated renewed attempts at cultivation and improvement to relieve post-war food shortages. Rather more now emphasised access, recreation and nature conservation. Both approaches were potentially in conflict, not only with each other but also with the rights of owners, common-right holders and trustees. To address these complex issues, a Royal Commission on Common Land was established in 1955 with a committee that included Hoskins and Stamp (much of their book was based on evidence heard by the Commission).[82] The Commission's report, published in 1958, concluded that:

> As the last reserve of uncommitted land in England and Wales, common land ought to be preserved in the public interest. The public interest embraces both the creation of wider facilities for public access and an increase in the productivity of the land.[83]

The Commission recommended that all commons should be registered, appropriate management schemes for each drawn up, and that the general public should be given legal rights of access to all commons. Seven years later the 1965 Commons Registration Act initiated the process which was to realise the first of these ambitions.[84]

As I have already noted on a number of occasions, the result was the registration, as 'common land', of much more than ancient commons, owned by manorial lord but exploited by a defined body of common-right holders. In Sarah Birtles' words, the Act:

> Was designed in such a way that the registers would be founded on modern fact without reference to historical records or tedious research. Moreover, they were likely to sweep up all land with amenity potential. In so doing, however, what the act actually achieved was a further redefinition of common land and the registration of a significant number of commons that could only be construed as such within this new definition.[85]

Crucial here was a distinction the act made between what it described as 'common land', which was 'land subject to rights of common', and 'waste land of a manor not subject to rights of common'. The latter was a new concept, invented primarily, it appears, to cover cases where common rights were unclaimed or had been forgotten about altogether (Section 9 of the act also provided for situations in which the owner was unknown, investing such land in the care of the parish council). The consequence, however, was to encourage the registration of much land, most notably poor's allotments, over which common rights had long since been extinguished but which lacked a single private owner and were locally deemed in some sense 'public', and which were freely accessible and uncultivated. This was compounded by the way in which the registration process was organised. Any individual could propose a particular parcel to the registration authority (in this case Norfolk County Council) for consideration, during a three-year period beginning on 2 January 1967 and ending 2 January

1970. Notification of the application was made in the local press but there was no organised attempt to examine the history of the land in question, to ascertain who owned it or to discover the character of the rights enjoyed over it, although these were duly noted where known or claimed. Assertion of an area's status as common land by a single individual was sufficient, if unopposed by a deadline of 1 August 1972, to ensure registration. Only where the true status of the land in question, or its precise boundaries, were disputed was any real evidence considered. Such disputed applications were referred to Commons Commissioners but these officials were solicitors and barristers without historical training, and cases were considered on the basis of evidence submitted, without further research or investigation.

In such circumstances it is hardly surprising that the registered land included poor's allotments, surveyors' pits, public staithes and other land over which common rights had long been terminated, and in some cases had never existed, as well as 'commons' created by enclosure acts of which the users were joint owners and the manorial lord had no proprietorial rights. What came to be registered (or otherwise) thus largely reflected local opinion, which had long been confused about such matters. In the 1850s the poor of Catfield, keen that the trustees should rent out part of the poor's allotment and disburse the income amongst themselves, described it as their 'common right', while as we have seen Clarke in 1909 bemoaned the widespread confusion and uncertainty over whether particular areas were, or were not, common land, including the tendency in Norfolk to call 'privately-owned heathland or any area with furze on it, "common"'. In many villages, he reported, 'parishioners give the most contradictory accounts of what is, and what is not, communal property'.[86]

Conclusion

Our 'registered' commons are thus in some ways an unusual, random collection. While all true commons of significant size were registered, the situation with 'allotted' commons is more uneven: Church Green in Old Buckenham and Shotesham Common were both registered, Kelling Heath and Salthouse Heath were not. The inclusion on the register of the smaller commons – tiny, 'pocket handkerchief' greens found at road junctions within settlements, and the long linear greens (little more than wide roads) which are a particular feature of the claylands in the south of the county – seems especially random. It is, for example, unclear why the wonderful Lath Green in Shotesham, which maintains a width of between 20 and 65 metres for more than half a kilometre, was omitted from the register while, less than a kilometre to the south-west in the adjacent parish of Saxlingham Nethergate, the narrower but otherwise identical 'green' which extends for a kilometre to the south-east of Saxlingham Green was included (Figure 6.3). But it is the registration or otherwise of parish pits, fuel allotments and the like which appears most arbitrary. In particular,

while some very diminutive examples were registered, including the village pond in Yelverton (a water-filled surveyors' pit covering 0.2 hectares: Figure 6.4), many of the larger poor's allotments in the county were not. The registration of the great East Ruston 'Common', for example, proposed by the Norfolk Naturalists Trust, was successfully opposed by the trustees. A significant number of such places, however, such as Hoe 'Common', now have permitted public access as 'open land' under the Countryside and Rights of Way Act of 2000, as indeed have some of the 'allotted commons', including Kelling Heath and Salthouse Heath, which were omitted from the Register. While further confusing and blurring classifications and categories, this has the advantage of allowing them to be included in the discussions presented in the following chapters.

FIG. 6.3. The long lane extending for more than 600 metres south-east from Saxlingham Green, Saxlingham Nethergate, forms part of the registered area of that common.

FIG. 6.4. The village pond at Yelverton, a flooded Highways Surveyors' pit, is one of the smallest registered commons in Norfolk.

However, although a further piece of legislation, the Commons Act of 2006, made provision for the registration and protection of some village greens not already registered as common land, these additional sites are not discussed. This is in part because of their often manicured, suburbanised character and in part because the principal qualification for inclusion – that they were land which had been used by a significant number of local people for recreation 'as of right' (i.e. without permission, without force and without secrecy) for at least 20 years – takes us too far from the commons, and poor's allotments, that are our primary concern.

Notes

1. Clarke, *Commons of Norfolk*, 55.
2. Clarke, *Natural History*, 297.
3. Clarke, *Commons of Norfolk*, 56.
4. 23 & 24 Vict., c. 136; 39 & 40 Vict. c. 56.
5. NRO P/CH1/29.
6. White, *Directory*, 794.
7. *Report of the Commissioners*.
8. NRO PD 111/44.
9. Williamson and Yardy, *Broadland*, 305.
10. *Report of the Commissioners*, 84.
11. White, *Directory*, 336, 341, 484 and 653.
12. White, *Directory*, 350.
13. NRO PD 531/63. I am grateful to Keith Bacon for all the information relating to Catfield poors' allotment.
14. Williamson and Yardy, *Broadland*, 307.
15. NRO DN/TA 722.

16 NHER 15993.
17 NRO DN/TA 425; NRO DN/TA 192; NRO DN/TA 222; NRO DN/TA 563.
18 NRO DN/TA 560.
19 NRO DUN (C) 56–57, 499X5; NRO /Sca 2/236. The common at Whitwell had been established as a stinted common by the enclosure of 1804.
20 Birtles, Green Space, 209.
21 Clarke, Commons of Norfolk, 64.
22 Clarke, Natural History, 298; Clarke, Commons of Norfolk, 60.
23 Clarke, Natural History, 298–300.
24 Clarke, Natural History, 298.
25 Clarke, Commons of Norfolk, 63, 65.
26 Clarke, Commons of Norfolk, 59.
27 Clarke, Commons of Norfolk, 66.
28 Clarke, Natural History, 298.
29 M.C.H. Bird, The Rural Economy, Sport and Natural History of East Ruston Common, *Transactions of the Norfolk and Norwich Naturalists' Society*, 8 (1904–1909), 631–66.
30 Bird, Rural Economy, 645.
31 Birtles, Green Space, 205–10; 236–40.
32 Birtles, Green Space, 237.
33 TNA MAFF 25/36.
34 Rackham, *History of the Countryside*, 303–4.
35 W.G. Clarke, Some Breckland Characteristics, *Transactions of the Norfolk and Norwich Naturalists' Society* 8 (1904–1909), 555–78, at 567.
36 W.H. Burrell and W.G. Clarke, A Contribution to a Vegetation Survey of Norfolk, *Transactions of the Norfolk and Norwich Naturalists' Society* 9 (1909–1914), 743–56, at 751–5.
37 Bird, Rural Economy, 645.
38 Clarke, Natural History, 308.
39 Clarke, Natural History, 305–6.
40 Clarke, Natural History, 308; Burrell and Clarke, Vegetation Survey, 749.
41 Burrell and Clarke, Vegetation Survey, 749.
42 E.T. Boardman, The Development of a Broadland Estate at How Hill, Ludham, Norfolk, *Transactions of the Norfolk and Norwich Naturalists' Society* 15 (1939–1943), 5–21, at 14; E.L. Turner, The Status of Birds in Broadland, *Transactions of the Norfolk and Norwich Naturalists' Society* 11 (1919–1924), 227–40, at 231–2.
43 C.P. Petch, Fenlands of West Norfolk, *Transactions of the Norfolk and Norwich Naturalists' Society* 16 (1944–1948), 317–22, at 317.
44 Petch, Fenlands, 318–9.
45 NRO C/C 10/15.
46 A. Douet, Norfolk Agriculture 1914–1972, unpublished PhD thesis, University of East Anglia, 1989, 40.
47 NRO C/C 10/15. NRO C/C 10/17.
48 NRO C/C 10/17. NRO DC 12/41.
49 MAFF Agricultural Returns. See S. Wade Martins and T. Williamson, *The Countryside of East Anglia: Changing Landscapes, 1870–1950* (Woodbridge, 2008), 25.
50 Douet, Norfolk Agriculture, 266.
51 TNA MAFF 80/1866, 80/1867, 80/1869; Birtles, Green Space, 250; J. Dominy, Commons of East and Westt Rudham, in M. Manning (ed.), *Commons in Norfolk* (Norwich, 1988), 29–35.

52 Birtles, Green Space, 260–1.
53 Birtles, Green Space, 261–3.
54 TNA MAFF 80/1873 and 80/1874.
55 Bitrles, Green Space, 252.
56 Oral history record, Norfolk Wildlife Trust, interview of June Batstone by Stephanie Witham, 2018.
57 M.C.B. Dawes, M.R. Devine, H.E. Jones and M.J. Post, *Calendar of Inquisitions Post Mortem: Vol. 16, Richard II* (London, 1974), 235.
58 Wade Martins and Williamson, *Countryside of East Anglia*, 91–5.
59 J. Sheail, *Rabbits and their History* (Newton Abbot, 1971), 111–15.
60 L.R. Haggard and H. Williamson, *Norfolk Life* (London, 1943).
61 NRO WLS LXVIII/26 479x3.
62 L.R. Haggard, *Norfolk Notebook* (London, 1946), 57.
63 W.A. Nicholson, *A Flora of Norfolk* (London, 1914), 24.
64 Sheail, *Rabbits*, 202–7.
65 Sheail, *Rabbits*, 204.
66 *Transactions of the Norfolk and Norwich Naturalists' Society* 19 (1958–1961), 142.
67 *Transactions of the Norfolk and Norwich Naturalists' Society* 20 (1962–1963), 102.
68 *Transactions of the Norfolk and Norwich Naturalists' Society* 21 (1966–1968), 150.
69 G. Garrod, Ringmere, *Transactions of the Norfolk and Norwich Naturalists' Society* 22 (1969–1973), 73–82.
70 Garrod, Ringmere, 81.
71 A. Bull, Bawdeswell Heath, *Transactions of the Norfolk and Norwich Naturalists' Society* 22 (1969–1973), 268–70.
72 8 & 9 Vict. c. 118.
73 *Hansard*, Vol LXXIII (1844), col. 975.
74 39 & 40 Vict. c. 56.
75 Birtles, Green Space, 235–6.
76 56 & 57 Vict. c. 57.
77 15 & 16 Geo. V c. 20, Section 19: Rights of Public over Commons and Waste Lands.
78 Clarke, Commons of Norfolk, 55.
79 Clarke, Natural History, 294.
80 Birtles, Green Space.
81 Dudley Stamp and Hoskins, *Common Lands*; L. Dudley Stamp, *The Land of Britain: Its Use and Misuse* (London, 1948).
82 *Commons Journal*, Vol. 544, Col. 990; Vol. 600, Col. 687.
83 *Report of the Royal Commission on Common Land, 1955–1958* (London, 1958), 131.
84 Commons Registration Act, 1965 c. 64.
85 Birtles, Green Space, 277.
86 Clarke, Commons of Norfolk, 294–5.

CHAPTER 7

Common Heaths

'Heath' is a term for a specific type of land, characterised by vegetation dominated by heather and acid grassland.[1] The word has no necessary legal implications; there were always areas of heathland that were private property, alongside those that were common land. This said, until the parliamentary enclosures of the eighteenth and nineteenth centuries the overwhelming majority of heaths in Norfolk were commons, and the majority of commons were heaths. Even today, most of the registered commons in the county – by number and by area – might be so categorised. They have a number of features that mark them out clearly from, in particular, the clayland commons which are examined in the next chapter. Perhaps the most obvious is their current condition. Most are at least partially overgrown with scrub and secondary woodland. They are, for the most part, rougher and wilder places than their clayland cousins. This impression of wildness is compounded by their relationship with the disposition of settlement in the landscape. Whereas clayland commons, even huge ones like Brisley Green or Hales Green, are usually surrounded by houses, this is much less true of common heaths. A few, such as Roydon Common, have houses densely clustered at one end only; rather more, including Church Hill Common in Ringland, have two or three dwellings attached to one side; but many lie quite detached or even remote from settlements. This is partly because a significant number, even of the larger examples like Bryant's Heath, are in reality poor's allotments, cut out of a common at enclosure and incorporating, at most, only limited lengths of its boundary. But it is also because, as discussed in Chapter 1, many heaths had never been a focus for settlement because the sands and gravels they overlie, extending beyond the boundaries of the common itself, were porous and thus failed to provide a dependable water supply of the kind available to the farms and cottages clustered on the margins of clayland commons. And there are other, more subtle characteristics which distinguish these two broad varieties of common. In particular, whereas few features of archaeological interest are usually preserved by the unploughed turf of clayland commons, common heaths often contain a range of distinctive and important earthworks.

The Nature of Common Heaths

Because they overlay acid substrates, usually sands and gravels, common heaths were until the late eighteenth century most continuous and extensive where these account for most of the surface area; in south-west Norfolk, in the area known as Breckland; in the north-west of the county, especially on the strip of land running north from King's Lynn, along the margins of the Wash; in the north, most notably on the gravel ridge that runs, a little inland from the coast, between Holt and Cromer; and on the extensive areas of glacial sands lying to the north of Norwich. But isolated examples of heathland commons could be found well outside these areas, in the south and east of the county, the outcome of local accidents of geological history. Between the late eighteenth century, and the late twentieth, enclosure, followed by the vagaries of the registration process, both massively reduced the area of common heathland in Norfolk, and changed its distribution. There was, in particular, a wholesale reduction in Breckland with the disappearance of examples like Swaffham Heath, Cley Heath, Cressingham Heath, Lynford Heath, Breccles Heath, Hockham Heath, Tottington Heath, Mundford Heath, Santon Heath, Croxton Heath, Larling Heath and Kilverstone and Brettenham Heath. Some of these initially survived enclosure, in ecological terms, as areas of private heathland but most were subsequently acquired by the Forestry Commission, in the 1920s and 30s, and planted with commercial conifers.[2] By the outbreak of the Second World War Barnham Cross Common in Thetford was the only surviving example, although Foulden Common on the northern edge of the district arguably displays some 'Breckland' characteristics. In contrast, in north Norfolk, on the Holt–Cromer ridge, there are large areas of common heaths either registered as common land or otherwise freely accessible to the public, including Salthouse Heath, Kelling Heath, Holt Lowes and Incleborough Hill in West Runton. This contrast is part of a wider change. In the eighteenth century a significant proportion of common heaths were to be found on fine sands, often of no great depth, overlying chalk. Today almost all are associated with coarser sands and gravels of fluvioglacial origin, especially those of the 'Britons Lane Member', usually forming considerable thicknesses and/or overlying solid formations, such as the Crag or the Sandringham Sands, which were themselves composed of sands and gravels.

Norfolk heaths are all varieties of what the National Vegetation Classification scheme categorises as H1 *Calluna vulgaris – Festuca ovina* heath, characterised by heather, grasses like sheep's fescue, and gorse.[3] But there were and are important differences between the heaths associated with these two broad geological conditions. Those formed over deep deposits of sand and gravel have a stronger wood-pasture tradition: it is on heaths of this kind that significant stands of woodland survived into the Middle Ages and in some cases beyond. The Breckland heaths, in contrast, and many of those in west Norfolk more generally where sands overlie chalk, seem to have been denuded of trees from an early date.[4] The reasons for this difference remain unclear but probably reflect the fact that the western heaths lay interspersed with tracts of light, calcareous soils that supported particularly dense populations of prehistoric, Roman and Anglo-Saxon farmers, resulting in high levels of grazing, limiting the opportunities for new trees to establish themselves as old ones were felled or died.

FIG. 7.1. Heather, gorse and acid grassland, intermixed with areas of scrub and bracken, on Kelling Heath.

This was later compounded by the widespread establishment of rabbit warrens and subsequently of feral rabbit populations on these sandy, well-drained soils, coupled with the presence of the vast folding flocks which characterised these quintessential areas of sheep-corn farming. In other parts of the county, in contrast, heaths were often surrounded by land that was less attractive to early farmers and overlay thicker and more gravelly deposits, sometimes featuring a high water table, making them less conducive to rabbit farming, and to the early development of large feral populations. Sheep were grazed on them, but not normally on the scale seen in the west of the county (above, p. 16).

Similar factors shaped other important differences. Heaths in Breckland, and to an extent elsewhere in the west, are often dominated by grass communities, acidic in nature over sands but calcareous where the chalk comes to the surface (CG7 *Festuca ovina – Hieracium pilosella – Thymus praecox* grassland), although areas of more 'normal', heather-covered heathland, and stands of gorse, also occur.[5] These grass communities are of particular ecological importance, for they can include – albeit to a lesser degree than a century ago – lichen-rich subcommunities and rare plant species usually associated with coastal dunes or even the European steppe, such as purple stemmed cat's tail (*Phleum phleoides*) and Spanish catchfly (*Silene otites*). These characteristics again arise from a combination of soils and geology and the intensity of grazing, especially by rabbits.

A number of heaths still survive in Breckland displaying these characteristics but mainly on land, in many cases managed as nature reserves, owned by private individuals or organisations like the Norfolk Wildlife Trust. The only registered common of this type, as already noted, is Barnham Cross Common to the south of Thetford, registered as a Site of Special Scientific Interest (SSSI) on account of the variety of butterflies, moths and birds (over 60 breeding species) supported by its diverse habitats, and because it sustains populations of a number of the rare Breckland plants just mentioned.[6] It boasts areas of calcareous chalk heath, especially towards the north-west, dominated by red fescue (*Festuca rubra*), sweet vernal grass (*Anthoxanthum odoratum*) and false oat grass (*Arrhenatherum elatius*), and featuring a wide variety of flowering herbs such as stemless thistle (*Cirsium acaule*), common bird's-foot-trefoil (*Lotus corniculatus*), purging flax (*Linum catharticum*) and kidney vetch (*Anthyllis vulneraria*). Acid grassland, with tall growths of sand sedge (*Carex arenaria*) – another Breckland speciality – or sheep's fescue (*Festuca ovina*) predominates elsewhere, accompanied by rather sparse populations of cat's ear (*Hypochoeris radicata*), harebell (*Campanula rotundifolia*), sheep's sorrel (*Rumex acetosella*) and common hemp nettle (*Galeopsis tetrahit*). Typically, heather is sparse – mainly concentrated towards the south of the common – and greatly outnumbered by gorse, which in places now forms dense thickets, a sign of the lack of grazing that has also led to the development of areas of tall, less interesting grassland, hawthorn and blackthorn scrub, and patches of woodland featuring oak and Scots pine.

The majority of common heaths in Norfolk traditionally carried more conventional heathland vegetation, dominated by heather rather than grasses. The former includes not only *Calluna vulgaris* but also bell heather (*Erica cinera*), which is absent from the heaths of Breckland and from many of those in the north-west of the county. Gorse is also an important component, including in some cases both common gorse (*Ulex europaeus*) and western gorse (*Ulex gallii*), likewise unknown in Breckland, and broom is often present. But acid grassland also occurs, in patches or as extensive areas, featuring grasses like sheep's fescue, common bent, (*Agrostis capillaris*) creeping soft grass (*Holcus mollis*), Yorkshire fog, wavy hair-grass (*Deschampsia flexuosa*), purple moor-grass (*Molinia caerulea*) and early hair-grass (*Aira praecox*). These are accompanied by a limited number of herb species such as sheep's sorrel, heath bedstraw (*Galium saxatile*), common bird's-foot-trefoil and cat's ear, alongside less common plants like heath milkwort (*Polygala serpyllifolia*) and heath woodrush (*Luzula multiflora*), and rare ones like heath dog violet (*Viola canina*). In a number of places, as on Bryant's Heath near North Walsham, the water table lies sufficiently close to the surface for 'wet heath' to occur, in which heather and bell heather are replaced by cross-leaved heath (*Erica tetralix*), purple moor-grass is usually the dominant grass and characteristic species such as common cotton-grass

(*Eriophorum angustifolium*) and heath rush (*Juncus squarrosus*) are found.[7] Heaths, especially those dominated by extensive stands of heather, may boast a relatively restricted range of plants but they can sustain a rich fauna which includes adder (*Vipera berus*), common lizard (*Lacerta Zootoca vivipara*), brown hare (*Lepus europaeus*), birds like nightjar (*Caprimulgus europaeus*), linnet (*Carduelis cannabina*), woodlark (*Lullula arborea*), Dartford warbler (*Sylvia undata*) and turtle dove (*Streptopelia turtur*), and butterflies including the green hairstreak (*Callophrys rubi*), purple hairstreak (*Neozephyrus quercus*), small heath (*Coenonympha pamphilus*), grayling (*Hipparchia semele*), small copper (*Lycaena phlaeas*), wall (*Lasiommata megera*), and beetles like the Minotaur beetle (*Typhaeus typhoeus*) and tiger beetle (*Cicindela campestris*).[8]

As noted earlier, many common heaths in the north and east of the county (and in the west of the county, in the area lying between King's Lynn and Hunstanton) carried, into the post-medieval period, significant numbers of trees, principally oak. The latter seem to have been widely scattered across the area of the common rather than being grouped, as was usually the case with clayland commons, around the margins. Faden's county map suggests that some common heaths retained a measure of tree cover even in the late eighteenth century. A number of trees are, for example, shown scattered across the north-eastern portion of Stock Heath and some of these survived its enclosure in the early nineteenth century and are preserved within Middle Heath Plantation near Gunthorpe Park. Thirty-five pollarded oaks remain here, their small size (most have circumferences of less than 5 metres) reflecting both the close nature of the planting and the poor, leached character of the soils. Other examples, generally of similar size but including one magnificent 'champion' tree with a girth of nearly 8 metres, survive on the edge of Stow Bedon Mere, and were apparently growing on Stow Bedon Common before its enclosure in 1816.[9] But no examples of old pollards appear to survive today on any of the county's heathland commons. Most now include at least some areas which are densely covered with trees, but this is the result of relatively recent developments.

Dereliction and Management

Indeed, the overgrown condition of heathland commons is, as already emphasised, one of the features that distinguishes them from those found on clay, most of which are largely clear of trees and scrub. Heather dominated heathland is an example of a 'plagio-climax' vegetation, maintained in an artificially stable state by regular cutting, grazing, digging and trampling. When economic exploitation (or conservation management) comes to an end, succession resumes although its progress in twentieth-century Norfolk was to some extent slowed until the 1950s and 60s, as we have seen, by large feral rabbit populations. Under present conditions, the 'climax' vegetation on heathland commons is oak-dominated woodland but this only develops after a number of stages which, due to a variety of 'natural' and historic factors, may occur at different rates, and take slightly different forms, on different sites. On most heaths, a decline of management is initially accompanied by the spread of bracken, invading rapidly by means of its deeply buried rhizomes or root system and outcompeting the heather, and by an increase in the quantity of gorse, soon joined by blackthorn, hawthorn and birch. But on some heaths, and on some parts of heaths, scrub – especially gorse thickets – may colonise heather and acid grassland largely unaccompanied by bracken. In some circumstances the transition to scrub, and then to woodland, occurs within a few decades but elsewhere it is a much slower process.

A range of factors appears to influence these different trajectories of development. Rabbits consume young bracken less readily than domestic livestock but will eagerly eat young woody plants, including gorse, so derelict heaths with significant rabbit populations will tend to remain infested with bracken but relatively free of trees and scrub for longer than others (although very dense rabbit populations may *retard* bracken spread, at least on grass heaths). Conversely, trees and shrubs spread most rapidly where there is an abundant seed supply; where the heath adjoins a wood or plantation or, in the case of gorse, where significant amounts of the plant were already present on the heath at the point when it began to decline into dereliction. Gorse was a valued commodity which may have been protected on parts of some, but not all, managed commons. It may even have been deliberately planted, as it certainly was on some of the fragments of common which, following enclosure, became poor's allotments.

Gorse often plays an important role in the development of vegetation on derelict heaths because it is a legume which fixes Nitrogen directly in the soil, making the land more suitable for the establishment of trees. It also forms dense thickets which protect seedling trees from the rabbits, deer and any domestic livestock still grazed on the heath. The hawthorn or, in particular, blackthorn scrub which develops in other circumstances has a similar effect. The normal succession is for birch to invade first, followed by oak, but there is a measure of variation and on some heaths colonisation by oak may be equally or more rapid. There is some evidence that this is, and was, a particular feature of heaths on which gorse had become dominant but it is mainly related to landscape context and seed supply – whether there are significant numbers of oak trees growing in woods and hedges in the immediate vicinity of the common. The character of neighbouring planting can affect the composition of the successional vegetation in other ways. On Barrow Common sycamore is prominent, with some Scots and Corsican pine; on Church Hill Common in Ringland, oak and birch are accompanied by both sycamore and sweet chestnut, the latter a prominent component of the eighteenth and nineteenth-century woods in the local area. Here, as on some other sites, hazel also occurs, spreading in from the ancient hedge on the common's eastern boundary. The understorey of the secondary woodland displays much variation, sometimes featuring grasses and herbs, sometimes thickets of bramble and blackthorn, sometimes bracken.

Because the rate at which trees succeeded bracken and scrub has varied, the size of the largest trees may provide a poor guide to when serious cutting and grazing on a particular common came to an end. Few trees found on common heaths in Norfolk, however – except for the occasional birch, fast colonising and fast growing – have girths at waist height that are much in excess of 1.5 metres, while their low-branching form attests that they have developed in the absence of large grazing animals. In places, examples of oak or birch with multiple stems rising from ground level, like coppice stools, mark efforts made in the past to control the encroaching scrub or take an opportunistic crop of firewood. Norfolk's heathland commons are in a wide range of conditions. A few are entirely derelict and overgrown but on many some conservation management takes place. This is usually directed primarily at the maintenance or re-establishment of open stands of heather but often simply at retarding or reversing the spread of woodland and scrub.

Several of Norfolk's common heaths now consist entirely, or very largely, of oak dominated woodland, such as School Common and Mill Common in Southrepps and Alderford Common in Swannington. Somewhat surprisingly, the latter has nevertheless the status of an SSSI but this is not on account of its heathland flora but rather for that found growing in the deepest of the extraction pits associated with the former lime kiln there, where the chalk underlying the sands and gravels has been exposed, which features lime-loving plants such as wild basil (*Clinopodium vulgare*), burnet saxifrage (*Pimpinella saxifraga*), larger wild thyme (*Thymus pulegoides*), and common spotted orchid (*Dactylorhiza fuchsii*).[10] This said, like many other overgrown commons Alderford also sustains an important population of breeding birds, benefitting in particular from dense areas of blackthorn and hawthorn scrub.

More usually, the larger heathland commons have become extensively colonised by woodland or scrub, but part of their area remains open through regular cutting as part of government-funded schemes. Crostwight Heath, an open expanse of grass and heather in the 1950s, was still largely free of trees in the 1980s, although increasingly infested with bracken and gorse. Today it is mainly secondary oak and birch woodland but a rigorous programme of management by the Honing estate keeps around a quarter of its area as a wide expanse of grass and heather (Figure 7.2). Church Hill Common in Ringland retains a central, open grassy area kept free of the trees that have otherwise engulfed it (Figure 7.3). Another variation is where a common comprises large areas of bracken as well as secondary woodland, again alongside an area maintained by cutting as grass and heather. Broome Heath, managed by the Ditchingham estate, now comprises around 6 hectares of woodland, 4 hectares of bracken and 3 hectares of grass and heather (along with 2.5 hectares of mown 'amenity' grass).

Such mosaics provide a greater range of habitats than heathland alone would do but they are also enforced by the difficulties of maintaining more extensive areas of heather and acid grassland where fencing costs and public access, including by dogwalkers, render grazing impractical. The war on trees, scrub and bracken can be never ending. Hoe Common was, by the early 1980s, almost entirely occupied by dense gorse scrub, birch and bracken. A major gorse fire then allowed a sudden resurgence of heather across a significant area, but by the end of the decade bracken, gorse and young trees had re-established themselves. Volunteers then cleared an extensive area but this rapidly became infested with bracken, against which a long battle was waged through the 1990s and early 2000s, accompanied by further clearance of birch. Soil was scraped from the surface to remove the bracken litter, and rhizomes, and areas were planted with heather seed brought from Roydon Common. But only in the 2010s was the war really won. Larger areas were scraped using a JCB and birch stumps removed using a mechanical grinder, then livestock fencing was erected and sheep introduced, initially on a periodic basis but more recently as semi-permanent residents. Removal of scrub and mechanical flattening and bruising of bracken continued, and continues, alongside this.[11] The Common now consists of a central open area of heathland vegetation, ringed by a band of oak and birch woodland, and sustains a diverse flora and fauna that includes nearly a hundred different plant species and important populations of adders, slow worms, common lizards, and of invertebrates including the small heath and copper butterflies and the green tiger beetle.[12]

FIG. 7.2. Crostwight Heath.

Gorse and other heathland vegetation is extremely combustible in dry conditions, especially in an overgrown state, and on some Norfolk heaths, especially those much used recreationally by outside visitors, sporadic summer fires helped slow the encroachment of scrub even after the collapse of rabbit populations, although, as at Hoe, any renewed growth of heather was normally soon swamped by bracken and scrub. Salthouse Heath suffered a series of serious fires in the post-war period and aerial photographs suggest extensive, but fluctuating, areas of open heather and bracken. Well into the 1980s more than half the heath was free of trees and scrub and stands of heather remained extensive but over the following decade the incidence of fires declined and the extent of tree cover and bracken steadily increased. From the late 1990s, in part with grants from English Nature's Tomorrow's Heathland project, the heath's trustees undertook more systematic work, clearing scrub and encouraging grasses and heather; work continued under a Higher Level Stewardship scheme and with further assistance from Norfolk County Council, Norfolk Wildlife Trust, and from 2016 with the help of North Norfolk District Council's herd of Bagot goats. The area is now a complex mosaic of heather and grasses, bracken, gorse scrub and woodland, the haunt of nightingales and nightjars.[13]

On nearby Kelling Heath, a designated SSSI, there has likewise been an overall increase in trees and scrub since the 1980s but extensive stands of heather

FIG. 7.3. Church Hill Common, Ringland.

exist, alongside large bracken-infested areas, again maintained by a programme of active management.[14] A similar combination of habitats, although rather more overgrown and with areas of grass more than heather, exists further along the coast on Barrow Common in Brancaster. This is maintained in its current state by a management committee, established in 2004, which mows the grass areas twice a year, to keep bramble and bracken growth under control, and removes young trees, gorse and other encroaching scrub from selected areas on a rotating basis.[15] A dedicated band similarly works tirelessly to maintain the 17-hectare SSSI of Bryant's Heath near North Walsham as a mix of heath, wet heath, scrub and woodland.[16] Arguably the best managed area of heathland in Norfolk, and the place we can get closest to experiencing something of the spacious emptiness of the county's vast common heaths as they would have been before the parliamentary enclosures, is Roydon Common near King's Lynn. This National Nature Reserve, owned and managed by the Norfolk Wildlife Trust, is again, to an extent, a mosaic of habitats (including fen) but the overwhelming majority of its 195 hectares comprises grass and heather, grazed by cattle and ponies, with only a light scatter of trees (above, Figure 1.3).

The Archaeology of Common Heaths: Prehistoric

Heaths are, in archaeological terms, the most important variety of common land in Norfolk and in particular the only type on which significant numbers of prehistoric monuments are to be found. Indeed, out of only four surviving Neolithic long barrows in the county, one – at West Rudham – is located on a registered common and a second on the noted 'pseudo common' of Broome Heath, Ditchingham.[17] These monuments – large rectangular mounds with lateral quarry ditches, normally ranged east–west and often slightly higher at their eastern end – were built between around 3,800 and 2,500 BC; most contained chambers of wood in which the bones of the dead were placed over several generations.[18] Round barrows are more numerous monuments, mainly of early and middle Bronze Age date (2200–1500 BC), and were raised over inhumations or cremations.[19] They sometimes cluster around long barrows but more usually occur in their absence, singly or in groups. What is probably the largest and certainly the best-preserved bell barrow in Norfolk, that is, a round barrow with a distinct bank running around the outer rim of the quarry ditch, stands on Weasenham Lyngs, a registered common which originated as a poor's allotment; it is accompanied by two further round barrows and the sites of three others, with at least seven more on what is now private land but which previously formed part of the wider area of common land out of which the allotment was cut.[20] Other round barrows can be found a short distance to the east of the long barrow just noted, on West Rudham Heath; on Kelling Heath; on Broome Heath in Ditchingham; probably on Barrow Common in Brancaster; and on Alderford Common in Swannington (Figure 7.4).[21] Salthouse Heath and its easterly extension, Gallow Hill Common, boasts the largest concentration of

FIG. 7.4. The round barrow on Alderford Common, Swannington.

barrows in Norfolk, with at least 15 upstanding examples including Gallow Hill, Three Halfpenny Hill and Three Farthing Hill; the name of the first reflects the fact that it later, in the Middle Ages, became an execution site and probably the meeting place for Holt Hundred (Figure 7.5).[22] The names of the others may reflect the disappointment of early treasure hunters. The heath also features a large number of 'mini barrows' covering slightly later, late Bronze Age burials, although these are not really visible on the ground in the bracken, gorse and other undergrowth.

The association of prehistoric barrows and common land, and especially common heaths, would have been much more apparent before the parliamentary enclosures of the late eighteenth and nineteenth centuries.[23] Careful examination of Faden's 1797 map of Norfolk shows that well over 80 per cent of barrows surviving in the landscape today – usually on private heathland, within plantation, or on poor's allotments that were never registered under the act – then stood on common land. This close relationship mainly reflects the fact that these earthworks are vulnerable to destruction, especially by later agricultural activity. Surviving barrows are part of a wider population, otherwise represented only by the distinctive crop marks of levelled examples, best revealed from the air, known to archaeologists as 'ring ditches'. By the thirteenth century most of the land in Norfolk was under cultivation and earthwork remains of earlier phases of history had either been destroyed by the plough or deliberately levelled to make way for it. Most of the unploughed areas were common land. Areas of waste enclosed as deer parks or to create managed woodland also remained unploughed, it is true, but these tended to occupy the heavier soils where prehistoric settlement had been sparse; most parks were anyway ploughed up in the post-medieval period. A few barrows, or possible barrows, are known from

FIG. 7.5. Bronze Age barrows on Gallow Hill Common, Kelling, looking west towards the main area of Salthouse Heath. The barrows to the south (left) of the road have recently been cleared of vegetation. 'Gallow Hill' is the large barrow to the north of the road.

within areas of ancient woodland, such as that within Swanton Novers Great Wood, but overall commons were, by the eighteenth century, the only places they were likely to survive.[24]

This is a neat, economical explanation but may not be the full story, for there is little evidence for other kinds of upstanding prehistoric earthworks, such as the low linear banks marking the remains of field systems, on heathland commons. To some extent the association may reflect the fact that barrows, and especially the larger groups of barrows, were like many commons located on the margins of the main cultivated areas. They may, indeed, have been deliberately placed towards the fringes of social territories based on lower, more fertile ground, perhaps as a symbolic assertion of ownership and control of marginal grazing grounds. In this context, attention might be drawn to the location of some of the most important concentrations of barrows in the county. The long barrow at West Rudham occupies a surviving fragment of West Rudham Common and is accompanied, to the east, by at least four round barrows located on other parts of the common, and within a plantation planted on a portion somehow severed from it immediately after the Second World War.[25] The common lies on the southern boundary of the parish and 200 metres to the south, in what was formerly Harpley Common, lies the truncated remains of another long barrow, accompanied by two further round barrows.[26] In the eighteenth century there was an extensive area of heathland here, and aerial photographs reveal the sites of numerous lost barrows. The way in which the boundaries of a number of parishes seem to stretch out to converge on the area from settlements based on lower ground – Harpley, West Rudham, East Rudham, Helhoughton, West Raynham, Weasenham St Peter, Weasenham All Saints and Little Massingham – emphasises its remote, liminal character and the importance to medieval communities of the resources it afforded, given that most of the land in the locality was under cultivation. Significantly, it lies on the watershed between the Babbingley River, draining west into the Wash, and the Wensum, flowing east to join the Yare in Norwich.

A similar situation occurs in the south of Weasenham All Saints. Here, as noted earlier, there is a cluster of barrows in the plantations around the Great Barrow on Weasenham Lyngs poor's allotment, all of which stood on Weasenham Heath before its enclosure in 1809.[27] Another example survives a few hundred metres to the east, on what was the adjoining common of Litcham Heath until its enclosure in 1856, and the sites of at least five lost barrows, marked by ring ditches, are scattered across the surrounding area.[28] Here, too, albeit less dramatically, parish boundaries – of Rougham, East Lexham, West Lexham, Litcham, Tittleshall, Wellingham and Weasenham – extended up to embrace the heath, which again occupied a topographically significant location, this time on the watershed between the Wensum and west-draining Nar. Less strikingly, the nine round barrows on Salthouse Heath are accompanied by further upstanding examples in adjacent plantations established on land enclosed from it in the 1780s, and are surrounded by a penumbra of ploughed-out examples appearing on aerial photographs. Heath, and barrows, occupy what is almost an island of high ground, with the sea to the north, river Glaven to the west, and minor valleys, largely dry, to south and east. The parishes of settlements on lower ground again extend up to reach it – Salthouse, Wiveton, Bayfield, Holt and Kelling.

The association of barrows and common heaths, while mainly arising from the character of the latter as unploughed spaces, may thus owe something to the tendency for major clusters of barrows to occur in the same topographically marginal locations as heathland, possibly because they were deliberately placed on the edges of the territories of communities whose fields and settlements occupied more fertile ground.[29] This said, clusters of barrows on common heaths are not only a feature of remote watersheds. The 'pseudo-common' of Broome Heath (above, p. 113) boasts a Neolithic long barrow, accompanied by two round barrows. There were once further examples: in 1858 Greville Chester reported how 'on the heath on the borders of Broome and Ditchingham, several tumuli existed until recently, when, with one or two exceptions, they have been carried away'.[30] At least two others survived into the twentieth century but were then destroyed by gravel extraction.[31] Occupying a site on low ground overlooking the river Waveney, this does not seem like an obviously 'marginal' site and indeed, in 1970 and 1971 a Neolithic settlement was excavated in the south-western section of the heath, little more than 100 metres from the long barrow.[32] It was marked by a scatter of postholes, pits and hearths, and produced over 9,000 sherds of Neolithic pottery (representing around 420 vessels) and more than 22,000 struck flint flakes: Bronze Age material was also present. This occupation area partly lies within an enclosure, measuring roughly 150 metres north–south and 100 metres east–west, defined by a C-shaped bank and ditch that never appears to have continued along its eastern side. Excavation revealed that the bank was originally faced with light timbers and carried a palisade or fence along the top, and that in places it was accompanied by a smaller outer bank and ditch. Pollen evidence suggests that the site already lay within an area of acid grassland, rather than woodland.[33] Broome Heath thus appears rather different to the places just discussed, a core area of settlement rather than a territorial margin. But it is possible that the excavated site, rather than being a permanently occupied settlement, in fact represents transient, seasonal occupation, related to feasting and ceremonies on the boundary between communities occupying different sections of the long Waveney valley.

The Archaeology of Common Heaths: Medieval and Later

Most of the archaeological features found on common heaths are significantly later in date, more humdrum in character and, superficially at least, less interesting than the prehistoric barrows just discussed. Indeed, even on those commons where barrows survive they are usually interspersed with medieval and post-medieval earthworks relating to the management and exploitation of heathland. On Broome Heath the long barrow has an unusual linear 'tail' that extends for some 43 metres from its south-eastern end, c. 5 metres wide and around 0.6 metres high. Geophysical survey reveals that it was added to the barrow at a later date. In size and shape it resembles a 'pillow mound', a type of earthwork used to accommodate rabbits on medieval and post-medieval warrens or, more usually in eastern England, to house pioneer populations when warrens were first established.[34] On Salthouse Heath there are, in addition to the barrows, a number of 'hollow ways' – erosion hollows marking the lines of early trackways – those where the ground falls away in the south-eastern corner of the common forming a complex, braided pattern. Such features are known from other common heaths in the county, including Kelling Heath; they are effectively undatable and while most are probably medieval a few could be much older. More intriguingly, in a number of places on Salthouse Heath, Lidar reveals patterns of parallel lines, varying in spacing but often closely set, some formed by low banks but others more vaguely defined and appearing, in the words of the Norfolk Historical Environment Record, 'more akin to ridge and furrow'.[35] The lines form blocks which lie on a number of different orientations. Similar patterns are apparent on Lidar images on other common heaths, including Barrow Common in Brancaster, where a number of blocks covering much of the heath again lie on different alignments; and Syderstone Common. All appear to be the archaeological traces of heathland 'doles' of medieval or post-medieval date, both defined and exploited in a variety of ways – cut for whins or dug for 'dry ground turf' (above, pp. 50–51).

The most frequently encountered archaeological features on heathland commons, however, are various kinds of pit. Few people would probably consider these as 'archaeological' at all but they have much to tell us about the character of common land and the rights exerted over it, and some examples may be of considerable antiquity. Abel Heath lies on the parish boundary between Blickling and Aylsham, most of its 6 hectares occupied by extraction pits. Like many commons located on boundaries, the heath was the subject of several disputes between the communities living on either side. One, in 1441, involved the digging of pits by the residents of Silver Street in Blickling on the Aylsham side of the heath; another, in 1622, led to the heath and parish boundary being surveyed.[36] The map clearly marks one of the larger of the pits which exists on the common today. Pits (and associated ponds) are also a characteristic feature of clayland commons but those on common heaths tend to be more widely scattered and to take up a much greater proportion of the area. Sometimes small, scattered, discrete pits occur but often deeper continuous or near-continuous quarries. It is impossible to date different patterns of extraction, or even to estimate the length of time over which they may have developed.

The various 6-inch and 25-inch Ordnance Survey maps from the late nineteenth and early twentieth centuries frequently mark extraction pits on common heaths but these must have been the most obvious examples, or those still in active use, for Lidar images almost invariably reveal more extensive workings, their scale often hard to appreciate on the ground because they are obscured by areas of gorse or other impenetrable scrub, or by dense secondary woodland. The First and Second Edition 6-inch maps, surveyed in 1885 and 1905 respectively, thus show a single discrete pit in the centre of Crostwight Heath, and a smaller one towards its northern edge, but Lidar suggests that nearly 30 per cent of its area has been quarried away (Figure 7.6). The same maps depict slightly more extensive workings on Bryant's Heath in Felmingham near North Walsham but give no indication that around two thirds of its surface area had been removed by quarrying, presumably before it became a poor's allotment, covering more than 40 acres (16 hectares), following the enclosure of Walsham Heath in 1814.[37]

In both these places the Ordnance Survey maps mark the excavations as 'sand pits' but here, and more generally, the principal material dug from heathland commons was gravel. Although sand was required by medieval and post-medieval communities for a wide range of purposes, there was a much

7. *Common Heaths* 157

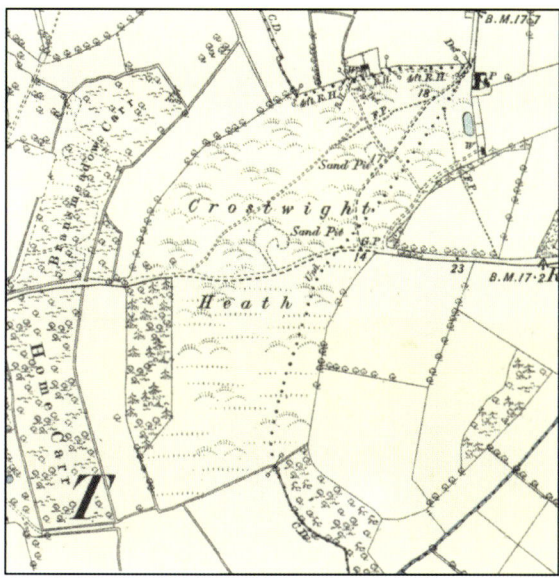 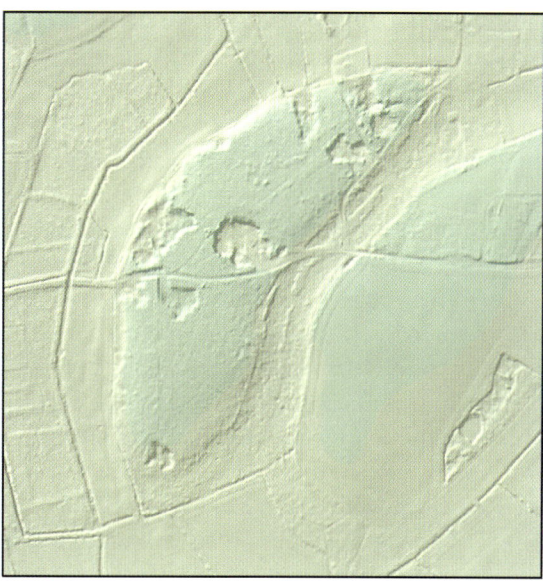

FIG. 7.6. Extraction pits on Crostwight Heath, as depicted on the First Edition Ordnance Survey 6-inch map of 1885 (left) and as revealed by Lidar (right).

greater need for gravel, vast quantities of which were, before the development of more sophisticated forms of road surfacing, required to maintain both public and private roads. This explains why, as we have seen, plots of land for the extraction of gravel were so frequently allotted to the parish highways surveyors by enclosure commissioners, a significant number of which came to be registered as common land under the 1965 Act. Many of these allotments probably enclosed pits on commons which were already being used for the purpose and most were fairly small, covering a hectare or less; that lying within the poor's allotment on Bryant's Heath, for example, comprised a little over an acre and a half. Much of the gravel removed over the centuries was probably taken by private individuals, to fulfil the obligations laid on them by law for the maintenance of public roads, or to surface their own private roads, carriage drives, yards and garden walks. Turnpike Trusts established from the late seventeenth century, in Norfolk as elsewhere, to improve and maintain the principal arterial roads, were also major consumers. The extent of excavations is thus to some extent a reflection of the power of manorial lords, owners of the 'soil' of the common, to sanction the kind of large scale excavation for private use that might reduce the amount of grazing or other resources available to commoners. This said, much material was probably dug from commons without formal permission, especially in the later stages of their history when manorial control, and interest, was often waning. The commons at Southrepps have been extensively dug for sand and gravel over an extended period of time. Extensive extraction scars exist on Bradfield Road Common while around half of the surface of School Common is occupied by pits of varying depth, the largest and deepest towards its western end. Perhaps not surprisingly, in 1883 the Lord of the Manor posted a notice, threatening 'stringent legal proceedings' on anyone found guilty of digging 'sand, gravel or other material … upon the land known as Southrepps Common' (Figure 7.7).[38]

Not all pits on heathland commons were dug solely or primarily to obtain sand or gravel. Some were for the exploitation of an underlying deposit, although the overburden was doubtless also used to advantage. One of the surviving commons in Hunworth consists entirely of a deep wooded pit, dug through sandy surface deposits to reach the fractured upper layers of the chalk, which could be spread on the fields to reduce the acidity of the soil. It was in existence by 1839, when it was recorded on the tithe map as 'Town Marl Pit'.[39] More dramatic is the case of Alderford Common in Swannington, already discussed (above, p. 74). The lime kiln shown here on Faden's map of Norfolk continued to operate into the twentieth century and nearly half the surface area of the 44-acre (17-hectare) common, now engulfed in woodland and scrub, is occupied by extraction pits of various sizes.

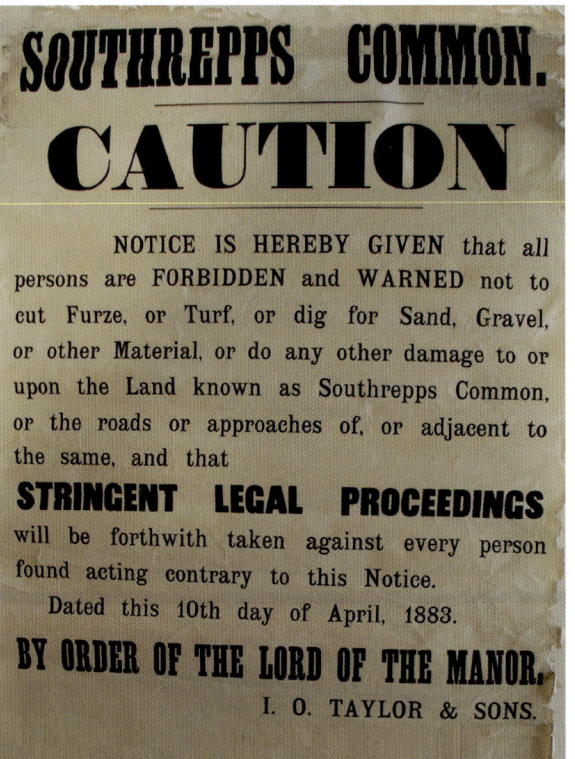

FIG. 7.7. Notice prohibiting removal of sand, gravel and gorse from the commons at Southrepps, 1883.

The most distinctive aspect of heathland commons and poor's allotments, and the one that distinguishes them most sharply from commons found on clay soils, is the large number that contain earthworks and other features relating to military activity in the First and, in particular, the Second World War. They form part of a wider population found, like the prehistoric monuments discussed earlier, on similar heathy land which passed into private ownership with the enclosures of the eighteenth and nineteenth centuries. A wide variety of features are represented. Some are built structures. Barrow Common in Brancaster, for example, boasts a concrete shed with iron framed windows, and an underground bunker, associated with a radar station that operated here between 1940 and 1944 (Figure 7.8). The northern section of Salthouse Heath is littered with the remains of another, including the footings of buildings, a blast shelter, and the four concrete bases of a large pylon aerial; while entrances to the collapsed concrete tunnels of a Second World War underground command centre can be seen on Incleborough Hill Common in West Runton.[40] Whin Common, Denver contains a pillbox and the meagre traces of a searchlight battery.[41] But most such remains take the form of earthworks – trenches and gun emplacements – dug for military training, by both the Home Guard and the regular army. Small 'foxholes' and 'weapons pits' dating from the Second World War are a common feature, with notable examples dug into the barrows on Broome Heath, Ditchingham.[42]

FIG. 7.8. The remains of the Second World War radar station on Barrow Common, Brancaster.

Narrow 'slit' trenches, like those on Holt Lows, are also often found, and wider examples are sometimes present. Most take simple, linear forms but more complex, 'zig-zag' and crenelated types occasionally occur. The dating of the latter is problematic. While often resembling the kinds of defences familiar from the First World War, some probably date from the early stages of the Second. Almost certainly of the former vintage is the magnificent complex on Hoe 'Common', comprising two groups of deep trenches, separate and symmetrical, each comprising two zig-zag trenches lying parallel and c. 25 metres apart which are linked by three zig-zag trenches running at right angles. To the south-west, and north-east, a series of parallel banks and ditches probably represent shooting butts (Figure 7.9).[43] The sophistication and regularity of the system suggests large scale training by the professional army. At the other extreme, the short, shallow and rather irregular stretch of trench on School Common in Southrepps seems to represent a practice machine-gun position dug by the local Home Guard during the Second World War (Figure 7.10). In many cases, such features are only really visible on the aerial photographs taken by the RAF shortly after the end of the war, for the areas in question are now engulfed in gorse, bracken and other vegetation. Little can be seen on the ground today, for example, of the extensive array of long slit trenches, gun emplacements and weapons pits dug within an extensive Second World War training area on Incleborough Hill in West Runton. More can be seen on Broome Heath, where parts of an extensive array of foxholes, and crenelated and zig-zag trenches, are visible where the vegetation is shorter, although much has been destroyed by post-war gravel extraction.

160   *The Landscapes of Common Land*

FIG. 7.9. First World War training trenches on Hoe Common, photographed by the RAF in 1946.

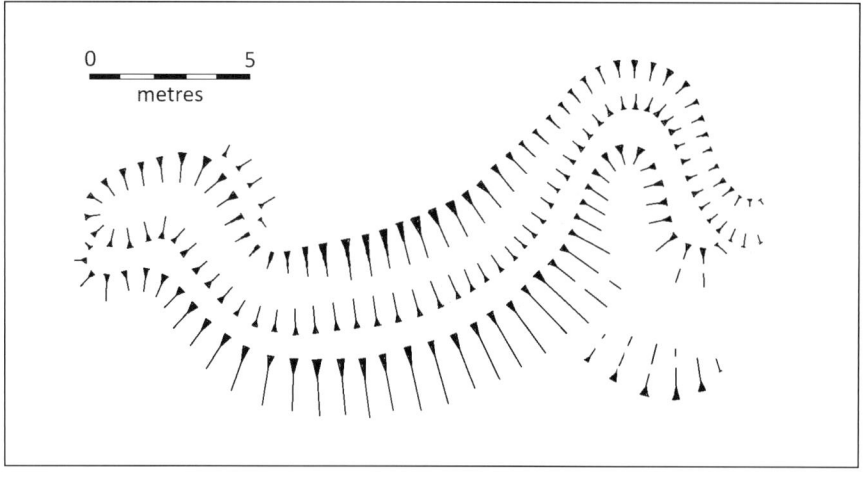

FIG. 7.10. Earthworks of probable Home Guard machine gun position, School Common, Southrepps.

The abundance of such remains on heathland commons must largely reflect the fact that by 1939, and to a significant extent even in 1914, they had effectively become economically redundant. Many were no longer regularly grazed, few were exploited for fuel or litter. Even at a time of blockades and rationing, few, as we have seen, were deemed worthy of cultivation. Yet at the same time they had not yet degenerated to secondary woodland, while on many examples even the spread of gorse and other scrub had only occurred to a limited extent, ensuring that they provided the open areas required for military purposes. Clayland commons, in contrast, still provided valuable grazing while a few, as we have seen, were drained and re-seeded, or ploughed up and used to grow crops. Heaths could best contribute to the war effort by providing spaces for training or other military installations, thus avoiding the loss of farmland.[44] In many parts of northern and western Norfolk commons and poor's allotments constituted only a small proportion of the poor quality heathy land that could be used for military purposes and here they might form a part of more extensive training areas which extended onto adjacent areas of private land. The pits and trenches on Incleborough Hill in West Runton, for example, represent one small section of a militarised zone that embraced not only nearby Town Hill Common (where practice trenches survive) but also more than a square kilometre of the surrounding heaths.[45] In contrast, across much of central and southern Norfolk heathland commons formed isolated pockets within what was, and is, more fertile land; places like Hoe Common and Broome Heath accordingly formed discrete 'islands' of military activity, and thus today of military archaeology.

There are other reasons why the north Norfolk heaths are so liberally strewn with wartime remains. They tend to occupy areas of gravel capping the highest ground, overlooking the sea, and thus made ideal locations, on this vulnerable coast, in which to place observation posts and radar stations, which required as clear and unimpeded a seaward view as possible – as amply provided by the sites on Barrow Common and Salthouse Heath (Figure 7.8). The vulnerability of the coast from attack by incoming aircraft was also reflected at the latter site by the presence of an anti-aircraft battery and a dummy or decoy airfield, alongside extensive training areas.[46]

The Character of Common Heaths

Heathland commons thus have an archaeological character all of their own and display a range of features that mark them out from other varieties of common land. While some of these remains are of relatively recent date, the prehistoric barrows found at places like Salthouse Heath seem to affirm the antiquity of the landscapes in which they are set. Yet in many ways Norfolk's heaths are the creation of the last century or so, their current appearance shaped by economic redundancy and dereliction to a greater extent than clayland commons. 'Dereliction' is, however, a loaded word. Common heaths have certainly *changed*, with few now providing the extensive panoramas of close-cropped grass and heather that would have been so familiar to Norfolk people in the eighteenth century. But even viewed as cultural landscapes, social artefacts, their current, more wooded appearance could in some ways be viewed as a return to the wood-pasture heathlands of the Middle Ages. And similar complexities confront us when we consider these areas in ecological terms, for the contribution they make to the maintenance of biological diversity. Beetley Common, covering over 9 hectares, was an open heath in the 1950s but is now almost completely wooded. Yet its importance as a habitat may not, on some measures, be any the less. More than 90 different plants, a mixture of woodland and relict heathland species, have been recorded there, as well as adders and slow worms.[47] Where commons are managed in such a way that they include both secondary woodland and areas of heathland, moreover, the number of species sustained will be significantly greater than it would be by either habitat alone. Common heaths thus raise important questions about how we should manage semi-natural landscapes like these, with a cultural and historical as well as an ecological importance: whether, that is, we should necessarily strive to maintain them in, or return them to, their open, grazed, 'traditional' condition, or embrace to a significant degree their new, 're-wilded' character. And the fact that we are called upon to make such choices highlights vividly both the essentially unnatural character of these seemingly 'wild' places, and how far we have come from the world of the agrarian, pre-industrial societies whose more practical needs first shaped them.

Notes

1 J. Parry, *Heathland* (London, 2003); Webb, *Heathlands*.
2 G. Backhouse, Thetford Forest, in H.L. Edlin (ed.) *East Anglian Forests* (London, 1972), 4–14; H.J. Joly de Lotbiniere, Afforestation in Breckland, *Transactions of the Norfolk and Norwich Naturalists' Society* 12 (1924–1928), 673–7; K. Skipper and T. Williamson, *Thetford Forest: Making a Landscape 1922–1997* (Norwich, 1997).
3 J.S. Rodwell (ed.), *British Plant Communities, Volume 2: Mires and Heaths* (Cambridge, 1992), 372–82.
4 G. Barnes, P. Dallas, H. Thompson, N. Whyte and T. Williamson, Heathland and Wood Pasture in Norfolk: Ecology and Landscape History, *British Wildlife* 18 (2007), 395–403.
5 Clarke, Some Breckland Characteristics; P. Dolman and W. Sutherland, The Ecological Changes of Breckland Grass Heath and the Consequences of Management, *Journal of Applied Ecology* 29, 2 (1992), 402–13; A.S. Watt, Studies in the Ecology of the Breckland IV: The Grass Heath, *Journal of Ecology* 28 (1940), 42–70.
6 Natural England citation, Barnhamcross Common: https://designatedsites.naturalengland.org.uk/PDFsForWeb/Citation/1000547.pdf, accessed online 23.8.2024.
7 Natural England citation, Bryant's Heath: https://designatedsites.naturalengland.org.uk/PDFsForWeb/Citation/1000770.pdf, accessed 3.6.2024.
8 Parry, *Heathland*; Webb, *Heathlands*.
9 G. Barnes and T. Williamson, *Ancient Trees in the Landscape; Norfolk's Arboreal Heritage* (Oxford, 2007), 108–10.
10 Natural England citation, Alderford Common: https://designatedsites.naturalengland.org.uk/PDFsForWeb/Citation/1000483.pdf, accessed 3.6.2024.
11 Hoe and Worthing Archive, http://www.hoeandworthingarchive.org.uk/common.html, accessed 4.6.2024.
12 Survey for Norfolk Wildlife Trust by J.M. Parmenter; R.M. Leaney & T. Doncaster, July 2019. http://www.hoeandworthingarchive.org.uk/hoe_common%20_2019_plant_list.pdf, accessed 5.6.2024

13 Site description, County Wildlife Site 2017; Salthouse History, https://www.salthousehistory.co.uk/heath2.html, accessed 6.7.2024; Norfolk Biodiversity Partnership, Lowland Heath Action Plan, https://www.norfolkbiodiversity.org/assets/Uploads/Lowland-heathland-and-dry-acid-grassland-HAP2.pdf, accessed 5.7.2024.
14 Natural England citation, Kelling Heath: https://designatedsites.naturalengland.org.uk/PDFsForWeb/Citation/1002812.pdfWildlife, accessed 5.7.2024.
15 Barrow Common, https://www.barrowcommonbrancaster.com/uploads/1/3/2/5/132570821/barrow_common_history.pdf, accessed 12.7.2024.
16 Bryant's Heath and Stow Heath, https://felminghampc.org.uk/bryants-and-stow-heaths/, accessed 12.7.24.
17 NHER 3611, 10597.
18 D. Field, *Earthen Long Barrows: The Earliest Monuments in the British Isles* (Stroud, 2006).
19 A. Woodward, *British Barrows: A Matter of Life and Death* (Stroud, 2000).
20 NHER 3658; 11282 and 25648; 3659, 3660, and 3662; and 3654, 3655, 3656, 3657, 25447, 25448 and 3688.
21 NHER 3628, 3624, 3625, 2626, 11287; 10611, 10624; 1363; 7705.
22 NHER 38629.
23 A.J. Lawson, E.A. Martin and D. Priddy, *The Barrows of East Anglia, East Anglian Archaeology* 12 (East Dereham, 1981), 53–62.
24 Barnes and Williamson, *Rethinking Ancient Woodland*, 232–35; NHER 40182.
25 NHER 3611, 3628, 3624, 3625, 2626, 11287.
26 NHER 3637, 3638, 3639.
27 NHER 3658; 11282 and 25648; 3659, 3660, and 3662.
28 NHER 3654, 3655, 3656, 3657, 25447, 25448 and 3688.
29 Lawson *et al.*, *Barrows of East Anglia*, 61–2, notes the relationship with commons but not with topography.
30 Proceedings of the Committee, *Norfolk Archaeology*, 5 (1859), 357–65, at 361–2.
31 NHER 10623, 10632
32 NHER 10602.
33 G.J. Wainwright, G.W. Dimbleby, A. Evans and J.G. Evans, The Excavation of a Neolithic Settlement on Broome Heath, Ditchingham, Norfolk, England, *Proceedings of the Prehistoric Society* 38 (1972), 1–97.
34 Giles Carey, Geophysical Survey, Ditchingham Long Barrow, GPR, and Magnetic Survey Report, unpublished report for the Prehistoric Society, 2017; R. Loveday and T. Williamson, Rabbits or Ritual? Artificial Warrens and the Neolithic Long Mound Tradition, *Archaeological Journal* 145 (1988), 290–313. It is, in fact, possible that the C-shaped enclosure, although considered by the excavator to be contemporary with the Neolithic settlement, is also associated in some way with rabbit farming; no firm dating evidence was produced by the excavations and the bank and ditch cut through, rather than simply enclose, the area of occupation.
35 NHER 27931 and 27957.
36 NRO FX 11/1; W. and M. Vaughan-Lewis, *Hearths and Heaths: Dispersed Settlements in Aylsham's Early Modern Landscape* (Itteringham, 2017), 76–7.
37 NRO C/Sce 1/1.
38 NRO GTN 3/7/6/4.
39 NRO DN/TA 370.
40 NHER 31786, 23386 and 30589.
41 NHER 32377.
42 NHER 43776.

43 NHER 30929.
44 T. Williamson, J. Bumstead, J. Frost, L. Owens and S. Pease, The Landscape Archaeology of Knettishall Heath, Suffolk and its Implications, *Landscapes* 18 (2017), 161–77.
45 NHER 38548.
46 NHER 27855 and 13566.
47 Site description, County Wildlife Site 1036.

CHAPTER 8

Fens, Greens and Marshes

This chapter discusses the character and current condition of registered commons in Norfolk other than heaths. These might, for convenience, be divided into three categories: 'clayland commons', often described as 'greens', mainly found on the poorly draining soils of the till plateau in the centre and south of the county; 'fens', overlying deposits of waterlogged peat on the floodplains of streams and rivers; and those commons, some described as 'marshes', occupying similar but more silty, alluvial land in such locations. These categories are useful and historically meaningful, in that they describe parcels of land exploited in particular ways, and which now display a specific range of ecological and archaeological characteristics. But they need to be used with caution. The boundaries between them have always been blurred, especially in the case of the floodplain or 'low' commons. An individual common, moreover, can extend over land in more than one category, or include in addition an area of heath; while the categories themselves are broad, embracing a range of variants or types.

Fens

Ecologists have defined a number of different kinds of 'fen' but all are essentially man-made (Figure 8.1). Without some kind of management, all will develop into something else and, eventually, into wet woodland, dominated by alder. As with heaths, traditional forms of exploitation, involving the cutting and removal of plant material and grazing, maintained the vegetation in a 'plagioclimax' or artificially stable state. Different forms of management also had their own specific impact. Mowing for litter or hay reduced the height and density of the taller plants and lowered nutrient levels, thus reducing the vigour of the more robust species and increasing the amount of light reaching the ground surface, ensuring the survival of lower growing species and increasing diversity. Where, more rarely, areas of fen were principally grazed the taller species were suppressed and grasses, low-growing plants and coarse rushes and sedges flourished.[1] And where areas containing a high proportion of reeds were regularly mown in the winter for thatching materials they tended to develop as ever purer stands, a dominance that might persist for more than a century after this form of management had been abandoned. But while the vegetation was shaped by how fens were exploited, this in turn was strongly influenced by natural factors. The wettest areas, where the water table remains at or above the ground surface for much of the year, were most likely to be cut for reeds and sedge, and least

FIG. 8.1. Boughton Fen, an SSSI, was created as an 'allotted' common by the parliamentary enclosure of 1803.

likely to be grazed. The driest areas tended to be managed as fen meadow, in which case they were often divided into privately owned strips and no longer treated as common land (above, p. 52).

Most fens lying between these extremes were predominantly managed by mowing, for litter or rough marsh hay, but some were mainly grazed. This was usually where the fen formed only one part of a common otherwise characterised by heath or some other kind of grazed land, or where the area of fen was so extensive that it would have provided more cut material than the commoners could use; in the latter circumstance part of the fen was grazed throughout the summer and measures taken to exclude livestock from mown areas until the harvest was over. Such diverse forms of management were still continuing in 1909, when Clark described how Bressingham Fen, Caldecote Fen and Broadwater Common in Thetford were managed by mowing but fens at Boughton, Flordon, Roydon near Diss, South Lopham and elsewhere were both regularly grazed *and* mown; while Foulden Common, around half of which comprises fen, was said to be grazed 'from May to Michaelmas'.[2] But many of these areas were poor's allotments, used in a different way to the commons of which they formed the remains, and the management of particular commons doubtless changed over time.

Common fens and, in particular, fuel allotments were dug for peat, and this also had a major impact on their ecology. In the first instance it led to the creation of areas of water. The 'broads' in east Norfolk were unusual in their depth and extent: even in this area peat extraction usually produced shallow 'turf ponds' less than 1.5 metres in depth, often in the form of narrow rectangular doles, which were immediately colonised by common reed (*Phragmites australis*), saw sedge (*Cladium mariscus*) and lesser bulrush (*Typha angustifolia*), soon joined by various herbaceous species in vigorous succession.[3] These together produced fresh peat at a rapid rate, as much as 1.5 cm per year, so that even nineteenth-century cuttings are usually so full of secondary peat that they are scarcely visible on the ground today.[4] But, as Jo Parmenter has demonstrated, they may still support vegetation which is markedly different from that growing over adjacent areas of solid peat, although taking a variety of forms due to variations in the way in which the terrestrialised areas were subsequently managed, coupled with various purely natural factors.[5]

The latter also had, and have, a more general influence on the vegetational composition of fens, especially the character of the water flowing into them; the extent to which it is derived from a stream or river, run-off from adjacent areas of higher ground, precipitation or valley side springs. These, in different locations and permutations, affect the salinity and nutrient levels within the fen, and also its acidity. Most fens are to some extent acidic, especially in their drier areas where the peat may be oxidising, but the ingress of alkaline groundwater from springs and seepage lines – in Norfolk, from a chalk aquifer or to a lesser extent some of the Crag deposits – can lead to the development of communities with a significant calciphile (lime loving) component, as on Honing Common, and, where areas are largely or only irrigated by such water, to the development of 'mires' only composed of such plants.[6]

A number of registered commons in Norfolk include fens of exceptional ecological character. Foulden Common is an SSSI with extensive areas of fen dominated by saw sedge, accompanied by reed, cotton grass (*Eriophorum angustifolium*) and marsh pennywort (*Hydrocotyle vulgaris*). There are also drier areas occupied by a form of fen meadow dominated by purple moor-grass, blunt-flowered rush (*Juncus subnodulosus*), black bog rush (*Schoenus nigricans*), and with early marsh orchid (*Dactylorhiza incarnata*) and purple small-reed (*Calamagrostis canescens*).[7] The common, which also includes much dry grassland, was by the early twentieth century grazed rather than mown but archaeological evidence for banks subdividing the western section of the fen and (less certainly) for peat digging suggests an earlier history of more varied and compartmentalised exploitation. Leziate Fen, part of a wider SSSI, is very different. Although significantly drier than it would have been in the past due to agricultural drainage of the adjacent land, this would always have been less waterlogged and the deposits of peat are thinner. It mainly comprises damp acid grassland with purple moor-grass, sheep's fescue, common bent, sheep's sorrel and soft rush (*Juncus effuses*), accompanied by a variety of plants characteristic of marshy meadows including marsh pennywort, devil's bit scabious (*Succisa pratensis*), tormentil (*Potentilla erecta*) and bottle sedge (*Carex rostrata*).[8] A fen in its own right, rather than forming part of a larger 'dry' common, it may have been largely grazed in the past but mowing for marsh hay, of certain parts and/or in certain periods, is also probable.

Different again is Southrepps Common, which includes an area of lowlying fen, flanking a stream called Fox's Beck or the Bradfield Beck, within a larger area of dry, heathy common. It was grazed in the recent past but may have an earlier history of mowing, and is regularly mown today. Here, too, the layers of peat are thin but the ground is more waterlogged and with water which, derived directly or indirectly from the Crag aquifer, is slightly alkaline in character. The vegetation – dominated by blunt-flowered rush to the north of the beck which bisects the common, and by a mixture of this and common reed to the south – thus includes a range of calcareous fen species which are relatively uncommon in Norfolk, such as grass of parnassus (*Parnassia palustris*), bog pimpernel (*Anagallis tenella*), marsh arrowgrass (*Triglochin palustris*), common quaking grass (*Briza media*) and flea sedge (*Carex pulicaris*), together with significant quantities of the uncommon marsh helleborine (*Epipactis palustris*) and fragrant orchid (*Gymnadenia conopsea* var. *densiflora*). There are, however, also low hummocks within the fen which feature plants more suited to acid conditions, including meadow thistle (*Cirsium dissectum*), heather, heath woodrush and common cotton-grass. Higher up the valley sides, in less waterlogged and less calcareous conditions, the vegetation is more like that within Leziate Fen, comprising damp grassland dominated by sheep's fescue and Yorkshire fog and featuring plants like yellow rattle (*Rhinanthus minor*), southern marsh orchid (*Dactylorhiza praetermissa*) and ragged robin (*Silene flos-cuculi*).[9]

The magnificent flora on Southrepps Common is maintained by a regular and rigorous regime of mowing carried out by the Norfolk Wildlife Trust and a team of local volunteers. Even here a broad strip of alder has developed to either side of the beck in the course of the twentieth century, while both Leziate Fen and Foulden Common have seen a marked increase in alder, and to an extent birch, since the 1940s; extensive areas of both these commons have, in effect, become secondary woodland, a development hastened in the former case by dehydration due to drainage, and water abstraction, on surrounding agricultural land. Although we may often be unclear about precisely how particular fens were exploited in the past, none survives long without some form of management. Boughton Fen, another SSSI, its reed, meadowsweet (*Filipendula ulmaria*) and great willowherb-dominated vegetation home to a range of rare moths (Figure 8.1); Irstead Holmes, a poor's allotment in Broadland; and Guist 'Common', also an SSSI, with reedbeds frequented by marsh harriers, hobbies, spotted flycatchers and a range of warblers are all only kept free of encroaching scrub through the efforts of dedicated local people, with varying degrees of support from Natural England and agro-environment schemes.

Most areas of fen registered as commons have not been so fortunate. Caldecote Fen, a fuel allotment in Oxburgh less than 2 kilometres from Boughton Fen, was no longer being cut for peat in 1910, although it was still being mown. The fen was still largely open in 1946 and in the 1960s was registered as an SSSI. But, now uncut and unmanaged, it had degenerated to wet woodland by the 1980s, and was deregistered, although it still boasts an important spider population.[10] Middleton 'Common', Pentney 'Common', Potter's Fen in East Dereham, Beetley 'Common', most of the Honing commons, Barton Fen and Horning Fen, are all now entirely wooded; Whitwell Common and Roydon

Fen near Diss are largely so. Almost all were open expanses of reed, sedge and other fen vegetation in the middle of the twentieth century. The fate of these registered commons has been shared by most of the rather more numerous areas of fen which are either privately owned or are poor's allotments which never came to be registered under the 1965 Act. This said, the wet woodland that has replaced some fens is not without ecological significance or interest, while many overgrown examples, such as Stow Bedon Fen, retain ponds or other habitats of importance. Nor, it should be emphasised, is freedom from encroaching scrub a guarantee of ecological health. Borough Fen in Foulden has few trees or shrubs but drainage, and intensive grazing, have destroyed most of its characteristic vegetation.

Fens are, perhaps unsurprisingly, rather lacking in above-ground archaeological features. But they are not entirely without interest in this respect. In a number of examples, including Borough Fen in Foulden, the northern part of Crostwight Common, Roydon Fen, several of the Honing Commons and less certainly Foulden Common, Lidar images reveal areas of faint, close-set parallel lines, of variable width and regularity but which are almost certainly the traces of peat 'doles'. Those at Honing replicate, in width and orientation, the residual pattern shown on the tithe map of 1843, although in places the boundaries have been widened, deepened and distorted, probably in an attempt to improve the drainage.[11] Much clearer are the examples in the western section of Leziate Fen (Figure 8.2), where strips of damp ground, featuring plants like creeping buttercup (*Ranunculus repens*), lesser spearwort (*R. flammula*), water mint (*Mentha aquatica*) and meadowsweet, are separated by ridges featuring a dry grassland dominated by red fescue. Elsewhere peat extraction has left rather different traces. On Irstead poor's allotment, established by the parliamentary enclosure of 1810, Lidar reveals traces of rectangular pits more regular in shape than the various turf ponds that now lie within the area while on Honing Common,

FIG. 8.2. Lidar image of the turf 'doles' in Leziate Fen.

on the boundary with East Ruston, a level, remarkably featureless area of fen beside the Hundred Stream marks the area of the lost Honing Broad, which is marked on a number of eighteenth-century maps but which had disappeared by the mid-nineteenth century. It is a reminder of how rapidly peat cuttings, even deep ones, can become filled with new peat, something that presumably explains why traces of 'doles', where they remain at all, are usually slight. It is noteworthy that the remarkably well-preserved examples at Leziate occupy a slightly drier, slightly higher, part of the fen, shown as rough pasture on the First Edition Ordnance Survey rather than as marsh, and fade out towards the lower, wetter ground. Peat formation may have ended here when the land lying adjacent to the north and east was severed from the common, and drainage ditches installed, and as already noted the local water table has dropped significantly over recent decades.

A few common fens contain low banks, or networks of banks, of uncertain age or purpose. On Southrepps Common a straight bank, around 0.5 metres or less in height, runs for c. 100 metres roughly parallel to, and around 60 metres to the south of, the stream which runs through the centre of its wetland section. A series of parallel banks run at right angles to it, north towards the stream (Figures 8.3 and 8.4). Several large hawthorn bushes grow on the banks but whether these represent the remnants of hedges, or simply self-sown specimens

FIG. 8.3. Part of the network of enclosures, defined by turf banks, on Southrepps Common.

which have benefitted from the drier conditions so provided, remains unclear. There is a similar series of enclosures on the north side of the stream, laid out in a similar relationship to a tributary watercourse that runs at right angles to it, although here defined in part by ditches rather than banks. The ruler-straight character of the earthworks suggests that they are not of any great antiquity but they do not correspond with anything shown on maps of the parish surveyed in 1784 and 1839.[12] If originally accompanied by a hedge or 'dead hedge', they may have served to keep stock out of areas in the lower part of the common at certain times of the year so that it could be cut for marsh hay or dug for peat, of which there is a significant thickness here: the uneven ground towards the east of the embanked areas to the south of the beck seems to be the result of peat cutting.

Traces of something similar are apparent on Foulden Common, another example that embraces both 'dry' common and fen. Here, however, a prominent bank and ditch which follows the approximate division between the two is accompanied by an outgrown hedge, and is shown as a boundary on the tithe map of 1839, with sections to either side separately named – as Tallon Common and Hothills Common respectively;[13] while the banks subdividing the fen define much larger areas than at Southrepps and are less easy to discern on the ground, because of the vegetation, and even on Lidar, due to the growth of peat. But here, too, the pattern suggests compartmentalisation, presumably associated with the exclusion of livestock from parts of the fen at certain times of the year.

Foulden Common is better known for undulations of an entirely natural kind, the 'pingos' – shallow pits or ponds, some enclosed by continuous banks – which form a dense 'shoal' across its central and northern portions (Figure 8.5). They were formed during the last Ice Age, in tundra conditions, as water from subsoil seepage lines gradually formed large blocks of ice.[14] These eventually expanded up through the ground surface, pushing the soil aside and, finally thawing, left behind these pits with their distinctive raised rims, the water filled examples here featuring species like greater bladderwort *Utricularia vulgaris* and fen pondweed *Potamogeton coloratus*.[15] Often, as here, pingos are accompanied by more amorphous undulations resulting from allied periglacial processes, often referred to as 'hummocky ground'. Similar features occur within a number of registered commons (Pentney Common, East Winch Common, Boughton Fen) or former commons (East Walton, Thompson) in the county.

FIG. 8.4. Plan of the earthworks on Southrepps Common.

FIG. 8.5. One of the many 'pingos' on Foulden Common. Note the distinctive raised outer rim.

Marshes

The various wetland commons that occupy less waterlogged sites, and less peaty, more alluvial soils of the Hanworth and Isleham Associations, than the 'fens' discussed in the previous section are something of a mixed bag. Some, such as Hanworth Common or Roughton Common, are located on relatively narrow floodplains and, partially surrounded by houses, differ little from clayland commons, other than in having a permanently high water table. Others, such as Castle Acre Common, occupy similar sites but without flanking houses. A few are found on the alluvial clays of former estuaries rather than on the floodplains of streams or rivers. What distinguishes them from fens, as already noted, is that they were all traditionally managed by grazing rather than by mowing, and were more productive and valuable land. Indeed, while most fens were commons, most of this less peaty, more alluvial floodplain land was privately owned and individually exploited, often as hay meadow rather than pasture, even in the Middle Ages. Moreover, whereas many of the fens that are registered commons are in reality poor's allotments, these are all 'true' commons. Four examples in the west of the county lie within areas reclaimed from coastal wetlands in the early Middle Ages: two bordering The Wash – Marsh Common and The Gongs in North Wooton to the north of King's Lynn – and two on the edge of the silt fens – Hardwick and West Winch Commons, to the south of the town. The others are thinly scattered along the floodplains of Norfolk's principal watercourses, including Wighton Common, or Wighton Town Green, beside the river Stiffkey; Castle Acre Common and Emmanuels' Common in Castle Acre, and George Common in Newton, beside the Nar; Ringland Low Common on the Yare; Brampton Common and Drabblegate Common in Aylsham on the Bure and Hanworth Common and Thwaite Common on its tributaries; and Shotesham Common on a tributary of the Tas.

Because commons of this type were traditionally grazed, rather than mown, they were probably less floristically diverse in the past than neighbouring areas of hay meadow, on which the removal of the hay repeatedly depleted nutrient levels, and where the exclusion of livestock during spring and early summer allowed tall, bulky plants to flower and set seed which would otherwise be browsed or trampled.[16] Those at North Wooton, West Winch and Hardwick are all still managed by grazing. West Winch and Hardwick both comprise relatively close-cropped unimproved grazing marsh and are included on Natural England's Inventory of this priority habitat. This is more important for bird populations (the high water table and consequent accessibility of invertebrates attracting waders and others in the winter) than for its flora, which is dominated by grasses like perennial rye-grass and Yorkshire fog, and rushes, accompanied by a few other relatively common species. But neither of these particular marshes is especially noted for its bird life. This is perhaps because they now lie well inland, separated from other areas of grazing marsh, and from mudflats and saltings, by arable farmland, and are flanked by large numbers of houses (West Winch is an expanding settlement close to King's Lynn) and, at the northern end of Hardwick, by a trading estate. Both are, nevertheless, important as survivors of the once extensive areas of grazing marsh in the area, otherwise private and largely ploughed up in the second half of the twentieth century. The two North Wooton Commons have less ecological interest, in part because they were ploughed up and re-seeded during the Second World War. They are not included on the Priority Habitat Inventory or even categorised as County Wildlife sites. Brampton Common, beside the Bure near Aylsham, and Ringland Low Common beside the Yare, are similarly grazed with some intensity, although here the drainage is poorer and larger areas are occupied by reed and rush.

In marked contrast, Castle Acre Common, an SSSI beside the river Nar, boasts a particularly rich and diverse flora. In part this reflects a greater range of soil and water conditions. While the common largely occupies broadly similar soils to those just discussed, there are more areas of waterlogged ground, some associated with springs and seepage lines, while the margins of the common extend onto a more acidic substrate. But in part it reflects the fact that the common is under conservation management and grazed at lower levels of intensity, and thus boasts more of the tall, bulky plants more usually associated with meadows. Much of the common's botanical interest comes from the areas of particularly waterlogged ground, which feature plants like bogbean *Menyanthes trifoliata*, marsh valerian *Valeriana dioica*, marsh pennywort, brown sedge *Carex disticha*, flat sedge *Blysmus compressus*, southern marsh orchid and blunt-flowered rush, and with stands of reed sweet-grass *Glyceria maxima*, common reed and lesser pond sedge *Carex acutiformis* beside the river. The drier ground features a diverse range of grasses but also a variety of herbs more usually associated with damp meadows than with grazed pastures, including devil's bit scabious, meadow thistle, meadow saxifrage *Saxifraga granulata*, yellow rattle, tormentil and heath bedstraw.[17] It is important to note, however, that the common was more intensively grazed and almost certainly better drained a century ago than it is today. The 1946 RAF vertical photographs show numerous straight surface drains, especially in the eastern half of the common, in addition to a deeper drainage ditch running through the western section; the grass appears close cropped and there were virtually no trees or bushes. Just over four decades later, aerial photographs taken in 1988 suggest a rougher and more varied sward, although even then only marginally more trees and shrubs. The latter have only proliferated over the last three decades, the consequence of less intensive grazing. The kinds of plants now present on the common were doubtless there a century ago but almost certainly in smaller numbers. The common has become a more diverse and wilder place.

The management of Shotesham Common, another SSSI, which occupies the floodplain of a tributary of the river Tas, deviates still further from that of the past (Figure 8.6). In the early twentieth century this was essentially grazed – Clarke in 1909 described it as 'pasture with *Juncus*' – but it is now very actively managed, by the local conservation group, through a combination of mowing and light grazing; essentially, as a hay meadow.[18] This is one

FIG. 8.6. Shotesham Common, recently cut for hay.

of the most biologically diverse places in Norfolk, a recent survey by Norfolk Wildlife Trust volunteers recording 195 plant species, 79 bird species and a rich invertebrate fauna including 18 species of bee, 8 of wasp, 26 of beetle, 17 of butterfly and 30 of moth.[19] In part this rich diversity arises from the fact that, over its 1.5 kilometre length, the common displays significant variations in soil and drainage. Beside the stream, but also towards the south-eastern end of the common, where there are springs, there is wet marshy grassland with a variety of rushes (blunt-flowered, sharp-flowered (*J. acutifloru*), soft (*J. effusus*) and hard (*J. inflexus*)), angelica (*Angelica sylvestris*) and meadowsweet, accompanied by bogbean, marsh marigold (*Caltha palustris*), ragged robin, southern marsh orchid and common spotted orchid, together with rarer species like marsh lousewort (*Pedicularis palustris*) and marsh helleborine. Away from the stream, where the ground is slightly drier, grass species typical of wet neutral conditions dominate – tufted hair-grass (*Deschampsia cespitosa*), Yorkshire fog and creeping bent – accompanied by herbs such as cowslip (*Primula veris*), common twayblade (*Listera ovata*) and adder's tongue (*Ophioglossum vulgatum*). Small areas of drier ground, on hummocks and toward the higher margins of the common, feature sweet vernal grass and Yorkshire fog, accompanied by meadow saxifrage, lady's bedstraw (*Galium verum*) and common quaking grass.[20] But while the common's rich fauna and flora is again in part a reflection of variations in soils and drainage, it is largely a consequence of recent and current management. Light grazing and regular mowing for hay allows plants to thrive which would have faced challenges when the area was used for grazing alone, at commercial levels of intensity.

Other wetland commons, similarly occupying alluvial soils or thin layers of peat, are less intensively managed than the examples just discussed. Wighton Common is the rump of a more extensive area of damp grassland that once occupied the floodplain of the river Stiffkey and, lying next to the village, will have been regularly and heavily grazed, as its nineteenth-century name 'Town Green' perhaps suggests. It is now mown, although not with strict regularity. It is accordingly dominated by plants characteristic of hay meadows – meadowsweet, cuckooflower (*Cardamine pratense*) and ragged robin. But it also features tall herbs more typical of roadsides and waste places, with stands of nettles and great willowherb (*Epilobium hirsutum*) and abundant hogweed (*Heracleum sphondylium*); while small areas of willow scrub are developing to the north-east and patches of bramble to the east. Lower growing plants characteristic of damp places also occur, including fen bedstraw (*Galium uliginosum*), soft and hard rush and marsh foxtail (*Alopecurus geniculatus*).[21] Town Green is essentially an area of damp pasture on which grazing has ceased, and enough mowing takes place to prevent the wholesale regeneration of scrub, but not to produce the rich diversity seen at Shotesham. It would not have looked like this a century ago, when this particular assemblage of plants would probably have been hard to find.

Brockdish Common beside the river Waveney is in a more derelict condition. There are some mown paths but otherwise it has been neither regularly cut nor grazed for years. Large areas are occupied by dense stands of nettle and bramble, accompanied by bindweed (*Convolvulus arvensis*) and cleavers (*Galium aparine*). Elsewhere, coarse grasses dominate, together with mugwort (*Artemisia vulgaris*), dock (*Rumex* sp.), great willowherb, hogweed and other plants characteristic of roadsides and waste land. In some parts willow or hawthorn scrub is developing and ash, sycamore and elder are becoming established. Only in a few, less overgrown areas can plants more characteristic of damp meadows and pastures still be found, including creeping thistle (*Cirsium arvense*), marsh thistle (*Cirsium palustre*) and marsh woundwort (*Stachys palustris*), although the banks of the Waveney support a typical riverside vegetation featuring pendulous sedge (*Carex pendula*), fool's watercress (*Helosciadium nodiflorum*), watermint (*Mentha aquatica*) and water forget-me-not (*Myosotis scorpioides*), together with a patch of Himalayan balsam (*Impatiens glandulifera*).[22] The development of scrub is now being held in check and the condition of the common improving, under the direction of the parish council. Emmanuel's Common in Castle Acre, and the neighbouring commons lying upriver on the Nar, Broadmeadow Common and George Common in Newton, have been less fortunate. All, ungrazed and uncut, are now characterised by rank vegetation which is fast becoming covered in willow, alder, ash and other trees.

The varied ecology of these different commons, all once used primarily for grazing and occupying broadly similar soils, is to an extent shaped by variations in drainage and other purely natural influences. But it is also the outcome of the ways in which they have been used and managed over recent decades. Where grazing has continued at a reasonably high intensity, a fairly impoverished flora, dominated by common grasses and rushes, can be found, probably providing some guide to conditions in the past. Where, at the other extreme, grazing has been abandoned and little other management takes place, a rank species-poor vegetation, infested with reed and common rushes, develops, followed by bramble and willow scrub, and ultimately woodland – with the speed of this progression being determined by natural factors, including the height of the water table. Regular mowing with the removal of the cut vegetation, in contrast, begins to move the flora in the direction of a hay meadow and increases the range of species present, while grazing at lower than traditional levels of intensity also allows taller meadow plants to survive and generally increases floral diversity. But neither of these, it should be emphasised, were probably how such commons were usually managed in the past. Most would have looked more like Brampton than Shotesham, although we should not forget the benefits that such species-poor grazing marshes bring in terms, in particular, of bird life.

The archaeology of these grazed wetland commons is generally less interesting than that of other types of common in Norfolk, with only a handful of exceptions. The wartime re-seeding of the two North Wooton commons was not sufficient to level a variety of important earthworks and undulations of historical importance. Those on Marsh Common include a number of sinuous depressions marking the courses of the tidal creeks which ran through the salt marshes from which the common, and the adjacent portions of drained private marsh, were reclaimed in the later Middle Ages (one, typically, has been re-used as a drainage ditch or 'dyke'). Before this happened, the area was a major salt-making centre. The method employed involved mixing salt-impregnated sand with sea water, slowly heating the resulting solution and skimming off the salt as it crystallised. The waste sand and silt was dumped beside the processing site, leading to the build-up of low mounds, one of which is preserved towards the western side of the common (Figure 8.7).[23] Surrounded by a ditch and rising 1.5 metres above the surrounding land, it later provided a site dry enough to be ploughed and cultivated, to judge from the slight traces of plough ridges visible on Lidar images. The common thus serves as an important 'island of preservation', fossilising features otherwise lost from the local landscape as, in the course of the twentieth century, the private grazing marshes on the margins of the Wash were progressively ploughed up. But not all the undulations in the surface of Marsh Common relate to this lost saltmarsh landscape. A pattern of long, shallow, ruler-straight surface drains, parallel and closely spaced, runs north–south through the southern section of the common. These almost certainly predate the wartime 'improvements' and appear contemporary with the equally straight drainage dykes dug across the common, probably of nineteenth-century date and clear evidence of the ability of commoners to work together to improve the value of their shared resource. There are traces

FIG. 8.7. The saltern mound on Marsh Common, North Wooton.

of another, rather sparser pattern of straight surface drains in the north-west of the common but here all undulations, including the salt marsh channels, have been blurred and smoothed, probably as a consequence of wartime reseeding. The final feature in this remarkable little palimpsest is the deep drain cutting through the northern section of the common, from north-east to south-west, which was dug in the 1850s as part of a scheme, initiated by a parliamentary act passed in 1846 and carried out by the Norfolk Estuary Company, to reclaim new land from the mudflats of the Wash, lying to the north and west of the existing grazing marshes.

The archaeology of North Wooton's other wet common, The Gongs, is broadly similar, featuring fossilised saltmarsh channels and post-medieval surface drains, although here the saltern mounds are large but seem less well defined, again probably due to wartime 'improvements'. The nearby West Winch Common and Hardwick Common have less to offer. There is no record of wartime ploughing but saltmarsh channels are less well defined, probably because the entire area of these narrow commons lay, before medieval reclamation, close to the 'uplands' and on the margins of the tidal marshes. Here there are fewer surface drains, but the ruler-straight drainage dykes which subdivide the marsh at intervals attest, once again, the ability of commoners to improve their shared resource.

Indeed, common grazing marshes were, and are, much more likely than fens to be dissected by ditches, drainage dykes and shallower surface drains. Often, as in the case of Ringland Low Common, Brampton Common, Emmanuel Common in Castle Acre and to some extent Shotesham Common, archaeological inspections reveals the traces of lost, silted examples, indicating that the network of ditches was denser in the past. There was greater potential for improving the drainage of such sites than was the case with the more doggedly waterlogged fens, and thus for improving the quality of the herbage. But it is possible that in a few cases dykes served as 'watery fences' which prevented livestock from straying into portions of the common, more peaty and waterlogged in character, that were mown for litter or hay; as I have emphasised, 'fen' and 'grazing marsh' were not discrete categories but lay on a continuum. Some of those on Flordon Common, for example, must surely have formed the division between the areas which Clarke in 1909 described as 'pasture' and 'mowing marsh'.[24] Most, but by no means all, of the drainage ditches on these floodplain commons have a ruler-straight character suggestive of a post-medieval origin.

The most striking earthworks present on any Norfolk floodplain common are, perhaps, the blocks of broad, regular, flat-topped, parallel ridges, orientated in a variety of directions, which occupy the north-eastern end of Emmanuel Common in Castle Acre, now engulfed in a tangle of woodland and scrub on the floodplain of the Nar. These are the remains of a 'floated' or irrigated water meadow, a complex system of leats, channels and slopes designed to warm the ground and encourage an early growth of grass in the spring and a bumper hay crop in the summer.[25] But they have nothing to do with the common. The meadow was laid out on private property, mainly in the adjacent parish of West Lexham but just extending west across the parish boundary, around 1804, to the design of the noted civil engineer and geologist William Smith.[26] The boundary of the registered common was, for reasons now unclear, drawn in such a way that it extended well beyond the area of the real common to embrace what was still, well into the twentieth century, a block of enclosed private land.

Clayland Commons

Clayland commons are, after heaths, the most numerous and extensive type of registered common land in Norfolk, and differ from them in a number of important respects. Mainly although not exclusively located on the till plateau in the centre and south of the county, almost all are 'true' commons, surviving in parishes unaffected by parliamentary enclosures or, like Church Green in Old Buckenham, recognised and allotted (and regulated) under the terms of an enclosure award. None are poor's allotments, a reflection of the limited use made by the poor of commons of this type prior to enclosure; they afforded little in the way of low value fuel, in the form of peat, gorse and heather and the grazing they provided, generally of reasonable quality, was in most cases monopolised by the commoners. Most are described as 'greens' on the modern Ordnance Survey maps – a word never used in the names of commons overlying freely draining substrates – and many of those now referred to as 'common' were so called in the past, such as Fritton Common, described in 1827 as the 'common pasture of Fritton called Fritton Green'.[27] Clayland commons lack the heather and bracken of heaths and are, on the whole, less wild, more domesticated spaces. Few are anything more than partially overgrown with scrub and secondary woodland and the majority have houses around one or more sides.

Clayland commons display much variation in terms of size. Some, such as Brisley Green or Hales Green, are vast expanses of pasture, their extent fully revealed by the paucity or absence of invading trees (Figure 8.8). At the other extreme, a number are tiny triangles of grass at road junctions, or wide verges beside lanes – both of which are accompanied by numerous examples, identical in character, which nobody got round to registering. They also vary in terms of their associated settlement. Some, including even very large examples like Church Green in Old Buckenham, have houses ranged all around their periphery. More usually dwellings congregate at one end, often around a 'funnel' entrance, and generally that lying in the direction of the parish church, as at Fritton. In some cases houses are densely clustered together but elsewhere, as at Hales, they are thinly and fairly evenly scattered around the margins of the common, with wide spaces in between.

The more open, managed aspect of clayland commons is largely a consequence of the fact that they often retained an agricultural role long after most heaths had become derelict. Indeed, many examples, including Hales Green, Wacton Common, Brisley Green and the nearby Harpers Green, are still grazed on a commercial or semi-commercial basis by the cattle of local farms (Figure 8.9). But it also arises from their intimate association with settlement. At places like Mulbarton, commons have developed a largely recreational role, with areas regularly mown almost like a municipal park to provide space for walking or informal play or – as at Swardeston – games like cricket (not a new use of such spaces: above, p. 82). Even where clayland commons are managed on less rigorously 'suburban' lines, regular mowing at less frequent intervals, often as part of a programme of conservation management, keeps what have effectively become public open spaces free of scrub. Where commons are surrounded by houses and are described as 'greens', local people understandably expect them to be used, and look, something like an idealised village green.

The relationship of clayland commons and settlement was even closer in the past; the edges of many examples were more densely settled in the Middle Ages than they are today. Fieldwalking by Alan Davison revealed, for example, that in the thirteenth century Hales Green was almost entirely surrounded by a continuous girdle of farms and cottages.[28] Rhees Green in Stratton St Michael now has only a single farm at its northern end but fieldwalking by Sylvia Addington suggests that this was once accompanied by at least four other dwellings.[29] In most cases contraction of greenside settlements occurred in the fourteenth and fifteenth centuries, part of the general late medieval demographic decline, but in some it continued well into the post-medieval period or even largely occurred

FIG. 8.8. Aerial view of Hales Green, one of the largest of Norfolk's surviving clayland commons (courtesy John Fielding).

8. Fens, Greens and Marshes

then. In the seventeenth century there were eight small farms and cottages clustered around Stubb's Green in Shotesham and in the early eighteenth century the settlement was important enough for its inhabitants to be accorded their own separate section in the parish tithe accounts, where they are described as the 'Stubb Green Dwellers'.[30] There were still seven dwellings here when the tithe map was surveyed in 1841.[31] By 1880, to judge from the First Edition Ordnance Survey 6-inch map, this had declined to five and by 1907 to three. By 1946 there were only two, as there are today.

The topography of surviving commons suggests a number of other medieval and post-medieval changes. A cottage stands within a small enclosure isolated in the centre of Wacton Common which at the time of tithe commutation in 1839 was still accompanied by a windmill; a slightly larger example shown on the tithe map in the centre of New Buckenham Common is now home to the Windmill Garage.[32] A number of clayland commons, including Hales Green, have irregular edges resulting from numerous small encroachments, made to provide gardens, sites for cottages or to expand farmyards or fields. Here, the most unusual encroachment disappeared in the inter war years leaving little obvious trace of its presence. The tithe map of 1838 shows an 'island' towards the southern end of the common, covering just 0.5 hectares and containing six tiny cottages and their gardens.[33] Five remained in 1906 when the Ordnance Survey 6-inch map

FIG. 8.9. Cattle grazing on Harpers Green, Brisley.

described them as 'Hole Houses'. They were demolished in the 1930s, probably under the terms of the 1930 Housing Act, which empowered District Councils to clear away insanitary or substandard housing.[34] Some encroachments on the margins of commons are signalled by the manner in which roads leading to the common appear to have been diverted around them. Wood Green in Stratton St Michael is approached from the south-east by a road, Wood Lane, leading from Morningthorpe Green. Only 100 metres before it arrives at the common it turns through two right-angle bends, only reaching its destination after running around the boundaries of closes attached to Wood Green Farm, which stands on the common edge but evidently on an intake which has blocked the original course of the road. The rear boundary of the property comprises a massive ditch which presumably represents the original common edge.

Indeed, as I emphasised in Chapter 2, the basic shapes of commons of all kinds, as much as the details, are best understood as the result of progressive encroachment; they were what remained after successive intakes had been made from more extensive and continuous areas of uncultivated 'waste'. When, in the period before the tenth and eleventh centuries, the wide clay plateau between the principal valleys still largely comprised wooded grazing grounds, there are signs that these were accessed via wide funnels of pasture running up from the more settled land below, which sometimes survived largely intact even after settlement had spread up onto the higher ground and the upland pastures largely converted to fields. That, at least, would explain the way that the great 'greens' at Hales and Fritton, in particular, have their long axes ranged at right angles to a major watercourse and extend for a little way down from the level plateau onto the better drained soils of its valley, gradually tapering as they do so (above, Figure 2.5). As the uplands were broken up, moreover, and replaced by intakes of private land at a variety of scales, ribbons of open ground were retained at their interstices to allow livestock to be moved to, or between, the rather larger surviving commons and greens. These account for many of the public roads that now exist on the claylands, a high proportion of which initially took, and some still retain, a distinctive form: lanes with very wide verges or narrow linear commons, depending on definition, typically between 15 and 30 metres in width and extending in some cases for several kilometres. Sometimes these were referred to as 'greens', but often not. The clay roads were almost impassable after heavy rain; extra width allowed pedestrians, riders, vehicles and driven livestock to pick a way between pools and quagmires. 'Ribbon commons' of this type seem to represent the articular routeways of the early agrarian landscape, commonly linking major centres of settlement to dwindling areas of woodland and grazing located on remote interfluves. Formal enclosure and narrowing, and piecemeal encroachment, have over the centuries converted many to lanes and roads of more normal form but a number still remain. Examples in Saxlingham Nethergate, Gissing and Shelfhanger were registered as commons under the 1965 Act. But many others, including Lath Green and Upgate Green in Shotesham and Cuttings

Road in Rushall were not: important and distinctive, but largely unnoticed, components of this ancient landscape.

Earthworks are generally easier to see in the grass, grazed or cut, of clayland commons, than in the bracken, scrub and woodland that characterises most common heaths. Here there are no examples of the Neolithic or Bronze Age burial mounds which form such dramatic elements in the landscapes of a number of heaths. But there are some early archaeological features, slighter but in some ways more important. The absence of early barrows probably reflects the fact that the claylands as a whole were only sparsely settled before the Iron Age, with farmsteads thinly scattered along the principal valleys cutting through the till plateau. Fieldwalking surveys indicate that settlement then intensified and in the Roman period farms were widely scattered across the heavy, poorly draining soils of the interfluves.[35] From the late fourth century settlement retreated again, retrenching to the principal valleys, and the more challenging land of the plateau was then exploited for several centuries as undivided tracts of woodland and pasture. Any Iron Age or Roman fields had been abandoned and long forgotten by the time that settlement and cultivation returned to the clay uplands at the end of the Anglo-Saxon period and their above-ground archaeological traces would have been subsequently levelled wholesale by medieval and post-medieval ploughing. Clayland commons are among the few areas that have remained unploughed since the late Roman period, and where the earthworks of late prehistoric and Roman fields might potentially survive; and there are indeed a few possible examples.

A network of shallow ditches, around 1.5–2 metres wide and accompanied by even slighter banks, extends across most of the area of Fritton Common, arranged in a regular pattern based on long axes ranged south-west–north-east (Figure 8.10). Some elements have been incorporated into later attempts to drain the common but most of these drainage ditches form an irregular pattern, determined by the location of ponds and the common's perimetre ditch, into which they discharged water. The network of fainter ditches in contrast can never have functioned primarily as a drainage system as its elements are poorly related to such receptacles and it includes features, such as right-angle bends, that would have impeded the free flow of water. It appears to represent the remains of a rectilinear, 'cohesive' field system of prehistoric or Roman date. There are suggestive traces elsewhere. On nearby Wood Green in Long Stratton there is a wide, enigmatic ditch or hollow way which runs roughly parallel with the western edge of the common. It now links two ponds and has clearly been adapted to improve drainage but it continues in slighter form for some distance beyond the more northerly of the two ponds and might conceivably be a fragment of an early system of land division. More intriguing is the pattern of slight ditches apparent on aerial photographs and Lidar images, but scarcely discernible on the ground, on Church Green, Old Buckenham, which appear to define another rectilinear field system.[36] Here, in contrast to the situation at Fritton, the earthworks appear to lie on a very similar alignment to the boundaries of

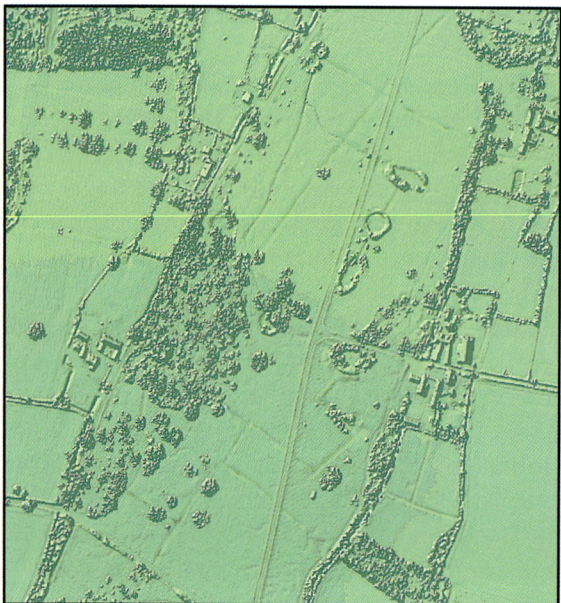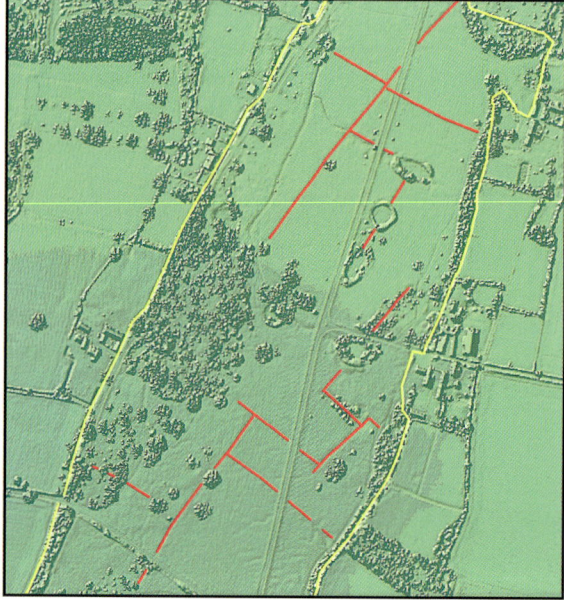

FIG. 8.10. Lidar image of earthworks on Fritton Common (left) and interpretation as a possible pre-medieval field system (right). Common edge in yellow.

the fields surrounding the common, possibly suggesting that the development of the latter was influenced by the same ancient framework. All these possible survivals are interesting and important. But so too is their rarity – the apparent *absence* of similar remains from other clayland commons. In part this may be because they often occupy the most poorly draining and intractable of the clay soils, which in the late prehistoric and Roman periods, as in the Middle Ages, probably comprised open land lying outside and beyond the areas divided into fields. It is also possible, however, that many of the pre-medieval settlements on the claylands recovered by fieldwalking were essentially pastoral establishments, outlying ranches set in largely open, undivided landscapes of pasture.

Most earthworks found on clayland commons clearly relate to their use and management as common land in the medieval or post-medieval periods. In particular, on many examples attempts have been made to remove surface water by digging shallow drains. The majority are relatively short in length and irregular in appearance, normally conducting water to a pit or pond or into the common's boundary ditch. A few, however, are more organised in layout, such as the system of shallow, ruler-straight, parallel drains, ranged south-west–north-east, which covers much of Hales Green. Such remains are of some importance in suggesting that commons were not simply neglected areas, casually exploited but otherwise left to their own devices, but that active steps might be taken to improve them. The grid of drains on Hales Green indicates a particularly ambitious and co-ordinated attempt, probably dating to the later eighteenth or nineteenth centuries, a period when landowners and farmers shared a fashionable interest in the improvement of land of all kinds through drainage.

In addition, clayland commons, like common heaths, are usually peppered with pits, but with important differences, the most obvious being that most, due to the nature of the subsoil, are at least seasonally filled with water. There is no doubt that the majority are man-made, something which is sometimes, but by no means always, clear from their form: they are accessed by a sloping 'ramp' which allowed carts to be loaded more easily with the extracted material. But it is possible that a significant minority are natural in character, and represent 'solution hollows'. Where the clay overlies chalk at no great depth, and includes (as it often does) significant lenses or pockets of sand and gravel, water seeping downwards and slightly acidic in character may have dissolved the underlying chalk, leading to some 'slumping' in the clay above.[37] It is noticeable that clay commons in the centre and west of the county, where the till overlies chalk, are often more liberally peppered with pits and ponds than those lying to the east, where it overlies the Pleistocene Crag. Wood Green is the most striking example, with seven large ponds scattered across its surface. In contrast, in the case of Hales Green, where Crag lies beneath the clay, pits and ponds not only take up far less of the area of the common: they are also very markedly concentrated towards the common edges. In all there are 14 ponds and 7 largely dry pits shown on the early Ordnance Survey maps, most of which remain fully intact today, of which around 80 per cent touch, or lie within c. 5 metres of, the common edge (Figure 8.11). Indeed, even where pits and ponds are more widely scattered across the area of a common, the majority will hug its edge. This suggests that most were dug to extract building materials, principally the clay required for the wattle-and-daub infill for timber-framed buildings, either still occupying these sites or their predecessors, although they doubtless served a useful function subsequently as watering ponds for livestock. Some peripheral ponds, it is true, no longer have houses near to them but these can sometimes be related, as at Rhees Green in Long Stratton, to the sites of lost medieval farms discovered by fieldwalking.[38] Many probably have medieval origins.

Other pits on clayland commons were dug to obtain clay for brick and tile kilns located either on the common or just beyond its edge, or to be used for road repairs (clay as well as gravel was required for this purpose: enclosure awards at a number of places, including Mundham, made separate allotments for gravel and clay to the parish highways surveyors).[39] Some may have been dug to extract other materials, for even the Lowestoft till in the centre and south of the county can include sizeable deposits of sand and gravel, while elsewhere the glacial clays can be more extensively mixed. There is a noticeable tendency for the larger extraction pits to be located close to where public roads enter the common (above, Figure 5.7).

Only a few earthworks of other kinds are found on clayland commons and these all appear to be of medieval or post-medieval date. The hollow way running east–west across the centre of Hales Green appears to be related to the exploitation of clay pits there; a much larger example on New Buckenham common marks the course of the old road to Norwich before this was straightened, on its present course, following the establishment of the Buckenham Turnpike Trust in 1772 (a limestone milestone stands on the common beside

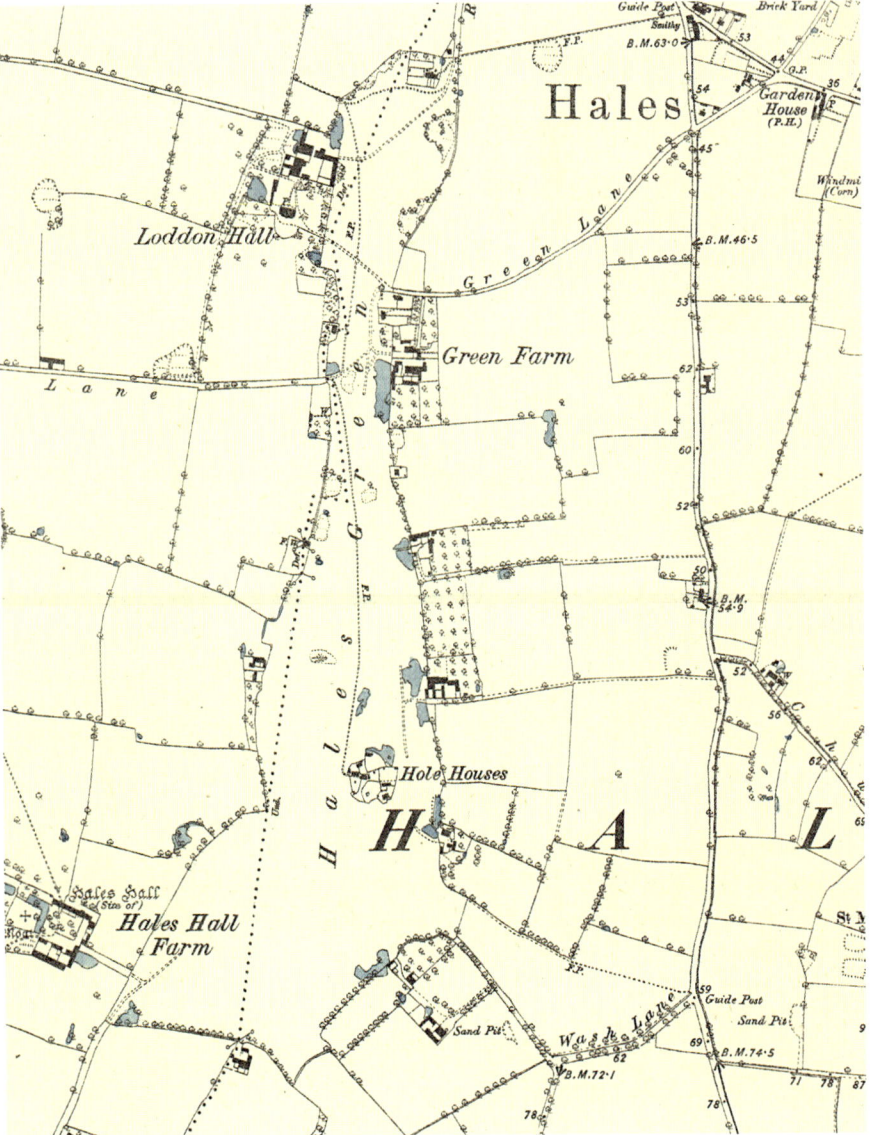

FIG. 8.11. Hales Green, as depicted on the First Edition Ordnance Survey 6-inch map of 1884. Note the concentration of pits and ponds towards the margins of the common.

the new road).[40] What particularly distinguishes clayland commons from commons and poor's allotments occupying heathy soils is the paucity of earthworks relating to military activity in the two world wars. As we have seen, heaths abound with such features. Clayland commons were used by the military – for observation posts, as on New Buckenham Common, where an example beside the Spitalmere is marked by amorphous earthworks and fragments of masonry.[41] But extensive use, for training, was directed towards heaths because these had already lost, or were losing, their economic or agricultural value. Most clayland commons still provided useful grazing, as we have seen, although the fact that practice trenches and the like soon filled with water on the clay soils may also have made them unsuitable as training areas.

Arguably of more importance than of any of these medieval and post-medieval earthworks is the 'living archaeology' of the old pollarded trees, the remains of 'plantings', which can still be seen on two of Norfolk's clayland commons. At Fritton, pollards of oak and ash, around 30 in all, are loosely scattered around the margins of the common, close to the houses, with all but one standing within 50 metres of the common edge. Most are oaks with girths in the range 2.5–5.5 metres, but there are also a number of ash (2.5–3.5 metres). At least half, to judge from their size, must have been planted and first cropped in the nineteenth century, and many were probably cut regularly into the twentieth. The most impressive are a group of oaks in the south-western corner of the common, hidden away amidst the younger scrub and woodland of birch and oak that has regenerated in relatively recent times due to a decline in regular grazing, which are clearly planted in straight lines (above, Figure 3.3). On Church Green in Old Buckenham the 'plantings' shown on the First Edition Ordnance Survey 25-inch map around the common's periphery are now mainly represented by a thin scatter of pollards of ash, together with some willow, oak and maple. Again the majority are fairly young trees, only a few with girths in excess of 4 metres and mostly between 2 and 3 metres: many appear to have been cropped well into the twentieth century. One area of 'planting' is, however, rather better preserved. On the southern edge of the common there is a narrow strip of woodland, covering an area of c. 0.8 hectares, which contains around 30 old oak pollards growing amidst a large number of younger trees which have mainly seeded from them. The pollards have girths that range from 2 to around 5 metres. As on Fritton Common, some appear to have been planted in lines (Figure 8.12). This is particularly clear on the northern edge of the wooded area, where a line of five pollards includes examples with girths ranging from 3 to 5 metres, perhaps suggesting that dead trees were replaced within an existing linear framework.

The large areas of scrub and secondary woodland running down the western side of Fritton Common, engulfing the oak pollards, are unusual, or at least atypical, in two respects. They contain a significant proportion of silver birch, alongside oak and hawthorn, reflecting the unusually acidic character of the common's soils; in the more neutral conditions found on most clayland commons birch is poorly represented and regeneration is dominated by hawthorn and blackthorn, soon joined by hazel, oak, ash, with some maple, and willow in damper areas. More importantly, most clayland commons, as already noted, have seen only limited development of woodland and scrub and most of the larger examples – Brisley Green, Church Green in Old Buckenham, New Buckenham Common, Wacton Common, Hales Green – remain grazed and almost entirely open. Some smaller examples, it is true, have fared less well. Crow Green in Long Stratton had already begun to tumble down to woodland before the end of the nineteenth century and is now, in effect, part of the adjacent Tyrell's Wood; Bracon Common and Marsh Green in Bracon Ash, and much of Swardeston Common, regenerated to woodland in the second half of the twentieth century. A number of medium-sized greens, such as Wood Green in Long

FIG. 8.12. Part of a 'planting' of pollarded oaks, Church Green, Old Buckenham.

Stratton, contain some areas of trees and scrub, albeit less extensive than those at Fritton. Their open, treeless aspect may be the most striking and distinctive aspect but, in terms of abandonment and dereliction, clayland commons still, to an extent, display a spectrum of conditions.

This is reflected in other aspects of their ecology. In broad terms, those examples managed over recent decades by commercial grazing tend to be the least biologically interesting. This is in part because of past efforts to improve the productivity of the sward – most drastically, as in the case of Wacton Common, by comprehensive wartime re-seeding. But it is mainly a consequence, as on the commons occupying alluvial soils, of the intensity of grazing. The vast but well-stocked Brisley Green, for example, has a sward dominated by a variety of grasses including crested dog's-tail (*Cynosurus cristatus*), red fescue and sweet vernal-grass (*Anthoxanthum odoratum*), and with much hairy sedge (*Carex hirta*). But herbs are not frequent, other than meadow buttercup (*Ranunculus acris*) and common sorrel (*Rumex acetosa*). Only where there is less grazing, along the sides of ditches and in naturally damp areas, can a more diverse flora be found, with tussocks of hard rush and soft rush and taller plants like greater bird's-foot-trefoil (*Lotus uliginosus*) and water mint.[42] Hales Green is likewise fairly intensively grazed and with little scrub. The sward, dominated by perennial rye grass, Yorkshire fog and meadow foxtail (*Alopecurus pratensis*), is again poor in herbs, those present predominantly low-growing species such as creeping cinquefoil (*Potentilla Reptans*), bulbous buttercup (*Ranunculus bulbosa*) and lesser bird's-foot-trefoil (*Lotus tenuis*), and mainly common ones like daisy

(*Bellis perennis*), dandelion (*Taraxacum officinale*) and white clover (*Trifolium repens*). Patches of nettles suggest high nitrogen levels. The grassland here has some botanical interest – spikes of common spotted orchid, bee orchid (*Ophrys apifera*) and pyramidal orchid (*Anacamptis pyramidalis*) have been recorded. But for the most part only the numerous ponds host a significant range of species, especially the 'intermittent' ones which only fill during the winter months, including great yellow cress (*Rorippa amphibia*), floating sweet grass (*Glyceris fluitans*), water mint, brooklime (*Veronica beccabunga*), fools water cress (*Apium nodiflorum*), and celery leaved buttercup (*Ranunculus sceleratus*). Where the ponds are much used by cattle, however, they may contain little beyond mud and water.[43]

As with grazed commons on alluvial floodplains, a lower level of grazing seems to increase diversity. Harpers Green in Brisley now features areas of gorse, blackthorn, hawthorn and bramble scrub, with self-seeded oak and ash, indicating many decades of relatively unintensive exploitation. These provide a habitat for turtle doves. The sward is rich in herbs like black knapweed (*Centaurea nigra*), autumn hawkbit (*Leontodon autumnalis*) and common mouse-ear (*Cerastium fontanum*), and in particular features taller growing species such as marsh dock (*Rumex palustris*), marsh cudweed (*Gnaphalium uliginosum*), marsh bedstraw (*Galium palustre*) and yellow rattle. In all, well over a hundred grassland species have been recorded from this relatively small, 9-hectare common, together with a range of waterplants in ponds and ditches, herbs of woods and hedges and a variety of trees and shrubs.[44] Once again it is important to emphasise that some of this diversity arises from purely natural factors – while some of the common is relatively dry there are numerous damp or waterlogged areas, and while the soils are mainly neutral the prominence of gorse amongst the scrub signals the presence of pockets of acidity. But less intensive grazing, even if in part enforced by these characteristics, is clearly a major influence on the common's ecology.

As with alluvial commons, replacing traditional management by grazing, with a regime of regular mowing for hay, seems to boost floristic diversity, as in the case of Langmere Green, where the sward contains almost equal proportions of grasses and flowering plants.[45] On Fritton Common mowing, with periods of light grazing, have maintained a rich flora characteristic of damp acidic grassland, dominated by common bent, red fescue and sweet vernal-grass, with abundant quantities of mat-grass (*Nardus stricta*), heath grass (*Danthonia decumbens*), purple moor-grass, heath bedstraw and tormentil, and with wetter areas characterised by soft rush, fleabane (*Pulicaria dysenterica*) and hairy sedge. Here, too, diversity is in part a consequence of purely natural influences, for in addition to these variations in drainage the common also includes areas of more calcareous soil which carry neutral grassland vegetation, dominated by creeping bent, Yorkshire fog and sweet vernal-grass accompanied by herbs such as green-winged orchid (*Orchis morio*), cowslip and lady's bed-straw.[46] It is also the case that the common's status as an SSSI owes much to the rich flora and fauna of its many ponds, and to the lichens associated with its ancient pollards. But once again, forms of management different from, and often less intensive than, those employed in the past are of crucial importance in sustaining biodiversity, allowing plants to thrive that are suppressed by intensive grazing and encouraging a mosaic of habitats that includes areas of scrub and secondary woodland. Yet at the same time, management is regular and rigorous enough to prevent wholesale woodland regeneration. These are very much habitats shaped and maintained by people and much of their biological interest derives from features like ponds and ditches created, for the most part, by human activity.

Notes

1. J. Treweek, P. José and P. Benstead, *The Wet Grassland Guide. Managing Floodplain and Coastal Wet Grassland for Wildlife* (Sandy, 1997); Williamson and Yardy, *Broadland*, 211–26.
2. Clarke, Commons of Norfolk, 62.
3. Williamson and Yardy, *Broadland*, 174–5, 202 and 225.
4. J. Gunn, *A Sketch of the Geology of Norfolk* (Norwich, 1864), 20.
5. J.M. Parmenter, The Development of the Wetland Vegetation of the Broadland Region: a Study of the Sociohistorical Factors which have Influenced and Modified the Development of Fen Vegetation In Broadland, unpublished PhD thesis, University of East Anglia, 2000.
6. *Ibid.*
7. Natural England citation, Foulden Common: https://designatedsites.naturalengland.org.uk/PDFsForWeb/Citation/1002450.pdf, accessed 24.6.2024.
8. Natural England citation, Leziate Fen: https://designatedsites.naturalengland.org.uk/PDFsForWeb/Citation/1002837.pdf, accessed 24.6.2024.
9. Natural England citation, Southrepps Common: https://designatedsites.naturalengland.org.uk/PDFsForWeb/Citation/1003281.pdf, accessed 25.6.2024.
10. E. Duffey and A. Feest, A Comparative Ecological Study of the Spider (Araneae) Faunas of East Anglian Fens, England: Regional Differences and Conservation, *Bulletin of the British Arachnology Society* 14, 8 (2009), 317–33.
11. NRO DN/TA 842.
12. NRO GTN 3/5/1/1; NRO DN/TA 190.
13. NRO ND/TA 302.
14. Rackham, *History of the Countryside*, 350–1.
15. Natural England citation, Foulden Common: https://designatedsites.naturalengland.org.uk/PDFsForWeb/Citation/1002450.pdf, accessed 24.6.2024.
16. J.J. Hopkins, British Meadows and Pastures, *British Wildlife* 1 (1990), 202–13, at 202–3; P. Marren, Harvests of Beauty: The Conservation of Hay Meadows, *British Wildlife* 6 (1995), 235–43.
17. Natural England citation, Castle Acre Common: https://designatedsites.naturalengland.org.uk/PDFsForWeb/Citation/1005965.pdf, accessed 2.7.2024.
18. Clarke, Commons of Norfolk, 67.
19. Unpublished survey report, archived with Norfolk Wildlife Trust.
20. Natural England citation, Shotesham Common; https://designatedsites.naturalengland.org.uk/PDFsForWeb/Citation/1000341.pdf, accessed 8.7.2024.
21. Unpublished survey report, archived with Norfolk Wildlife Trust.

22 Unpublished survey report, archived with Norfolk Wildlife Trust.
23 G. Clarke, *Salt-Winning on the Lyn: Anglo-Saxon and Medieval Industry at Gaywood's North Marsh, King's Lynn*, East Anglian Archaeology 180 (2023); A.M. and A.P. Fielding, *Salt Works and Salinas. The Archaeology, Conservation and Recovery of Salt Making Sites and their Processes* (Marston, 2005).
24 Clarke, Commons of Norfolk, 62.
25 S. Wade Martins and T. Williamson, Floated Water-Meadows in Norfolk: A Misplaced Innovation, *Agricultural History Review* 42 (1994), 20–37.
26 W. Smith, *Observations on the Utility, Form, and Management of Water Meadows* (Norwich, 1806), 112–16; Wade Martins and Williamson, Floated Water-Meadows, 24.
27 S. Addington and B. Cushion, Landscape and Settlements in South Norfolk Prehistoric to Post-medieval: Tasburgh-Fritton Area, with Particular Reference to Hedge Dating, *Norfolk Archaeology* 38 (1982), 97–139; at 99.
28 Davison and Fenner, *Evolution of Settlement*, 20–2, 33–6.
29 Addington and Cushion, Landscape and Settlements, 106.
30 NRO FEL 1076; NRO FEL 480, 553X1.
31 NRO DN/TA 558.
32 NRO DN/TA 501.
33 NRO DN/TA 157.
34 20 & 21 Geo. V c. 9; Wade Martins and Williamson, *The Countryside of East Anglia*, 162; NRO DC 4/2.
35 Davison and Fenner, *Evolution of Settlement*; D. Gurney, Roman Norfolk, in T. Ashwin and A. Davison (eds), *An Historical Atlas of Norfolk*, 3rd edn. (Chichester, 2005), 28–9; N. Hutcheson and T. Ashwin, Iron Age Norfolk, in T. Ashwin and A. Davison (eds), *An Historical Atlas of Norfolk*, 3rd edn. (Chichester, 2005), 22–5; A. Rogerson, *Fransham: People and Land in a Central Norfolk Parish from the Palaeolithic to the Eve of Parliamentary Enclosure*, East Anglian Archaeology 176 (2022), 23–35.
36 NHER 57347.
37 H. Prince, The Origin of Pits and Depressions in Norfolk, *Geography* 49 (1964), 15–32; Rackham, *History of the Countryside*, 349.
38 The pond on the south-western edge of the green lies next to a scatter of medieval sherds: Addington and Cushion, Landscape and Settlements, 106.
39 NRO C/Sca 2/259; NRO DN/TA 530.
40 NHER 41289.
41 NHER 44362.
42 County Wildlife Site, site description, 1044.
43 County Wildlife Site, site description, 141.
44 County Wildlife Site, site description, 1047.
45 County Wildlife Site, site description, 25.
46 Natural England citation, Fritton Common: https://designatedsites.naturalengland.org.uk/PDFsForWeb/Citation/1000352.pdf, accessed 10.8.2024.

CHAPTER 9

Comparisons and Conclusions

Commons and Contexts

The examination of common land in the county of Norfolk presented in this book has hopefully served to highlight key aspects of its character, some already familiar but others perhaps more surprising and somewhat neglected in the past. Commons became defined and fixed in the landscape in the two centuries following the Norman Conquest; they represent the remnants of once more extensive tracts of uncultivated land – something which explains much about their morphology – and generally survived unploughed because the soils they occupied were acidic, permanently waterlogged, or both. Comparatively few were to be found on poorly draining clays, which evidently posed less of a challenge to medieval farmers. A high proportion thus carried a heathy vegetation, but trees were also numerous; many commons appear to have initially been at least partly wooded and a surprising number retained a respectable covering of trees into the eighteenth or nineteenth centuries. Commons played an important role in the rural and domestic economy and accordingly attracted farms to their margins in order to allow the more convenient exploitation of the grazing, fuel and other resources they afforded, in the increasingly arable world on the twelfth and thirteenth centuries. Commons form the bones of Norfolk's settlement pattern, even underlying the plan forms of some of the nucleated villages in its more 'champion' areas.

The resources provided by commons were not freely available to all; nor were they shared equally amongst those entitled to exploit them. Their use was usually regulated in such a way that the wealthiest commoners received the greatest benefits. The poorest members of the community, in contrast, might derive some marginal resources from them but usually on sufferance rather than by right. Commons were not communal property. Common rights resembled shares, owned in varying quantities by private individuals according to their landed wealth, and might be colonised by pieces of private property, like the 'plantings' of pollarded trees widely established by commoners, especially in the county's claylands. But in the final analysis commons were owned by the manorial lord, whose freedom to use them for his own profit varied with the independence and economic strength of the commoner community but was always considerable. Lordly owners could plant trees on commons, allow industrial enterprises to be established there, or even permit portions to be enclosed. Some such actions might notionally require the formal consent of commoners in the manorial court, but this was likely to be forthcoming. Relations between the wealthier commoners, and manorial lord, were not necessarily antagonistic, not least because they needed to jointly defend their rights against the encroachments of neighbouring individuals and communities, and of the poor in their own parishes.

This is not to deny that commons also had a communal aspect. They came to be used, in particular, to fulfil parochial obligations concerning the care of the poor both formally – by providing sites for poor houses and allotments – and informally – as places where the poor might gather fuel. Nor is it to deny that commoners and their lords frequently came into conflict, leading on occasions to legal cases, direct action, even violence. But these were essentially disputes over property rights, not struggles between rich and poor. And while enclosure of common land is often seen as disastrous for small landowners and the landless poor, the reality was more complex. The fortunes of these groups declined through the post-medieval period for a host of reasons associated with the rise of an increasingly market-oriented society, of which enclosure was only one. There is no evidence that the disappearance of commons, in Norfolk at least, led to the wholesale demise of small owners, and there was clearly a widespread belief that the poor should receive meaningful compensation for the uses they had made of common land, even where these had been exercised without legal right.

Commons were, throughout their history, intensively used and probably, for the most part, well managed. They were highly unnatural environments, their ecology fundamentally structured by repeated cutting and grazing. But there are dangers in thinking of them solely in agrarian terms. Gravel and other materials were dug from them, often on an awesome scale. A range of industrial enterprises might be sited on or beside them, exploiting the fuel or mineral resources they provided (Figure 9.1). Above all, they provided accessible open spaces, fully integrated with the public road network, which could be used to host a range of recreational activities, and for fairs and markets; commons have structured the morphology of urban as much as of rural settlement.

Common land thus has a long and complex history. Yet at the same time the commons present in the landscape of today are essentially a creation of the last century and a half. Legislative developments have radically changed the rights enjoyed over them, not least in ensuring universal public access, and have redefined 'common land' so that it now includes a host of areas over which common rights were formally extinguished long ago or, in a few cases, may never have existed. Most commons, moreover, have experienced a long decline into dereliction which has ensured that, as habitats and environments, they often bear only a passing resemblance to how they were in the late nineteenth century. And where they are managed, it is often in different ways, and to achieve different ends, from in the past, for most commons in Norfolk are now valued primarily as wildlife habitats and as a recreational resource.

Large parts of the story I have presented unquestionably have a wider relevance, to other areas of England, not least because they concern aspects of national law. But others do not because they are the outcome of specific local circumstances. Commons are firmly embedded in their natural and social contexts, entangled in the environments and histories of particular areas and regions. To take an obvious example, the presence of extensive deposits of combustible peat gave commons in Norfolk an importance as a fuel resource that they did not necessarily possess elsewhere. The study of commons exemplifies a more general problem in environmental and social history in England, one noted in the Introduction. Particular institutions or phenomena can only be understood through in-depth studies of restricted areas, for only these can illuminate the complexity of the influences that shaped them. Yet every area, every locality is different, calling into question the wider relevance of the conclusions of such studies. It is true that Norfolk is a large and diverse county and that this allows us to examine, for example, the differing character and development of common land on the poor acid soils of Breckland and the rich moist clays in the south-east of the county. But a brief look at the history of common land in some other parts of the country, emphasising the differences as much as the similarities with the Norfolk experience, will – while

FIG. 9.1. Windmill and former brickpits on the common at Brill, Buckinghamshire.

Common Land in Hertfordshire

Hertfordshire makes a useful comparison, since it is geologically different from Norfolk but not radically so. Most of the county overlies chalk but this is mainly obscured by later deposits and only exposed in the major river valleys which have cut through them and, more extensively, on the long escarpment of the Chiltern Hills and their more muted north-easterly continuation beyond Hitchin, which broadly correspond with the county's north-western boundary.[1] In south Hertfordshire the principal overlying deposit is the heavy, impermeable London Clay.[2] This covers much of the area to the south of Watford, Hatfield and Hertford, and is capped on the highest ground by spreads of acid gravels – the 'Pebble Gravels' – and sporadic deposits of boulder clay, all giving rise to some of the worst soils in the county: principally those of the Essendon and Windsor Associations, which are both seasonally waterlogged and acidic.[3] Similar Tertiary deposits originally also extended across the north and west of the county but here they were first eroded by surface streams and then weathered during the intense cold of the Ice Ages to form the Plateau Drift, a variable mixture of sandy clays with pebbles. These give rise to a range of soils – principally those of the Batcombe, Hornbeam 2 and Hornbeam 3 Associations – which are again acidic and generally poorly draining, although significantly less so than those in the south of the county.[4] The east of the county, in contrast, is characterised by the same glacial till which dominates the geology of central and southern Norfolk, although here more calcareous in nature.[5] The dominant soils, those of the Hanslope Association, while poorly draining and seasonally waterlogged, are lime-rich and fertile.[6] Domesday shows this as by far the most densely populated part of the county, a position only slowly eroded during the following centuries by the expansion of clearance and cultivation on the more challenging soils to the south and west.[7]

Even at the time of Domesday, however, the boulder clay soils still largely comprised uncultivated woodland and pasture, and the dense population of the area largely reflected the extent to which it was dissected by valleys in which freely draining soils were found. Indeed, everywhere in the county early settlement was concentrated on the lower ground, including not only the principal river valleys but also a broad area of low-lying land, the Vale of St Albans, running roughly east–west through the county on the northern flank of the London Clay uplands.[8] This marks the course of the old, pre-glacial Thames and is characterised by sands and gravels largely deposited by glacial meltwaters, overlain in places by silty drift and till, giving rise to a diverse range of well-drained and moderately fertile soils.[9] In the period between the tenth and the thirteenth century, settlement and cultivation expanded out from Vale and valley, creating a complex scatter of hamlets and isolated farms across the heavier soils of the interfluves: Hertfordshire is a mainly 'woodland' county and only a narrow strip of land, along the chalk escarpment and on the Gault clay below it, extends into the 'champion' Midlands, with its landscapes of nucleated villages and extensive, continuous open fields, although broadly similar arrangements could be found in some of the larger valleys in the north-east of the county.[10]

In Hertfordshire, as in Norfolk, common land represents the fragments of 'waste' that survived after the great medieval expansion and displays the same irregular shapes, curving boundaries and tapering, funnel entrances. But its distribution in the period before the parliamentary enclosures of the late eighteenth and nineteenth centuries is more difficult to reconstruct because Hertfordshire lacks an eighteenth-century county map as detailed and accurate as William Faden's Norfolk survey. Its equivalent, Dury and Andrew's map of 1766, is a much more schematic affair.[11] While it shows, with tolerable accuracy, most of the larger commons then extant, distinctly shaded, the presence of others is only implied – by a name on the map and the presence of 'unbounded' roads, as in the case of Bernards Heath to the north of St Albans – while a significant minority, mainly the smaller examples, are omitted altogether.[12] But the location, size and morphology of many of these can, with some confidence, be reconstructed using a wide range of more local maps from the seventeenth, eighteenth and early nineteenth centuries, allowing useful comparisons with Norfolk to be made (Figure 9.2).

Compared with Norfolk, Hertfordshire was, by the eighteenth century, not well endowed with common land. Dury and Andrew's map shows it occupying only 4.1 per cent of the county's surface area, a figure which rises, but only to 4.5 per cent, if the various known omissions are taken into account. These are by no means complete but this suggests, nevertheless, that area for area eighteenth-century Hertfordshire possessed between a third and half the amount of common land of Norfolk. While in both counties a significant proportion had been lost through encroachment and enclosure over the preceding five centuries, this difference is unlikely to have changed significantly since commons first became fixed and defined in the landscape. The explanation for it probably lies, in large part, in the character of the soils found in the two counties. In Hertfordshire, as in Norfolk, medieval settlement and land use were not significantly constrained by poor drainage; commons were numerous but small and scattered on the boulder clay soils of the Hanslope Association in the east of the county (Figure 9.3). It was soil acidity that encouraged the survival of commons and repelled the expansion of fields and farms and here, as in Norfolk, the area of common heaths and acid grassland greatly exceeded, and exceeds, that of clayland 'greens'. But while across the rest of the county the soils are mainly acidic in nature, only on the highest ground and on interfluves between major drainage basins, in the north-west (on the crest of the Chilterns) and in the far south (where Pebble Gravels capped the London Clay), are they comparable in this respect with soils like those of the Newport 4 Association,

9. *Comparisons and Conclusions* 197

FIG. 9.2. Probable extent of common land in Hertfordshire at the end of the eighteenth century (above), and registered commons today (below) (old county boundary above, modern below).

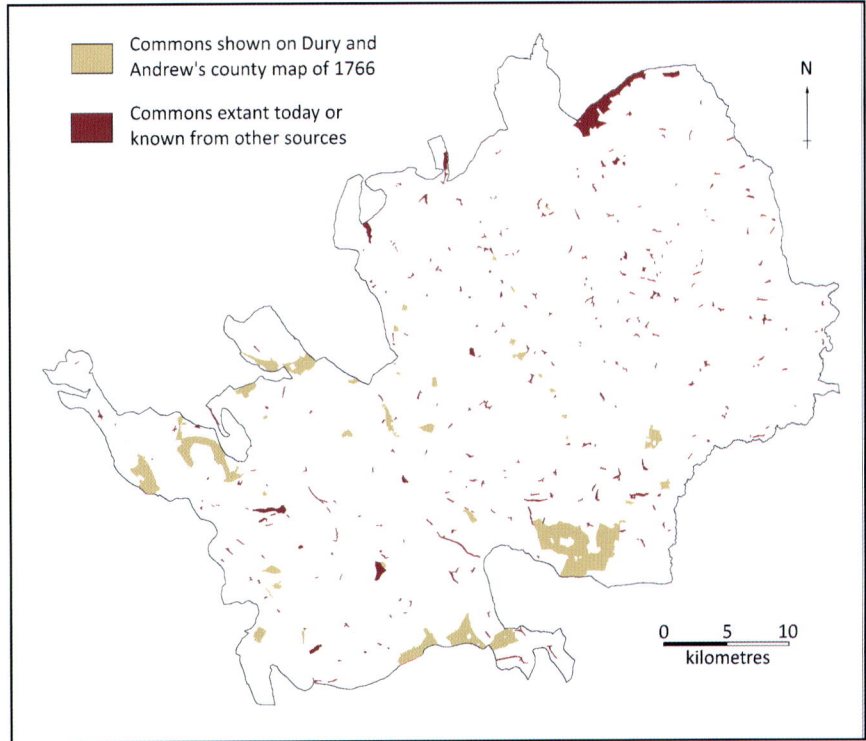

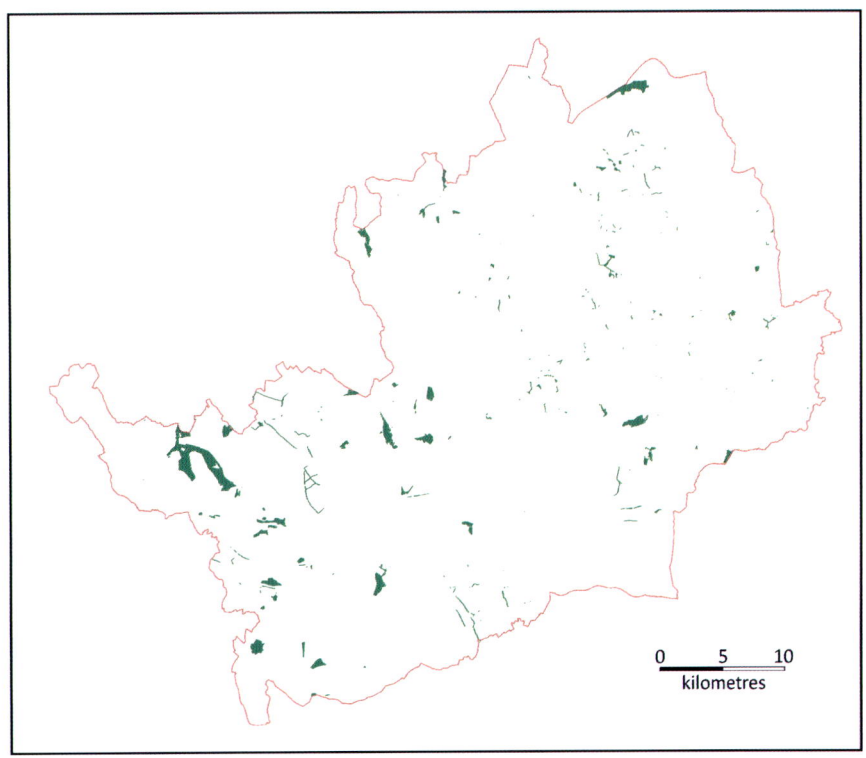

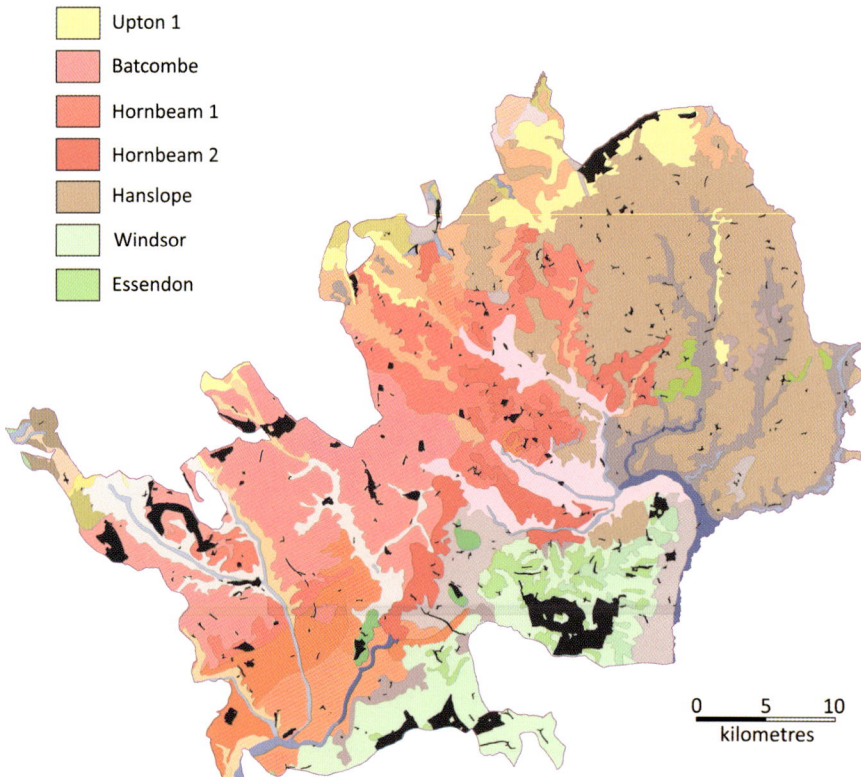

FIG. 9.3. Hertfordshire: commons and soils. Only the most important soil associations, or those closely associated with common land, are shown on the key.

formed in glacial sands and gravels, which blanket much of Norfolk's land surface. In these places vast commons carrying a heathy vegetation of gorse and heather could accordingly be found. In the south these included Bushey Heath and Elstree, Barnet, Northaw and Cheshunt Commons; on the crest of the Chiltern Hills in the north-west the commons of Caddington, Kensworth, Studham, Tring, Berkhamsted and Aldbury (Figure 9.3).

In Hertfordshire, as in Norfolk, many heaths appear to have been wood pastures, covered to varying extents with trees that were mostly pollarded, in the Middle Ages, gradually becoming more open in the course of the post-medieval centuries. Even in the middle of the eighteenth century the Finnish visitor Pehr Kalm described Northaw Common as:

> Covered with tufts of ling, between which bracken flourished and swamps abounded. But there was scarcely any grass. Sheep grazed here. In places *Carpinus* (hornbeam) grew fairly densely to a height of six feet, and the tops of it were cut for fuel.[13]

The rate at which such commons lost their trees displayed much variation. Berkhamsted Frith, wooded in the Middle Ages, was marked on a map of 1638 as 'Barkhamsteed Heathe with out trees'.[14] Barnet Common was described at the end of the seventeenth century as 'formerly a wood, but … of recent years laid waste, and used as a common'.[15] Nearby Northaw Common in contrast was still densely treed when enclosed by a parliamentary act of 1803, the draft Ordnance Survey Drawings made two years later showing it almost as a wood but inscribed with the words 'Clearing for Inclosure'.[16]

Even where they lacked trees Hertfordshire's heaths, like those in Norfolk, were a significant source of fuel, as well as grazing. Its extraction was carefully regulated, in a manner that should by now be familiar, in order to preserve supplies, prevent householders from taking more than their due share, and deny use by people living outside the parish. In 1764 the manor court at Aldbury, for example, prohibited the cutting of furze or fern on the commons between 31 July and 1 September, that is, the summer growing season;[17] at Bushey in 1707 the court ordered a closed period between 'May Day and Michaelmas' and in October 1600 forbade the selling of furze cut from the waste to anyone living outside the manor.[18] In the late seventeenth century the tenants of the manor of Berkhamsted were similarly forbidden from selling furze gathered from the commons to any 'Forrainer' and also from cutting it using a bill with a double blade or with a handle that was more than 12 inches long, although exceptions were made for those who were aged over 60 or under 14, or were disabled.[19] At Tring in the same period the manor court ruled that 'no person [was] to carry any scrubbs [sic] or heath [heather] out of the commons upon carts carriages or on horse back' but only as much as 'they can carry upon their backs'.[20] Such examples could be endlessly multiplied: these were intensive exploited and managed environments and there was nothing very 'wild' about them. In 1748 Pehr Kalm reported that much of Berkhamsted common 'was overgrown with *Genista spinosa* [gorse], which was here not much over a hand's breadth high because the poor people are continually cutting it down to the ground and taking it home as fuel'.[21]

Many other parallels, and similarities, between the commons of the two counties could be instanced. In Hertfordshire as in Norfolk, commons, especially heaths, have served to preserve a range of important early earthworks within what is otherwise a largely arable or urbanised landscape. The county is not rich in prehistoric barrows but the two best barrow cemeteries are on common land – on Chipperfield Common and Therfield Heath – while the unusual Roman barrow cemetery called the 'Six Hills' in Stevenage occupies almost the entire area of a small common, now marooned somewhat incongruously within the New Town. The Chiltern commons in the west of the county are particularly important in this respect. Earthworks of Iron Age and Roman enclosures, fields and lanes have been discovered on Aldbury and Berkhamsted Commons, while the latter boasts the best preserved stretch of the linear earthwork called Grimms Ditch to survive in the county – as well as a remarkable series of First World War practice trenches.[22]

In Hertfordshire as much as in Norfolk, moreover, the development of settlement was intimately connected with that of common land. As, in the course of the eleventh, twelfth and thirteenth centuries, clearance and cultivation expanded on to the difficult soils of the 'uplands', a high proportion of farms and cottages clustered around the margins of surviving fragments of 'waste', although perhaps to a greater degree than in Norfolk their subsequent encroachment, often at a late date, has obscured this relationship, especially on the eastern claylands (Figure 9.4). Only in situations where water was difficult to obtain were common edges settled sparsely, or not at all. In the east of the county the attraction of farms and cottages to greens often suppressed the development of existing settlements located on the margins of the clay plateau, leaving parish churches marginalised (Rushden, Meesden) or completely isolated (Sacombe). Some examples of this exist elsewhere in the county (Sarratt, Little Gaddesden). But in these poorer and less populous areas parish churches were generally established at a later date than in the east of the county, or in Norfolk – alongside, rather than before, the great expansion of settlement. More of them therefore stand away from major valleys, beside upland commons or former commons to which settlement had already migrated (Aldbury, Wigginton, Abbots Langley, Monken Hadley). In some major valleys in the north-east of the county, and on and below the chalk escarpment, 'champion' landscapes of nucleated villages surrounded by extensive open fields tended to develop, hydrological conditions precluding dispersal of settlement into the immediately surrounding area. In such circumstances, as in west Norfolk, village plans seem sometimes to have developed through the progressive infilling of a green or common pasture, as at Willian or Weston. All in all, the intimate relationship between rural settlement and common land may be less immediately obvious in Hertfordshire than in Norfolk but it is no less pervasive and important.

The same is true of common land and urban settlement. Hertfordshire commons were used for fairs from an early date – the name of Chipperfield Common in Kings Langley means something like 'the open area used by traders' – and most of its medieval towns, like those in Norfolk, were ranged around marketplaces morphologically indistinguishable from commons, and with no sign of a planned origin. Some, often the earliest like those at St Albans or Hitchin, comprised (before partial infilling in the course of the Middle Ages) large triangles of land; others, such as Watford or Stevenage, were irregular widenings in a main road. At Watford the church stands beside the marketplace and appears to have been established after it had come into existence, probably in the reign of Henry I.[23] At Stevenage, in contrast, the church stands beside the manor house nearly a kilometre from the medieval town and its marketplace, which developed on the Great North Road some time before 1281. The growth of the town presumably suppressed that of the original settlement beside the church, or even drew houses away from it.[24] Chipping Barnet and probably Royston are among other Hertfordshire examples of 'common edge' towns.[25]

Once again, in Hertfordshire as in Norfolk, we find common land used in a wide variety of other non-agricultural ways. Commons heaths are often scattered with pits for the extraction of sand, gravel or some underlying deposit of chalk or brickearth, most notably perhaps Bernards Heath in St Albans; the clayland greens in the east of the county, such as Roe Green in Sandon, tend

FIG. 9.4. Aston End, Hertfordshire, as shown on the tithe map of 1840 (with green shading added for clarity). Late medieval and post-medieval encroachments often removed the close association of farms and commons on the claylands in the east of the county. Unusually, this map distinguishes between enclosed land, surviving commons (brown) and areas of 'waste' (green) occupied and improved at some unknown time in the past, making it clear that the farms shown all once fronted directly on a network of linear 'greens'.

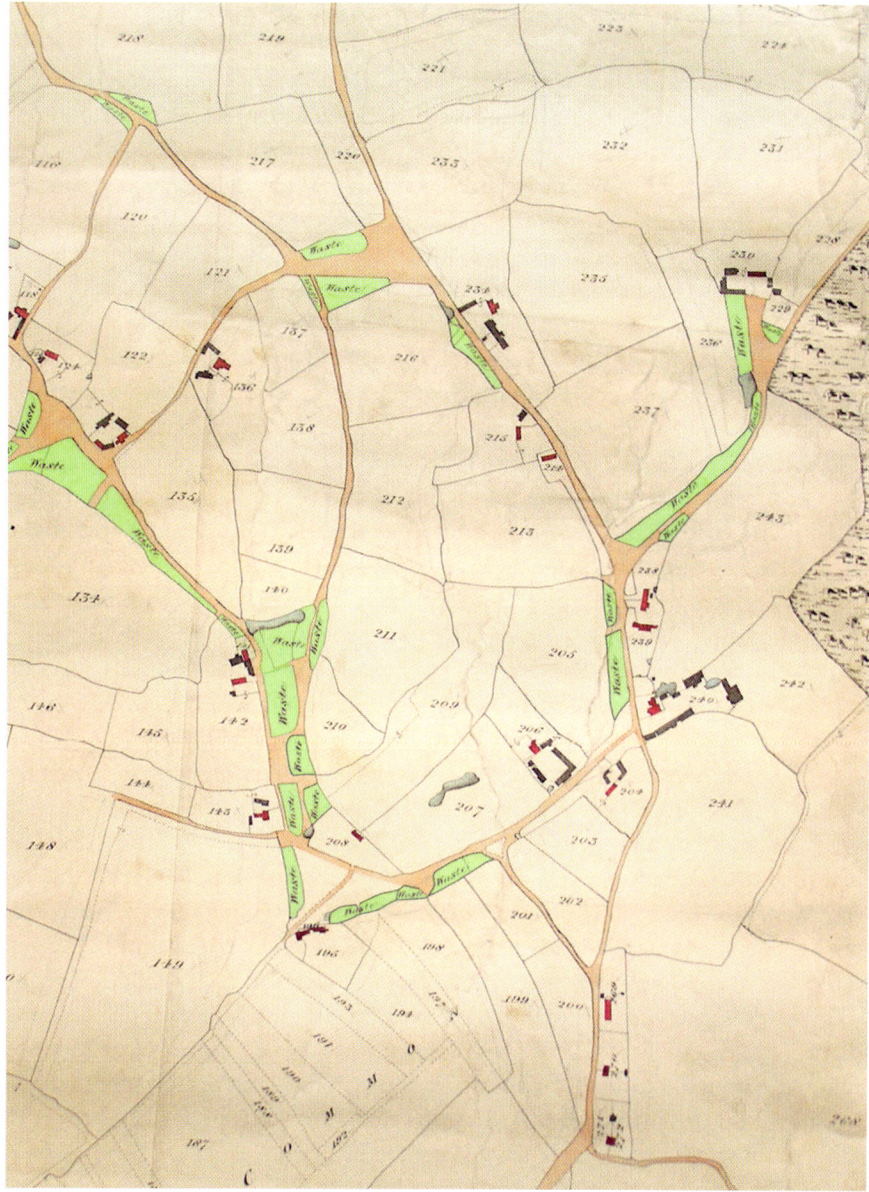

like those in south and central Norfolk to only have them along the perimeter, close to farms or sites of former farms. Windmills were often built on intakes from common land, as on Bushey Heath, Patmore Heath in Albury, Cheshunt Common, Chipperfield Common, Colney Heath, Northaw Common, Roe Green at Sandon, Bernards Heath in St Albans and elsewhere, although the relationship is not quite as strong as in Norfolk.[26] Brickworks gravitated to the margins of commons, as at Bernards Heath or Harpenden, or occupied intakes within them, as on Aldbury, Berkhamsted, Northaw or Barnet Commons.[27] And here, too, common land was extensively used from an early date for a range of essentially recreational activities. The brickworks at Barnet and Northaw both shared their respective commons with 'medicinal wells', which doubtless benefitted from the proximity of London. Celia Fiennes, visiting Barnet in the 1680s, described how 'the houses are made commodious to entertain the company that comes to drink the waters', but decided against sampling them herself after noting that the well was 'full of leaves and dirt'.[28] There was also a race course here in the eighteenth century ('such an exhibition of bad horses, and worse riders … not to be seen at any other course in England'), which continued in use until 1870.[29] Another existed at Odsey in the far north of the county, on the great common to the west of Royston, where races were said to be 'frequent' in 1751 but had been discontinued before the end of the century.[30] In Hertfordshire, as in Norfolk, we fail to appreciate the full role of commons if we concentrate only on farms and farming, commoners and common rights.

In Hertfordshire as in Norfolk, commons had lost most of their economic importance by the start of the twentieth century, but maps and aerial photographs suggest only limited regeneration of woodland before the drastic decline of rabbit populations following the introduction of myxomatosis. In the Chiltern Hills, Berkhamsted Common, Pitstone Common and Aldbury Common were still mainly open ground at the end of the Second World War. But by the 1970s they were all largely wooded, and the same is true of most of the smaller commons scattered across the Chiltern dipslope, such as Chipperfield Common or Bernards Heath in St Albans. All this may be reflected in the official statistics for woodland in a county in which (unlike Norfolk) there was little deliberate planting, by private individuals or the Forestry Commission, before the end of the twentieth century. In 1905 woodland cover was estimated as 6.5 per cent of the land area, in 1913 at 5.2 per cent, in 1924 at 6.4 per cent and in 1949 at 6.6 per cent. By 1959, however, it had leapt to 7.5 per cent; by 1980 the figure was 7.7 per cent; and by 1998 it had reached around 9 per cent.[31] Amenity planting in a rapidly suburbanising county and regeneration over abandoned mineral working accounts for much of this increase but the development of woodland on derelict commons, no longer held in check by large numbers of rabbits, must have made a significant contribution.

Further broad parallels might be drawn between the two counties in terms of the character and development of common land. But the differences are perhaps more interesting and illuminating. In Hertfordshire, as in Norfolk, present-day legally recognised commons, registered under the 1965 act, include some pieces of land that were not traditionally common land. In Kings Langley for example one of the five was a privately owned meadow in 1844 and another a 'pleasure ground and garden'.[32] Meadows at Hertford have also been registered, and at Wigginton three ponds that were all privately owned in 1910.[33] But there are few such cases: almost all registered commons in Hertfordshire are 'real' commons, largely because very few poor's allotments, or highways surveyors' pits were registered here. There are a number of reasons for this. The first and most important is that these types of land were created by the parliamentary enclosure of common 'waste' and in Hertfordshire such enclosures were comparatively rare. Outside the 'champion' areas of the county most open fields disappeared at an early date and a high proportion of the county's commons escaped enclosure and survive to this day. Secondly, the poor do not seem to have used commons as a source of fuel to the same extent as in Norfolk so that when such land was enclosed by act they were not considered to require any compensation for its loss. The county abounded in managed woodland and in hedges which, in Arthur Young's words, were planted and managed more 'for fuel than fences'.[34] While much firewood was sent to London, much was burned locally, particularly the twiggy growth, bound into faggots, probably largely by the poor. Conversely, deposits of peat were restricted and only in two areas were there extensive tracts of true heath, affording an abundance of gorse and heather, enclosed by parliamentary act; on the crest of the Chilterns, and on the high ground in the far south of the county. Here, significantly, enclosure awards did sometimes make provision for the poor. In the Chilterns, a fuel allotment of 100 acres was made when Tring Common was enclosed in 1804 and one of 10 acres at the enclosure of Wigginton in 1854.[35] In the south, allotments were made at Chipping Barnet (1818) and Elstree (1777), while a fund was established to benefit the poor in Totteridge, in compensation for losses experienced from the enclosure of Barnet Common.[36]

But coal, long used by the wealthy, became relatively cheap and more widely used in the county with the completion of the Grand Junction canal in the 1790s and of the London–Birmingham railway in the 1840s, while proximity to London ensured an active market in, and high rents for, land. Trustees responded accordingly. The allotments at Tring, Barnet and Elstree were all being rented out by 1841; the second and third of these had been sold off, and the proceeds invested, by the end of the century; while that at Tring was exchanged with Sir Nathan Meyer de Rothschilde for 15 acres of land elsewhere in the parish and £5,000 of investments, the rents and dividends from which were used to purchase coal.[37] High land prices generally ensured that other varieties of land allotted by awards, which in Norfolk continued as increasingly derelict open spaces, ultimately considered suitable for registration, were here sold off or given defined roles – only one parish gravel pit, at Standon, appears to have been registered under the 1965 act. At Cheshunt, enclosed in 1804, the cottagers were provided with an allotment of 100 acres as a 'stinted common', but vestiges of peasant economy must have been out of place in this suburbanising area so close to London and by the end of the century it was being leased out and the income distributed.[38]

The relative paucity of enclosure acts dealing with common 'waste' in Hertfordshire has the corollary that large areas of such land survived up until the time of the registration process. Indeed, with the notable exception of the great common heaths in the far south of the county, the majority of commons existing in the mid-eighteenth century escaped enclosure and remain extant. Quite why this should be is a complex question that requires more research; what is clear is that commons, at least by the nineteenth century, did not play the central role in the lives of the poor and small landowners often suggested by historians; nor did their survival bring these groups any very obvious advantages. Poverty remained 'endemic among the labouring population and a constant threat to hard-pressed farmers'.[39] It was the expansion of industrial and semi-industrial by-employments such as straw plaiting, and a gradual increase in the provision of allotment gardens, rather than the continued exploitation of the meagre and marginal resources afforded by common land, that raised the living standards of rural workers in the course of the nineteenth century.[40] Moreover, while there were major and sometimes violent protests against the enclosure of common land in the sixteenth and seventeenth century – as at Aldenham, Shenley and North Mymms – all were against illegal, unilateral enclosures by manorial lords, and no similar actions attended the parliamentary enclosures of the eighteenth and nineteenth centuries.[41] Indeed, the only major dispute in this period again involved an illegal manorial initiative. In 1865 Earl Brownlow enclosed around a third of Berkhamsted Common with iron fences, having bought out most, but not all, of the commoners: Augustus Smith, a wealthy local resident, still retained his rights and on 7 March 1866 brought 120 labourers by train from London to break them down. In a subsequent court case, in which the newly formed Commons Preservation Society was much involved, the Earl was defeated.[42] In the increasingly suburbanised south and west of the county common land was already, by the middle of the nineteenth century, making the transition from local agrarian resource, to mainly recreational space, no doubt contributing significantly to the survival of those examples that had so far escaped enclosure. The intensity of subsequent urban development further enhanced their value in this respect, and also in terms of nature conservation, often presenting significant management challenges. By the 1920s many were already under pressure from visitors, especially in the Chilterns, with cars and motorbikes being driven long distances from the public roads. The main Chiltern commons are now carefully managed by the National Trust; many others, including Hertford Heath, Patmore Heath and Therfield Heath, are SSSIs or local nature reserves in the care of the Hertfordshire and Middlesex Wildlife Trust or some other body (Figure 9.5). A significant number, such as Watford Heath, are mown areas little different from any other municipal open space.

Northamptonshire

My second case study, Northamptonshire, could scarcely be more different. It was a largely 'champion' county, its medieval landscape characterised by nucleated villages and extensive, communally regulated open fields.[43] Space precludes any detailed discussion of this landscape, still less of the county's soils and geology, beyond noting that this was characterised by a complex range of

FIG. 9.5. Patmore Heath, Albury, now a nature reserve managed by the Herts and Middlesex Wildlife Trust.

pre-Cretaceous deposits on lower ground, mainly clays and mudstones, blanketed by boulder clay on the higher. Traditionally, historians have emphasised the paucity of uncultivated common land in 'champion' areas, the vast extent of the arable, and this impression is superficially borne out by the fact that Northamptonshire is today poorly endowed with registered commons, with only around two dozen examples, mostly tiny pieces of land covering less than an acre.[44] Some – at Broughton, Pitsford, Brafield, Culworth, Houghton, Weston, Weedon Lois and Kingsbury – are small greens of the kind frequently found in Northamptonshire villages; at Kingscliff a 'public wash dyke' was registered; and at Evenley a larger area of common land. But once again registered areas include land considered fully private in 1910 (at Woodnewton, Isham, Aynho, Brafield and Apethorpe), together with such things as a gravel pit at Nassington, village pounds at Yarwell and Crick and allotment gardens at Grendon.[45] It is true that at Ailsworth, now part of Peterborough but formerly in the county, there is the large Ailsworth Heath and a number of other commons; it is also true that there are several large village greens, at Great Creaton, Badby, Helidon and elsewhere, which survive but were never registered. But the contrast with Norfolk and Hertfordshire is, nevertheless, a marked one.

Historians of Northamptonshire have highlighted the three royal forests, all occupying clay-covered uplands between major drainage basins, as the main areas where extensive commons, broadly similar to those so far discussed, were to be found: Whittlewood and Salcey in the south of the county (and extending well beyond its borders), and Rockingham in the north-east (Figure 9.6).[46]

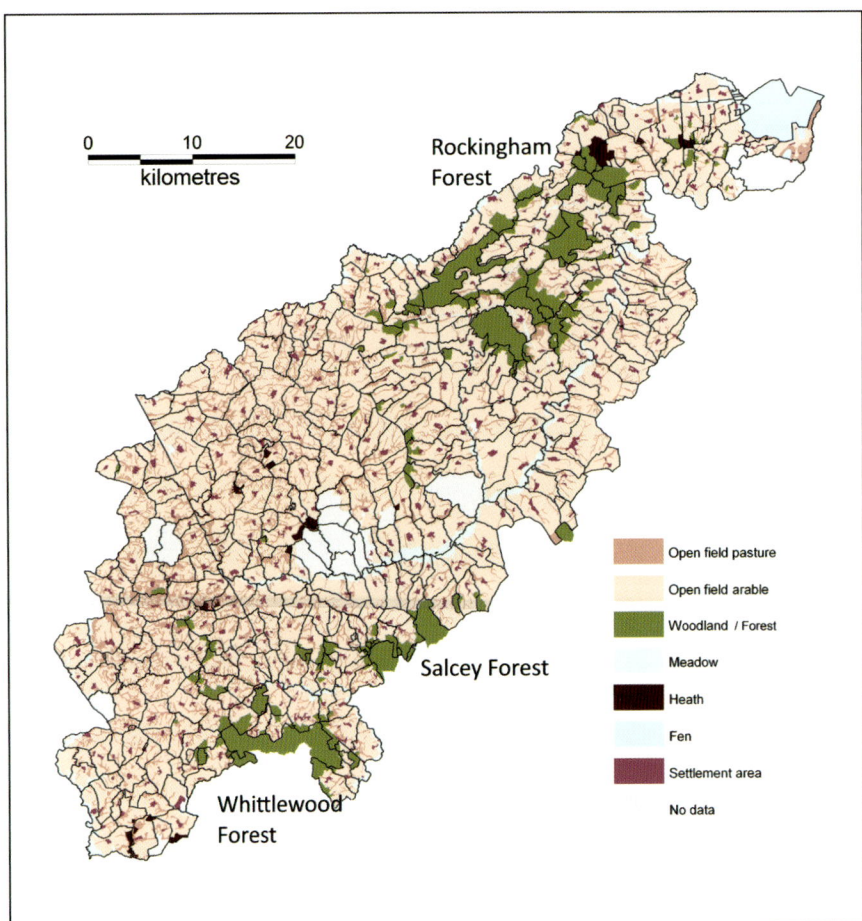

FIG. 9.6.
Northamptonshire: medieval land use.

Their core areas, belonging to the Crown, were in part extra-parochial and comprised blocks of enclosed woodland separated by areas of common pasture. The forest bounds extended beyond these, however, with forest law – regulations designed to protect the deer and their habitats – being applied to the farmland of many surrounding townships. In some of the pasture areas – the 'ridings' and 'plains' – the inhabitants of villages in and around the forests grazed cattle, and sometimes pigs, alongside the king's deer and enjoyed other common rights. They could also graze many of the woods in the later stages of the coppice rotation. The largest single block of grazing comprised the combined plains of Benefield, Weldon and Deenethorpe in Rockingham Forest, which amounted in all to c. 1200 hectares. Most of this land had probably comprised wood-pasture in the early Middle Ages and some continued to carry a scatter of pollards well into post-medieval times. In Rockingham the grazing season ran from 29 April to 11 November; in Salcey from Old May Day to 22 November; and in Whittlewood from 5 April to 11 November in the case of the 'in-towns', and from 4 May to 25 September in the case of the 'out towns'.

The latter phrase references the fact that common rights in all the forests were shared between large numbers of parishes, some of which lay well away from the wooded 'core'. Geddington Chase in Rockingham Forest for example was grazed by the inhabitants of Geddington itself, Brigstock, Stanion and Newton Willows; Whittlewood by Whitfield and Silverstone (the 'in-towns') and by Syresham with Crowfield, Wappenham, and Slapton (the 'out-towns').[47] Commoners were also permitted to collect 'sere and broken' wood – fallen boughs and the like, rather than poles cut from the enclosed coppices. As in other contexts, common rights were not universally enjoyed, but in each village were attached to particular commonable tenements. Their owners generally constituted a declining proportion of the population, for forest villages grew at a higher than average rate, in part perhaps because they absorbed people displaced from enclosed and depopulated townships in the surrounding 'champion' areas. In Whittlewood, by the seventeenth century, those with common rights frequently constituted only 20–25 per cent of the population; in Rockingham the proportion was generally lower.

The forests were organisationally complex landscapes, administered by royal officials and officers, and their management became more difficult as, over time, areas of woodland were alienated into private hands, and permission given to make assarts or create deer parks. Through the post-medieval period the basic rules and regulations governing the forests were increasingly flouted. By the sixteenth century sheep, as well as cattle, were being grazed on the plains; the coppices were grazed out of season; and overstocking was endemic. When Rockingham was enclosed, many commoners claimed the right to graze unlimited numbers of animals 'all year round'.[48] Deer were poached on a large scale and were continually disturbed by people entering the woods while nutting. A notice printed in 1819 declared that as 'the deer … have of late years have been much disturbed by people gathering nuts', offenders would be prosecuted.[49] The right to collect 'sere and broken' wood was often interpreted as green and growing wood, either from trees or, more damagingly, from coppices.[50] There were numerous disputes between, as well as within, villages over grazing and other rights.

Much has been written about these distinctive landscapes of commoning, almost with the implication that they comprised islands of unploughed ground in what were otherwise uninterrupted seas of arable. But careful mapping of the cartographic and archaeological evidence – the latter in the form of the plough ridges which, following enclosure, were widely preserved in the landscape until recently by the large scale conversion of land to permanent pasture – suggests that, even at its greatest extent, arable accounted for no more than 66 per cent of Northamptonshire's land surface.[51] The rest comprised, in addition to the forests and a scatter of woods outside them, areas of common fen in the far east of the county; meadows (mostly held as intermingled strips) beside the major rivers; and innumerable areas of pasture land lying *within* the open fields, running as bands between the furlongs, along the boundaries between townships, and flanking minor watercourses (Figure 9.6). These varied in form and extent – ranging from narrow, irregular ribbons to substantial blocks, as much as a kilometre across.[52] They could be found throughout the county but were particularly numerous and extensive in the west, and especially in a block of 30 contiguous townships extending from Byfield and West Farndon in the south-west to Long Buckby and Welton in the north-east, where several townships had less than 60 per cent of their land in cultivation (Figure 9.7). These ribbons of open-field pasture were, in a sense, common land, freely accessed and exploited, like the adjacent areas of arable, by those holding land in the common fields. But they were not, in these open landscapes, enclosed from the adjacent arable by hedges. When this lay under crops the larger areas could be grazed by livestock, but only under close supervision, and cut for hay.

Such areas were also exploited in other ways. In some places they coincided with pockets of acidic soils and comprised heathland – especially around Wittering, on either side of the Kingsthorpe Brook near Northampton, and in the south-west of the county around Croughton, Evenley and Hinton (only the

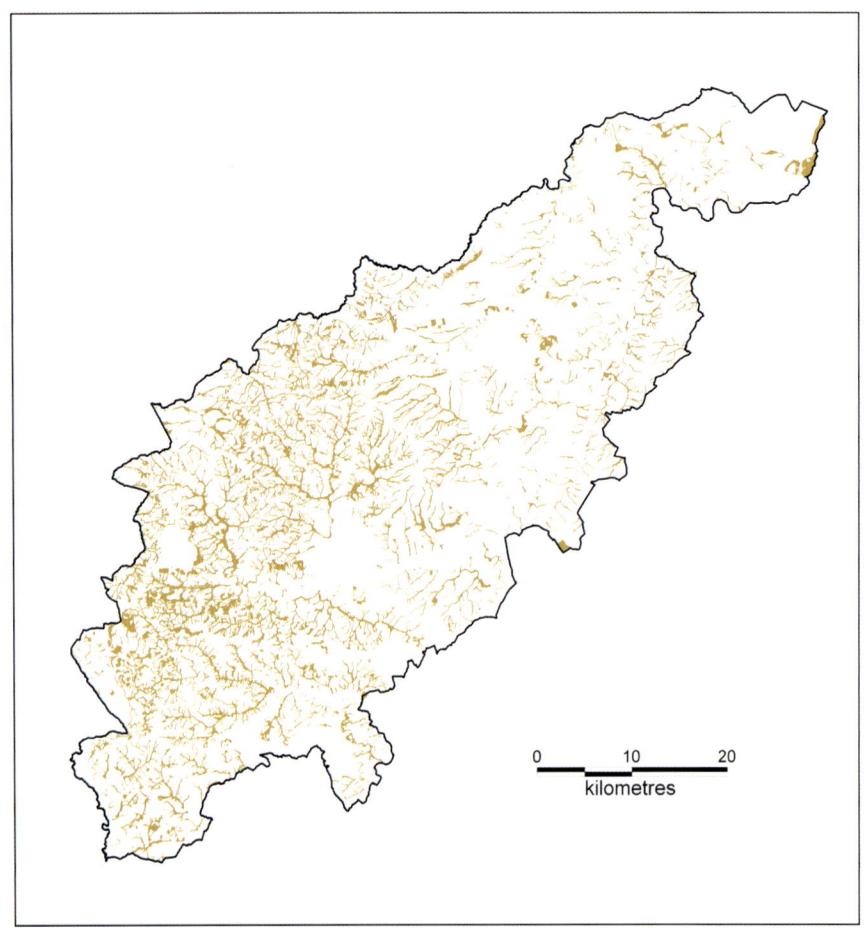

FIG. 9.7.
Northamptonshire: 'open-field pasture'.

larger areas of heathland are shown in Figure 9.6).⁵³ These provided, in a way that should by now be familiar, fuel and animal bedding as well as grazing. In 1635, at Burton Latimer, furze and thorns were allotted in faggots at the rate of 120 for a yardland, 60 for each ancient cottage and 30 for each newly built cottage.⁵⁴ Court rolls, such as those for East Haddon in 1664, include prosecutions for cutting out of season.⁵⁵ In some places portions of the heath were 'doled', as at Harlestone Heath in the thirteenth century.⁵⁶ In 1767 each yardland in the township had the right to take a load of turf and a 'lot' of brakes from the heath.⁵⁷ What is particularly striking is the similarity between the morphology of these areas of unploughed ground within the Midland open fields and common land of more conventional form. Comparing the layout of commons portrayed on William Faden's 1797 map of Norfolk, with that of the pastures running through the open fields of Northamptonshire, we see the same rambling, interconnected ribbons of unploughed ground, varying in width, surrounding irregular, indented rectangles and ovoids of arable (Figure 9.7 and 9.8).

There were other important, underlying similarities. Close examination of the morphology of Northamptonshire villages suggest that many, as in the more 'champion' areas of Norfolk and Hertfordshire, were formed by the dispersal of farms around the margins of areas of unploughed ground left amidst the arable fields, forming for a time a settlement with a large 'green'; followed by the spread of houses onto the green itself, leading to its fragmentation, erosion or complete obliteration. Many Northamptonshire villages are, like Yardley Hastings or Wappenham, ranged around a number of small, separate greens, connected by curving roads (Figure 9.9). There seems little doubt that this plan was formed

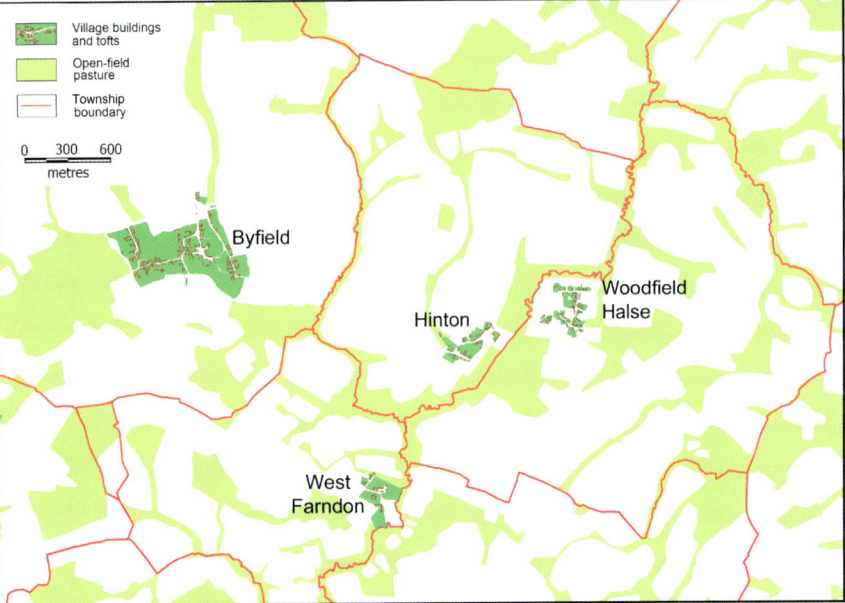

FIG. 9.8. The configuration of 'open-field pasture' in the area around Byfield and Hinton, west Northamptonshire.

by the progressive colonisation of what was once a large, single open space. Indeed, the numerous diminutive 'greens' so characteristic of Northamptonshire villages make little sense as areas of common grazing in their own right. Most clearly represent the truncated remains of larger commons, which themselves had once formed part of (and provided access to) wider areas of pasture which ran, and to some extent continued throughout the Middle Ages to run, through the surrounding open fields. Unsurprisingly, urban settlements, as in the other counties, display an intimate association with common land, with marketplaces at Higham Ferrrers, Rothwell and elsewhere generally indistinguishable, in morphological terms, from the larger village greens.

FIG. 9.9.
Northamptonshire: village plans in the nineteenth century (left) and interpretation as infilled greens (right). Above, Wappenham. Below, Yardley Hastings.

Of the approximately 400 historic townships in the pre-modern county of Northamptonshire, around a third were wholly enclosed, by a variety of means, before 1727, the date of the first enclosure by parliamentary act. The remainder were enclosed by acts which mainly fell within the first wave of parliamentary enclosure, peaking in the 1770s, as was typical on the Midland clays, although a significant minority fell within the second, during the Napoleonic Wars. The enclosure of the Forests, however, generally came later. Brigstock Bailiwick and Cliffe Bailiwick in Rockingham Forest were enclosed in 1805 and 1806, under acts passed in 1795 and 1796, respectively. But the act for Salcey Forest was passed in 1825, with the award coming the following year; that for the remainder of Rockingham in 1832, with the award in 1837; while Whittlewood was enclosed in two stages, with awards in 1826 and 1856. These acts generally made some provision for the poor, allocating parcels of land to the churchwardens or overseers to be rented out and the income used to purchase coals; and some parishes on the edge of the forests separately enclosed, such as Aldwinkle, Burton Latimer, Duddington, Kettering, Oundle, Piddington, Syresham and Whitfield, also received allotments for the poor.[58] Following usual practice, the allocation of allotments broadly reflected the use that the poor had made of the pre-enclosure landscape, in these cases the collection of fallen wood for fuel. Elsewhere allotments were more thinly scattered, generally restricted to parishes where areas of heath had provided a supply of gorse or heather, such as Croughton, Cold Higham and King's Sutton. Most enclosure acts in the county in fact allocated parcels of land to be used for the benefit of the poor but these were mainly allotted in lieu of parish or charity land used for this purpose which already existed in the open fields, rather than as compensation for the loss of resources afforded by the commons.

Most of the county's poor's allotments were leased out, probably from the time of the award, rather than being directly exploited by the poor; some, as at Burton Latimer, were eventually sold and the money invested. The contrast with Norfolk is probably the consequence of three factors; the earlier penetration of coal into the local economy resulting from the proximity of the Warwickshire coalfield and navigable rivers, coupled with a shortage of firewood and peat (John Morton in 1712 emphasised how 'the remotest part of the county is not twenty miles from the seats of coal, either of the inland or of the Newcastle sort'); the late date of the forest enclosures; and, perhaps, the fact that Northamptonshire parishes were generally more firmly under the control of large, tidy-minded landowners than those in Norfolk. Whatever the explanation, as in Hertfordshire, poor's allotments did not generally survive as neglected, freely accessible, 'public' land when the commons registration process began in the 1970s.

Northamptonshire formed the focus for Jeanette Neeson's *Commoners: Common Right, Enclosure and Social Change in England 1700–1820*, published in 1993, a powerful reframing of the argument that parliamentary enclosure had a significant negative impact on the less wealthy members of rural society. She argued that rights of grazing and gleaning across the open fields were of considerable economic value to small landowners and the poor, while around one acre in six in unenclosed parishes in the mid-eighteenth century comprised common 'waste' which afforded them grazing, fuel and wild foods such as nuts and berries.[59] Enclosure dealt these groups a terrible blow, a point she demonstrated statistically through an analysis of the Land Tax for the years 1780–1815, comparing changes in ownership in 17 parishes affected by parliamentary enclosure and six that were not. The contrasts were marked, Neeson concluding that 'many smallholders sold all their land at enclosure and most sold some of it' as a direct consequence of the economic challenges resulting from the costs of enclosure and the loss of common rights.

As Ginter has shown, however, the Land Tax Returns are an unreliable source for this kind of enquiry, consistently confusing owners, leaseholders and rent-payers.[60] Comparing the data from enclosure awards and tithe awards for the relatively few Northamptonshire parishes which possess the latter suggests a more variable picture. When Abthorpe, for example, was enclosed in 1823, 13 individuals received an allotment; by 1840 there were 25 owners with more than 5 acres of land, and no less than 14 with 15 acres or more. In some parishes the numbers of owners declined between enclosure and the tithe award but the pattern of increased land sales following individual awards detected by Neeson can probably be explained, at least in part, by the fact that enclosed land was worth significantly more than open.[61] Act and Award were separated, on average, by three years, but discussion of enclosure had presumably continued for several years before this. Enclosures were thus followed by a cascade of sales, which had hitherto been delayed by the expectation that land prices would rise. As Moore-Colyer has shown at Great Oakley and Corby, many of the smaller occupiers had a variety of by-employments and did not always define themselves as 'farmers'.[62] In some cases land sales following enclosure may have served to liberate capital required for their other business.

The impact of enclosure on the landless poor of the county was examined statistically by Keith Snell, who included Northamptonshire in the research underpinning his *Annals of the Labouring Poor* of 1983. He clearly established that the numbers claiming poor relief tended to rise significantly following a parliamentary enclosure. But in Northamptonshire, as elsewhere in the Midlands, the enclosure of open field was often followed by the laying of land to pasture and it may have been this, rather than enclosure *per se*, which mainly increased unemployment. Eden, discussing Kibworth Beauchamp – just over the county boundary in Leicestershire – in 1797, explained how the poor rates were 'said to have been not one-third of their present figure before the enclosure'. But he added:

> Before the fields were enclosed they were solely applied to the production of corn; the Poor had then plenty of employment in weeding, reaping, thrashing etc., and would also collect a great deal of cash by gleaning, but ... the fields being now in pasturage, the farmers have little occasion for labourers and the Poor being thereby thrown out of employment, must of course be supported by the parish.[63]

In Northamptonshire, as elsewhere, enclosure did the poor few favours. At Raunds the enclosure of 1797 was fiercely opposed by the poorer members of the village community on the basis that they would be:

> Deprived of an inestimable Privilege, which they now enjoy, of turning a certain Number of Cows, Calves, and Sheep, on and over the said lands; a Privilege that enables them ... to maintain themselves and their families in the Depth of Winter.[64]

But, as already noted, it was one of many hostile forces that assailed them. Michael Turner's study of landownership in neighbouring Buckinghamshire concluded that changes in the number of landowners were much the same in old-enclosed parishes as they were in those affected by parliamentary enclosure.[65]

A consideration of these issues in a county characterised by the large-scale enclosure of open *arable* is perhaps a distraction from the story of common land which forms the subject of this book. It is hard, in particular, to disentangle the negative impacts on the poor of the two forms of loss. It seems unlikely, however, that – outside the royal forests – many areas of uncultivated ground provided the copious reserves of fuel and food suggested by Neeson. By the eighteenth century they afforded grazing for those who had a right, or were permitted, to use them, and who could afford to keep livestock, but probably provided few other resources.

Conclusion

The cases of Hertfordshire and Northamptonshire briefly discussed in the previous pages, combined with the more extended treatment of Norfolk, suggest that the landscapes of common land are best understood, not as examples of a recurrent pattern, so much as variations on a number of shared themes. Throughout the country, commons contain pre-medieval earthworks, archaeological evidence of medieval and post-medieval industrial activities, or – as at Cockfield Fell in County Durham – both.[66] Even urban commons, usually much 'municipalised', constitute an important archaeological resource.[67] In all areas, commons have for centuries provided open, accessible places that could be used for trading, public meetings, protests; which could be used for recreation and sports such as horseracing;[68] or exploited for military training. Everywhere commons display the same distinctive range of morphological characteristics – funnel entrances, inward-curving boundaries, islands of encroachment, castellated edges. And, while by no means all commons have settled margins, in all areas medieval settlement had an intimate relationship with common land; even in the heart of the 'champion' Midlands, lost greens seem to underlie the plans of many villages.

Common land is closely entwined with many aspects of early landscape history. Yet at the same time commons as we see them today are very much the product of relatively recent developments. Parliamentary enclosures in the eighteenth and nineteenth century not only led to the wholesale removal of common land but also, because that removal was to an extent selective, changed the relative numbers of commons of different ecological characters. They also, to an extent that is often perhaps underestimated by historians, served to preserve, regulate and redefine many commons. More importantly, combined with twentieth-century legal changes and the character of the associated registration process, they created in the long term many new areas of common land, in the form of poor's allotments, surveyors' pits and the like. Above all, recent history has radically shaped the appearance and ecological character of many lowland commons, with fens and heaths in particular experiencing the effects of redundancy and dereliction, leading ultimately to the regeneration of secondary woodland. Largely in spite of this neglect, but to an extent because of it, commons now play a crucial role in sustaining biodiversity. Throughout England, common land accounts for a very high proportion of National Nature Reserves, SSSIs, and the like.[69]

The commons of upland counties, it is true, display a number of distinctive features – not least in terms of extent and current management – which distinguish them from the commons of lowland England which have been the principal focus of this book. The reader is referred, in particular, to Angus Winchester's various discussions of this subject.[70] But even these, as landscapes, display many familiar features, in terms of their morphology, relationship with settlement, archaeology, and the ways they were used in the past. Common land in England as a whole certainly exhibits a bewildering diversity, born of particular social and environmental circumstances, but also an underlying unity, structured by the prescriptions of national law; shared concepts of ownership, and of the public and private; by the practicalities of farming; and by recurrent patterns in the ways that societies, at various stages of development and in varied forms, have interacted with the natural environment.

Within lowland England at least, differing histories of common land can usually be related to environmental variations, and the social and agrarian conditions these engendered. But not always, or at least obviously, and some aspects of this fascinating subject remain mysterious. The distribution of poor's allotments is a case in point. In Norfolk these form an important part of the history of common land, and account for a significant proportion of modern, 'registered' commons. But elsewhere they are much less prominent, as we have seen in the discussions of Hertfordshire and Northamptonshire. The contrast, like the variations *within* each of these counties in the provision of allotments, can largely be explained in terms of the extent of common land removed by parliamentary enclosure, and the extent and character of the uses made of it by the poor prior to enclosure. But at a national level there are many exceptions to this pattern. Poor's allotments were certainly large and numerous in many areas where commons had been extensive, and had afforded an abundance of fuel for the poor, such as heathlands of Surrey and East Berkshire or the Isle of Axholme in Lincolnshire, where a total of 400 acres (162 hectares) was allotted as turbary for the four parishes there at the enclosure of 1795.[71] Yet there are others where they were not. While certainly not unknown in Lincolnshire and Cambridgeshire, such allotments are comparatively infrequent in parishes flanking the great peat levels of Fenland, even though a high proportion were enclosed by parliamentary acts.[72] Few if any counties could boast the number of allotments provided in Norfolk. Whether this reflects the peculiarly assertive character of the county's poor, the particular practices of local enclosure commissioners, or other essentially 'cultural' factors, remains unclear.

What does seem clear, from the evidence and discussion presented in this brief study, is that much about common land is misunderstood, or oversimplified, in popular discourse, by contemporary commentators and policy makers, even by some researchers and academics. Commons, for all their wild appearance today, were in the past intensively managed, rather unnatural, sometimes busy and even industrial places. Their modern management for nature conservation requires care, thought and in some cases more research. The species of flora and fauna most closely associated with common heaths, for example, benefit most from the continuation or reinstatement of 'traditional' management, and this is usually interpreted as grazing sufficiently intense to maintain an open landscape of grass and heather. But heaths in the past were often more disturbed environments, with areas of bare earth constantly being created by the stripping of heather and 'flags', the excavation of sand and gravel, and the burrowing of rabbits. And as Dolman and colleagues have observed, many of the rarer heathland 'specialists', both flora and invertebrate fauna, in East Anglia as elsewhere depend for their survival on bare and disturbed ground, of the kind provided by current management at Kelling Heath but few other commons.[73] To complicate matters further, the range of species present on a heath is increased, and in particular the presence of birds like nightjar and woodlark encouraged, by adopting less intensive forms of management which lead to the development of a rougher landscape and a habitat mosaic including woodland and scrub – the *de facto* situation on most common heaths today. Such an approach is contrary to documented management practices in the past, and produces landscapes very different to those of heaths as illustrated or described in recent centuries, although in historical terms, might be justified as representing a return to the wood-pasture heaths of more ancient times. Similar questions, problems and contradictions attend wildlife conservation on other varieties of common. Levels of biodiversity on clayland and alluvial commons, as we have seen, are unquestionably boosted by forms of use and management radically different to those of the past (above, pp. 173–6, 188–90).

History can inform decisions about how particular types should be managed, but it cannot provide rules for future management because the wholesale replication of past practices, even if possible, might well produce commons inappropriate to the modern world, poorly equipped to deal with the biodiversity crisis that has been caused by the urbanisation and agricultural intensification affecting the wider landscape. Management should be designed to benefit wildlife, more than to follow perceived historical precedent. That is not to deny that some commons, or parts of commons, should be maintained in or restored to something like their 'traditional' form, both because this is necessary to sustain biodiversity and also for essentially cultural reasons. This is particularly true of heathland, on which a number of rare invertebrates, and birds like the stone curlew, depend for their survival, and which, as Oliver Rackham reminded us, are 'a special responsibility of England' because of the success of our European neighbours in destroying this important habitat.[74] But as already noted heaths as currently maintained may differ in important respects from those of the past, and in more general terms maintaining commons in their 'traditional' form involves more than the adoption of particular regimes of grazing or cutting. It would be good, for example, to see the reinstatement of some of the 'plantings', peripheral bands of pollarded trees, which have been almost completely lost from Norfolk's clayland commons.

Whatever we choose to do with particular examples, all commons require some kind of active management. In this as in most other contexts, 're-wilding', the idea that biodiversity is best enhanced by leaving nature to its own devices, is a nonsense. A derelict common that has regenerated in its entirety to mature secondary woodland does not, in biodiversity terms, represent the best use of the land in question; and the rarer species associated with common heaths, in particular, in their traditional state are there because of, not in spite of, management. Commons have always existed in a very human world. It is a fitting paradox that, as they became economically redundant, the downward spiral of their 'traditional' vegetation to scrub and woodland was for a while retarded by the rabbit, an alien species originally introduced as a semi-domesticate. The 'wildness' that so often eventually triumphed is more akin to that of the long-abandoned industrial site than to that of the virgin rain forest.

The characterisation of commons as 'wild' places, while not entirely misleading, is certainly over simple and problematic. Much the same can be said of the other main way we like to think about common land. Commons were never really 'our' land, shared equally by all. And while their enclosure may have been an ecological disaster it was not really a simple act of upper class 'theft' which drove the poor from the land and impoverished small landowners. Commons were always the property of the landed elite and rights to use them were never universally or equally shared; the principal beneficiaries were the 'middling sort' and the propertied, not the poor and the landless. Enclosure may have harmed the poorer elements of society but it was not a major cause of their woes and there is no evidence that they flourished where commons survived unenclosed.

Myths about the past can be helpful in challenging the inequalities of the present, and are particularly enduring and pervasive when they can be linked to the physical landscape, that ever-present 'memory palace'. But the future can be shaped without such references to a supposedly more equal past, and some aspects of this familiar narrative about common land are arguably harmful. In particular, it wilfully conflates the interests of the propertied, middling groups in society and the poor, in order to place the blame for all social ills firmly at the door of 'the rich'. Such a view is convenient for, and appealing to, the middle-class groups from whom the bulk of liberal social commentators (and professional historians) are drawn, but it oversimplifies the complex realities of social relations, both as they were in the past, and as they are in the present.

Notes

1. J. Catt (ed.), *Hertfordshire Geology and Landscape* (Welwyn Garden City, 2010).
2. J. Catt and J. Doyle, The Palaeogene Period, in Catt (ed.), *Geology and Landscape*, 62–3; D. Millward, R.A. Ellison, R.D. Lake and B.S. Loorlock, *The Geology of the Country Around Epping: Memoir for the 1:50,000 Sheet 240 of the British Geological Survey* (Keyworth, 1987), 10–12.
3. Hodge *et al.*, *Soils and their Use*, 121–2, 184–6, 358–61.
4. Hodge *et al.*, *Soils and their Use*, 111–15, 220–4.
5. J. Catt and A. Cheshire, Quaternary Deposits and Later Landscape Development, in Catt (ed.), *Geology and Landscape*, 152–5.
6. Hodge *et al.*, *Soils and their Use*, 209–12.
7. H.C. Darby, *The Domesday Geography of South-East England* (Cambridge, 1962), 63–71.
8. A. Rowe and T. Williamson, *Hertfordshire a Landscape History* (Hatfield, 2013), 10–12.
9. Catt and Cheshire, Quaternary Deposits, 140–50.
10. Rowe and Williamson, *Hertfordshire*, 32–58.
11. A. Dury and J. Andrews, *A Topographical Map of Hartford-shire* (London, 1766); available online at www.duryandrewsmapofhertfordshire.co.uk.
12. A. Macnair, A. Rowe and T. Williamson, *Dury and Andrews' Map of Hertfordshire: Society and Landscape in the Eighteenth Century* (Oxford, 2016), 110–15.
13. W.R. Mead, *Pehr Kalm: A Finnish Visitor to the Chilterns in 1748* (Aston Clinton, 2003), 43–4.
14. HALS 1985 photograph of a map of 'Barkhampsted Parke', c. 1638 (original at The National Archives).
15. W. Page, *Victoria County History of Hertfordshire* Vol. 2 (London, 1907), 331.
16. British Library, Ordnance Survey Drawings, sheet 149.
17. HALS AH/2790.
18. HALS 6398; HALS 6442.
19. HALS DE/Hn/Z5.
20. HALS DE/X1010/M1.
21. Mead, *Pehr Kalm*, 84.
22. N. Groves, From Berkhamsted to Battlefield: WWI Training Trenches on Berkhamsted Common, in Chiltern Conservation Board, *Our Common Heritage: Essays About the Social History of Chiltern Commons* (Chinnor, 2015), 84–98; M. Morris and A. Wainwright, Iron Age and Romano-British Settlement and Economy in the Upper Bulbourne Valley, Hertfordshire, in R. Holgate (ed.), *Chiltern Archaeology: Recent Work* (Dunstable, 1995), 68–75.

23 Page, *Victoria History* Vol. 2, 451.
24 W. Page, *Victoria County History of Hertfordshire* Vol. 3 (London, 1912), 141.
25 T. Slater, Roads, Commons and Boundaries in the Topography of Hertfordshire Towns, in T. Slater and N. Goose (eds), *A County of Small Towns: The Development of Hertfordshire's Urban Landscape to 1800* (Hatfield, 2008), 67–95, at 81–2.
26 C. Moore, *Hertfordshire Windmills and Windmillers* (Sawbridgeworth, 1999).
27 Dury and Andrews, *Topographic Map*; Ordnance Survey 6-inch, First Edition, Hertfordshire sheets 26, 27 and 34.
28 C. Morris (ed.), *The Journeys of Celia Fiennes* (London, 1949), 120–1.
29 W. Toldervy, *England & Wales Described in a Series of Letters* 1 (London, 1762), 114–17.
30 S. Whatley, *England's Gazetteer or an Accurate Description of All the Cities*, Vol. 2 (London, 1751), unpaginated; Racecourses, Here Today and Gone Tomorrow.
31 Board of Agriculture Statistics, 1910, 56; Board of Agriculture Statistics, 1914, 92; Forestry Commission 4th Annual Report, 1924, 25.
32 HALS D/P64/27/1–27/4.
33 1910 Finance Act, St Albans Office, TNA.
34 A. Young, *General View of the Agriculture of Hertfordshire* (London, 1804), 49.
35 Page, *Victoria History* Vol. 2, 293 and 317.
36 Page, *Victoria History* Vol. 2, 337 and 351.
37 *Digest of the Reports Made by the Commissioners of Inquiry into Charities: County of Hertford* (London, 1841); Page, *Victoria History* Vol. 2, 293.
38 Page, *Victoria History* Vol. 3, 452; Young, *General View Hertfordshire*, 45.
39 N. Agar, *Behind the Plough: Agrarian Society in Nineteenth-century Hertfordshire* (Hatfield, 2005), 25.
40 Agar, *Behind the Plough*.
41 A.C. Jones, 'Commotion Time': The English Risings of 1549 (unpublished PhD thesis, University of Warwick, 2003), 33; Page, *Victoria History* Vol. 2, 151–2; *Journal of the House of Commons* 3, 1643–4 (London, 1802), 94.
42 B. Cowell, The Commons Preservation Society and the Campaign for Berkhamsted Common, 1866–70, *Rural History* 13 (2002), 145–61.
43 T. Williamson, R. Liddiard, and T. Partida, *Champion: The Making and Unmaking of the English Midland Landscape* (Exeter, 2013).
44 DEFRA, MAGIC website, Access, Registered Commons, https://magic.defra.gov.uk/, accessed 10.1.2025.
45 TNA, 1910 Finance Act: IR 58 and IR 121–35.
46 The following discussion is based on: G. Baker, *The History and Antiquities of The County of Northamptonshire* Vol. 2 (London, 1822), 74–86; D. Hall, The Woodland Landscapes of Southern Northamptonshire, *Northamptonshire Past and Present* 54 (2001), 33–46; M. Page, The Extent of Whittlewood Forest and the Impact of Disafforestation in the Later Middle Ages, *Northamptonshire Past and Present* 56 (2003), 22–34; P.A. Pettit, *The Royal Forests of Northamptonshire: A Study of their Economy 1558–1714* (Northampton, 1968); C. Wise, *Rockingham and the Watsons* (London, 1891), 128–79.
47 Nmptn RO G3909. In-towns had right of common for their cattle from 25 March to 1 November; Out-towns from 23 April to 25 September.
48 Nmptn RO Brooke of Oakley 318/1.
49 Nmptn RO Brooke of Oakley 313/21.
50 Pettit, *Royal Forests*, 125.

51 Williamson *et al.*, *Champion*, 106.
52 Williamson *et al.*, *Champion*, 109–16.
53 J. Morton, *The Natural History of Northamptonshire* (London, 1712), 9.
54 Nmptn RO 55P/233.
55 Nmptn RO Box X6155.
56 Nmptn RO A12 and A17.
57 Nmptn RO Encl Award Vol B p. 46 seq.
58 Williamson *et al.*, *Champion*, 147; *Digest of the Reports Made by the Commissioners of Inquiry into Charities: County of Northampton* (London, 1841)
59 J.M. Neeson, *Commoners: Common Right, Enclosure and Social Change in England 1700–1820* (Cambridge, 1993), 158–84.
60 D. Ginter, *A Measure of Wealth: the English Land Tax in Historical Analysis* (London, 1992). There are often marked differences between the number of owners listed in the Land Tax returns, and in the enclosure awards. In Chelveston, for example, Neeson notes that there were 27 landowners five years before enclosure, but the award allocated land to only eight people; for Rushden the figures are 101 and 60.
61 Williamson *et al.*, *Champion*, 157.
62 R. Moore-Colyer, Land and People in Northamptonshire: Great Oakley, *c*.1750–1850, *Agricultural History Review* 45 (1957), 149–64, at 150.
63 W.G. Hoskins, The Leicestershire Crop Returns of 1801, in W.G. Hoskins (ed.) *Studies in Leicestershire Agricultural History* (Leicester, 1949), 134.
64 Snell, *Annals of the Labouring Poor*, 178.
65 M.E. Turner, Parliamentary Enclosure and Landownership Change in Buckinghamshire, *Economic History Review* 28 (1975), 565–81.
66 B. Roberts, Cockfield Fell, *Antiquity*, 49, 193 (1975), 38–50.
67 M. Bowden, G. Brown and N. Smith, *An Archaeology of Town Commons in England. 'A Very Fair Field Indeed'* (Swindon, 2009).
68 R.W. Tomlinson, A Geography of Flat Racing in Great Britain, *Geography* 71, 3 (1968), 228–39.
69 J. Aitcheson, K. Crowther, M. Ashby and L. Redgrave, *The Common Lands of England: A Biological Survey* (Aberystwyth, 2000).
70 Winchester, *Common Land*; A. Winchester, *The Harvest of the Hills: Rural Life in Northern England and the Scottish Borders 1400–1700* (Edinburgh, 2000).
71 Winchester, *Common Land*, 229–34.
72 *Digest of the Reports Made by the Commissioners of Inquiry into Charities: County of Cambridge* (London, 1841); *Digest of the Reports Made by the Commissioners of Inquiry into Charities: County of Lincoln* (London, 1841).
73 P.M. Dolman, C. Panter and H.L. Mossman, *Securing Biodiversity in Breckland: Guidance for Conservation and Research. First Report of the Breckland Biodiversity Audit* (Norwich, 2010); P.M. Dolman, C. Panter and H.L. Mossman, The Biodiversity Audit Approach Challenges Regional Priorities and Identifies a Mismatch in Conservation, *Journal of Applied Ecology* 49 (2012), 986–97; R.J. Fuller, T. Williamson, G. Barnes and P. Dolman, Human Activities and Biodiversity Opportunities in Pre-Industrial Cultural Landscapes: Relevance to Conservation, *Journal of Applied Ecology* 54 (2017), 459–69.
74 Rackham, *History of the Countryside*, 302.

Bibliography

Books and Articles

Addington, S. and Cushion, B. 1982. Landscape and Settlements in South Norfolk Prehistoric to Post-medieval: Tasburgh-Fritton Area, with Particular Reference to Hedge Dating, *Norfolk Archaeology* 38, 97–139.

Agar, N. 2005. *Behind the Plough: Agrarian Society in Nineteenth-century Hertfordshire*. University of Hertfordshire Press, Hatfield.

Aitcheson, J., Crowther, K., Ashby, M. and Redgrave, L. 2000. *The Common Lands of England: A Biological Survey*. University of Aberystwyth, Aberystwyth.

Allison, K.J. 1957. The Sheep-Corn Husbandry of Norfolk in the Sixteenth and Seventeenth Centuries, *Agricultural History Review* 5, 12–30.

Angus, I. 2023. *The War Against the Commons: Dispossession and Resistance in the Making of Capitalism*. NYU Press, New York.

Apling, H. 1984. *Norfolk Corn Windmills*. Norfolk County Council, Norwich.

Ayers, B. 2005. Medieval Planned Towns. In T. Ashwin and A. Davison (eds), *An Historical Atlas of Norfolk*, 3rd edn, 74–5. Phillimore, Chichester.

Backhouse, G. 1972. Thetford Forest. In H.L. Edlin (ed.), *East Anglian Forests*, 4–14. HMSO, London.

Bailey, M. 1988. The Rabbit and the Medieval East Anglian Economy, *Agricultural History Review* 36, 1–20.

Bailey, M. 1989. *A Marginal Economy? East Anglian Breckland in the Later Middle Ages*. Cambridge University Press, Cambridge.

Bailey, M. 1990. Sand into Gold: The Evolution of the Foldcourse System in West Suffolk, 1200–1600, *Agricultural History Review*, 38, 40–57.

Baker, A.R.H. and Butlin, R. (eds) 1973. *Studies of Field Systems in the British Isles*. Cambridge University Press, Cambridge.

Baker, G. 1822. *The History and Antiquities of The County of Northamptonshire*, Vol. 2. John Bower, Nichols and Son, London.

Barnes, G. and Williamson, T. 2007. *Ancient Trees in the Landscape; Norfolk's Arboreal Heritage*. Windgather Press, Oxford.

Barnes, G. and Williamson, T. 2015. *Rethinking Ancient Woodland: The Archaeology and History of Woods in Norfolk*. University of Hertfordshire Press, Hatfield.

Barnes, G., Dallas, P., Thompson, H., Whyte, N. and Williamson, T. 2007. Heathland and Wood Pasture in Norfolk: Ecology and Landscape History, *British Wildlife* 18, 395–403.

Barringer, C. 2005. Markets and Fairs in the 18th and 19th Centuries. In T. Ashwin and A. Davison (eds), *An Historical Atlas of Norfolk*, 3rd edn, 138–9. Phillimore, Chichester.

Belcher, J. 2020. *The Foldcourse and East Anglian Agriculture and Landscape, 1100–1900*. Boydell, Woodbridge.

Beresford, J. (ed.) 1924. *The Diary of a Country Parson: The Reverend James Woodforde, Vol. 1, 1758–1781*. Oxford University Press, Oxford.

Beresford, J. (ed.) 1926. *The Diary of a Country Parson: The Reverend James Woodforde, Vol. 2, 1782–1787*. Oxford University Press, Oxford.

Beresford, M. 1967. *New Towns of the Middle Ages*. Lutterworth, London.

Bird, M.C.H. 1904–1909. The Rural Economy, Sport and Natural History of East Ruston Common, *Transactions of the Norfolk and Norwich Naturalists' Society* 8, 631–66.

Birtles, S. 1998. The Impact of Commons Registration: A Norfolk Study, *Landscape History* 20, 83–97.

Birtles, S. 1999. Common Land, Poor Relief and Enclosure: The Use of Manorial Resources in Fulfilling Parish Obligations 1601–1834, *Past and Present* 165, 74–106.

Blomefield, F. 1805–1810. *An Essay Towards a Topographical History of the County of Norfolk*, 11 Vols. London.

Boardman, E.T. 1939–1943. The Development of a Broadland Estate at How Hill, Ludham, Norfolk, *Transactions of the Norfolk and Norwich Naturalists' Society* 15, 5–21.

Boulton, G.S., Cox, F., Hart, J. and Thornton, M. 1984. The Glacial Geology of Norfolk, *Bulletin of the Geological Society of Norfolk* 34, 103–22.

Bowden, M., Brown, G. and Smith, N. 2009. *An Archaeology of Town Commons in England. 'A Very Fair Field Indeed'*. English Heritage, Swindon.

Bracton, H. 1977. *On the Laws and Customs of England*, ed. and trans. S.E. Thorne, Vol. 3. Harvard University Press, Cambridge, MA.

Brian, A. 1999. The Allocation of Strips in Lammas Meadows by the Casting of Lots, *Landscape History* 21, 1, 43–58.

Bull, A. 1969–1973. Bawdeswell Heath, *Transactions of the Norfolk and Norwich Naturalists' Society* 22, 268–70.

Burrell, W.H. and Clarke, W.G. 1909–1914. A Contribution to a Vegetation Survey of Norfolk, *Transactions of the Norfolk and Norwich Naturalists' Society* 9, 743–56.

Campbell, B.M.S. 1980. Commonfield Origins – the Regional Dimension. In T. Rowley (ed.), *The Origins of Open Field Agriculture*, 112–29. Croome Helm, London.

Catt, J. (ed.) 2010. *Hertfordshire Geology and Landscape*. Hertfordshire Natural History Society, Welwyn Garden City.

Catt, J. and Cheshire, A. 2010. Quaternary Deposits and Later Landscape Development. In J. Catt (ed.), *Hertfordshire Geology and Landscape*, 118–82. Hertfordshire Natural History Society, Welwyn Garden City.

Catt, J. and Doyle, J. 2010. The Palaeogene Period. In J. Catt (ed.), *Hertfordshire Geology and Landscape*, 61–78. Hertfordshire Natural History Society, Welwyn Garden City.

Clarke, G. 2023. *Salt-Winning on the Lyn: Anglo-Saxon and Medieval Industry at Gaywood's North Marsh, King's Lynn, East Anglian Archaeology* 180, Gressenhall.

Clarke, W.G. 1904–1909. Some Breckland Characteristics, *Transactions of the Norfolk and Norwich Naturalists' Society* 8, 555–78.

Clarke, W.G. 1909–1914. The Commons of Norfolk, *Transactions of the Norfolk and Norwich Naturalists' Society* 9, 52–70.

Clarke, W.G. 1914–1919. The Natural History of Norfolk Commons, *Transactions of the Norfolk and Norwich Naturalists' Society* 10, 294–318.

Cornford, B. 1988. The Commons of Flegg in the Middle Ages and Early Modern Periods. In M. Manning (ed.), *Commons in Norfolk*, 14–20. Norfolk Research Group, Norwich.

Cousins, E.F. and Honey, R. 2012. *Gadsden on Commons and Greens*. Sweet and Maxwell, London.

Cowell, B. 2002. The Commons Preservation Society and the Campaign for Berkhamsted Common, 1866–70, *Rural History* 13, 145–61.

Cox, A. 1979. *A Survey of Bedfordshire Brickmaking: History and Gazetteer*. Bedford County Council, Bedford.

Cromwell, T.K. 1829. *Excursions in the County of Norfolk*. 2 Vols. London.

Crowley, J. and Reid, A. (eds) 1983. *The Poor Law in Norfolk, 1700–1850*. EARO, Ely.

Dallas, P. 2010. Sustainable Environments: Common Wood Pastures in Norfolk, *Landscape History* 31, 23–36.

Darby, H.C. 1962. *The Domesday Geography of South-East England*. Cambridge University Press, Cambridge.

Davison, A. 1994. The Field Archaeology of Bodney, and the Stanta Extension, *Norfolk Archaeology* 42, 57–79.

Davison, A. and Cushion, B. 1999. The Archaeology of the Hargham Estate, *Norfolk Archaeology* 53, 257–74.

Davison, A. and Fenner, A. 1990. *The Evolution of Settlement in Three Parishes in South-East Norfolk, East Anglian Archaeology* 49, Gressenhall.

Davison, A. and Joby, R. 2005. Early Roads and Turnpikes. In T. Ashwin and A. Davison (eds), *An Historical Atlas of Norfolk*, 3rd edn, 154–5. Phillimore, Chichester.

Dawes, M.C.B., Devine, M.R., Jones, H.E. and Post, M.J. 1974. *Calendar of Inquisitions Post Mortem: Vol. 16, Richard II*. HMSO, London.

Digby, A. 2005. Poor Law Unions and Workhouses, 1834–1930. In T. Ashwin and A. Davison (eds), *An Historical Atlas of Norfolk*, 3rd edn, 148–9. Phillimore, Chichester.

Dodgshon, R. 1980. *The Origins of British Field Systems: An Interpretation*. Academic Press, London.

Dolman, P. and Sutherland, W. 1992. The Ecological Changes of Breckland Grass Heath and the Consequences of Management, *Journal of Applied Ecology* 29, 2, 402–13.

Dolman, P.M., Panter, C. and Mossman, H.L. 2010. *Securing Biodiversity in Breckland: Guidance for Conservation and Research. First Report of the Breckland Biodiversity Audit*. University of East Anglia, Norwich.

Dolman, P.M., Panter, C. and Mossman, H.L. 2012. The Biodiversity Audit Approach Challenges Regional Priorities and Identifies a Mismatch in Conservation, *Journal of Applied Ecology* 49, 986–97.

Dominy, J. 1988. Commons of East and West Rudham. In M. Manning (ed.), *Commons in Norfolk*, 29–35. Norfolk Research Committee, Norwich.

Dudley Stamp, L. 1948. *The Land of Britain: Its Use and Misuse*. Geographical Publications, London.

Dudley Stamp, L. and Hoskins, W.G. 1963. *The Common Lands of England and Wales*. Collins, London.

Duffey, E. and Feest, A. 2009. A Comparative Ecological Study of the Spider (Araneae) Faunas of East Anglian Fens, England: Regional Differences and Conservation, *Bulletin of the British Arachnology Society* 14, 8, 317–33.

Dury, A. and Andrews, J. 1766. *A Topographical Map of Hartford-shire*. London; available online at www.duryandrewsmapofhertfordshire.co.uk.

Dyer, C. 2006. Conflict in the Landscape: The Enclosure Movement in England, 1220–1349, *Landscape History* 28, 21–4.

Dymond, D. 1985. *The Norfolk Landscape*. Hodder and Stoughton, London.

Dymond, D. 1993. Workhouses Before 1834. In P. Wade-Martins (ed.), *An Historical Atlas of Norfolk*, 142–3. Norfolk County Council, Norwich.

Dymond, D. 2005. Medieval and Later Markets. In T. Ashwin and A. Davison (eds), *An Historical Atlas of Norfolk*, 3rd edn, 76–7. Phillimore, Chichester.

Dymond, D. 2021. The Game of Camping in Eastern England, *The Local Historian* 51, 2–15.

Eyre, S.R. 1955. The Curving Ploughland Strip and its Historical Implications, *Agricultural History Review* 3, 80–94.

Faden, W. 1797. *A Topographical Map of the County of Norfolk*. London.

Faulkner, N., Rossin, G. and Robinson, K. (eds) 2014. *Digging Sedgeford: A People's Archaeology*. Poppyland, North Walsham.

Field, D. 2006. *Earthen Long Barrows: The Earliest Monuments in the British Isles*. Tempus, Stroud.

Fielding, A.M. and Fielding, A.P. 2005. *Salt Works and Salinas. The Archaeology, Conservation and Recovery of Salt Making Sites and their Processes*. Lion Salt Works Trust, Marston.

Fuller, R.J., Williamson, T., Barnes, G. and Dolman, P. 2017. Human Activities and Biodiversity Opportunities in Pre-Industrial Cultural Landscapes: Relevance to Conservation, *Journal of Applied Ecology* 54, 459–69.

Funnell, B.M. 2005. Geological Background. In T. Ashwin and A. Davison (eds), *An Historical Atlas of Norfolk*, 3rd edn, 4–5. Phillimore, Chichester.

Garrod, G. 1969–1973. Ringmere, *Transactions of the Norfolk and Norwich Naturalists' Society* 22, 73–82.

Ginter, D. 1992. *A Measure of Wealth: The English Land Tax in Historical Analysis*. McGill-Queen's Press, London.

Gray, H.L. 1915. *English Field Systems*. Harvard University Press, Cambridge, MA.

Groves, N. 2015. From Berkhamsted to Battlefield: WW I Training Trenches on Berkhamsted Common. In *Our Common Heritage: A Collection of Six Essays About the Social History of Chiltern Commons*, 84–98, Chilterns Conservation Board, Chinnor.

Gunn, J. 1864. *A Sketch of the Geology of Norfolk*. Norwich.

Gurney, D. 2005. Roman Norfolk. In T. Ashwin and A. Davison (eds), *An Historical Atlas of Norfolk*, 3rd edn, 28–9. Phillimore, Chichester.

Haggard, L.R. 1946. *Norfolk Notebook*. Faber and Faber, London.

Haggard, L.R. and Williamson, H. 1943. *Norfolk Life*. Faber and Faber, London.

Hall, D. 2001. The Woodland Landscapes of Southern Northamptonshire, *Northamptonshire Past and Present* 54, 33–46.

Hall, D. 2020. *The Open Fields of England*. Oxford University Press, Oxford.

Hammond, J.L. and Hammond, B. 1911. *The Village Labourer, 1760–1832*. British Publishers' Guild, London.

Hardin, G. 1968. The Tragedy of the Commons, *Science* 162, 3859, 1243–8.

Harting, J.E. 1898. *The Rabbit*. Longmans, Green and Co., London.

Hassell Smith, A. and Baker, J. (eds) 1983. *The Papers of Nathaniel Bacon of Stiffkey*, Vol. 2. University of East Anglia, Norwich.

Higgins, D. 1988. West Winch Common. In M. Manning (ed.), *Commons in Norfolk*, 21–8. Norfolk Research Committee, Norwich.

Hodge, C.A.H., Burton, R.G.O., Corbett, W.M.C., Evans, R. and Seale, R.S. 1984. *Soils and their Use in Eastern England*. Soil Survey, Harpenden.

Hoggett, R. 2018. *New Buckenham, Norfolk: Landscape and Heritage Statement*. New Buckenham Parish Council, New Buckenham.

Holderness, B.A. 1984. East Anglia and the Fens. In J. Thirsk (ed.), *The Cambridge Agrarian History of England and Wales Vol. 5*, 197–238. Cambridge University Press, Cambridge.

Homans, G.C. 1941. *English Villagers of the Thirteenth Century*. Harvard University Press, Cambridge, MA.

Homans, G.C. 1969. The Explanation of English Regional Differences, *Past and Present* 42, 1, 18–34.

Hopkins, J.J. 1990. British Meadows and Pastures, *British Wildlife* 1, 202–13.

Hoskins, W.G. 1949. The Leicestershire Crop Returns of 1801. In W.G. Hoskins (ed.), *Studies in Leicestershire Agricultural History*. The Leicestershire Archaeological Society, Leicester.

Hutcheson, N. and Ashwin, T. 2005. Iron Age Norfolk. In T. Ashwin and A. Davison (eds), *An Historical Atlas of Norfolk*, 3rd edn, 22–5. Phillimore, Chichester.

Jarvis, C. 2024. The Making of the Broads. In T. Williamson and A. Yardy, *Broadland: Shaping Marsh and Fen*, 197–208. University of Hertfordshire Press, Hatfield.

Joly de Lotbiniere, H.J. 1924–1928. Afforestation in Breckland, *Transactions of the Norfolk and Norwich Naturalists' Society* 12, 673–7.

Kent, N. 1794. *General View of the Agriculture of Norfolk*, 2 Vols. London.

Kerridge, E. 1969. *Agrarian Problems in the Sixteenth Century and After*. Allen and Unwin, London.

Larwood, G.P. and Funnell, B.M. (eds) 1961. *The Geology of Norfolk; Transactions of the Norfolk and Norwich Naturalists' Society* 19, 6.

Lawson, A.J., Martin, E.A. and Priddy, D. 1981. *The Barrows of East Anglia, East Anglian Archaeology* 12, Norwich.

Leake, G.F. 1991. *The Commons of East and West Runton*. Norfolk County Council, Norwich.

Lee, J.R., Woods, M.A. and Moorlock, B.S.P. (eds) 2015. *British Regional Geology: East Anglia*, 5th edn. British Geological Survey, Keyworth.

Lewis, C., Mitchell-Fox, P. and Dyer, C. 2002. *Village, Hamlet and Field: Changing Settlements in Central England*. Windgather Press, Macclesfield.

Liddiard, R. 2005. The Castle Landscapes of Anglo-Norman East Anglia: A Regional Perspective. In C. Harper-Bill (ed.), *Medieval East Anglia*, 33–51. Boydell, Woodbridge.

Lilley, K. 2002. *Urban Life in the Middle Ages 1000–1450*. Macmillan, Basingstoke.

Linebaugh, P. 2014. *Stop, Thief!: the Commons, Enclosures, and Resistance*. PM Press, Oakland, CA.

Louverre, A.G. 2010. The Atlas of Rural Settlement GIS, *Landscapes* 11, 2, 21–44.

Loveday, R. and Williamson, T. 1988. Rabbits or Ritual? Artificial Warrens and the Neolithic Long Mound Tradition, *Archaeological Journal* 145, 290–313.

Lucas, R. 2000. Brickmaking on Norfolk Commons, *Norfolk Archaeology* 43, 457–68.

MacMaster, N. 1990. The Battle for Mousehold Heath 1857–1884: 'Popular Politics' and the Victorian Public Park, *Past and Present* 127, 117–54.

Macnair, A., Rowe A. and Williamson, T. 2016. *Dury and Andrews' Map of Hertfordshire: Society and Landscape in the Eighteenth Century*. Windgather Press, Oxford.

Macnair, A. and Williamson, T. 2010. *Wiliam Faden and Norfolk's 18th-Century Landscape*. Windgather Press, Oxford.

Maine, H.S. 1871. *Village-Communities in the East and West*. John Murray, London.

Malster, R. 1993. *The Broads*. Phillimore, Chichester.

Manning, M. (ed.) 1988. *Commons in Norfolk*. Norfolk Research Committee, Norwich.

Marren, P. 1995. Harvests of Beauty: The Conservation of Hay Meadows, *British Wildlife* 6, 235–43.

Marshall, W. 1787. *The Rural Economy of Norfolk*, Vol. 2. London.

Martin, E. and Satchell, M. 2008. *Wheare most inclosures be. East Anglian Fields, History, Morphology and Management, East Anglian Archaeology* 124. Ipswich.

Mason, A. and Parry, J. 2010. *The Warrens of Breckland*. The Breckland Society. Thetford.

Mead, W.R. 2003. *Pehr Kalm: A Finnish Visitor to the Chilterns in 1748*. W.R. Mead, Aston Clinton.

Millward, D., Ellison, R.A., Lake, R.D. and Moorlock, B.S. 1987. *The Geology of the Country Around Epping: Memoir for the 1:50,000 Sheet 240 of the British Geological Survey*. British Geological Survey, Keyworth.

Mingay, G.E. 1997. *Parliamentary Enclosure in England: An Introduction to its Causes, Incidence and Impact 1750–1850*. Longman, London.

Moore, C. 1999. *Hertfordshire Windmills and Windmillers*. Windsup Publishing, Sawbridgeworth.

Moore-Colyer, R. 1957. Land and People in Northamptonshire: Great Oakley, *c*.1750–1850, *Agricultural History Review* 45, 149–64.

Morris, C. (ed.) 1949. *The Journeys of Celia Fiennes*. Cresset, London.

Morris, M. and Wainwright, A. 1995. Iron Age and Romano-British Settlement and Economy in the Upper Bulbourne Valley, Hertfordshire. In R. Holgate (ed.), *Chiltern Archaeology: Recent Work*, 68–75. The Book Castle, Dunstable.

Morris, R. 1989. *Churches in the Landscape*. Phoenix, London.

Morton, J. 1712. *The Natural History of Northamptonshire*. Knaplock & Wilkin, London.

Murphy, E. 2021. Brockdish Common, Norfolk: Historical Research for Present-Day Community Benefit, *Local Historian* 51, 1, 47–56

Neeson, J.M. 1993. *Commoners: Common Right, Enclosure and Social Change in England, 1700–1820.* Cambridge University Press, Cambridge.

Nicholson, W.A. 1914. *A Flora of Norfolk.* West, Newman & Co., London.

Ostrom, E. 1990. *Governing the Commons: The Evolution of Institutions for Collective Action.* Cambridge University Press, Cambridge.

Page, M. 2003. The Extent of Whittlewood Forest and the Impact of Disafforestation in the Later Middle Ages, *Northamptonshire Past and Present* 56, 22–34.

Page, W. 1907. *Victoria County History of Hertfordshire*, Vol. 2. University of London, Institute of Historical Research, London.

Page, W. 1912. *Victoria County History of Hertfordshire*, Vol. 3. University of London, Institute of Historical Research, London.

Pannett, D. 2020. Commons of the Stiperstones Mining District, *Shropshire History and Archaeology* 95, 61–82.

Parry, J. 2003. *Heathland.* National Trust, London.

Petch, C.P. 1944–1948. Fenlands of West Norfolk, *Transactions of the Norfolk and Norwich Naturalists' Society* 16, 317–22.

Pettit, P.A. 1968. *The Royal Forests of Northamptonshire: A Study of their Economy 1558–1714.* Northamptonshire Record Society, Northampton.

Postgate, M.R. 1957. The Field Systems of Breckland, *Agricultural History Review* 10, 80–101.

Prince, H. 1964. The Origin of Pits and Depressions in Norfolk, *Geography* 49, 15–32.

Rackham, O. 1986. *The History of the Countryside.* J.M. Dent, London.

Rackham, O. 1986. The Ancient Woods of Norfolk, *Transactions of the Norfolk and Norwich Naturalists' Society* 27, 161–77.

Records Commission, 1810. *Statutes of the Realm*, Vol. 1, House of Commons, London.

Reynolds, A. 1997. The Definition and Ideology of Anglo-Saxon Execution Cemeteries. In D. Boe and F. Verhaeghe (eds), *Death and Burial in Europe*, 33–41. Instituut voor het archeologisch patrimonium, Bruges.

Roberts, B. 1975. Cockfield Fell, *Antiquity*, 49, 193, 48–50.

Roberts, B.K. and Wrathmell, S. 2000. *An Atlas of Rural Settlement in England.* Historic England, London.

Roberts, B.K. and Wrathmell, S. 2000. Peoples of Wood and Plain: An Exploration of National and Local Regional Contrasts. In D. Hooke (ed.), *Landscape: The Richest Historical Record*, 85–96. Society for Landscape Studies, Birmingham.

Roberts, B.K. and Wrathmell, S. 2002. *Region and Place; A Study of English Rural Settlement.* English Heritage, London.

Rodwell, J.S. (ed.) 1992. *British Plant Communities, Volume 2: Mires and Heaths.* Cambridge University Press, Cambridge.

Rogerson, A. 2007. Wymondham Before 1107. In P. Cattermole (ed.), *Wymondham Abbey: A History of the Monastery and Parish Church*, 2–15. Wymondham Abbey, Wymondham.

Rogerson, A. 2022. *Fransham: People and Land in a Central Norfolk Parish from the Palaeolithic to the Eve of Parliamentary Enclosure, East Anglian Archaeology* 176, Gressenhall.

Rowe, A. and Williamson, T. 2013. *Hertfordshire a Landscape History.* University of Hertfordshire Press, Hatfield.

Rutledge, P. and Rutledge, T. 2002. *New Buckenham: A Moated Town.* Poppyland, New Buckenham.

Scull, C., Brookes, S. and Williamson, T. 2024. *Lordship and Landscape in East Anglia AD 400–800: The Royal Centre at Rendlesham, Suffolk and its Contexts.* Society of Antiquaries, London.

Sheail, J. 1971. *Rabbits and their History.* David and Charles, Newton Abbot.

Simmons, I.G. 2003. *The Moorlands of England and Wales: An Environmental History, 8000 BC–AD 2000.* Edinburgh University Press, Edinburgh.

Skipper, K. and T. Williamson, T. 1997. *Thetford Forest: Making a Landscape 1922–1997.* Centre of East Anglian Studies, Norwich.

Slack, P. 1990. *The English Poor Law, 1531–1782.* Cambridge University Press, Cambridge.

Slater, T. 2008. Roads, Commons and Boundaries in the Topography of Hertfordshire Towns. In T. Slater and N. Goose (eds), *A County of Small Towns: The Development of Hertfordshire's Urban Landscape to 1800*, 67–95. University of Hertfordshire Press, Hatfield.

Smith, A.H. 1956. *English Place Name Elements*, Vol. 2. Cambridge University Press, Cambridge.

Smith, W. 1806. *Observations on the Utility, Form, and Management of Water Meadows.* John Harding, Norwich.

Snell, K.D.M. 1985. *Annals of the Labouring Poor: Social Change and Agrarian England, 1660–1900.* Cambridge University Press, Cambridge.

Suffling, E.R. 1885. *The Land of the Broads*. Upcott Gill, London.

Tarlow, S. 2015. The Landscape of the Gibbet, *Landscape History* 36, 1, 71–88.

Tate, W.E. and Turner, M. 1978. *A Domesday of English Enclosure Acts and Awards*. University of Reading, Reading.

Thirsk, J. 1966. The Common Fields, *Past and Present* 29, 3–29.

Thompson, E.P. 1991. *Customs in Common*. The New Press, London.

Toldervy, W. 1762. *England & Wales Described in a Series of Letters* 1. London.

Tomlinson, R.W. 1968. A Geography of Flat Racing in Great Britain, *Geography* 71, 3, 228–39.

Treweek, J., José, P. and Benstead, P. 1997. *The Wet Grassland Guide. Managing Floodplain and Coastal Wet Grassland for Wildlife*. Royal Society for the Protection of Birds, Sandy.

Turner, E.L. 1919–1924. The Status of Birds in Broadland, *Transactions of the Norfolk and Norwich Naturalists' Society* 11, 227–40.

Turner, M.E. 1975. Parliamentary Enclosure and Landownership Change in Buckinghamshire, *Economic History Review* 28, 565–81.

Turner, M.E. 1980. *English Parliamentary Enclosure*. Dawson Publishing, Folkestone.

Turner, M.E. 2005. Parliamentary Enclosure. In T. Ashwin and A. Davison (eds), *An Historical Atlas of Norfolk*, 3rd edn, 130–2. Phillimore, Chichester.

Vaughan-Lewis, W. and Vaughan-Lewis, M. 2017. *Hearths and Heaths: Dispersed Settlements in Aylsham's Early Modern Landscape*. Wordpress, Itteringham.

Vinogradoff, P. 1892. *Villainage in England*. Clarendon Press, Oxford.

Wade-Martins, P. 1990. *Village Sites in the Launditch Hundred, East Anglian Archaeology* 10, Norwich.

Wade Martins, S. and Williamson, T. 1994. Floated Water-Meadows in Norfolk: A Misplaced Innovation, *Agricultural History Review* 42, 20–37.

Wade Martins, S. and Williamson, T. (eds) 1995. *The Farming Journal of Randall Burroughes of Wymondham, 1794–99*, Norfolk Record Society Vol. 58. Norwich.

Wade Martins, S. and Williamson, T. 1999. *Roots of Change; Farming and the Landscape in East Anglia, c. 1700–1870*. British Agricultural History Society, Exeter.

Wade Martins, S. and Williamson, T. 2008. *The Countryside of East Anglia: Changing Landscapes, 1870–1950*. Boydell, Woodbridge.

Wainwright, G.J., Dimbleby, G.W., Evans, A. and Evans, J.G. 1972. The Excavation of a Neolithic Settlement on Broome Heath, Ditchingham, Norfolk, England, *Proceedings of the Prehistoric Society* 38, 1–97.

Warner, P. 1987. *Greens, Commons and Clayland Colonization*. Leicester University Press, Leicester.

Warner, P. 1989. Shared Churchyards, Freemen Church Builders and the Development of Parishes in Eleventh-century East Anglia, *Landscape History* 8, 39–52.

Watt, A.S. 1940. Studies in the Ecology of the Breckland IV: The Grass Heath, *Journal of Ecology* 28, 42–70.

Webb, N. 1986. *Heathlands*. Collins, London.

Wells, C. 2000. Post-Medieval Turf-digging in Norfolk, *Norfolk Archaeology*, 43, 3, 469–82.

Wells, C. 2001. The Role of Turf and Associated Fuels in the Nineteenth-Century Rural Economy of Norfolk, *Norfolk Archaeology* 43, 4, 630–42.

Whatley, S. 1751. *England's Gazetteer or an Accurate Description of All the Cities*, Vol. 2. London.

White, W. 1845. *History, Gazetteer, and Directory of Norfolk, and the City and County of Norwich*. Privately printed, Sheffield.

Whitelock, D. (ed.) 1955. *English Historical Documents. Vol. I, c.500–1042*. Eyre and Spottiswoode, London.

Whyte, N. 2003. The Deviant Dead in the Norfolk Landscape, *Landscapes* 4, 1, 24–39.

Williamson, T. 1998. *The Archaeology of the Landscape Park; Garden Design in Norfolk, England, c.1680–1840*. British Archaeological Report 268, Oxford.

Williamson, T. 2000. Understanding Enclosure, *Landscapes* 1, 56–79.

Williamson, T. 2007. *Rabbits. Warrens and Archaeology*. Tempus, Stroud.

Williamson, T. 2007. The Landscape. In P. Cattermole (ed.), *Wymondham Abbey: a History of the Monastery and Parish Church*, 172–85. Wymondham Abbey, Wymondham.

Williamson, T. 2013. *Environment, Society and Landscape in Early Medieval England*. Boydell and Brewer, Woodbridge.

Williamson, T. and Yardy, A. 2024. *Broadland: Shaping Marsh and Fen*. University of Hertfordshire Press, Hatfield.

Williamson, T., Bumstead, J., Frost, J., Owens, L. and Pease, S. 2017. The Landscape Archaeology of Knettishall Heath, Suffolk and its Implications, *Landscapes* 18, 161–77.

Williamson, T., Liddiard, R. and Partida, T. 2013. *Champion: The Making and Unmaking of the English Midland Landscape*. Exeter University Press, Exeter.

Winchester, A. 2000. *The Harvest of the Hills: Rural Life in Northern England and the Scottish Borders 1400–1700*. Edinburgh University Press, Edinburgh.

Winchester, A. 2022. *Common Land in Britain: A History from the Middle Ages to the Present Day*. Boydell and Brewer, Woodbridge.

Wisdom, A.S. 1979. *The Law of Rivers and Watercourses*. Shaw and Son, London.

Wise, C. 1891. *Rockingham and the Watsons*. E. Stock, London.

Witney, K.P. 1998. The Woodland Economy of Kent, 1066–1348, *Agricultural History Review* 38, 20–39.

Wood, A. 2007. *The 1549 Rebellions and the Making of Modern England*. Cambridge University Press, Cambridge.

Woodward, A. 2000. *British Barrows: A Matter of Life and Death*. Tempus, Stroud.

Yelling, J.A. 1977. *Common Field and Enclosure in England 1450–1850*. Macmillan, London.

Young, A. 1804. *General View of the Agriculture of the County of Norfolk*. Sherwood, Neely and Jones, London.

Young, A. 1804. *General View of the Agriculture of Hertfordshire*. Sherwood, Neely and Jones, London.

Unpublished Theses and Dissertation

Bacon, K. 2003. Landholding and Enclosure in the Hundreds of East Flegg, West Flegg and Happing in Norfolk, 1695 to 1832, unpublished PhD thesis, University of East Anglia.

Birtles, S. 2003. A Green Space Beyond Self-interest: The Evolution of Common Land in Norfolk, c.750–2003, unpublished PhD thesis, University of East Anglia.

Bull, A. 2020. Five Clayland Commons: The Development, Survival and Ecology of a Relic Landscape, unpublished MA dissertation, School of History, University of East Anglia.

Buxton, C. 2005. Eighteenth and Early Nineteenth-Century Race Grounds in Norfolk and Suffolk, unpublished MA dissertation, School of History, University of East Anglia.

Dallas, P. 2005. Wood Pasture in Norfolk: The Relationship Between Trees, Animal Husbandry and the Changing Agricultural Landscape from the First Millennium AD to the Age of Improvement, unpublished MA dissertation, University of East Anglia.

Douet, A. 1989. Norfolk Agriculture 1914–1972, unpublished PhD thesis, University of East Anglia.

Jones, A.C. 2003. 'Commotion Time': The English Risings of 1549, unpublished PhD thesis, University of Warwick.

King, C. 2015. The Leisure Activities of the Rural Working Classes with Special Reference to Norfolk 1840–1940, unpublished PhD thesis, University of East Anglia.

Morley, K.E. 2003. The Origins and Development of Common Land in the Boulder Clay Region of Norfolk, unpublished MA dissertation, School of History, University of East Anglia.

Parmenter, J.M. 2000. The Development of the Wetland Vegetation of the Broadland Region: A Study of the Sociohistorical Factors which have Influenced and Modified the Development of Fen Vegetation in Broadland, unpublished PhD thesis, University of East Anglia.

Rogerson, A. 1995. Fransham: An Archaeological and Historical Study of a Parish on the Norfolk Boulder Clay, unpublished PhD thesis, University of East Anglia.

Whyte, N. 2005. Perceptions of the Norfolk Landscape c. 1500–1750, unpublished PhD thesis, University of East Anglia.

Government Reports

Board of Agriculture, Statistics for England and Wales, 1910 (London, 1911).

Board of Agriculture, Statistics for England and Wales, 1914 (London, 1915).

Digest of the Reports Made by the Commissioners of Inquiry into Charities: County of Cambridge (London, 1841).

Digest of the Reports Made by the Commissioners of Inquiry into Charities: County of Lincoln (London, 1841).

Digest of the Reports Made by the Commissioners of Inquiry into Charities: County of Northampton (London, 1841)

Digest of the Reports Made by the Commissioners of Inquiry into Charities: County of Hertford (London, 1841).

Forestry Commission 4th Annual Report (London, 1924).

Journal of the House of Commons 3, 1643–4 (London, 1802).

Report of the Commissioners Concerning Charities and Education of the Poor in England and Wales, Vol. XXIII, Norfolk (London, 1832).

Report of the Royal Commission on Common Land, 1955–1958 (London, 1958), 131.

Websites and Online Resources

Association of Commons Registration Authorities, Reference 225/U/242, Billingford Common: https://acraew.org.uk/sites/default/files/uploads/Norfolk/BILLINGFORD%20COMMON%20-%20BRECKLAND%20D%20NO.CL.96.pdf, accessed 1.6.2024.

Barrow Common: https://www.barrowcommonbrancaster.com/uploads/1/3/2/5/132570821/barrow_common_history.pdf, accessed 12.7.2024.

DEFRA, MAGIC website, Access, Registered Commons: https://magic.defra.gov.uk/, accessed 10.1.2025.

Felmingham Parish Council, Bryant's Heath and Stow Heath: https://felminghampc.org.uk/bryants-and-stow-heaths/, accessed 12.7.24

Norfolk Biodiversity Partnership, Lowland Heath Action Plan: https://www.norfolkbiodiversity.org/assets/Uploads/Lowland-heathland-and-dry-acid-grassland-HAP2.pdf, accessed 5.7.2024.

Racecourses, Here Today and Gone Tomorrow: http://www.greyhoundderby.com/Closed%20Courses%20New.html, accessed 14.11.2024.

Salthouse History: https://www.salthousehistory.co.uk/heath2.html, accessed 6.7.2024.

Hoe and Worthing Parish Archive

Hoe Common: http://www.hoeandworthingarchive.org.uk/common.html, accessed 4.6.2024.

Vegetation Survey for Norfolk Wildlife Trust by J.M. Parmenter; R.M. Leaney and T. Doncaster, July 2019: http://www.hoeandworthingarchive.org.uk/hoe_common%20_2019_plant_list.pdf, accessed 5.6.2024

Norfolk Windmills Trust

Wood Norton Mill: https://www.norfolkmills.co.uk/Windmills/wood-norton-smockmill.html, accessed 12.9.2024.

New Buckenham Mill: https://www.norfolkmills.co.uk/Windmills/new-buckenham-postmill.html, accessed 11.11.2024.

Natural England SSSI Citations

Alderford Common: https://designatedsites.naturalengland.org.uk/PDFsForWeb/Citation/1000483.pdf, accessed 3.6.2024.

Barnhamcross Common: https://designatedsites.naturalengland.org.uk/PDFsForWeb/Citation/1000547.pdf, accessed 23.8.2024.

Bryant's Heath: https://designatedsites.naturalengland.org.uk/PDFsForWeb/Citation/1000770.pdf, accessed 3.6.2024.

Castle Acre Common: https://designatedsites.naturalengland.org.uk/PDFsForWeb/Citation/1005965.pdf, accessed 2.7.2024.

Foulden Common: https://designatedsites.naturalengland.org.uk/PDFsForWeb/Citation/1002450.pdf, accessed 24.6.2024.

Fritton Common: https://designatedsites.naturalengland.org.uk/PDFsForWeb/Citation/1000352.pdf, accessed 10.8.2024.

Kelling Heath: https://designatedsites.naturalengland.org.uk/PDFsForWeb/Citation/1002812.pdf, accessed 5.7.2024.

Leziate Fen: https://designatedsites.naturalengland.org.uk/PDFsForWeb/Citation/1002837.pdf, accessed 24.6.2024.

Shotesham Common: https://designatedsites.naturalengland.org.uk/PDFsForWeb/Citation/1000341.pdf, accessed 8.7.2024.

Southrepps Common: https://designatedsites.naturalengland.org.uk/PDFsForWeb/Citation/1003281.pdf, accessed 25.6.2024.

Unpublished Reports and Similar

Giles Carey, Geophysical Survey, Ditchingham Long Barrow, GPR, and Magnetic Survey Report, unpublished report for the Prehistoric Society, 2017.

Norfolk Biodiversity Information Service, County Hall, Norwich Wildlife Site Descriptions, sites 25, 141, 1044, 1047 and 2017.

Norfolk Wildlife Trust, Bewick House, Norwich; volunteer surveys of Brockdish, Shotesham and Wighton Commons; oral history trascript, interview of June Batstone by Stephanie Witham, 2018.

Index

Abbots Langley, Herts. 200
Abthorpe, Northants. 212
Addington, Sylvia 180
Ailsworth, Peterborough 205
Aldbury Common, Herts. 198, 202
Aldbury, Herts. 199, 200, 202
Aldeby, Norfolk 68, 73, 92
Aldenham, Herts. 204
Alderford Common, Swannington, Norfolk 73–5, 101, 131, 148, 151–2, 158
Aldwinkle, Northants. 211
Ant, River 15, 21, 48, 54, 107, 109, 110
Apethorpe, Northants. 205
Ashby, Norfolk 68
Ashill, Norfolk 107, 111, 130
Ashmanaugh, Norfolk 105
Ashwellthorpe, Norfolk 85, 104
Aston End, Herts. 201
Attleborough, Norfolk 23, 49, 58, 68, 109
Axholme, Isle of, Lincs. 214–15
Aylmerton, Norfolk 58, 93
Aylsham, Norfolk 77, 156, 173
Aynho, Northants. 205

Babbingley, River 154
Bacon, Keith 10
Bacton, Norfolk 68
Badby, Northants. 205
Banham, Norfolk 23, 59, 75, 109
Banningham, Norfolk 68
Barnet Common, Herts. 198, 202, 203
barrows 60, 82, 114, 151–5, 158, 161, 183, 199
Bayfield, Norfolk 82, 154
Bedingham 68
Beechamwell, Norfolk 72
Beeston Heath, Norfolk 72
Beeston Regis, Norfolk 124
Beetley, Norfolk 106, 162, 168
Beighton, Norfolk 105, 112–13
Berkhamsted Common, Herts. 198, 199, 202, 204
Besthorpe, Norfolk 49, 57
Billingford, Norfolk 68–71, 99, 101
Billockby, Norfolk 59
Binham, Norfolk 39, 41
Bird, Maurice 126–7, 130
Birtles, Sarah 9, 135–6
Blickling, Norfolk 72, 73, 156
Blo Norton, Norfolk 104–5, 123, 126
Blofield, Norfolk 68, 73
Blomefield, Francis 48, 53, 55, 75, 76, 93–4
Bodham, Norfolk 128
Boughton, Norfolk 98, 101, 126, 166, 168, 171
bracken 12, 27, 72, 73, 126–7, 130–1, 133–4, 144, 147–51, 152, 159, 179, 183, 198

Bracon Ash, Norfolk 101, 131, 187
Bradenham, Norfolk 35, 45, 81
Brafield, Northants. 205
Brampton, Norfolk 101, 173, 176, 178
Brancaster, Norfolk 98, 121, 147, 151, 156, 158–9, 161
Breckland 14, 16, 17, 18, 21–2, 25, 48, 59, 94, 101, 109, 131, 142–6, 194
Bressingham, Norfolk 48, 60, 68, 95, 104, 110, 126, 166
Brettenham, Norfolk 49, 143
brickmaking 12, 71–4, 84, 116–17, 185, 194, 200–2
Bridgham, Norfolk 109
Brigstock, Northants. 207, 211
Brill, Bucks. 194
Brisley, Norfolk 9, 35, 56, 57, 82, 101, 102, 129, 142, 179, 181, 187–8, 189
Briston, Norfolk 75, 68
Broadland 10, 15, 18, 21, 44, 48, 52, 79–80, 92, 95, 101, 107, 109, 113, 125, 168
Brockdish, Norfolk 87, 99, 175
Broome Heath, Ditchingham, Norfolk 9, 113–14, 148, 151, 154–5, 158, 159, 161
Broughton, Northants. 205
Brumstead, Norfolk 126
Bull, Alan 10
Bure, River 15, 21, 35, 173
Burgh St Margaret, Norfolk 44, 59, 106, 109, 126
Burgh St Peter, Norfolk 113
Burnham Overy, Norfolk 68
Burroughes, Randall 27
Burston, Norfolk 68, 87
Burton Latimer, Northants. 209, 211
Bushey Heath, Herts. 198, 201
Bushey, Herts. 199
Byfield, Northants. 208, 209

Caddington Common, Herts. 198
Caistor, Norfolk 69, 123
camping 82
Cantley, Norfolk 48, 62
Carbrooke, Norfolk 69, 109
Carleton Rode, Norfolk 23, 60
Castle Acre, Norfolk 126, 172–3, 176, 178
Castle Rising, Norfolk 126
Catfield, Norfolk 29, 48, 73, 106, 109, 113, 123–4, 137
Cawston, Norfolk 14, 25, 63, 68, 72, 109
champion 36–41, 93, 146, 192, 196, 200, 203, 204–9, 213
Charitable Trusts Act (1860) 122
Chedgrave, Norfolk 49, 79
Cheshunt Common, Herts. 198, 201, 203
Chet, River 15
Chilterns 3, 195, 196, 198, 199, 202–4
Chipperfield Common, Herts. 199–202
Chipping Barnet, Herts. 200, 203
Clarke, W. G. 9, 121, 126, 127–8, 130, 135, 137, 174, 178
clayland commons 10, 12, 27, 33, 53, 96, 101, 122, 128–31, 142, 146, 156, 161, 165, 172, 179–90, 216

Cley, Norfolk 75, 143
Clippesby, Norfolk 45, 73, 92
Cockfield Fell, Co. Durham 213
Cockley Cley, Norfolk 59
Cold Higham, Northants. 211
Colkirk, Norfolk 36
Coltishall, Norfolk 79, 101
common rights 4, 6–8, 28, 34–7, 44–60, 75, 92–4, 97–9, 101, 102–4, 128, 135–7 192–3, 202, 206–7
Commons Acts (1876 and 1899) 122, 134–5
Commons Preservation Society 134, 204
Commons Registration Act (1965) 7, 136
Corby, Northants. 212
Cornford, Barbara 45, 59
Corpusty, Norfolk 124
Countryside and Rights of Way Act (2000) 9, 113, 138
Cranworth, Norfolk 68, 111
Crick, Northants. 205
cricket 82–3, 180
Cringleford, Norfolk 83
Crostwick, Norfolk 82, 125, 130
Crostwight, Norfolk 75, 101, 130–1, 148, 149, 156–7, 169
Croughton, Northants. 208, 211
Crowfield, Northants. 207
Culworth, Northants. 205

Dallas, Patsy 10
Davison, Alan 180
deer 147, 206, 207
deer parks 7, 17, 35, 152, 207
Denton, Norfolk 52
Denver, Norfolk 24, 45, 70, 158
Deopham, Norfolk 58, 102
Dersingham, Norfolk 99
Dickleburgh, Norfolk 86, 95, 115
Diss, Norfolk 33, 53, 68, 75–6, 82, 166, 169
Docking, Norfolk 39, 51
doles 6, 50–53, 100, 156, 166–7, 169–70, 209
Dolman, Paul 215
Domesday Book 5, 6, 17, 34–5, 195
donkeys 27, 83, 111, 124–5, 127
Downham Market, Norfolk 15, 109
Duddington, Northants. 211
Dury and Andrews 196
Dyer, Christopher 35

Earsham, Norfolk 45–6, 49, 52, 62, 63
East Dereham, Norfolk 77–8, 98, 101, 106, 127, 129–30
East Harling, Norfolk 68, 72, 109
East Lexham, Norfolk 154
East Rudham, Norfolk 68, 154
East Ruston, Norfolk 9, 99, 107, 109, 112, 126–7, 129, 138, 170
East Winch, Norfolk 101, 171
East Wretham, Norfolk 82
Eccles, Norfolk 27, 82
Edgefield, Norfolk 82
Ellingham, Norfolk 68, 109
Elstree, Herts. 198, 203
enclosure 69, 71, 72, 79, 82, 83, 86–7, 91–118, 121–5, 128, 134–5, 137, 142, 143, 146, 147, 151, 152, 154, 156, 157, 158, 166, 169, 179, 182, 185, 193, 196, 203–4, 207, 211–15, 216
encroachment 39, 49, 56–9, 65, 76, 85, 91, 92, 124, 127, 181–2, 193, 200–1, 213

English Nature 150
Epping Forest 3
Evenley, Northants. 205, 208

Faden, William 21–6, 31, 33, 35–6, 53, 68–9, 71, 73, 81, 85–6, 91, 93, 117, 121, 146, 152, 158, 196, 209
fairs 75–7, 80, 81, 193, 200
Fakenham, Norfolk 68, 75, 111
Felmingham, Norfolk 156
Felthorpe, Norfolk 14, 109, 126, 128, 131
Feltwell, Norfolk 48, 81, 104, 109
Fenland 13, 15, 25, 26, 40, 69, 98, 215
fens 6, 10, 13, 21, 27–8, 36, 48, 50–1, 54, 62, 92, 95, 101, 109, 117, 122, 126, 128–9, 130, 165–73, 178, 214
Fersfield, Norfolk 53–5, 109
field systems, prehistoric 153, 183–4
Fiennes, Celia 202
Fincham, Norfolk 62, 105, 111
Flegg, Norfolk 44, 45, 59, 85
Fleggburgh, Norfolk 50
Flitcham, Norfolk 60, 61
Flordon, Norfolk 126, 166, 178
foldcourses 16, 17, 18, 27, 34, 59, 63, 93
Forestry Commission 143, 202
Foulden Common, Norfolk 9, 98, 126, 143, 166, 167, 168, 169, 171–2
Frettenham, Norfolk 68, 71
Fritton, Norfolk 24, 27, 31, 33, 47, 55, 62, 64, 100, 101, 179, 182, 183–4, 187–8, 189
Fulmondeston, Norfolk 35, 56, 105, 123

gallows 80–2
Garboldisham, Norfolk 53, 69, 71
Garrod, George 133–4
Gaywood, Norfolk 69, 105, 128
Geddington, Northants. 207
geese 27–8, 45–7, 62, 106, 107, 111, 124–5, 126
Geldeston, Norfolk 113
'ghost commons' 113–18
gibbets 80–2, 85, 86, 88
Gilbert's Act (1782) 85
Gillingham, Norfolk 51–2, 72, 73
Ginter, D. 212
Glaven, River 35, 154
goings 46–7, 52, 62
gorse 27, 45, 50, 51, 72–73, 106, 108, 123, 126–7, 130–31, 143–45, 147, 149, 158, 189, 198–99, 203, 211
gravel 4, 8, 12, 14, 24, 62, 75, 109, 113, 117, 143, 155, 156–61, 185, 193, 200, 203, 205
Gray, Howard 38
Great Bircham, Norfolk 126
Great Dunham, Norfolk 69
Great Ellingham, Norfolk 49
Great Massingham, Norfolk 39, 41, 126
Great Melton, Norfolk 92, 115–17
Great Oakley, Northants. 212
Great Ringstead, Norfolk 106
Great Yarmouth, Norfolk 11, 15, 62, 124
Grendon, Northants. 205
Gressenhall, Norfolk 28, 33, 53–4, 75, 85
Grimms Ditch 199
Grimston, Norfolk 73, 104, 106, 109
Griston, Norfolk 109

Guist, Norfolk 72, 124, 126, 168
Gunthorpe, Norfolk 35, 146

Hales Green, Norfolk 24, 101, 142, 179–81, 184–6, 187–8
Halvergate Marshes, Norfolk 15
Hanworth, Norfolk 101, 172, 173
Happisburgh, Norfolk 105, 107, 123
Hardley, Norfolk 92
Hardwick, Norfolk 172–3, 178
Hargham, Norfolk 49, 82, 92
Harleston, Norfolk 79, 124
Harlestone Heath, Northants. 209
Harpenden, Herts. 201
Harpley, Norfolk 72, 154
Hassingham, Norfolk 106
Heacham, Norfolk 39, 72
heath 12, 14, 21, 24–6, 34, 51, 61, 63, 82–4, 85, 86, 87, 92, 94, 101, 113, 128, 130, 142–62, 165, 166, 203, 209, 211, 215
heather 12, 27, 51, 72–3, 106, 130–31, 143–51, 179, 198, 199, 203, 211, 215
Heckingham, Norfolk 85
Helhoughton, Norfolk 154
Helidon, Northants. 205
hemp 68, 103, 145
Hempstead, Norfolk 107
Hemsby, Norfolk 50–51
Hertford Heath, Herts. 204
Hertford, Herts. 195, 202
Hertfordshire and Middlesex Wildlife Trust 204
Hethersett, Norfolk 115
Hevingham, Norfolk 104, 109
Hickling, Norfolk 109, 124
Higham Ferrers, Northants. 210
Hindolveston, Norfolk 35, 85
Hingham, Norfolk 76
Hinton, Northants. 208–9
Historic Environment and Biodiversity Information Service 9
Hockwold, Norfolk 48
Hoe, Norfolk 72, 138, 149, 150, 159–61
Holkham, Norfolk 82, 94
Holme Hale, Norfolk 45, 47, 81
Holt, Norfolk 35, 76, 78, 81, 83, 85–6, 99, 126, 152, 154, 159
Holt-Cromer ridge 14, 25, 117, 143
Honing, Norfolk 51, 52, 69, 72, 100, 130, 148, 167–70
Horning, Norfolk 113, 168
Horsey, Norfolk 105
Horsford, Norfolk 109, 127–8
Horsham St Faith's, Norfolk 109, 127
Hoskins, W. G. 2, 135–6
Houghton Hall, Norfolk 82, 94
Houghton, Northants. 205
Hunstanton, Norfolk 13, 15, 146

Illington, Norfolk 49
Ingham, Norfolk 105
Irstead, Norfolk 28, 48, 54, 108, 113, 168, 169–70
Isham, Northants. 205

Kalm, Pehr 198, 199
Kelling Heath, Norfolk 100, 137–8, 143–4, 150, 151, 155, 215
Kelling, Norfolk 82, 99, 121, 153, 154
Kempstone, Norfolk 59
Kenninghall, Norfolk 53, 55, 69
Kensworth Common, Herts. 198

Kent, Nathaniel 21
Kett, Robert 63, 87, 92–3
Kettering, Northants. 211
Kibworth Beauchamp, Leics 212
Kilverstone, Norfolk 49, 94, 143
King's Lynn, Norfolk 11, 13, 77, 123, 143, 146, 151, 172, 173
King's Sutton, Northants. 211
Kings Langley, Herts. 202
Kingscliff, Northants. 205

Land Utilisation Survey 135
Langhale, Norfolk 73
Langley, Norfolk 52, 72, 92
Larling, Norfolk 49, 143
Law of Commons Amendment Act (1893) 135
Law of Property Act (1925) 135
Leziate Fen 167–70
Linebaugh, Peter 3
Litcham, Norfolk 59, 87, 99, 101, 123, 129, 154
Little Cressingham, Norfolk 105
Little Ellingham, Norfolk 112, 126
Little Gaddesden, Herts. 200
Little Massingham, Norfolk 154
Little Melton, Norfolk 115–16
Little Plumstead, Norfolk 105
Long Stratton, Norfolk 87, 183, 185, 187
Lopham, Norfolk 104, 111
Lucas, Robin 72
Ludham, Norfolk 28, 29, 48, 106, 109, 123
Lynford, Norfolk 72, 143

MacMaster, N. 83
Macnair, Andrew 22
Maine, Henry 6
Marham, Norfolk 104, 109, 128
Marlingford, Norfolk 69, 112
Marshall, W. 28
Marsham, Norfolk 34, 93, 109, 126, 129
marshes 27, 36, 62, 92, 95, 129, 165, 172–9
Martham, Norfolk 50, 59, 62, 107, 109
Mattishall, Norfolk 53, 69, 81
Meesden, Herts. 200
Melton Constable, Norfolk 35
Merton, Statute of (1236) 7, 21, 35, 56, 58, 63, 93, 134, 135
Methwold, Norfolk 14, 24, 48, 81
Middleton, Norfolk 56, 75, 93, 168
Monken Hadley, Herts. 200
Moore-Colyer, R. 212
Morley, Karen 10
Morley, Norfolk 31, 33, 58
Morningthorpe, Norfolk 87, 101, 102
Morston Quay, Norfolk 79
Moulton, Norfolk 69, 103–4, 113
Mousehold Heath, Norwich, Norfolk 24, 34, 48, 51, 69, 72, 73, 81, 83, 87, 111
Mulbarton, Norfolk 69, 83, 101, 127, 131, 180
Mundham, Norfolk 69, 185

Nar, River 35, 154, 172, 173, 176, 178
Nassington, Northants. 205
Natural England 168, 173
Neatishead, Norfolk 48, 54, 108
Necton, Norfolk 45, 69

Needham Market, Norfolk 72
Neeson, Jeanette 3, 211–13, 219
New Buckenham Common, Norfolk 12, 60, 69–70, 79, 130, 181, 185–6, 187
New Buckenham, Norfolk 69, 79
New Poor Law (1834) 85
Newton St Faith, Norfolk 113
Newton Willows, Northants. 207
Norfolk County Council 131, 136, 150
Norfolk Wildlife Trust 9, 11, 52, 145, 150, 151, 168, 175
North Elmham, Norfolk 35, 69, 99
North Lopham, Norfolk 109
North Mymms, Herts. 204
North Norfolk District Council 150
North Runcton, Norfolk 98, 101
North Tuddenham, Norfolk 112
North Walsham, Norfolk 75, 77, 81, 145, 151, 156
North Wooton, Norfolk 101, 129, 172, 173, 176–8
Northampton, Northants. 208
Northaw Common, Herts. 198–9, 201–2
Northwold, Norfolk 62, 109
Norwich, Norfolk 9, 11, 13, 14, 25, 34, 48, 54, 75, 81, 83, 87, 109, 143, 154, 185

Odsey, Herts. 202
Old Buckenham, Norfolk 23, 62, 79, 96–7, 101, 102, 108, 126, 137, 179, 183, 187–8
open fields 2, 6, 95–6, 103, 208–9, 212
Ormesby, Norfolk 92, 113
Ostrom, E. 63
Oulton, Norfolk 69
Oundle, Northants. 211
Ovington, Norfolk 62
Oxburgh, Norfolk 126, 168

Parmenter, Jo 10, 167
Patmore Heath, Herts. 201, 204–5
peat extraction 4, 28, 50–1, 105–6, 107, 108, 122–3, 126–7, 128, 166–7, 168, 169–70, 171, 179, 194
Pentney, Norfolk 108, 109, 123, 168, 171
pingos 171–2
pits 8, 9, 12, 62, 68, 73–5, 100, 112–17, 121, 135, 137, 148, 156–9, 161, 169, 171, 184–6, 200–201, 203, 214
Pitsford, Northants. 205
plantings 53–4, 55, 62, 64, 96–7, 128, 187–8, 192, 216
Plumstead, Norfolk 69
Pockthorpe, Norfolk 84
poor houses 84–6, 116–17, 193
Poor Laws (1597 and 1601) 84–5
poor's allotments 9, 86–7, 94–5, 99, 100, 101, 102–3, 121–5, 126–8, 130, 133–8, 142, 147, 152, 158, 161, 166, 169, 172, 179, 186, 203, 211, 214
Poringland, Norfolk 69
Potter Heigham, Norfolk 27, 29, 44, 48, 72, 107, 109
Pulham, Norfolk 53, 68, 72, 86

Quidenham Hall, Norfolk 82

rabbits 21–3, 58–9, 63, 86, 131–4, 144, 146, 147, 150, 202, 216
racecourses 83, 85, 86
Rackham, Oliver 2, 38, 216
Rackheath Hall, Norfolk 82
Ranworth, Norfolk 69
Raunds, Northants. 213

Raynham, Norfolk 94
Redenhall, Norfolk 79
Redgrave, Suffolk 109
Reedham, Norfolk 79
Report of the Commissioners into Charities (1832) 106, 108, 109
Repps-with-Bastwick, Norfolk 107, 113
re-wilding 4, 216
Reymerston, Norfolk 111
Rider Haggard, Lilias 131
Ringland, Norfolk 69, 101, 124–5, 131, 142, 147, 148, 150, 172–3, 178
riots 93, 110–11
Rockingham Forest, Northants. 205, 206, 207, 211
Rockland All Saints, Norfolk 104
Rockland St Andrew, Norfolk 104
Rockland St Mary, Norfolk 52
Rollesby, Norfolk 59, 85, 103–4
Rothwell, Northants. 210
Roudham, Norfolk 49
Rougham, Norfolk 154
Royal Commission on Common Land (1955) 136
Roydon Common, Norfolk 9, 11, 142, 149, 151, 166, 168–9
Royston, Herts. 200, 202
Runham, Norfolk 105
Rushall, Norfolk 182–3
Rushden, Herts. 200

Sacombe, Herts. 200
Saham Toney, Norfolk 62,, 109
St Albans, Herts. 195, 196, 200–201, 202
Salcey Forest, Northants. 205, 206, 211
Salhouse, Norfolk 105
Salthouse Heath, Norfolk 9, 82, 137–8, 143, 150, 151–2, 153, 154, 155–6, 158, 161
Salthouse, Norfolk 99, 154
Sandon, Herts. 200–201
Sarratt, Herts. 200
Saxlingham Nethergate, Norfolk 137–8, 182
Saxthorpe, Norfolk 72
Scarning, Norfolk 106
Scottow, Norfolk 69
Sea Palling, Norfolk 123
Sedgeford, Norfolk 41
Shelfhanger, Norfolk 60, 87, 182
Shelton, Norfolk 101
Shenley, Herts. 204
Shipdham, Norfolk 44–5, 53, 109
Shotesham, Norfolk 99, 101, 121, 125, 137, 173–5, 176, 178, 181, 182
Shouldham, Norfolk 59, 103, 109
Shropham, Norfolk 49, 109
Simmons, Ian 2
Slapton, Northants. 207
Smallburgh, Norfolk 85, 93, 126, 129
Smith, William 179
Snell, Keith 212
Snetterton, Norfolk 46, 49, 62, 82
Snettisham, Norfolk 77, 105
South Creake, Norfolk 39–41
South Lopham, Norfolk 69, 108, 109, 126, 166
South Wooton, Norfolk 72
Southrepps Commons, Norfolk 75, 131, 133, 148, 157–60, 167, 168, 170–1
Sporle, Norfolk 105
sports 82–4, 213
staithes 79–80, 112–113, 123, 124, 137

Stalham, Norfolk 109
Stamp, L. Dudley 2, 135, 136
Standon, Herts. 203
Stanion, Northants. 207
Stanninghall, Norfolk 92
Stevenage, Herts. 199, 200
Stibbard, Norfolk 56, 74
Stiffkey, River 35, 172, 175
stints 45–47, 62–3, 99, 125
Stock Heath, Norfolk 24, 34, 35, 53, 72, 146
Stody, Norfolk 113
Stoke Ferry, Norfolk 13, 106
Stokesby, Norfolk 79–80, 95, 110–11
Stradsett, Norfolk 40
Stratton St Mary, Norfolk 101
Stratton St Michael, Norfolk 101, 180, 182
Stratton Strawless, Norfolk 53
Strumpshaw, Norfolk 69
Studham Common, Herts. 198
Surlingham, Norfolk 52, 105, 123
Sustead, Norfolk 73
Sutton, Norfolk 109, 123
Swaffham, Norfolk 77, 83, 111, 143
Swainsthorpe, Norfolk 62, 125
Swanton Novers, Norfolk 35, 153
Swardeston, Norfolk 46–7, 180, 187
Syresham, Northants. 207, 211

Tas, River 31, 173, 174
Taverham, Norfolk 34
Thelveton, Norfolk 23, 93–4
Therfield Heath, Herts. 199, 204
Thetford, Norfolk 23, 82, 109, 127, 143, 145, 166
Thompson Common, Norfolk 69, 72, 171
Thorpe St Andrew, Norfolk 79, 83
Thurne, Norfolk 107
Thurne, River, Norfolk 15, 21, 48, 107, 109
Thursford, Norfolk 35
Thwaite Common, Norfolk 86, 124, 129, 173
Tibbenham, Norfolk 25
timber 35, 36, 53, 58
Tittleshall, Norfolk 130, 154
Toft Monks, Norfolk 87
Tottenhill, Norfolk 106
Tottington, Norfolk 109, 143
Transactions of the Norfolk and Norwich Naturalists' Society 9, 121
Tring, Herts. 198, 199, 203
Tunstead, Norfolk 69
Turner, Michael 95, 213

Upton, Norfolk 51–2

Vinogradoff, Paul 6

Wacton Common, Norfolk 101, 102, 129, 179, 181, 187, 188
Walsham Heath, Norfolk 53, 156
Wappenham, Northants. 207, 209, 210
War Agricultural Committee (WAC) 129
War Agricultural Executive Committee (WAEC) 129, 130
Warner, Peter 36
warrens 21–3, 58–9, 63, 86, 131, 144
Wash, the 13, 15, 25, 40, 143, 154, 172, 177, 178

Waterman, Thomas 25, 28, 33, 54
Watford, Herts. 195, 200, 204
Watton, Norfolk 69
Waveney, River 15, 109, 155, 175, 176
Weald, The 36
Weasenham, Norfolk 104, 130, 151, 154
Webb, Nigel 2
Weedon Lois, Northants. 205
Weeting, Norfolk 69, 72
Wellingham, Norfolk 130, 154
Wells, C. 106
Welton, Northants. 208
Wensum, River 35, 154
Wereham, Norfolk 41
West Bradenham Common, Norfolk 45, 81
West Farndon, Northants. 208
West Harling, Norfolk 48
West Lexham, Norfolk 106, 154, 179
West Newton, Norfolk 60
West Raynham, Norfolk 154
West Rudham, Norfolk 129, 151, 153–4
West Runton, Norfolk 68, 72, 87, 143, 158, 159, 161
West Wereham, Norfolk 75
West Winch, Norfolk 126, 172, 173, 178
Westminster, Statute of (1285) 7
Weston, Herts. 200
Weston Longville, Norfolk 81
Weston, Northants. 205
Wheatacre, Norfolk 69, 113
Whitfield, Northants. 207, 211
Whittlewood Forest, Northants. 205–7, 211
Whitwell, Norfolk 98, 125, 168
Whyte, Nicola 10, 81–2
Wicklewood, Norfolk 85
Wigginton, Herts. 200, 202, 203
Wighton, Norfolk 40, 101, 172, 175
Wilby, Norfolk 49
Willian, Herts. 200
Wilton, Norfolk 48, 131
Wimbotsham, Norfolk 41
Winchester, Angus 2, 7, 214
windmills 60, 68–71, 95, 106, 181, 194, 201
Winfarthing, Norfolk 59
Witney, K. P. 36
Wittering, Northants. 208
Witton, Norfolk 69
Wiveton, Norfolk 154
Wood Norton, Norfolk 105
Woodforde, Parson 81, 87
Woodnewton, Northants. 205
World Wars 129–30, 135, 143, 154, 173, 202
World Wars, archaeology of 158–61, 199
Wramplingham, Norfolk 69, 115–17
Wretton, Norfolk 106
Wymondham, Norfolk 27, 47, 58, 69, 75–6, 92–3, 105, 109, 115–17

Yardley Hastings, Northants. 209–10
Yare, River 15, 154, 173
Yarwell, Northants. 205
Yelverton, Norfolk 69, 138–9
Young, Arthur 27, 45, 47, 62, 102, 104, 109, 111